american VIRGIN

AROUND THE WORLD

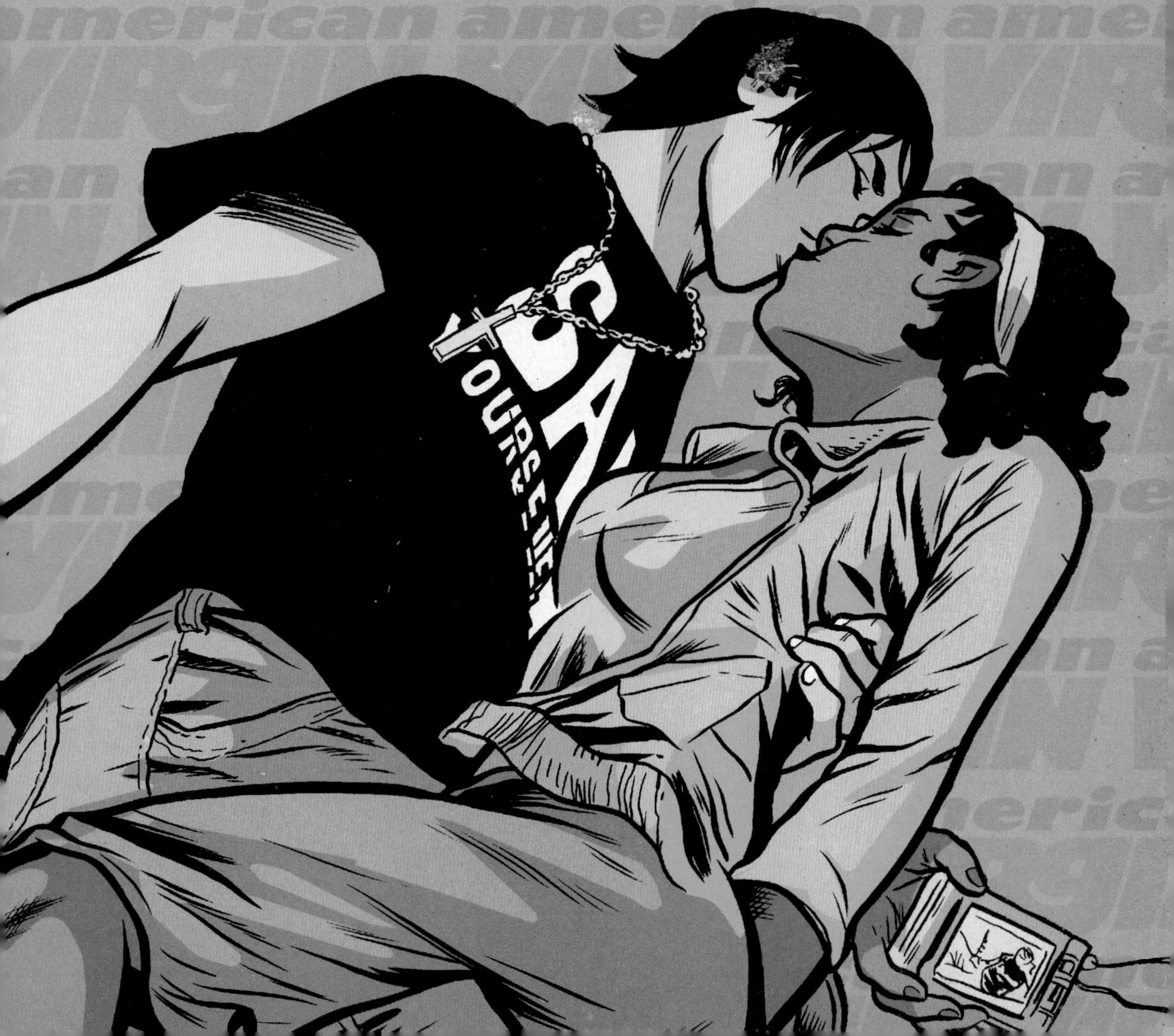

PAB

american VIRGIN AROUND THE WORLD

STEVEN T. SEAGLE WRITER

BECKY CLOONAN & RYAN KELLY PENCILLERS

JIM RUGG & JASEN LEX INKERS

BRIAN MILLER COLORIST JARED K. FLETCHER LETTERER

CELIA CALLE ORIGINAL SERIES COVERS

AMERICAN VIRGIN CREATED BY STEVEN T. SEAGLE AND BECKY CLOONAN

Karen Berger Senior VP-Executive Editor Shelly Bond and Casey Seijas Editors-original series
Bob Harras Editor-collected edition Robbin Brosterman Senior Art Director Paul Levitz President & Publisher
Georg Brewer VP-Design & DC Direct Creative Richard Bruning Senior VP-Creative Director Patrick Caldon Executive VP-Finance & Operations
Chris Caramalis VP-Finance John Cunningham VP-Marketing Terri Cunningham VP-Managing Editor Alison Gill VP-Manufacturing
David Hyde VP-Publicity Hank Kanalz VP-General Manager, WildStorm Jim Lee Editorial Director-WildStorm
Paula Lowitt Senior VP-Business & Legal Affairs MaryEllen McLaughlin VP-Advertising & Custom Publishing
John Nee Senior VP-Business Development Gregory Noveck Senior VP-Creative Affairs Sue Pohja VP-Book Trade Sales
Steve Rotterdam Senior VP-Sales & Marketing Cheryl Rubin Senior VP-Brand Management
Jeff Trojan VP-Business Development, DC Direct Bob Wayne VP-Sales

Cover illustration by Celia Calle. Logo design by Steve Cook. Publication design by Amelia Grohman.

DC Comics, 1700 Broadway, New York, NY 10019. A Warner Bros. Entertainment Company.
Printed in Canada. First Printing. ISBN 13: 978-1-4012-1831-7

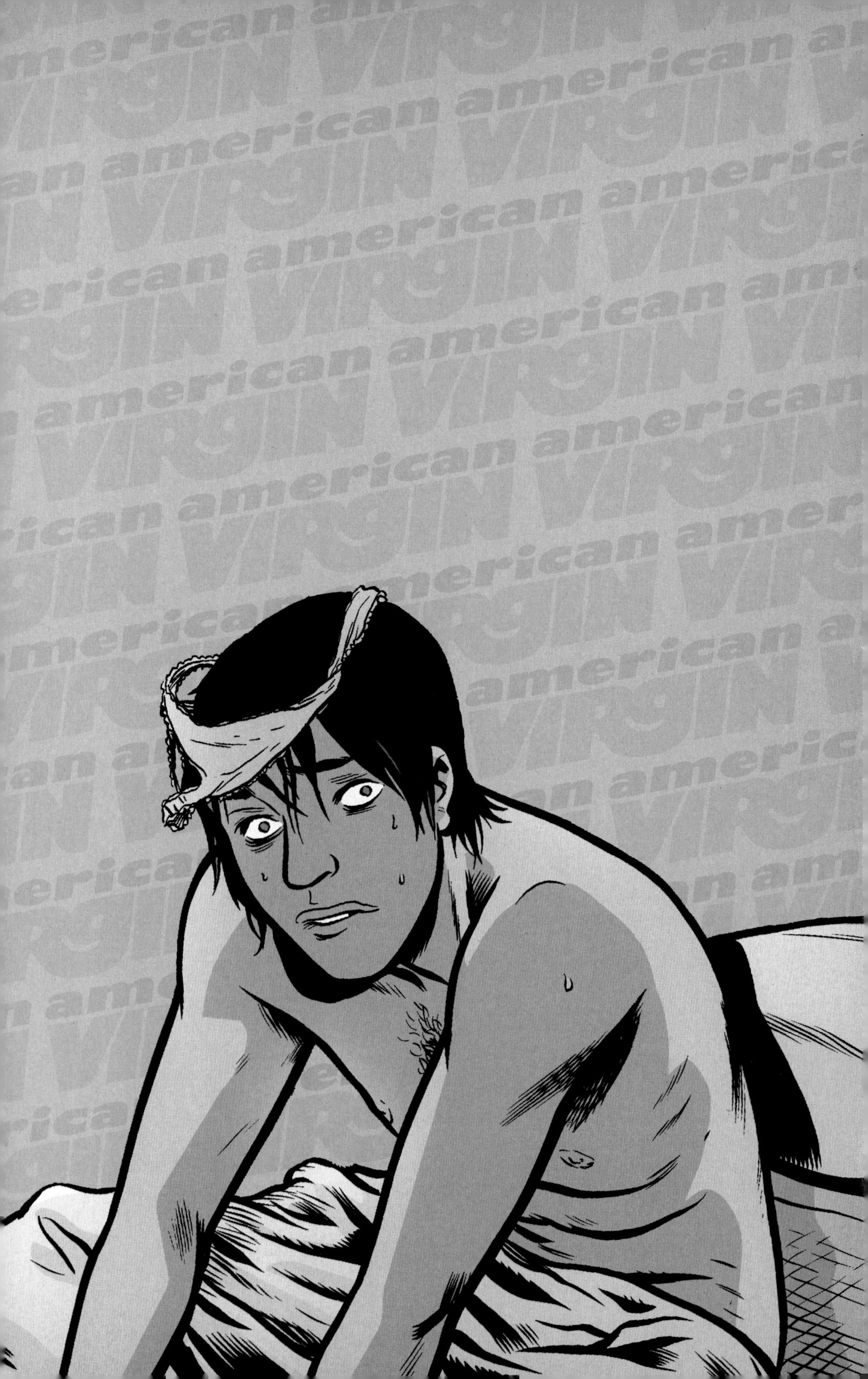
american
VIRGIN

PREVIOUSLY IN AMERICAN VIRGIN...

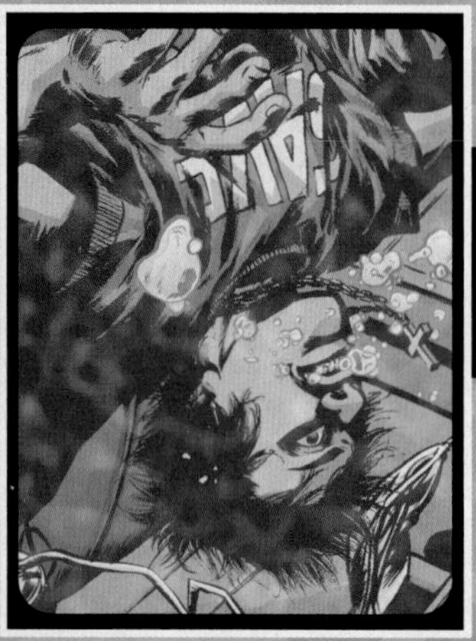

Returning to his Youth Virginity Ministry in Miami, ADAM CHAMBERLAIN's plane slid off the runway and into a swamp.

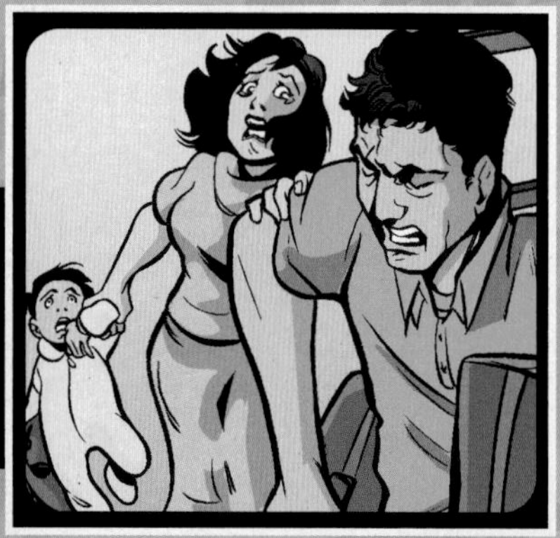

Adam's short life flashed before his eyes, reminding him of both his long-absent natural father, REYDEL, and the tarnished path taken by his family en route to becoming part of Miami's polished set.

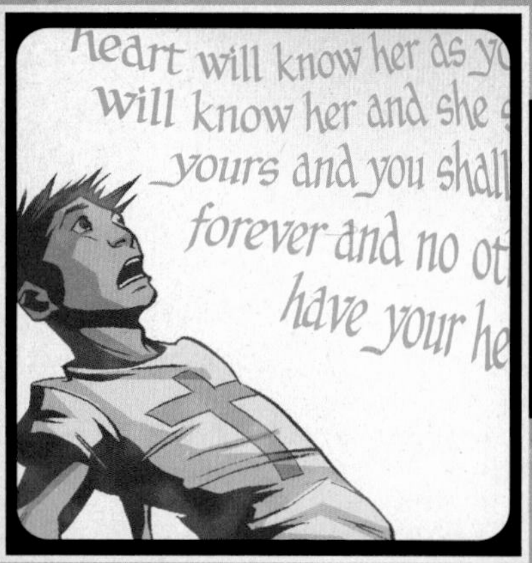
heart will know her as
Will know her and she
yours and you shall
forever and no
have your

A vision from GOD led Adam to believe that he may have incorrectly identified his murdered fiancée, CASSIE, as his one true love, so he set out to find the other likely candidates to determine if any of them might be the actual "chosen one."

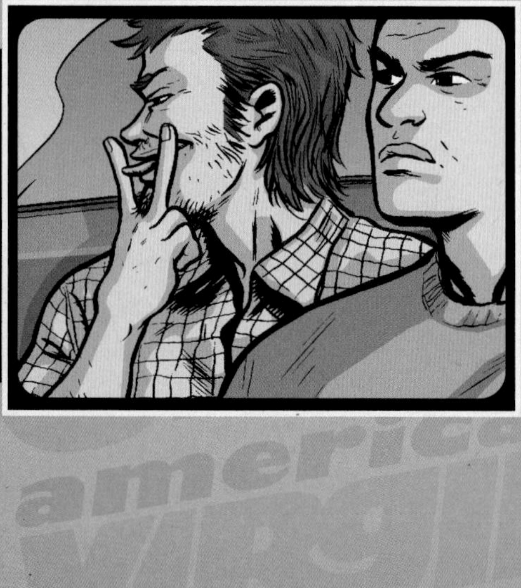

Hiring his lascivious stepcousins LEVI and MORGAN to find the women – all former contestants in the Miss Teen Miami Beach Pageant – Adam agreed to host this year's contest while navigating a broad sea of moral corruption in Miami's underworld in order to seek out the girl of his vision.

But from nude encounter groups, to swingers parties, to first-hand experience of the miracle of birth – Adam's inaugural view of the mysteries of woman – Adam still came up short on his own mystery.

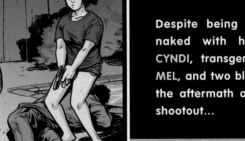

Despite being caught half-naked with his stepsister CYNDI, transgender hit man MEL, and two bloody thugs in the aftermath of a backyard shootout...

...Adam managed to quell the concerns of his mother MAMIE and continue his quest.

In the chaos of a hurricane that threatened to dismantle the pageant he was hosting, Adam felt a calm certainty – that one of the pageant assistants might just be the woman God intended him to experience the carnal mysteries with...

...VANESSA COLEMAN...

Adam is now set to follow his heart by following Vanessa around the world...

CHAPTER ONE

Chapter pencils by Becky Cloonan   Chapter inks by Jim Rugg

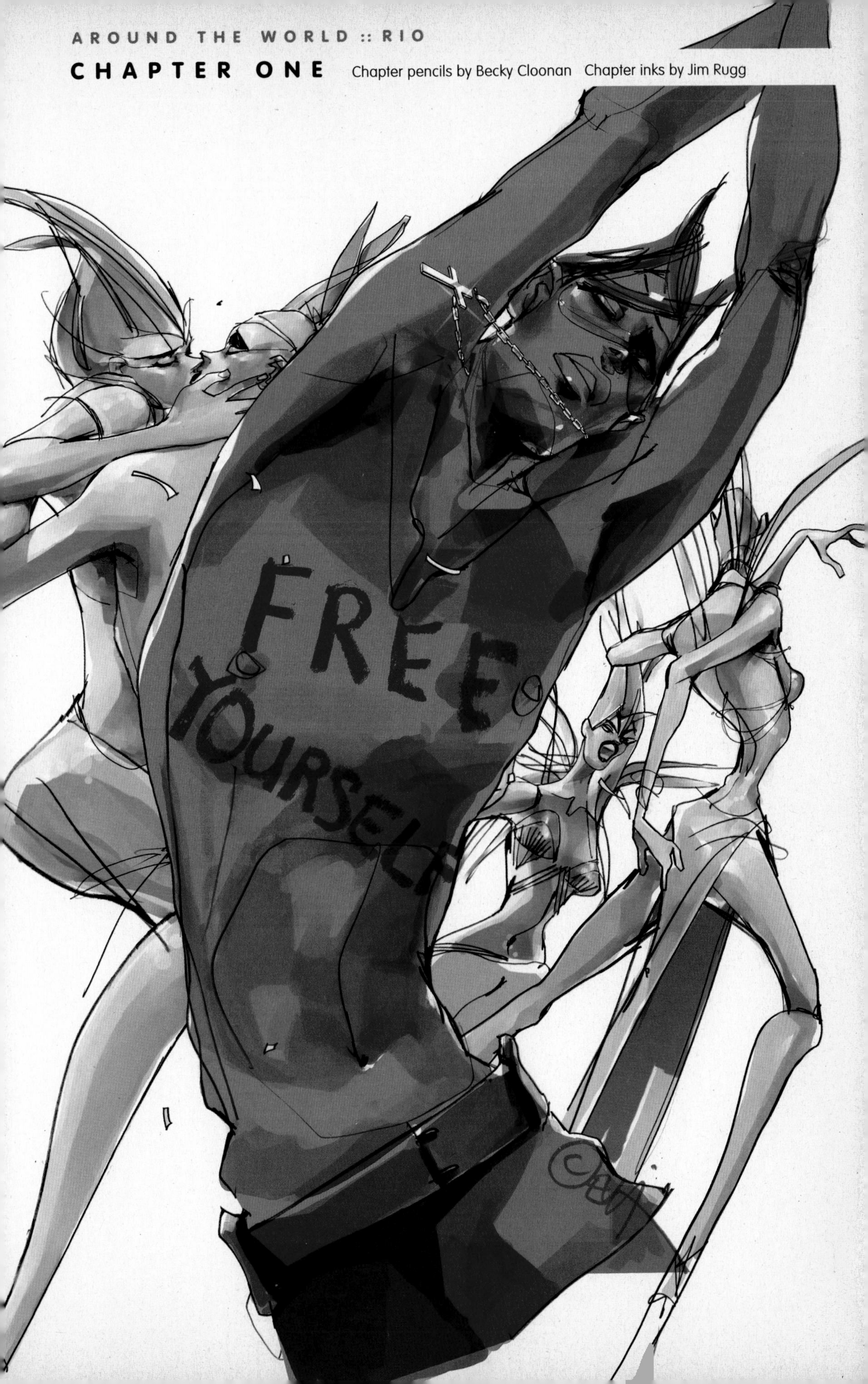
FREE YOURSELF

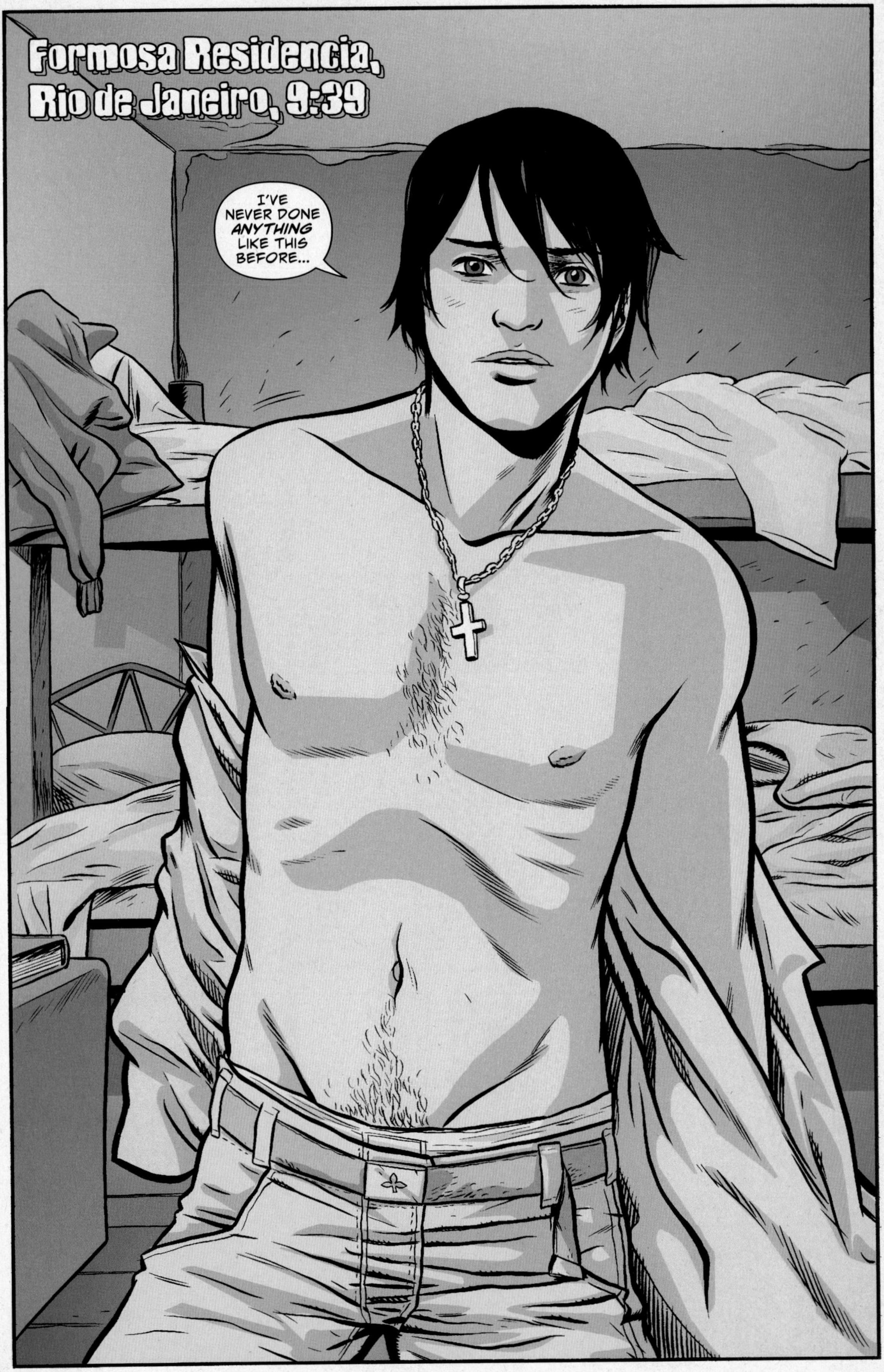
Formosa Residencia, Rio de Janeiro, 9:39
I'VE NEVER DONE *ANYTHING* LIKE THIS BEFORE...

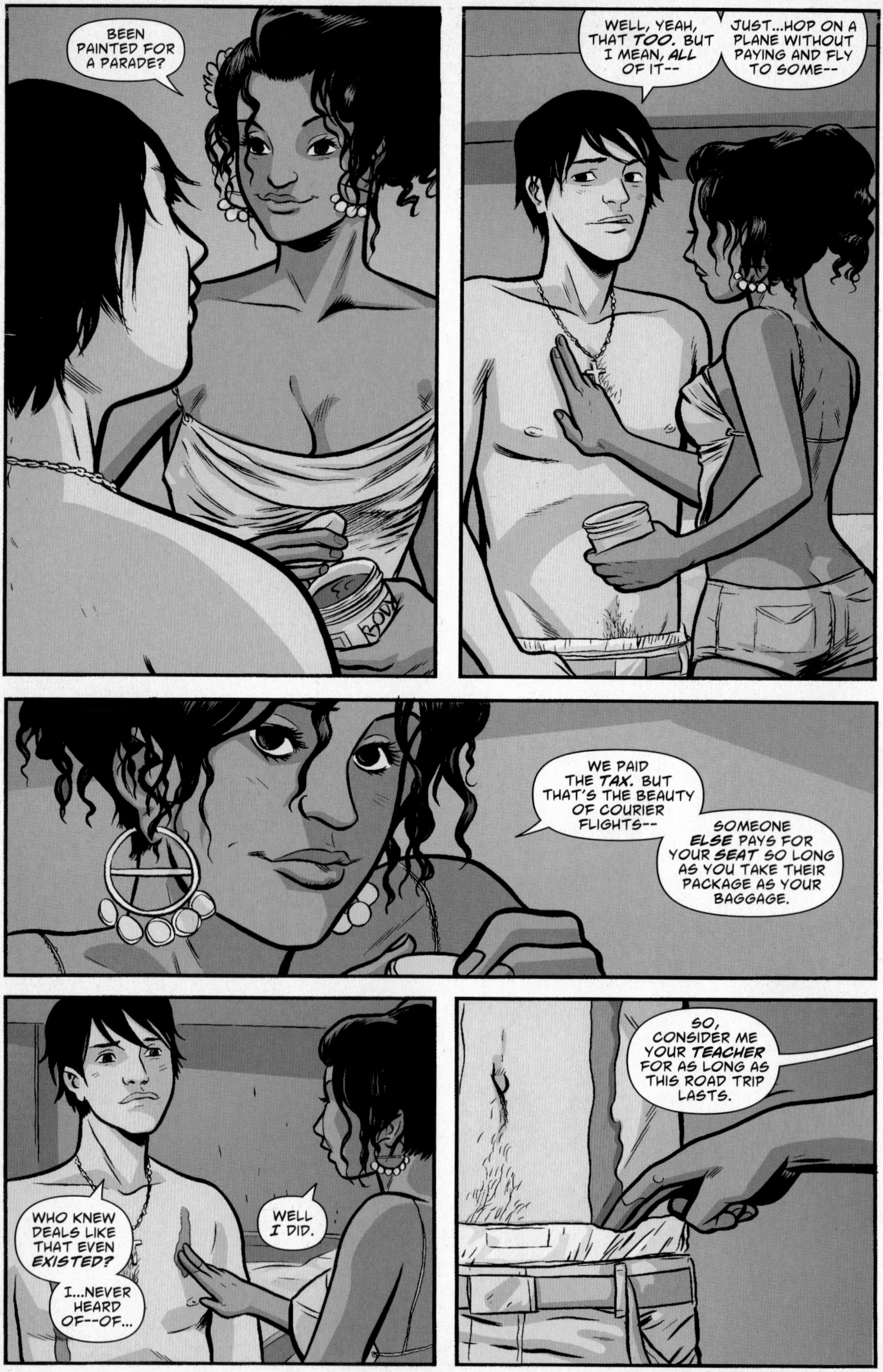
BEEN PAINTED FOR A PARADE?
WELL, YEAH, THAT TOO. BUT I MEAN, ALL OF IT--
JUST...HOP ON A PLANE WITHOUT PAYING AND FLY TO SOME--
WE PAID THE TAX. BUT THAT'S THE BEAUTY OF COURIER FLIGHTS--
SOMEONE ELSE PAYS FOR YOUR SEAT SO LONG AS YOU TAKE THEIR PACKAGE AS YOUR BAGGAGE.
WHO KNEW DEALS LIKE THAT EVEN EXISTED?
I...NEVER HEARD OF--OF...
WELL I DID.
SO, CONSIDER ME YOUR TEACHER FOR AS LONG AS THIS ROAD TRIP LASTS.

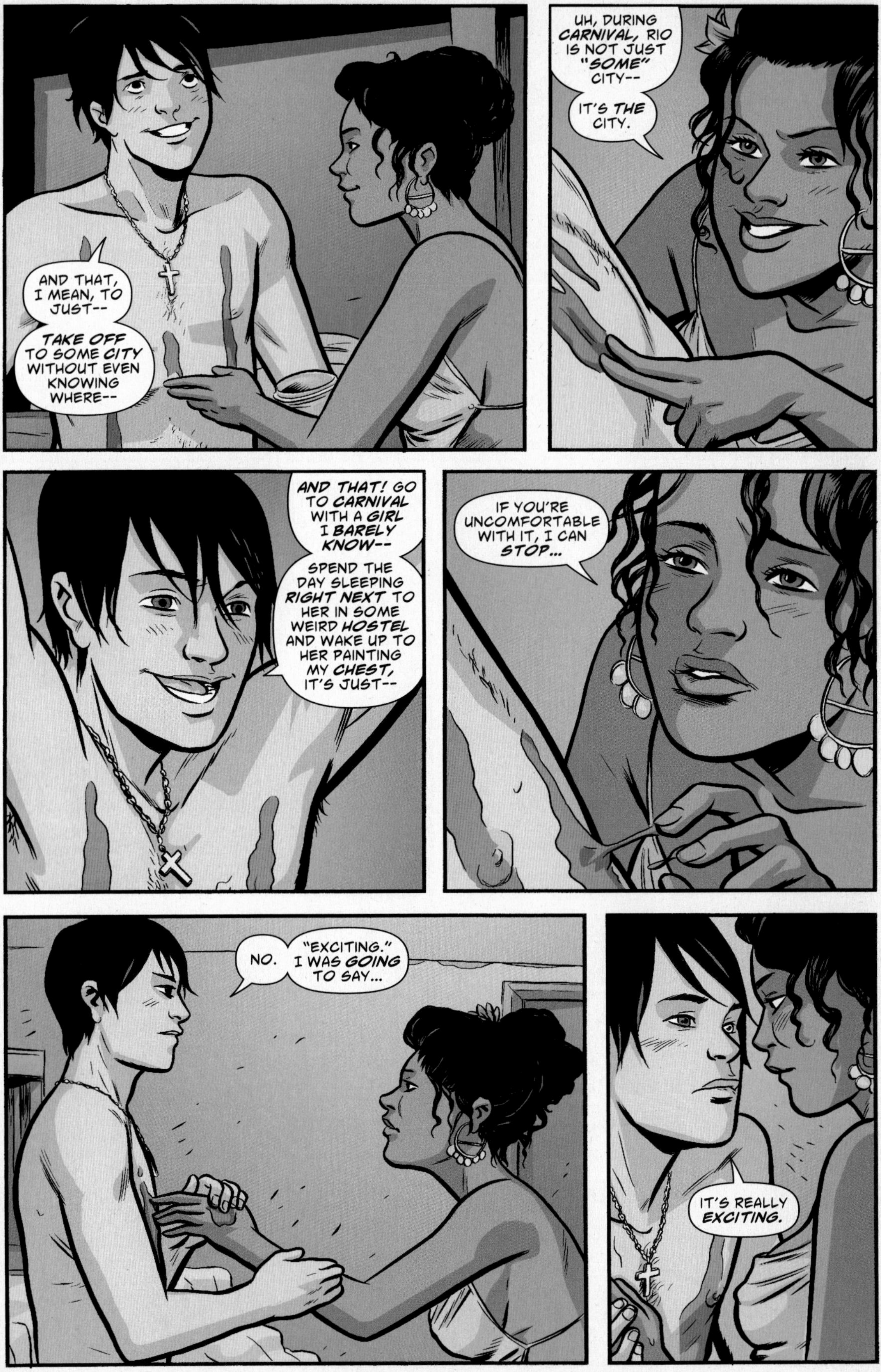
AND THAT, I MEAN, TO JUST--
TAKE OFF TO SOME CITY WITHOUT EVEN KNOWING WHERE--
UH, DURING CARNIVAL, RIO IS NOT JUST "SOME" CITY--
IT'S THE CITY.
AND THAT! GO TO CARNIVAL WITH A GIRL I BARELY KNOW--
SPEND THE DAY SLEEPING RIGHT NEXT TO HER IN SOME WEIRD HOSTEL AND WAKE UP TO HER PAINTING MY CHEST, IT'S JUST--
IF YOU'RE UNCOMFORTABLE WITH IT, I CAN STOP...
NO.
"EXCITING." I WAS GOING TO SAY...
IT'S REALLY EXCITING.

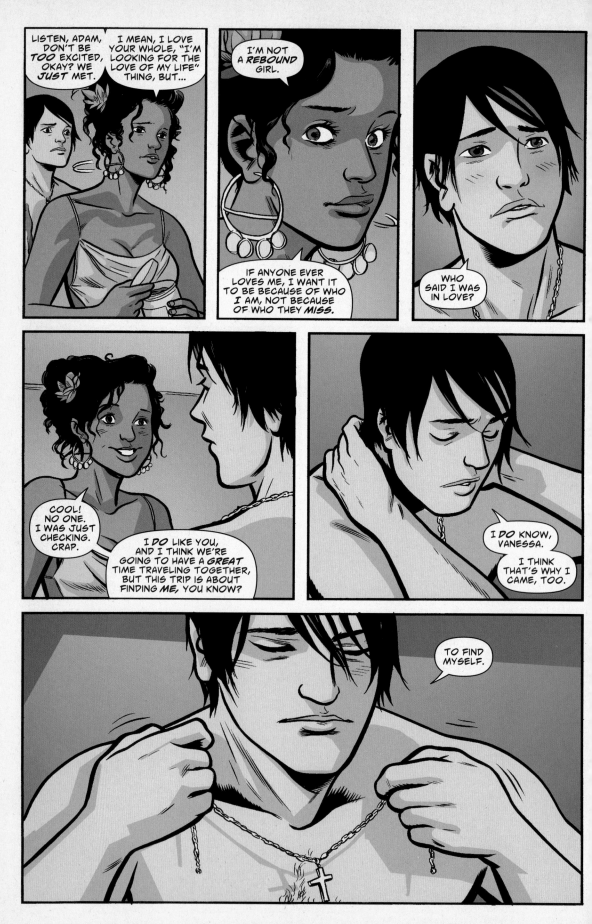

LISTEN, ADAM, DON'T BE *TOO* EXCITED, OKAY? WE *JUST* MET.

I MEAN, I LOVE YOUR WHOLE, "I'M LOOKING FOR THE LOVE OF MY LIFE" THING, BUT...

I'M NOT A *REBOUND* GIRL.

IF ANYONE EVER LOVES ME, I WANT IT TO BE BECAUSE OF WHO *I* AM, NOT BECAUSE OF WHO THEY *MISS*.

WHO SAID I WAS IN LOVE?

COOL! NO ONE. I WAS JUST CHECKING. CRAP.

I *DO* LIKE YOU, AND I THINK WE'RE GOING TO HAVE A *GREAT* TIME TRAVELING TOGETHER, BUT THIS TRIP IS ABOUT FINDING *ME*, YOU KNOW?

I *DO* KNOW, VANESSA.

I THINK THAT'S WHY I CAME, TOO.

TO FIND MYSELF.

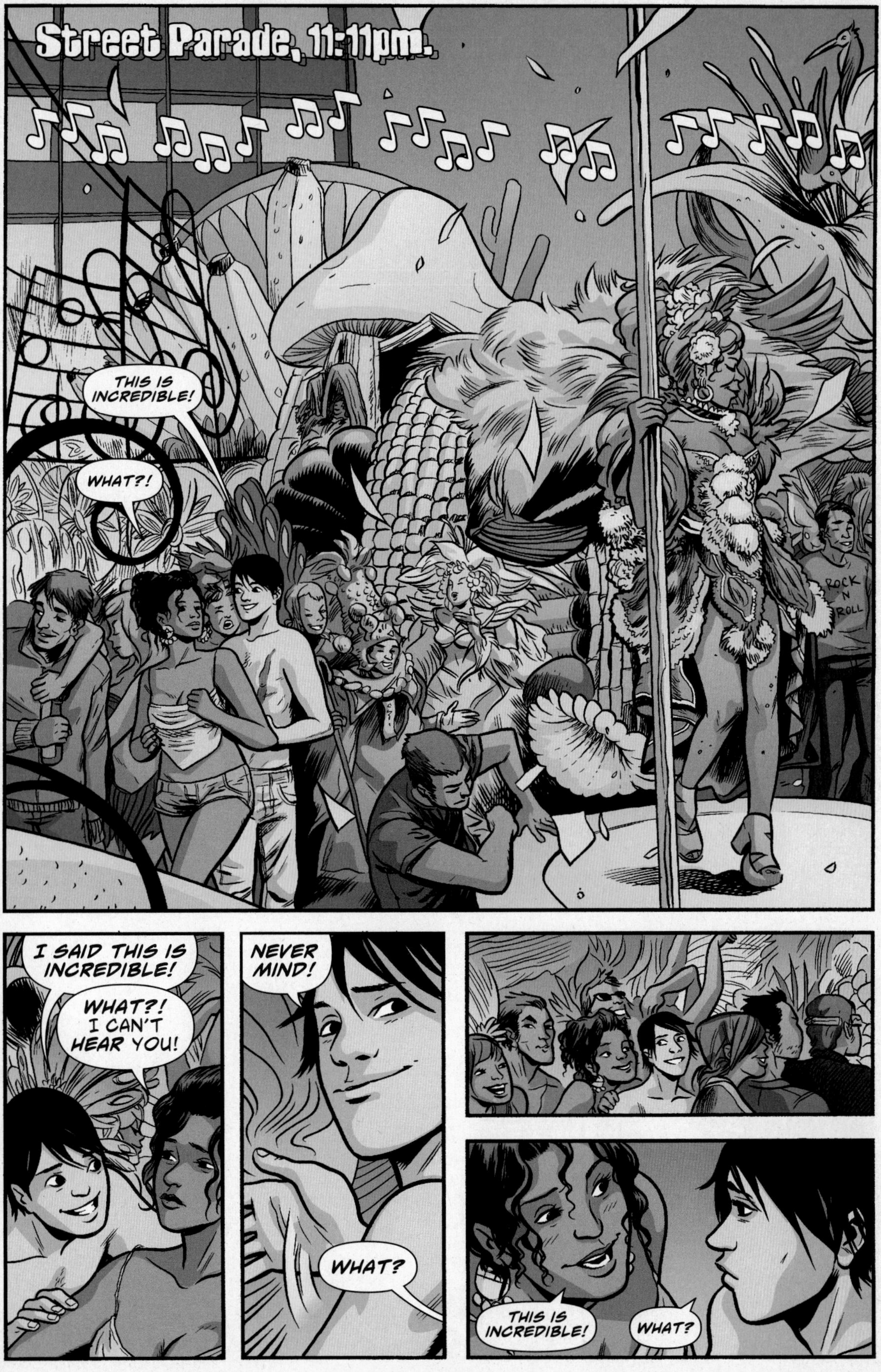
Street Parade, 11:11pm.
THIS IS INCREDIBLE!
WHAT?!
ROCK 'N' ROLL
I SAID THIS IS INCREDIBLE!
WHAT?! I CAN'T HEAR YOU!
NEVER MIND!
WHAT?
THIS IS INCREDIBLE!
WHAT?

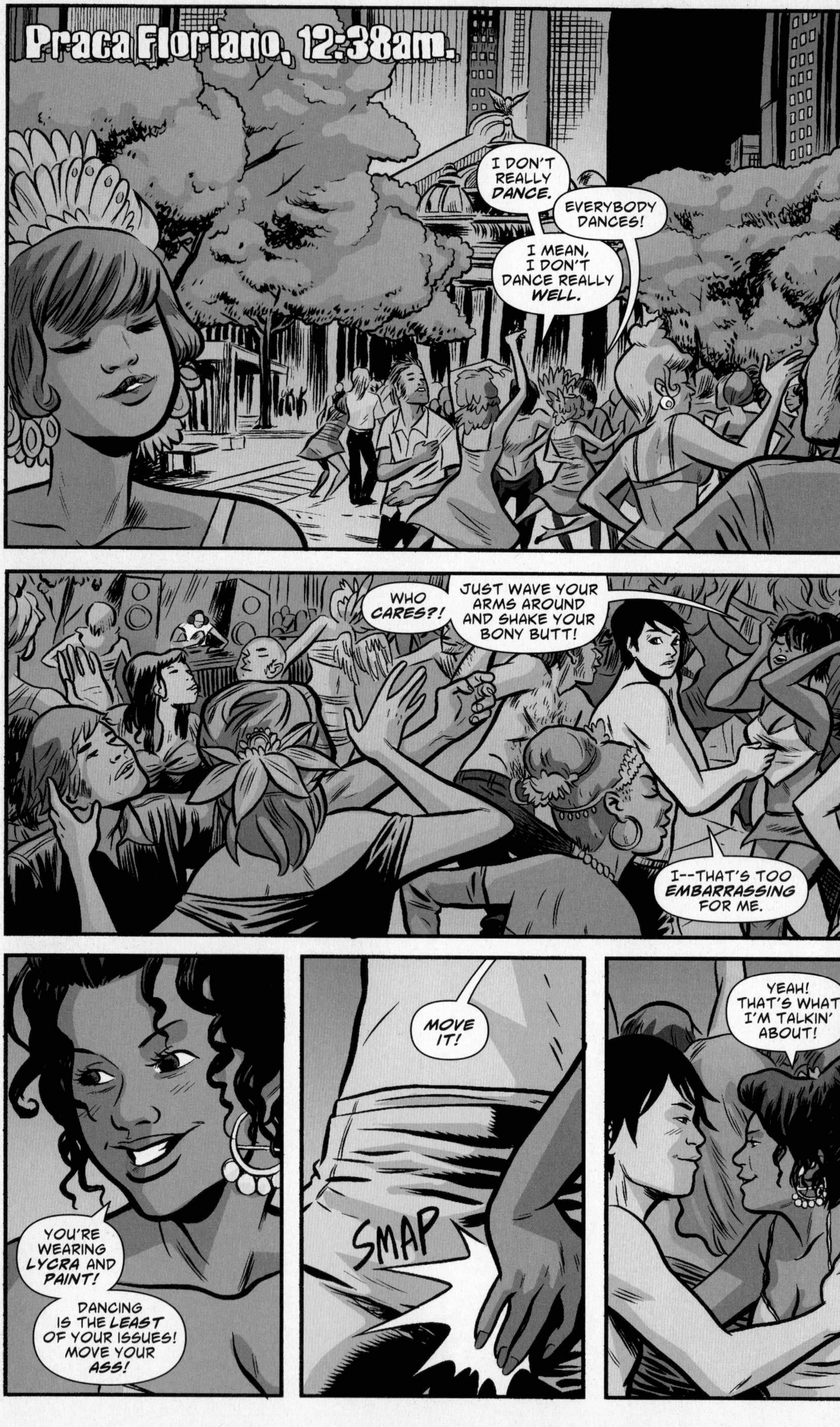
Praca Floriano, 12:38am.
I DON'T REALLY DANCE.
EVERYBODY DANCES!
I MEAN, I DON'T DANCE REALLY WELL.
WHO CARES?!
JUST WAVE YOUR ARMS AROUND AND SHAKE YOUR BONY BUTT!
I--THAT'S TOO EMBARRASSING FOR ME.
YOU'RE WEARING LYCRA AND PAINT!
DANCING IS THE LEAST OF YOUR ISSUES! MOVE YOUR ASS!
MOVE IT!
SMAP
YEAH! THAT'S WHAT I'M TALKIN' ABOUT!

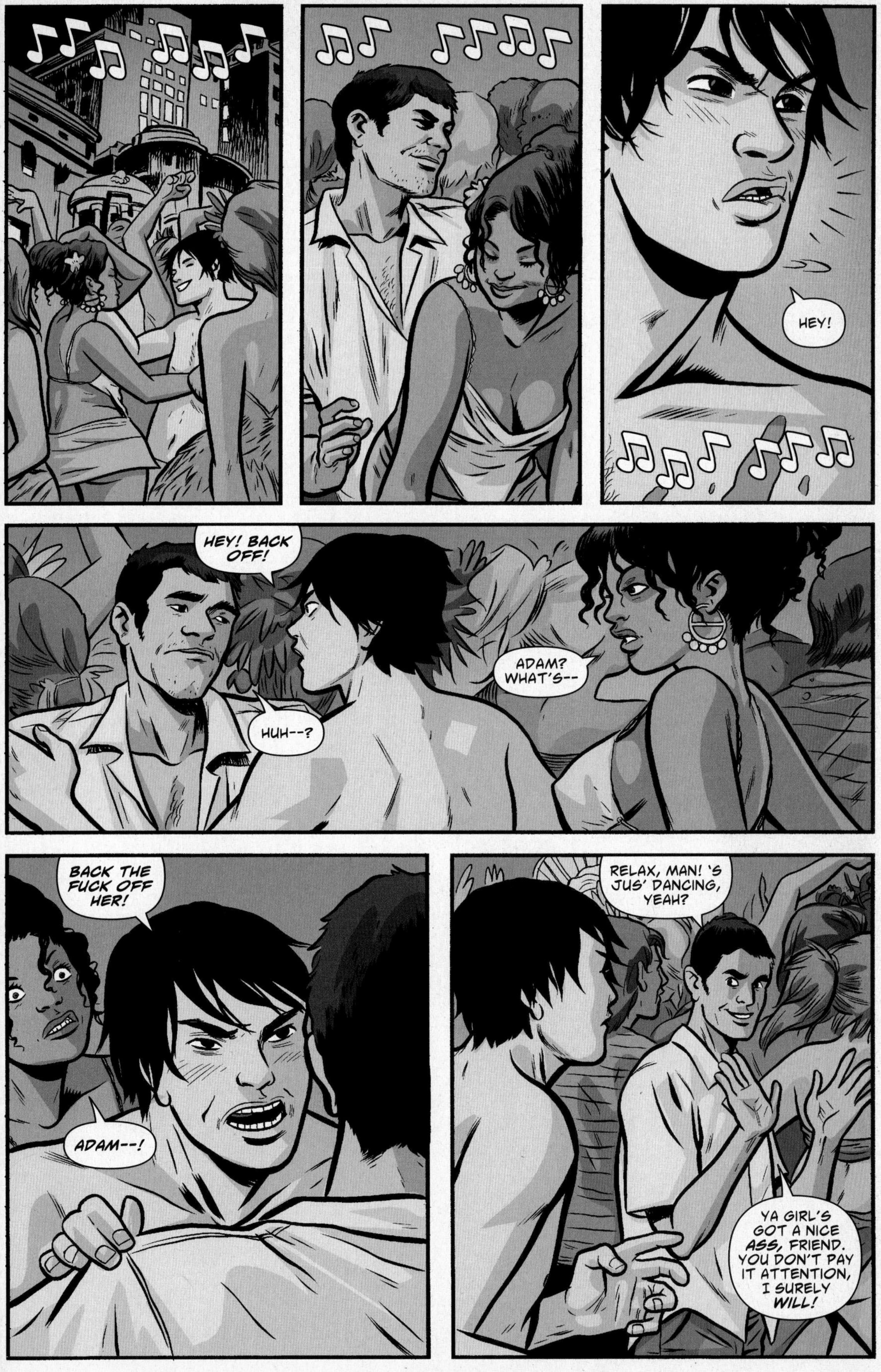
HEY!
HEY! BACK OFF!
HUH--?
ADAM? WHAT'S--
BACK THE FUCK OFF HER!
ADAM--!
RELAX, MAN! 'S JUS' DANCING, YEAH?
YA GIRL'S GOT A NICE ASS, FRIEND. YOU DON'T PAY IT ATTENTION, I SURELY WILL!

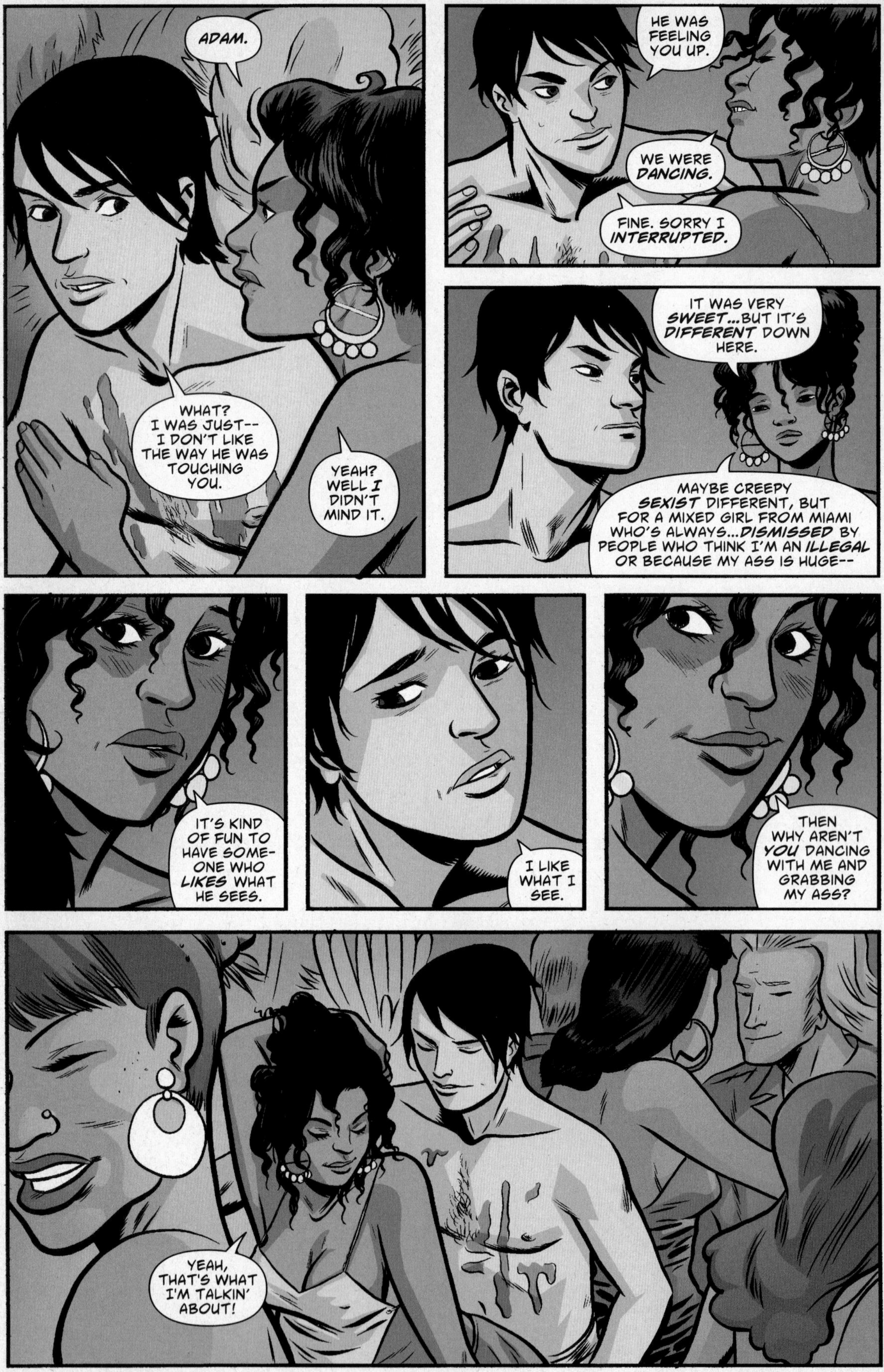
ADAM.
WHAT? I WAS JUST-- I DON'T LIKE THE WAY HE WAS TOUCHING YOU.
YEAH? WELL I DIDN'T MIND IT.
HE WAS FEELING YOU UP.
WE WERE DANCING.
FINE. SORRY I INTERRUPTED.
IT WAS VERY SWEET...BUT IT'S DIFFERENT DOWN HERE.
MAYBE CREEPY SEXIST DIFFERENT, BUT FOR A MIXED GIRL FROM MIAMI WHO'S ALWAYS...DISMISSED BY PEOPLE WHO THINK I'M AN ILLEGAL OR BECAUSE MY ASS IS HUGE--
IT'S KIND OF FUN TO HAVE SOME-ONE WHO LIKES WHAT HE SEES.
I LIKE WHAT I SEE.
THEN WHY AREN'T YOU DANCING WITH ME AND GRABBING MY ASS?
YEAH, THAT'S WHAT I'M TALKIN' ABOUT!

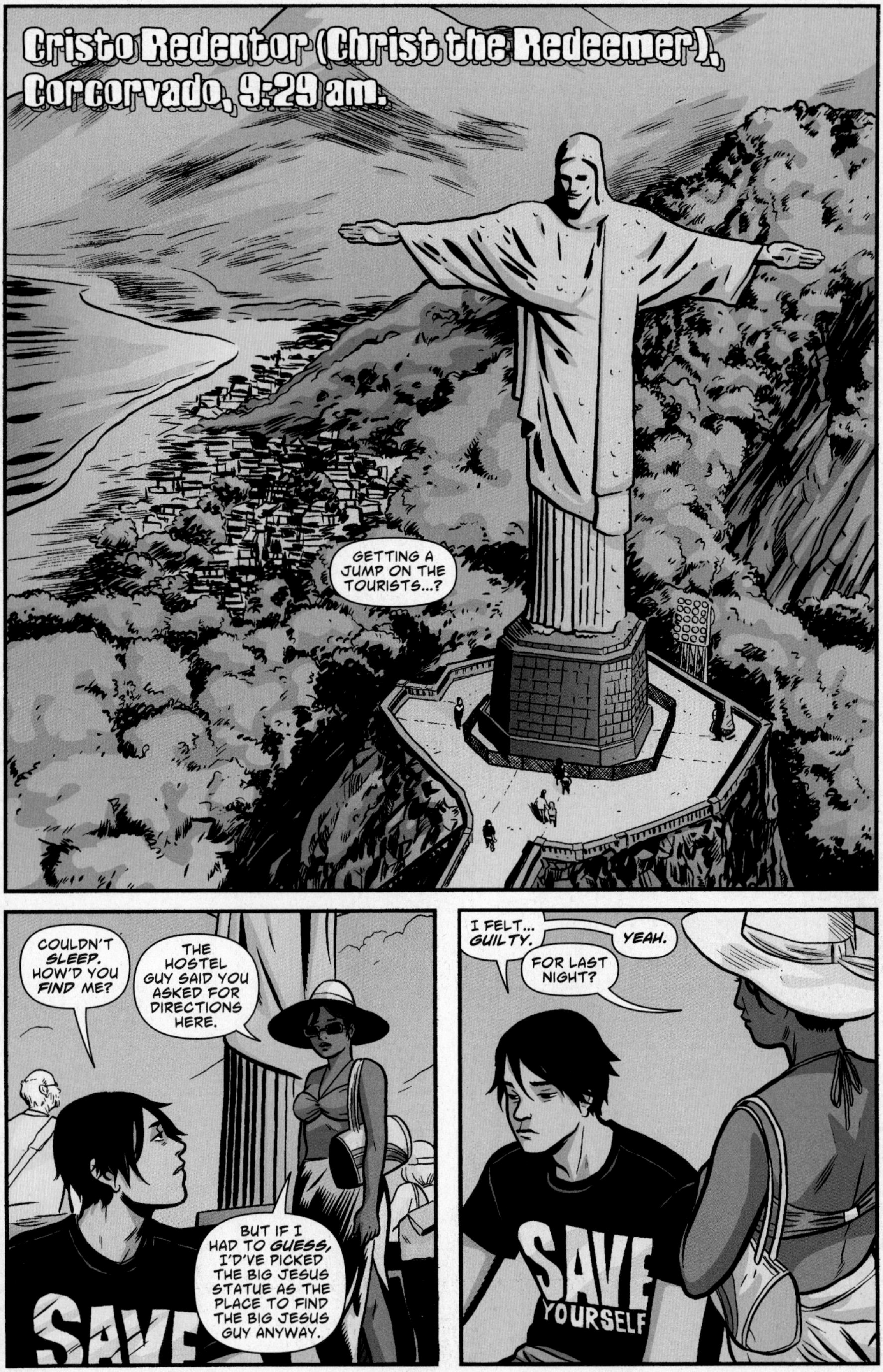
Cristo Redentor (Christ the Redeemer), Corcorvado, 9:29 am.
GETTING A JUMP ON THE TOURISTS...?
COULDN'T SLEEP. HOW'D YOU FIND ME?
THE HOSTEL GUY SAID YOU ASKED FOR DIRECTIONS HERE.
BUT IF I HAD TO GUESS, I'D'VE PICKED THE BIG JESUS STATUE AS THE PLACE TO FIND THE BIG JESUS GUY ANYWAY.
SAVE
I FELT... GUILTY.
FOR LAST NIGHT?
YEAH.
SAVE YOURSELF

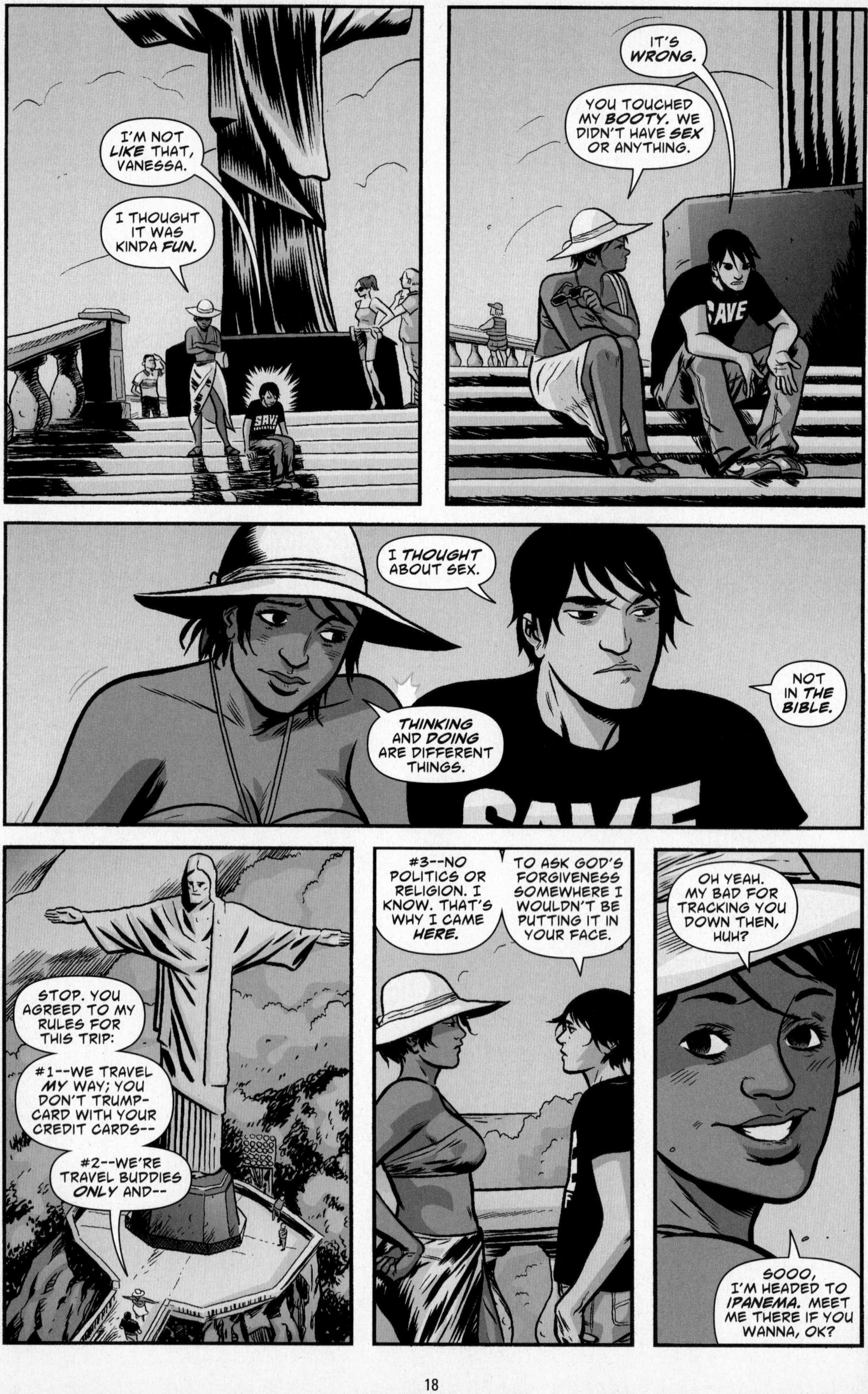
I'M NOT LIKE THAT, VANESSA.
I THOUGHT IT WAS KINDA FUN.
SAVE
IT'S WRONG.
YOU TOUCHED MY BOOTY. WE DIDN'T HAVE SEX OR ANYTHING.
SAVE
I THOUGHT ABOUT SEX.
THINKING AND DOING ARE DIFFERENT THINGS.
NOT IN THE BIBLE.
STOP. YOU AGREED TO MY RULES FOR THIS TRIP:
#1--WE TRAVEL MY WAY; YOU DON'T TRUMP-CARD WITH YOUR CREDIT CARDS--
#2--WE'RE TRAVEL BUDDIES ONLY AND--
#3--NO POLITICS OR RELIGION. I KNOW. THAT'S WHY I CAME HERE.
TO ASK GOD'S FORGIVENESS SOMEWHERE I WOULDN'T BE PUTTING IT IN YOUR FACE.
OH YEAH. MY BAD FOR TRACKING YOU DOWN THEN, HUH?
SOOO, I'M HEADED TO IPANEMA. MEET ME THERE IF YOU WANNA, OK?

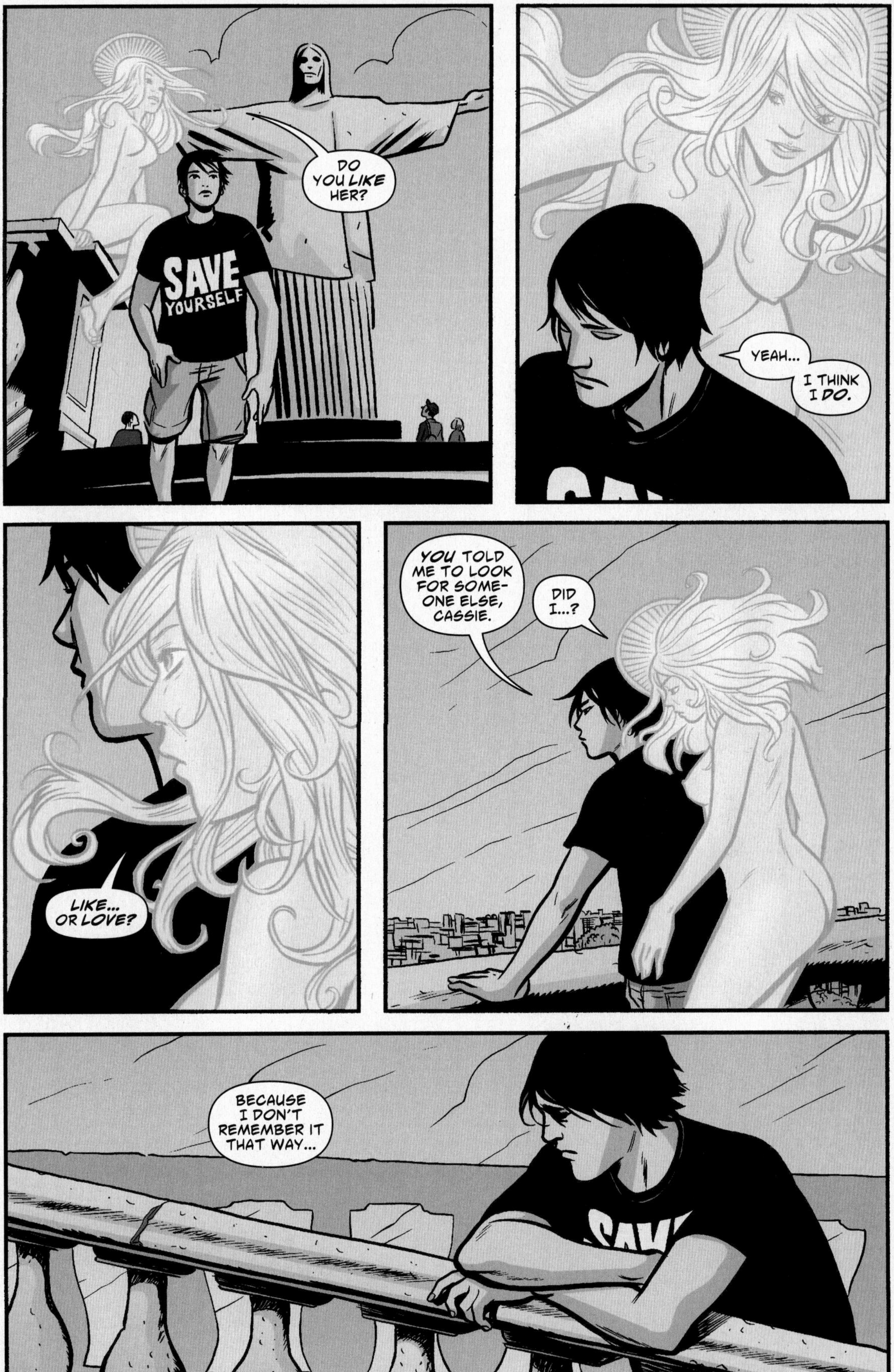
DO YOU LIKE HER?
SAVE YOURSELF
YEAH... I THINK I DO.
LIKE... OR LOVE?
YOU TOLD ME TO LOOK FOR SOME-ONE ELSE, CASSIE.
DID I...?
BECAUSE I DON'T REMEMBER IT THAT WAY...

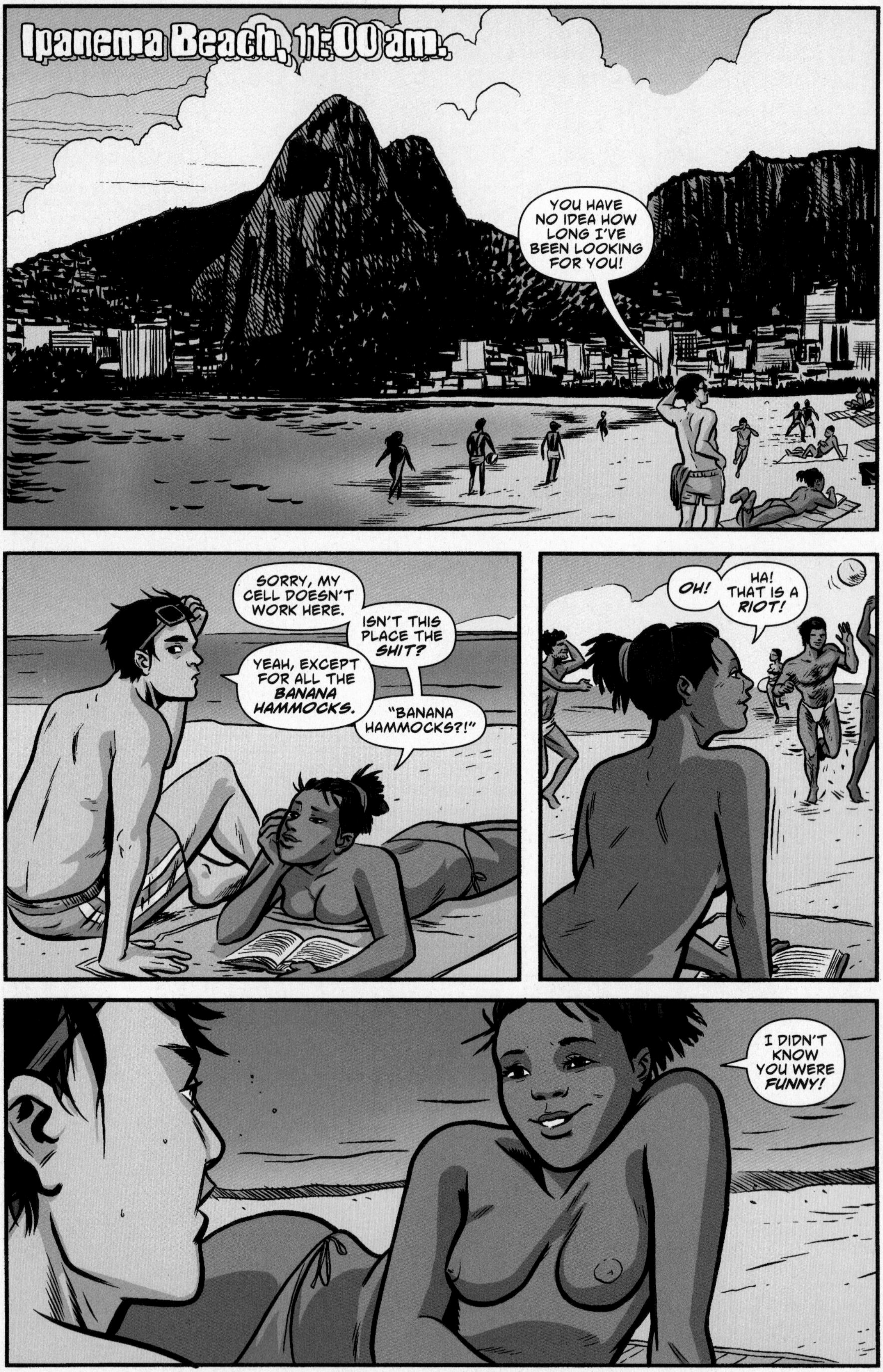
Ipanema Beach, 11:00 am.
YOU HAVE NO IDEA HOW LONG I'VE BEEN LOOKING FOR YOU!
SORRY, MY CELL DOESN'T WORK HERE.
ISN'T THIS PLACE THE *SHIT?*
YEAH, EXCEPT FOR ALL THE *BANANA HAMMOCKS.*
"BANANA HAMMOCKS?!"
OH!
HA! THAT IS A *RIOT!*
I DIDN'T KNOW YOU WERE *FUNNY!*

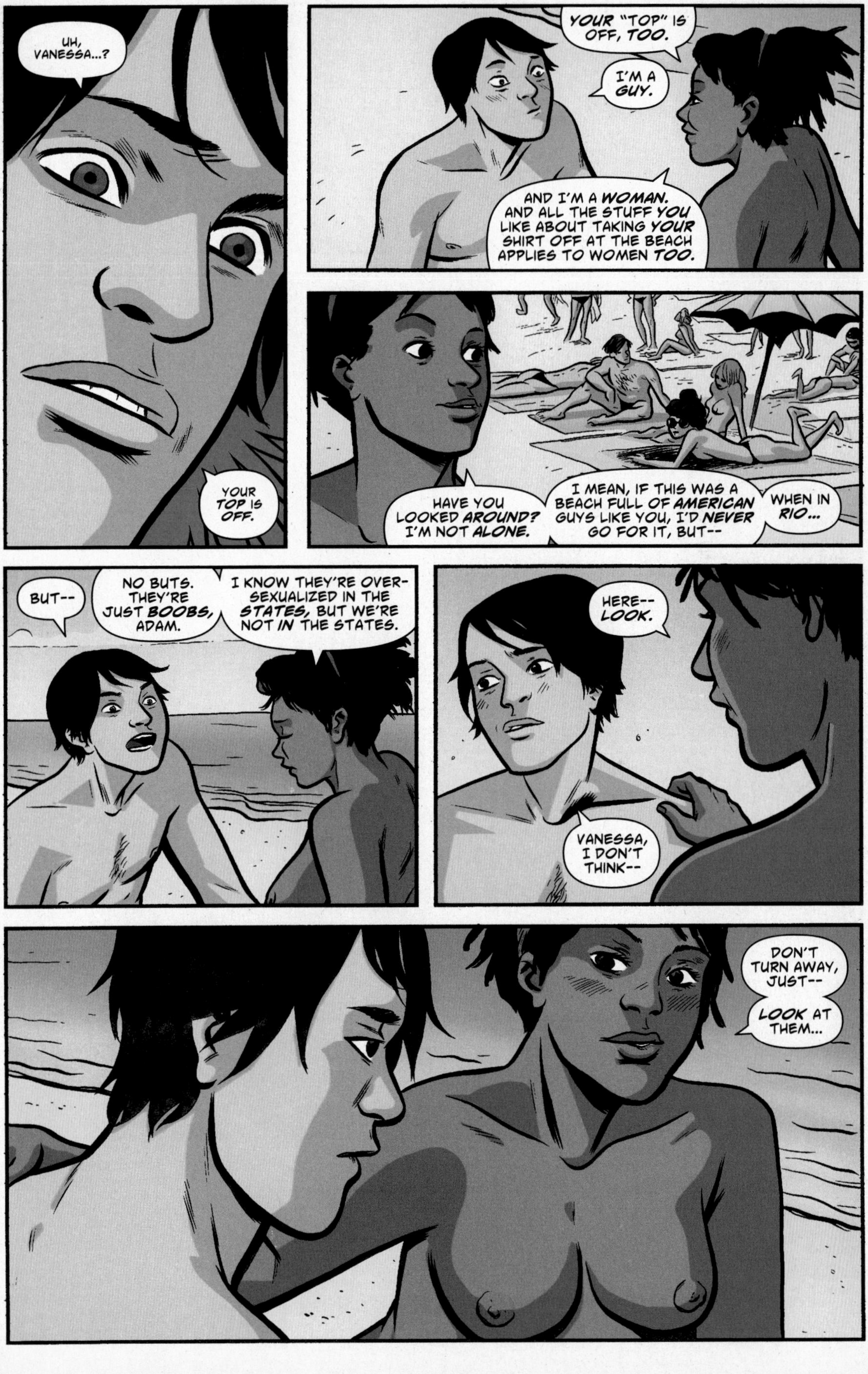

UH, VANESSA...?
YOUR TOP IS OFF.
YOUR "TOP" IS OFF, TOO.
I'M A GUY.
AND I'M A WOMAN. AND ALL THE STUFF YOU LIKE ABOUT TAKING YOUR SHIRT OFF AT THE BEACH APPLIES TO WOMEN TOO.
HAVE YOU LOOKED AROUND? I'M NOT ALONE.
I MEAN, IF THIS WAS A BEACH FULL OF AMERICAN GUYS LIKE YOU, I'D NEVER GO FOR IT, BUT--
WHEN IN RIO...
BUT--
NO BUTS. THEY'RE JUST BOOBS, ADAM.
I KNOW THEY'RE OVER-SEXUALIZED IN THE STATES, BUT WE'RE NOT IN THE STATES.
HERE-- LOOK.
VANESSA, I DON'T THINK--
DON'T TURN AWAY, JUST--
LOOK AT THEM...

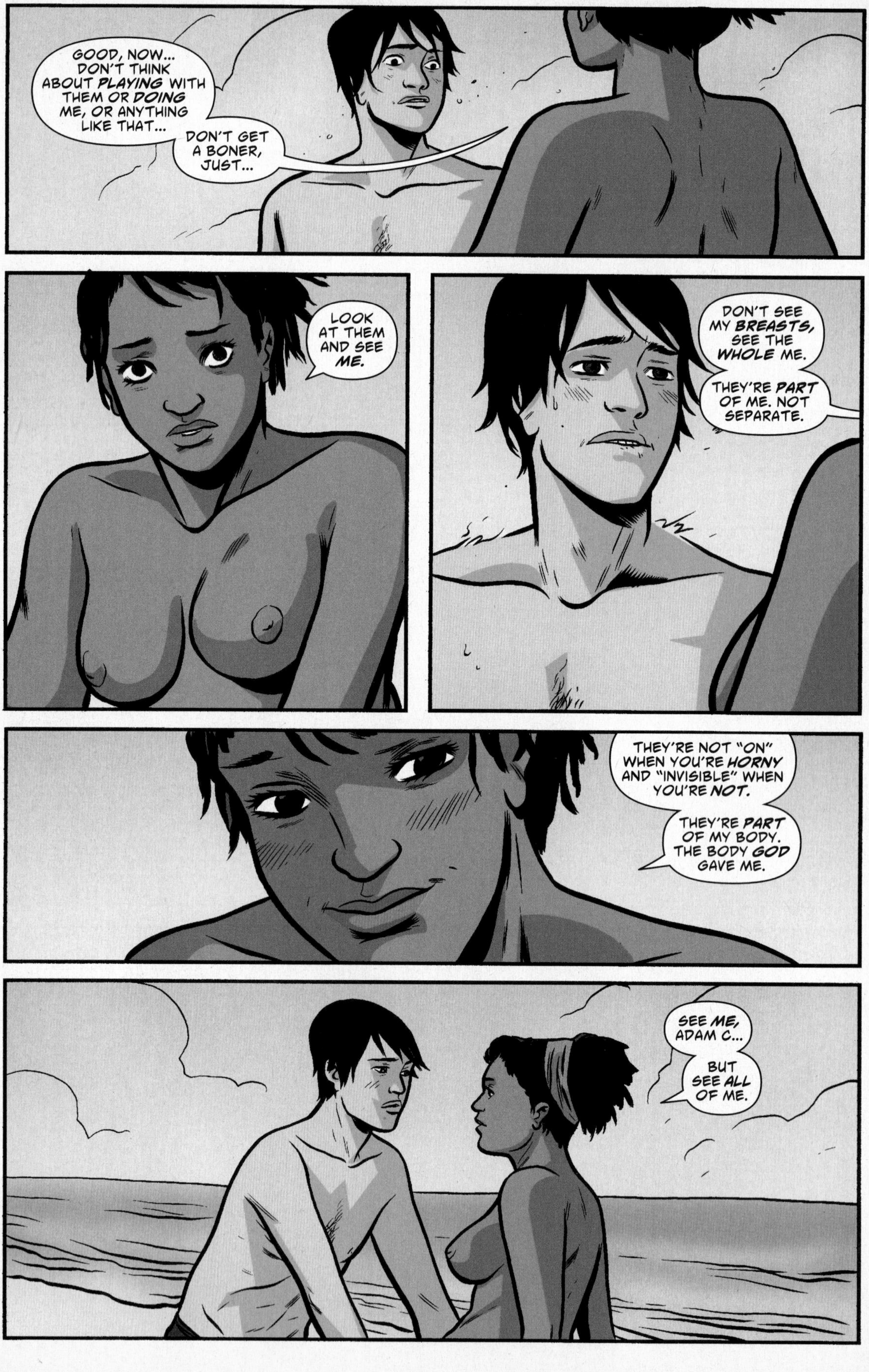
GOOD, NOW... DON'T THINK ABOUT PLAYING WITH THEM OR DOING ME, OR ANYTHING LIKE THAT...
DON'T GET A BONER, JUST...
LOOK AT THEM AND SEE ME.
DON'T SEE MY BREASTS, SEE THE WHOLE ME.
THEY'RE PART OF ME. NOT SEPARATE.
THEY'RE NOT "ON" WHEN YOU'RE HORNY AND "INVISIBLE" WHEN YOU'RE NOT.
THEY'RE PART OF MY BODY. THE BODY GOD GAVE ME.
SEE ME, ADAM C...
BUT SEE ALL OF ME.

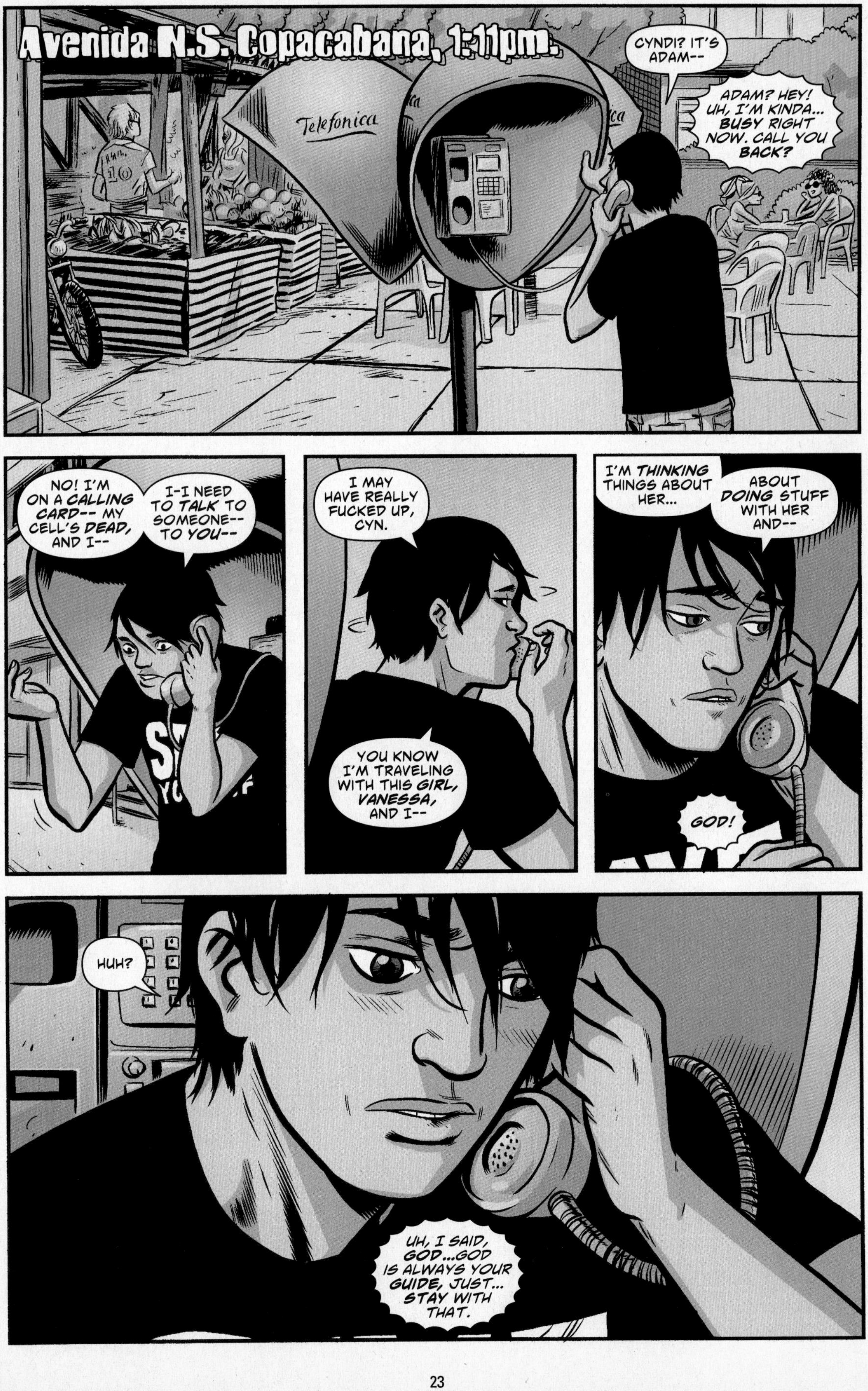
Avenida N.S. Copacabana, 1:11pm.
Telefonica
CYNDI? IT'S ADAM--
ADAM? HEY! UH, I'M KINDA... BUSY RIGHT NOW. CALL YOU BACK?
NO! I'M ON A CALLING CARD-- MY CELL'S DEAD, AND I--
I-I NEED TO TALK TO SOMEONE-- TO YOU--
I MAY HAVE REALLY FUCKED UP, CYN.
YOU KNOW I'M TRAVELING WITH THIS GIRL, VANESSA, AND I--
I'M THINKING THINGS ABOUT HER...
ABOUT DOING STUFF WITH HER AND--
GOD!
HUH?
UH, I SAID, GOD...GOD IS ALWAYS YOUR GUIDE, JUST... STAY WITH THAT.

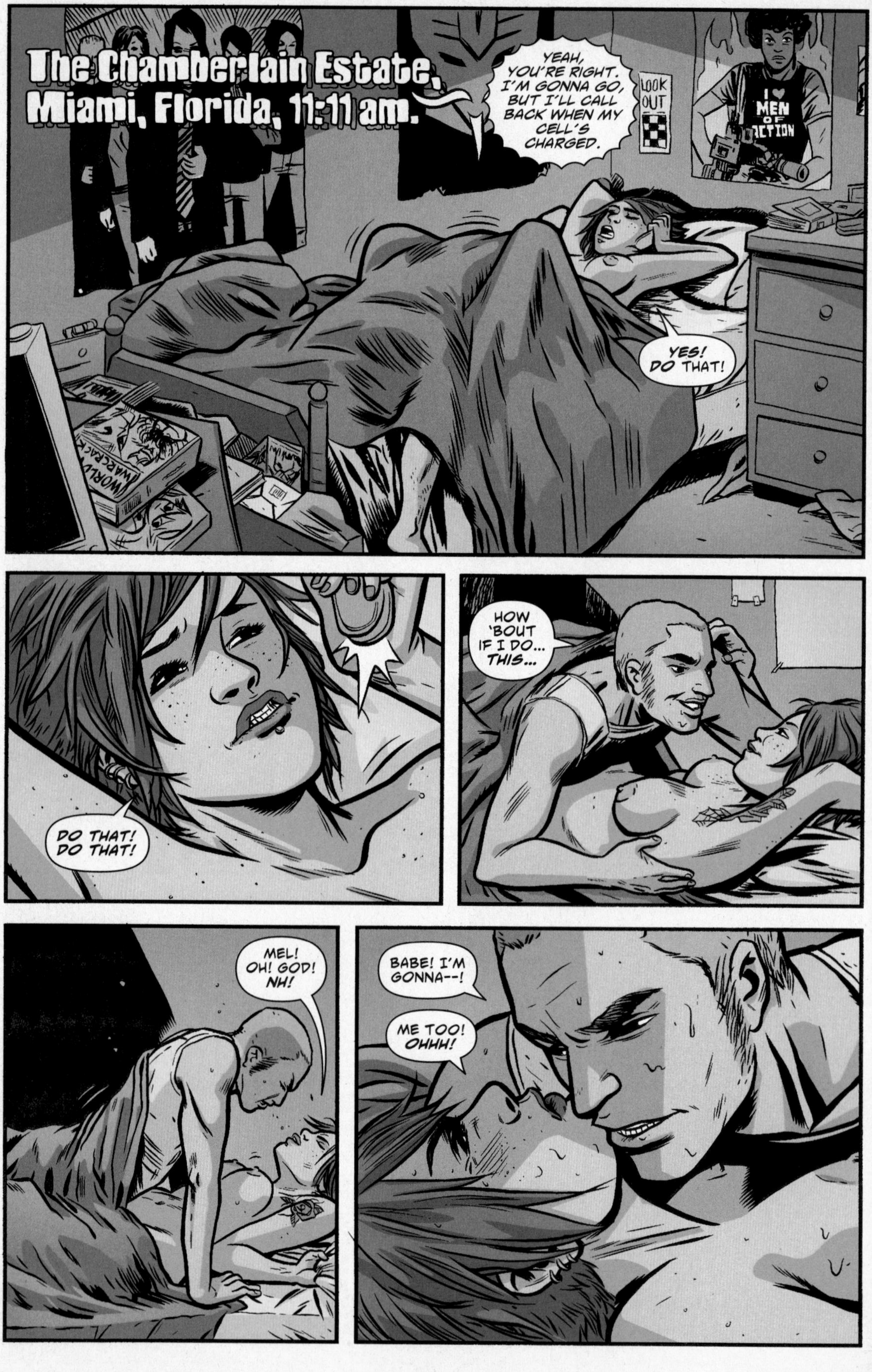
The Chamberlain Estate, Miami, Florida, 11:11 am.
YEAH, YOU'RE RIGHT. I'M GONNA GO, BUT I'LL CALL BACK WHEN MY CELL'S CHARGED.
LOOK OUT
YES! DO THAT!
DO THAT! DO THAT!
HOW 'BOUT IF I DO... THIS...
MEL! OH! GOD! NH!
BABE! I'M GONNA--!
ME TOO! OHHH!

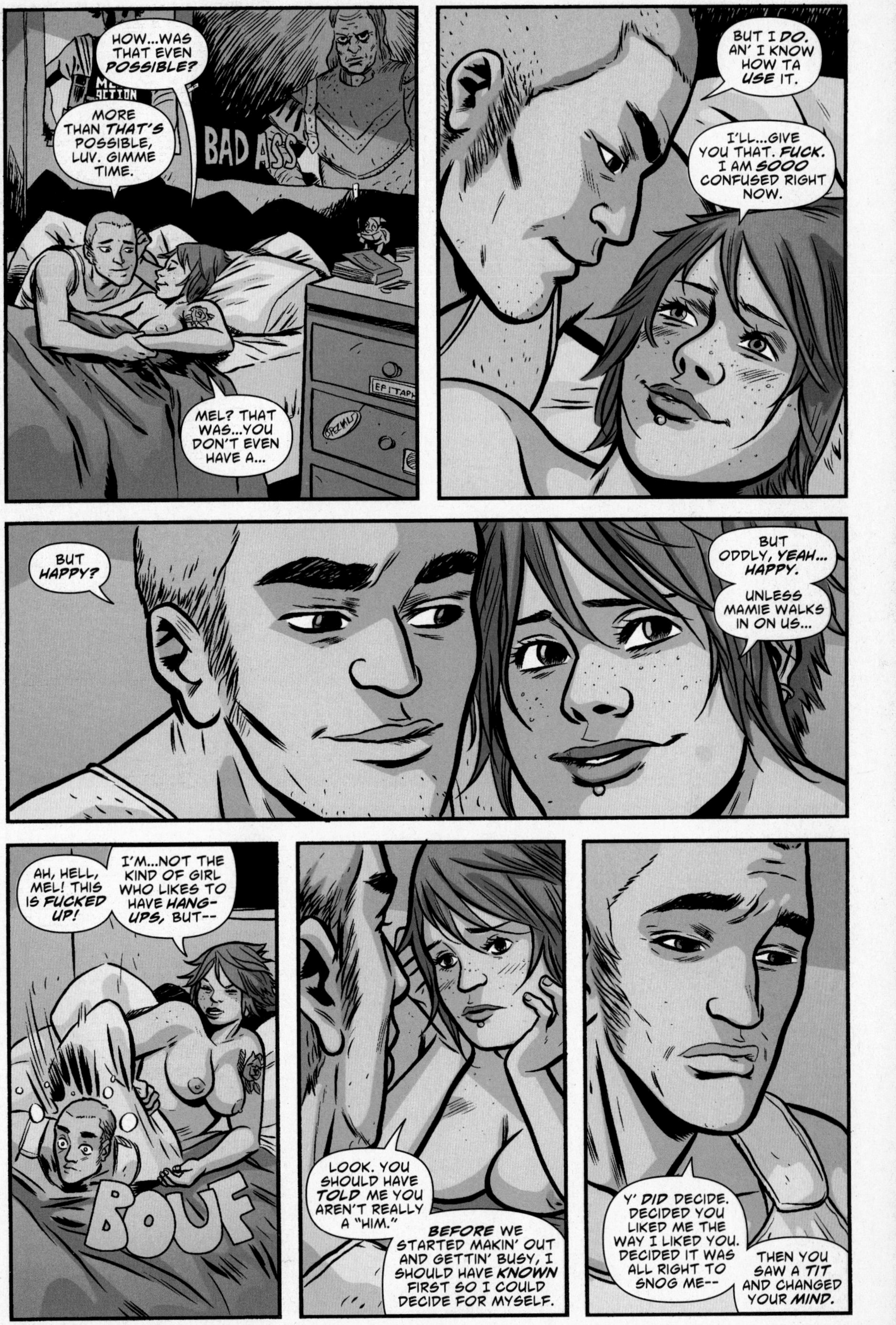
ME
ACTION
BAD ASS
HOW...WAS THAT EVEN POSSIBLE?
MORE THAN THAT'S POSSIBLE, LUV. GIMME TIME.
EPITAPH
MEL? THAT WAS...YOU DON'T EVEN HAVE A...
BUT I DO. AN' I KNOW HOW TA USE IT.
I'LL...GIVE YOU THAT. FUCK. I AM SOOO CONFUSED RIGHT NOW.
BUT HAPPY?
BUT ODDLY, YEAH... HAPPY.
UNLESS MAMIE WALKS IN ON US...
AH, HELL, MEL! THIS IS FUCKED UP!
I'M...NOT THE KIND OF GIRL WHO LIKES TO HAVE HANG-UPS, BUT--
BOUF
LOOK. YOU SHOULD HAVE TOLD ME YOU AREN'T REALLY A "HIM."
BEFORE WE STARTED MAKIN' OUT AND GETTIN' BUSY, I SHOULD HAVE KNOWN FIRST SO I COULD DECIDE FOR MYSELF.
Y' DID DECIDE. DECIDED YOU LIKED ME THE WAY I LIKED YOU. DECIDED IT WAS ALL RIGHT TO SNOG ME--
THEN YOU SAW A TIT AND CHANGED YOUR MIND.

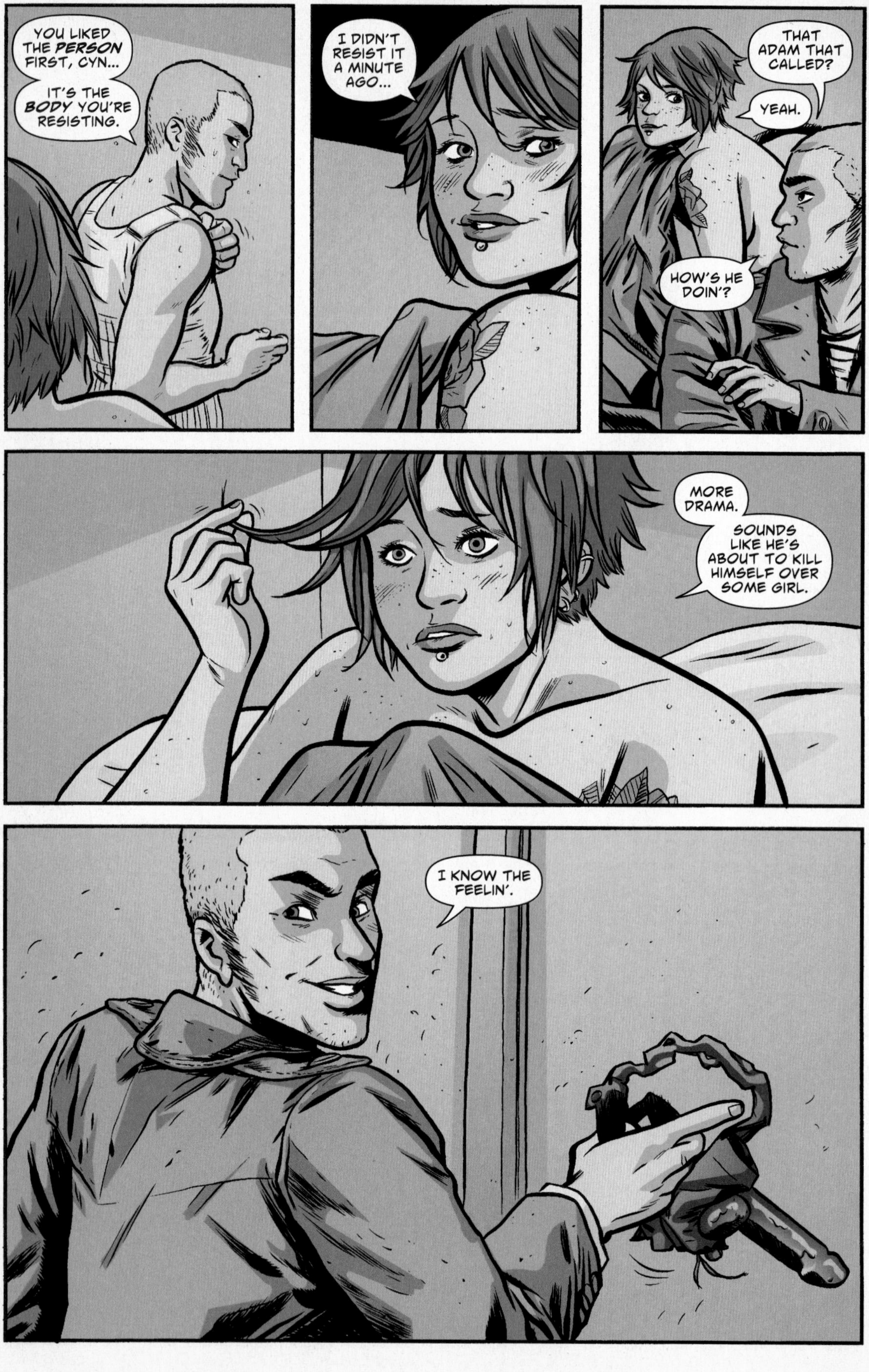
YOU LIKED THE PERSON FIRST, CYN...
IT'S THE BODY YOU'RE RESISTING.
I DIDN'T RESIST IT A MINUTE AGO...
THAT ADAM THAT CALLED?
YEAH.
HOW'S HE DOIN'?
MORE DRAMA.
SOUNDS LIKE HE'S ABOUT TO KILL HIMSELF OVER SOME GIRL.
I KNOW THE FEELIN'.

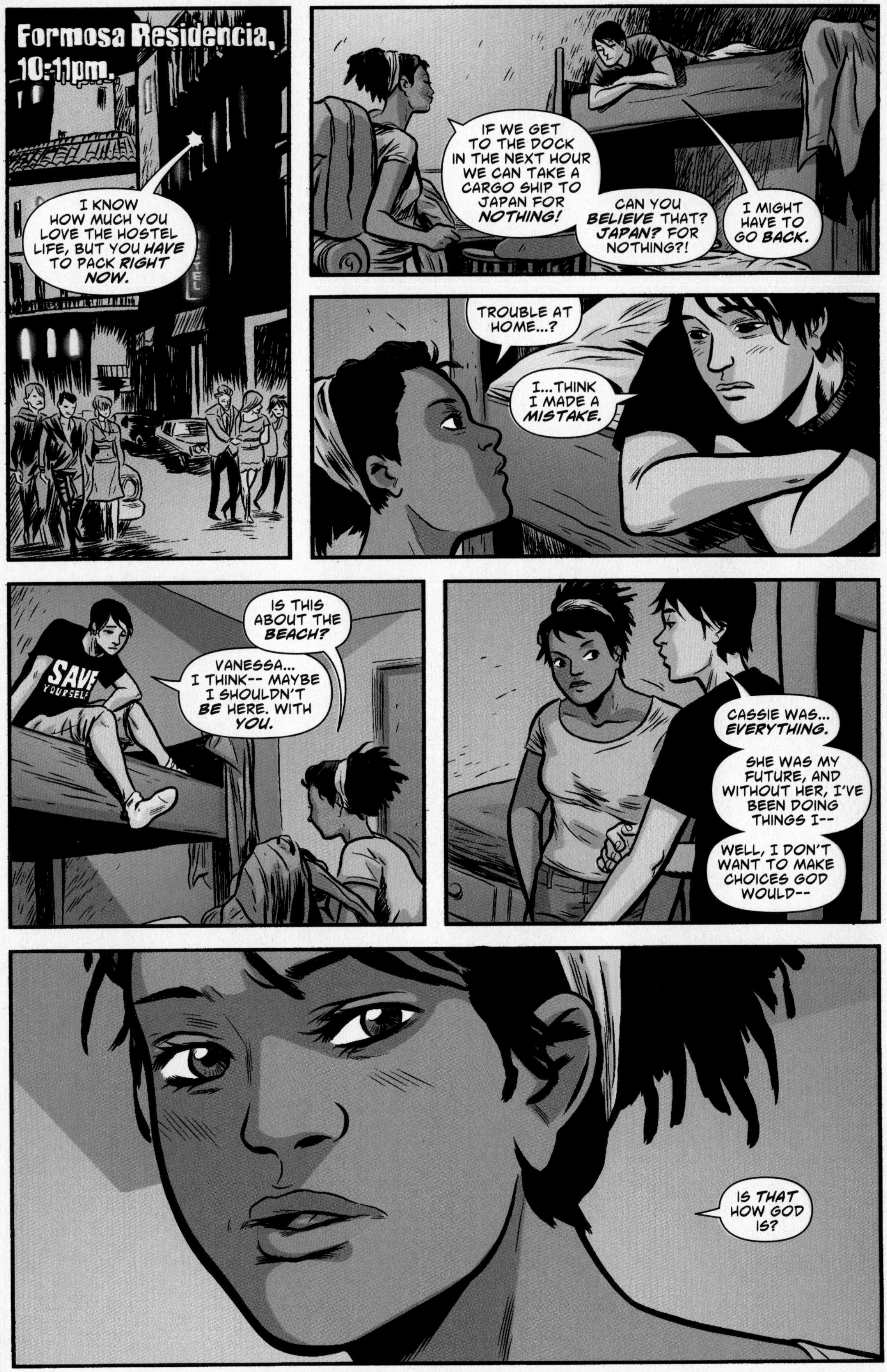

Formosa Residencia, 10:11pm.
I KNOW HOW MUCH YOU LOVE THE HOSTEL LIFE, BUT YOU *HAVE* TO PACK *RIGHT NOW.*
HOSTEL
IF WE GET TO THE DOCK IN THE NEXT HOUR WE CAN TAKE A CARGO SHIP TO JAPAN FOR *NOTHING!*
CAN YOU *BELIEVE* THAT? *JAPAN?* FOR NOTHING?!
I MIGHT HAVE TO GO *BACK.*
TROUBLE AT HOME...?
I...THINK I MADE A *MISTAKE.*
SAVE YOURSELF
IS THIS ABOUT THE *BEACH?*
VANESSA... I THINK-- MAYBE I SHOULDN'T *BE* HERE. WITH *YOU.*
CASSIE WAS... *EVERYTHING.*
SHE WAS MY FUTURE, AND WITHOUT HER, I'VE BEEN DOING THINGS I--
WELL, I DON'T WANT TO MAKE CHOICES GOD WOULD--
IS *THAT* HOW GOD IS?

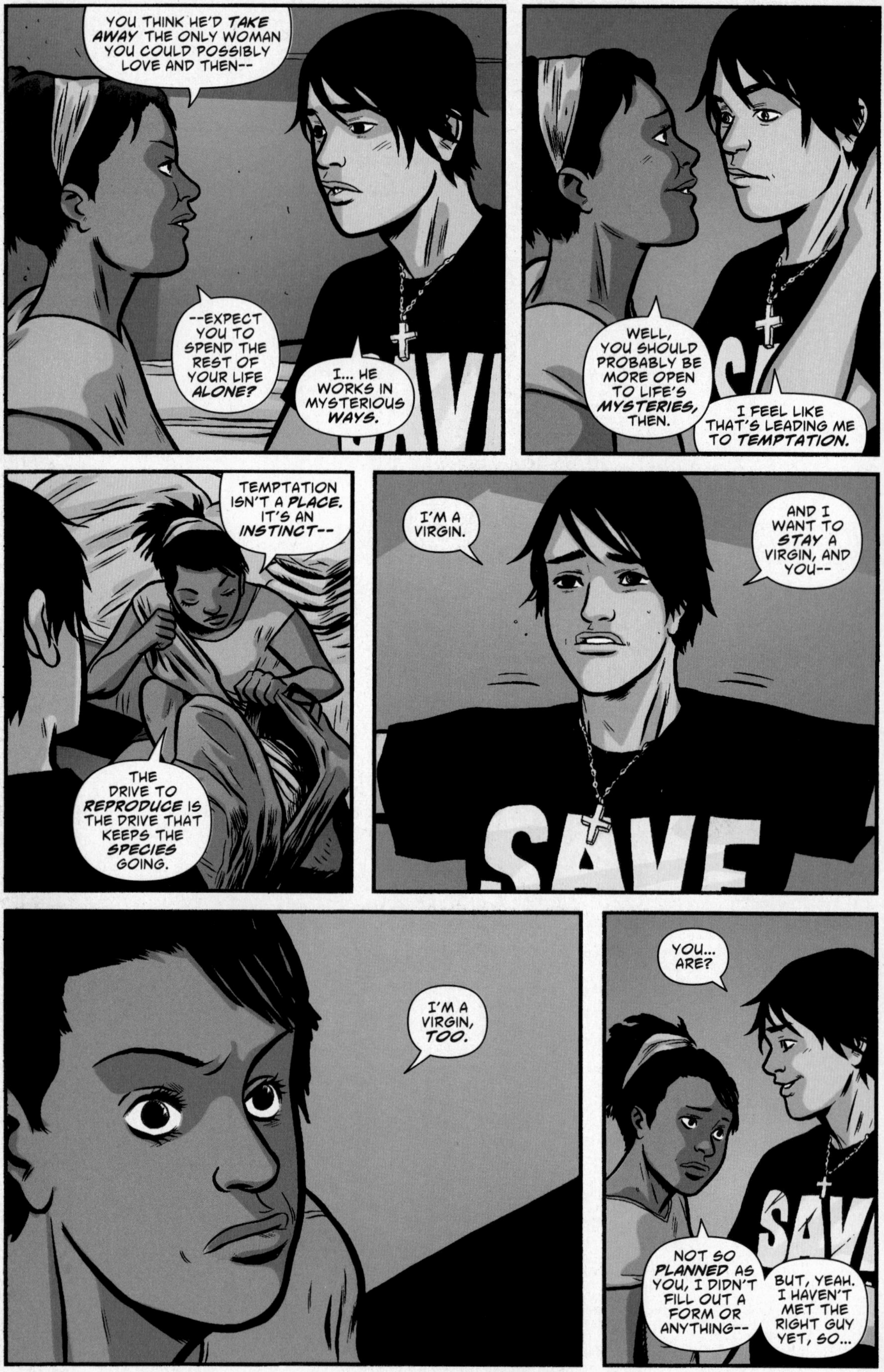
YOU THINK HE'D TAKE AWAY THE ONLY WOMAN YOU COULD POSSIBLY LOVE AND THEN--
--EXPECT YOU TO SPEND THE REST OF YOUR LIFE ALONE?
I... HE WORKS IN MYSTERIOUS WAYS.
WELL, YOU SHOULD PROBABLY BE MORE OPEN TO LIFE'S MYSTERIES, THEN.
I FEEL LIKE THAT'S LEADING ME TO TEMPTATION.
TEMPTATION ISN'T A PLACE. IT'S AN INSTINCT--
THE DRIVE TO REPRODUCE IS THE DRIVE THAT KEEPS THE SPECIES GOING.
I'M A VIRGIN.
AND I WANT TO STAY A VIRGIN, AND YOU--
I'M A VIRGIN, TOO.
YOU... ARE?
NOT SO PLANNED AS YOU, I DIDN'T FILL OUT A FORM OR ANYTHING--
BUT, YEAH. I HAVEN'T MET THE RIGHT GUY YET, SO...

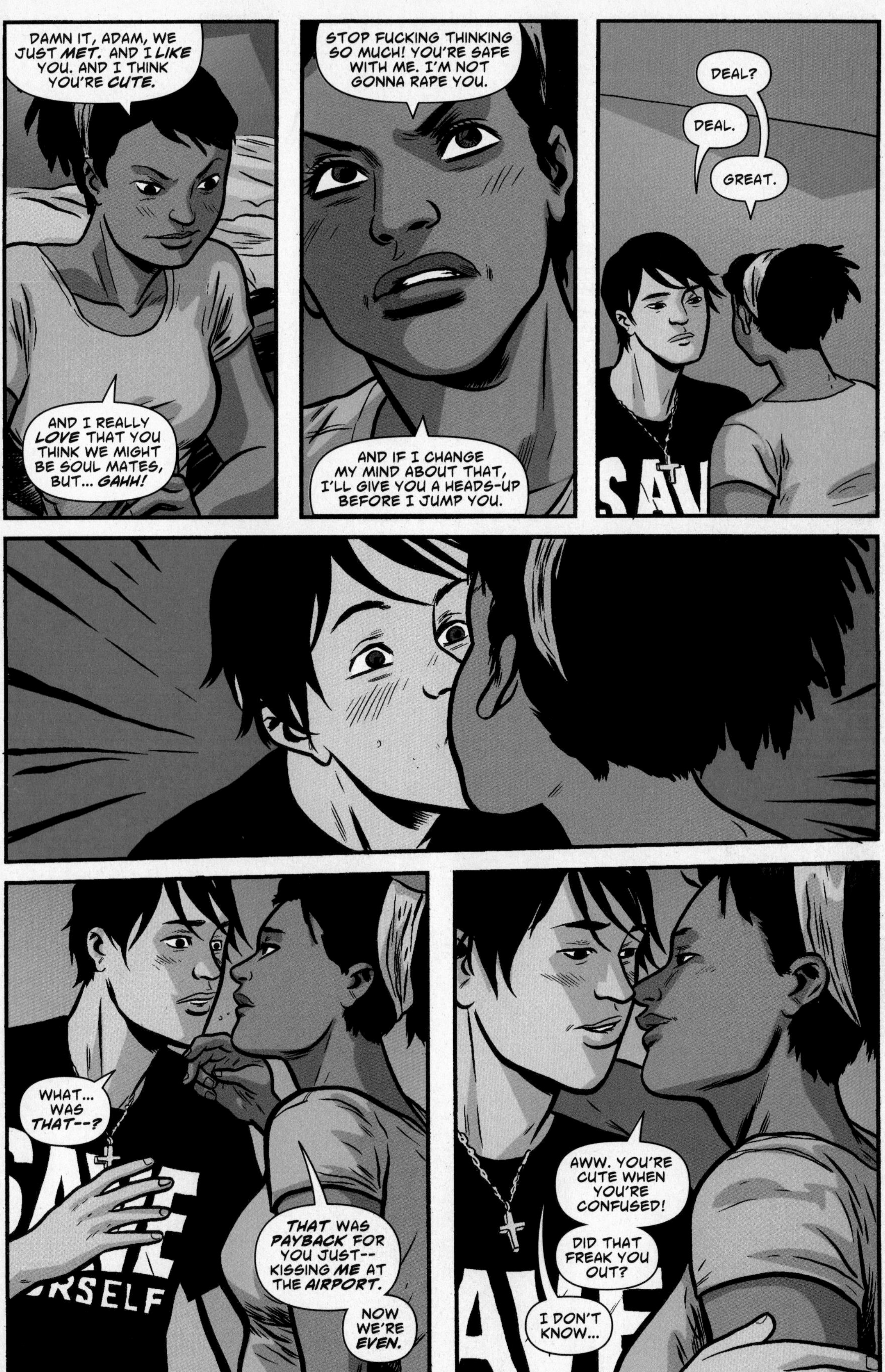
DAMN IT, ADAM, WE JUST MET. AND I LIKE YOU. AND I THINK YOU'RE CUTE.
AND I REALLY LOVE THAT YOU THINK WE MIGHT BE SOUL MATES, BUT... GAHH!
STOP FUCKING THINKING SO MUCH! YOU'RE SAFE WITH ME. I'M NOT GONNA RAPE YOU.
AND IF I CHANGE MY MIND ABOUT THAT, I'LL GIVE YOU A HEADS-UP BEFORE I JUMP YOU.
DEAL?
DEAL.
GREAT.
WHAT... WAS THAT--?
THAT WAS PAYBACK FOR YOU JUST--KISSING ME AT THE AIRPORT.
NOW WE'RE EVEN.
AWW. YOU'RE CUTE WHEN YOU'RE CONFUSED!
DID THAT FREAK YOU OUT?
I DON'T KNOW...

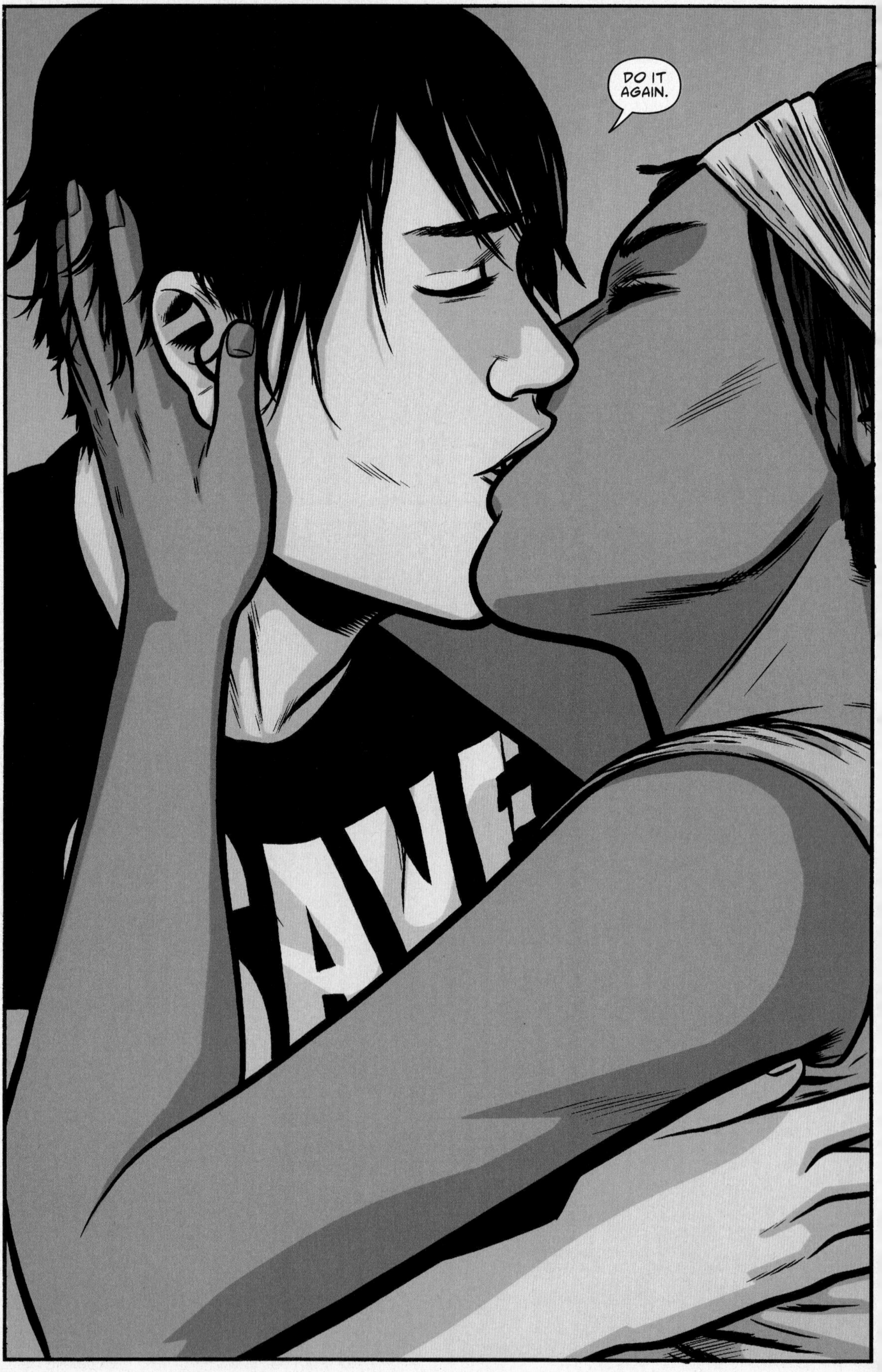
DO IT AGAIN.

CHAPTER TWO

Chapter pencils by Becky Cloonan   Chapter inks by Jim Rugg

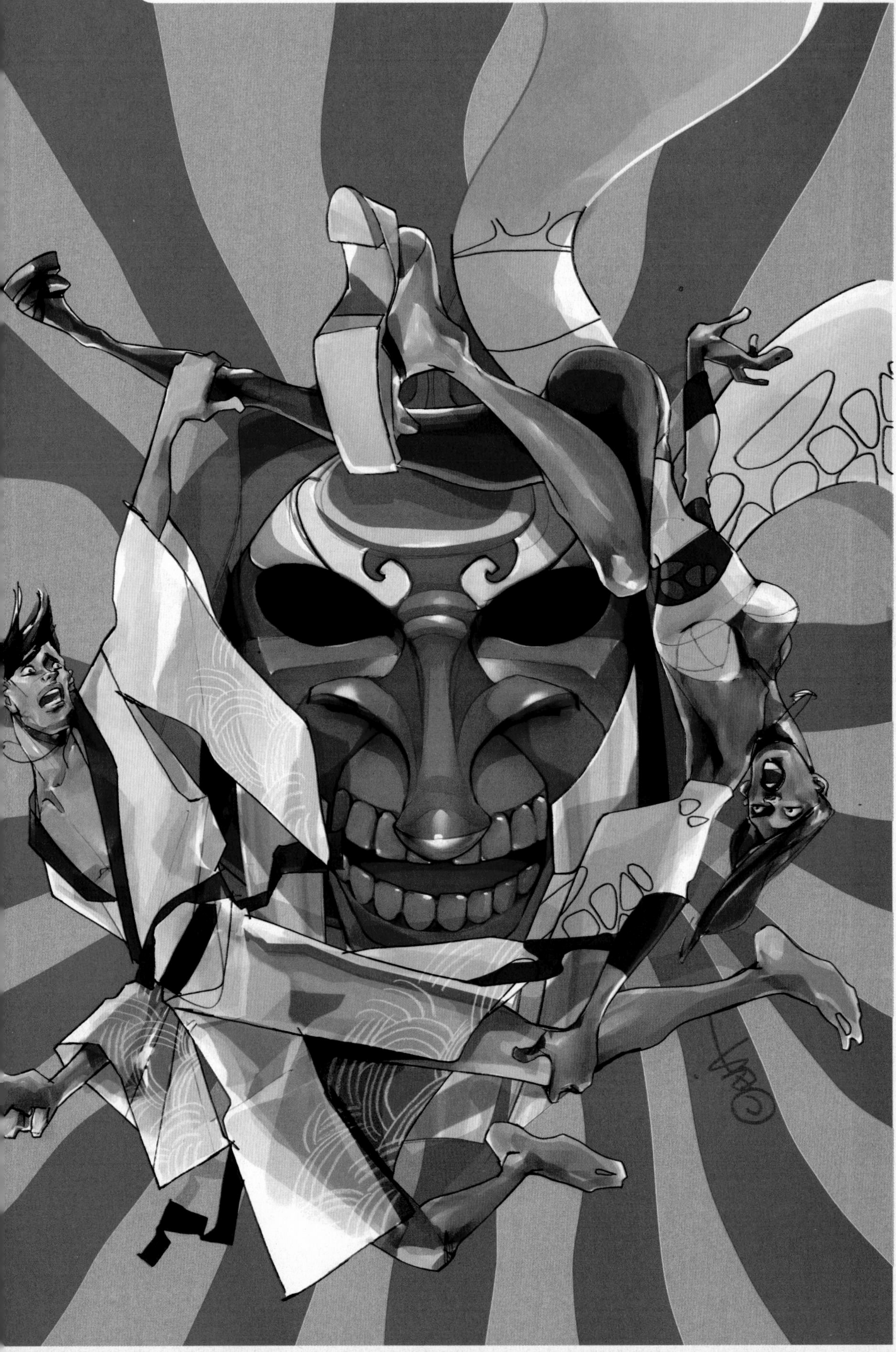

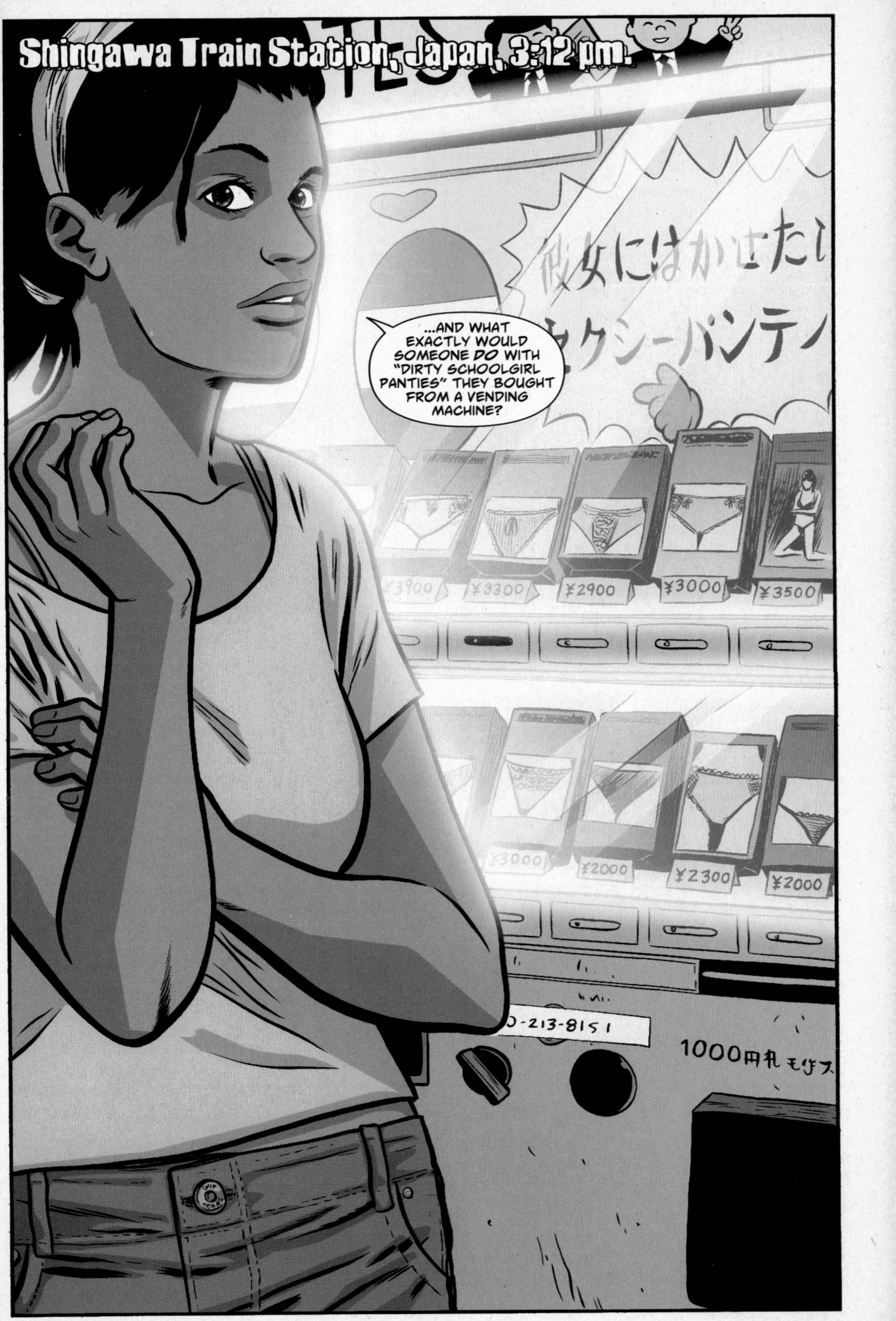
Shingawa Train Station, Japan, 3:12 pm.
...AND WHAT EXACTLY WOULD SOMEONE *DO* WITH "DIRTY SCHOOLGIRL PANTIES" THEY BOUGHT FROM A VENDING MACHINE?

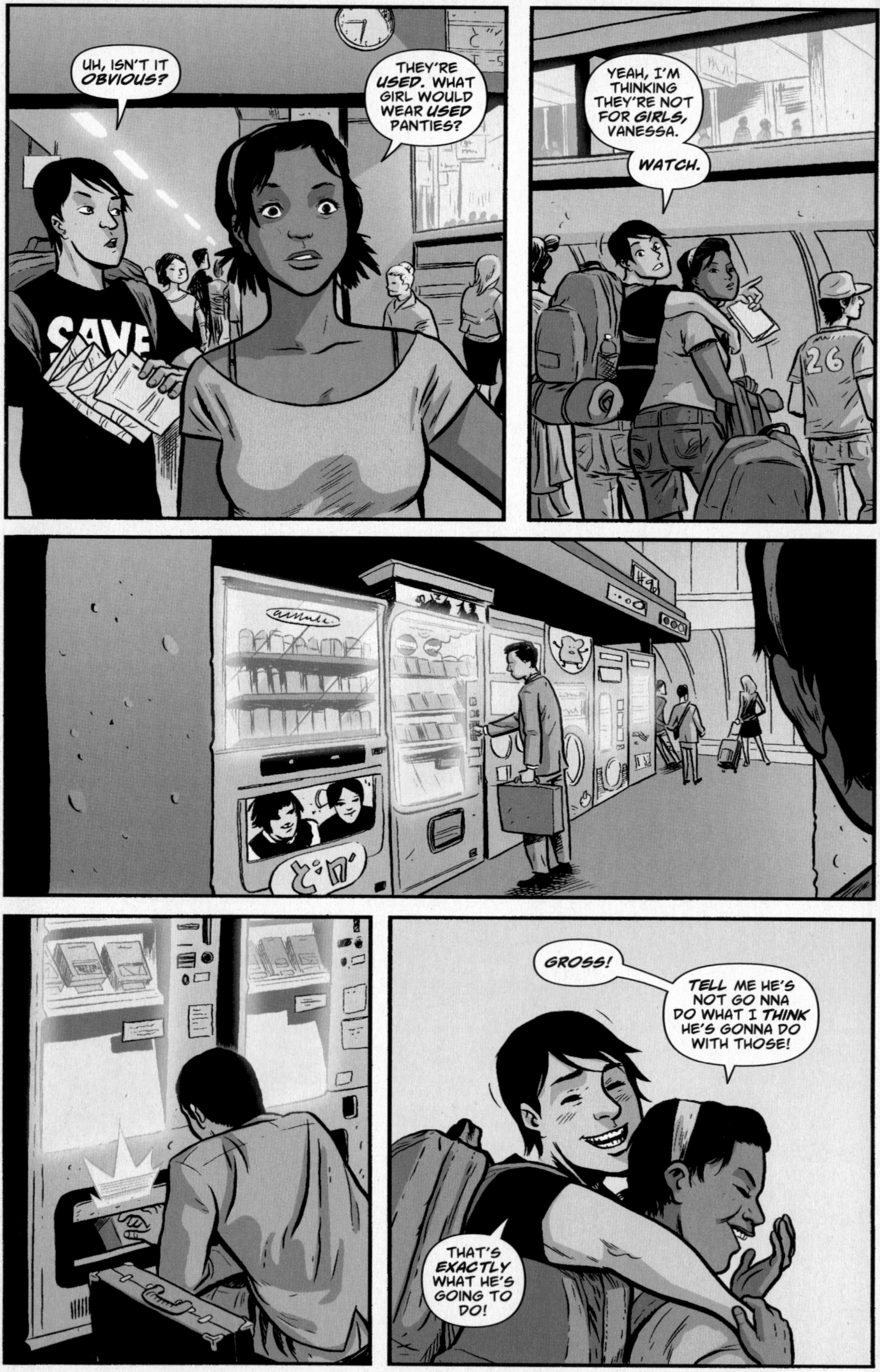
UH, ISN'T IT OBVIOUS?
THEY'RE USED. WHAT GIRL WOULD WEAR USED PANTIES?
YEAH, I'M THINKING THEY'RE NOT FOR GIRLS, VANESSA.
WATCH.
GROSS!
TELL ME HE'S NOT GO NNA DO WHAT I THINK HE'S GONNA DO WITH THOSE!
THAT'S EXACTLY WHAT HE'S GOING TO DO!

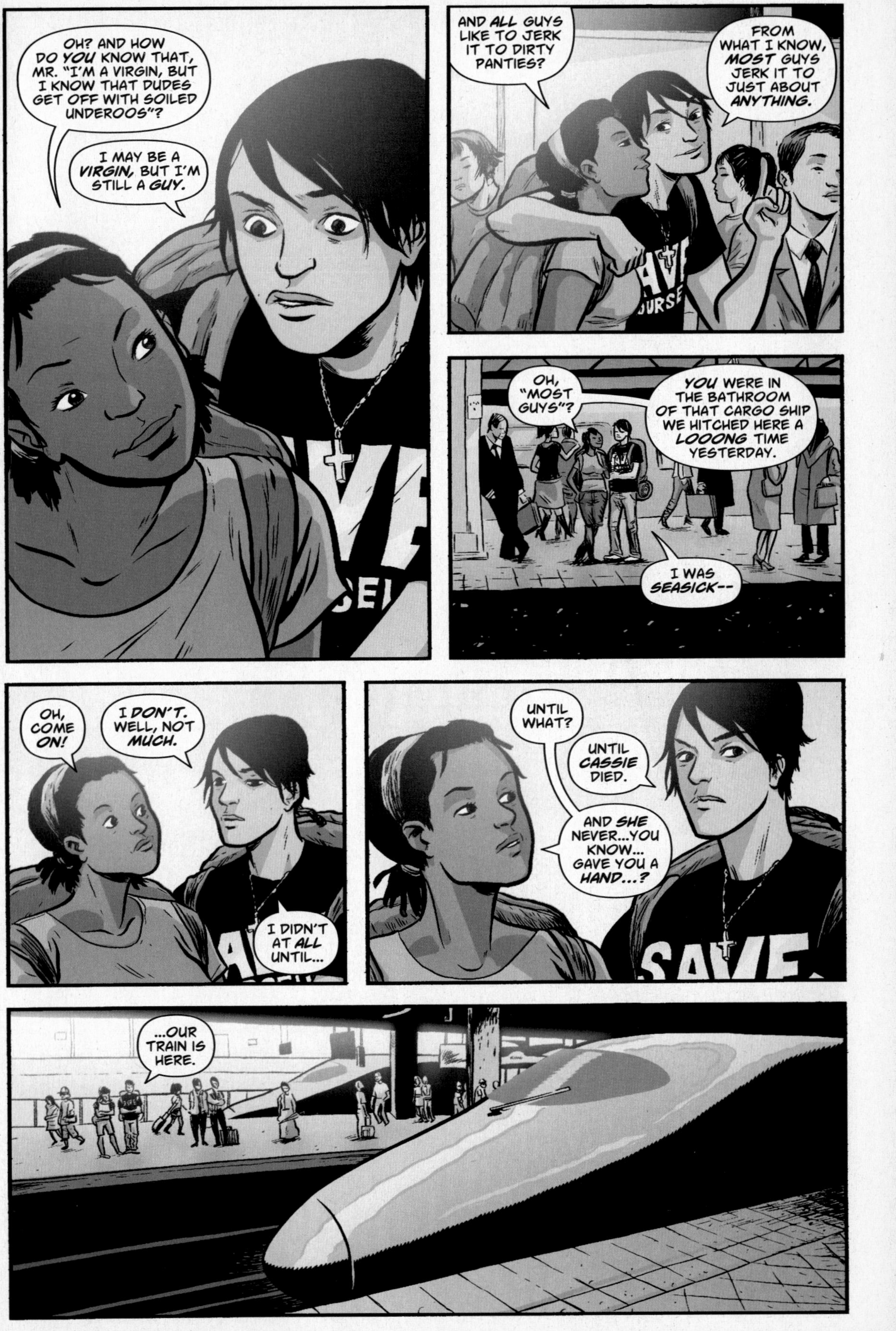
OH? AND HOW DO YOU KNOW THAT, MR. "I'M A VIRGIN, BUT I KNOW THAT DUDES GET OFF WITH SOILED UNDEROOS"?
I MAY BE A VIRGIN, BUT I'M STILL A GUY.
AND ALL GUYS LIKE TO JERK IT TO DIRTY PANTIES?
FROM WHAT I KNOW, MOST GUYS JERK IT TO JUST ABOUT ANYTHING.
OH, "MOST GUYS"?
YOU WERE IN THE BATHROOM OF THAT CARGO SHIP WE HITCHED HERE A LOOONG TIME YESTERDAY.
I WAS SEASICK--
OH, COME ON!
I DON'T. WELL, NOT MUCH.
I DIDN'T AT ALL UNTIL...
UNTIL WHAT?
UNTIL CASSIE DIED.
AND SHE NEVER...YOU KNOW... GAVE YOU A HAND...?
...OUR TRAIN IS HERE.

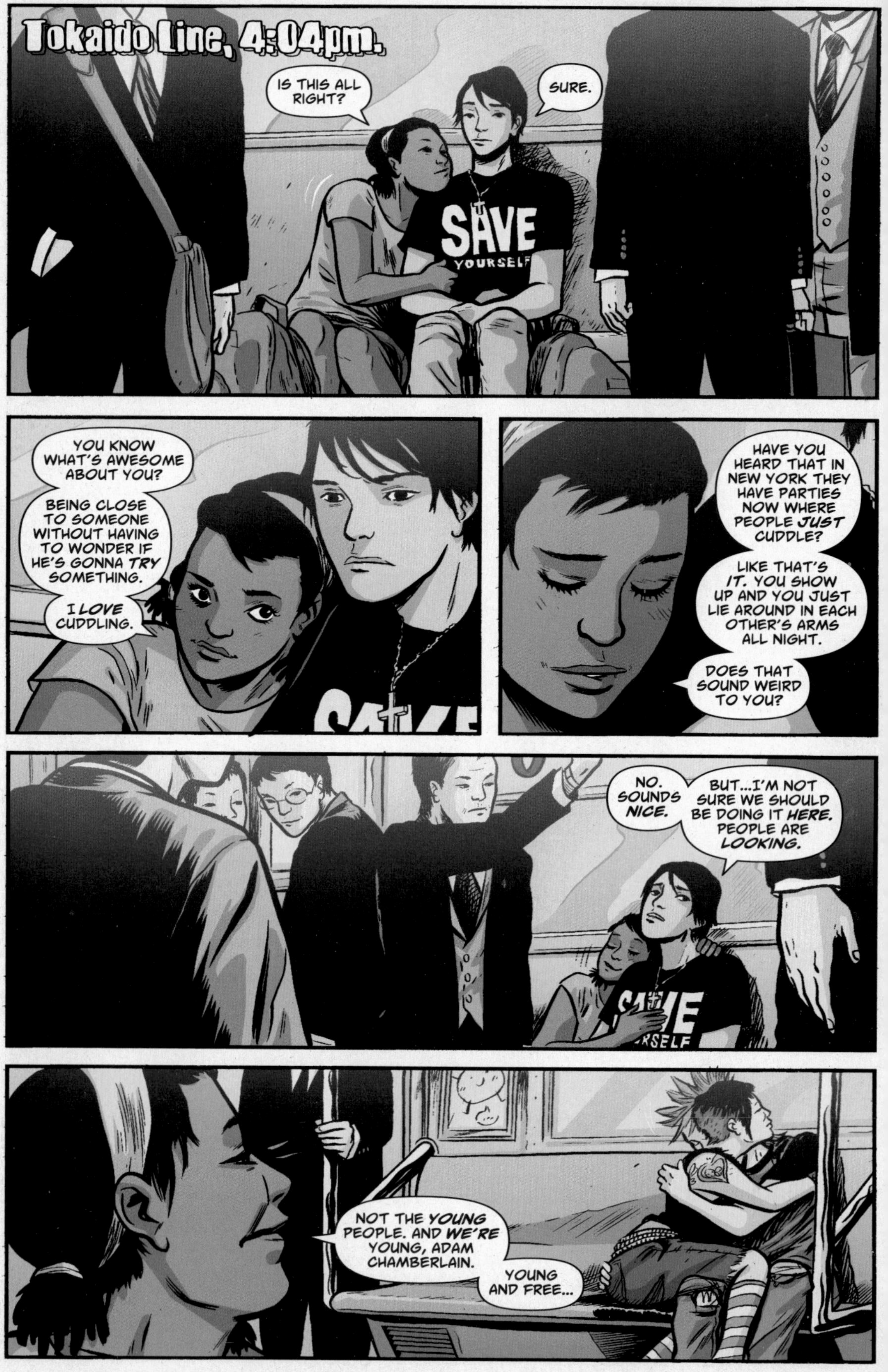
Tokaido Line, 4:04pm.
IS THIS ALL RIGHT?
SURE.
SAVE YOURSELF
YOU KNOW WHAT'S AWESOME ABOUT YOU?
BEING CLOSE TO SOMEONE WITHOUT HAVING TO WONDER IF HE'S GONNA TRY SOMETHING.
I LOVE CUDDLING.
HAVE YOU HEARD THAT IN NEW YORK THEY HAVE PARTIES NOW WHERE PEOPLE JUST CUDDLE?
LIKE THAT'S IT. YOU SHOW UP AND YOU JUST LIE AROUND IN EACH OTHER'S ARMS ALL NIGHT.
DOES THAT SOUND WEIRD TO YOU?
NO. SOUNDS NICE.
BUT...I'M NOT SURE WE SHOULD BE DOING IT HERE. PEOPLE ARE LOOKING.
NOT THE YOUNG PEOPLE. AND WE'RE YOUNG, ADAM CHAMBERLAIN.
YOUNG AND FREE...

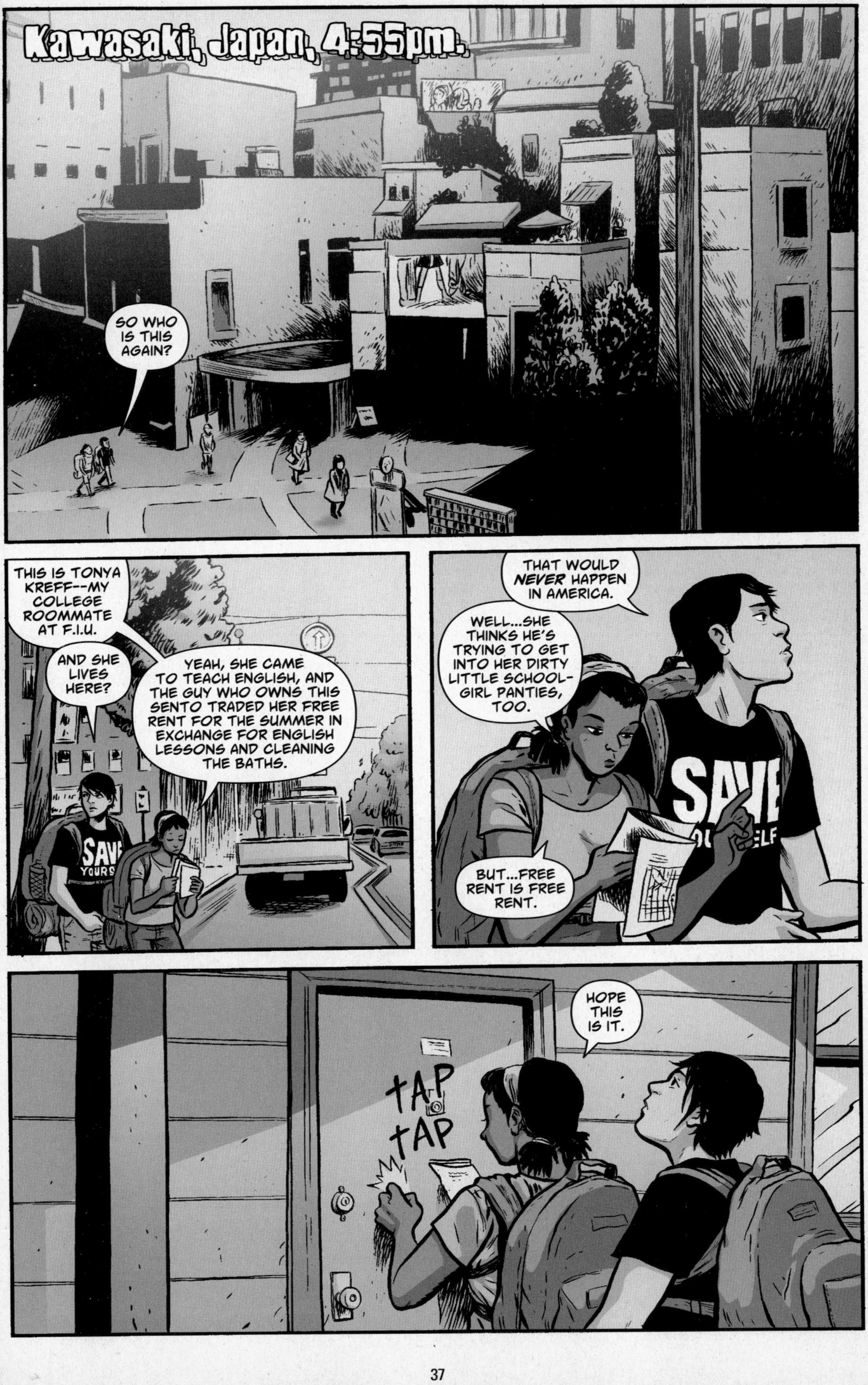
Kawasaki, Japan, 4:55pm.
SO WHO IS THIS AGAIN?
THIS IS TONYA KREFF--MY COLLEGE ROOMMATE AT F.I.U.
AND SHE LIVES HERE?
YEAH, SHE CAME TO TEACH ENGLISH, AND THE GUY WHO OWNS THIS SENTO TRADED HER FREE RENT FOR THE SUMMER IN EXCHANGE FOR ENGLISH LESSONS AND CLEANING THE BATHS.
THAT WOULD *NEVER* HAPPEN IN AMERICA.
WELL...SHE THINKS HE'S TRYING TO GET INTO HER DIRTY LITTLE SCHOOL-GIRL PANTIES, TOO.
BUT...FREE RENT IS FREE RENT.
TAP TAP
HOPE THIS IS IT.

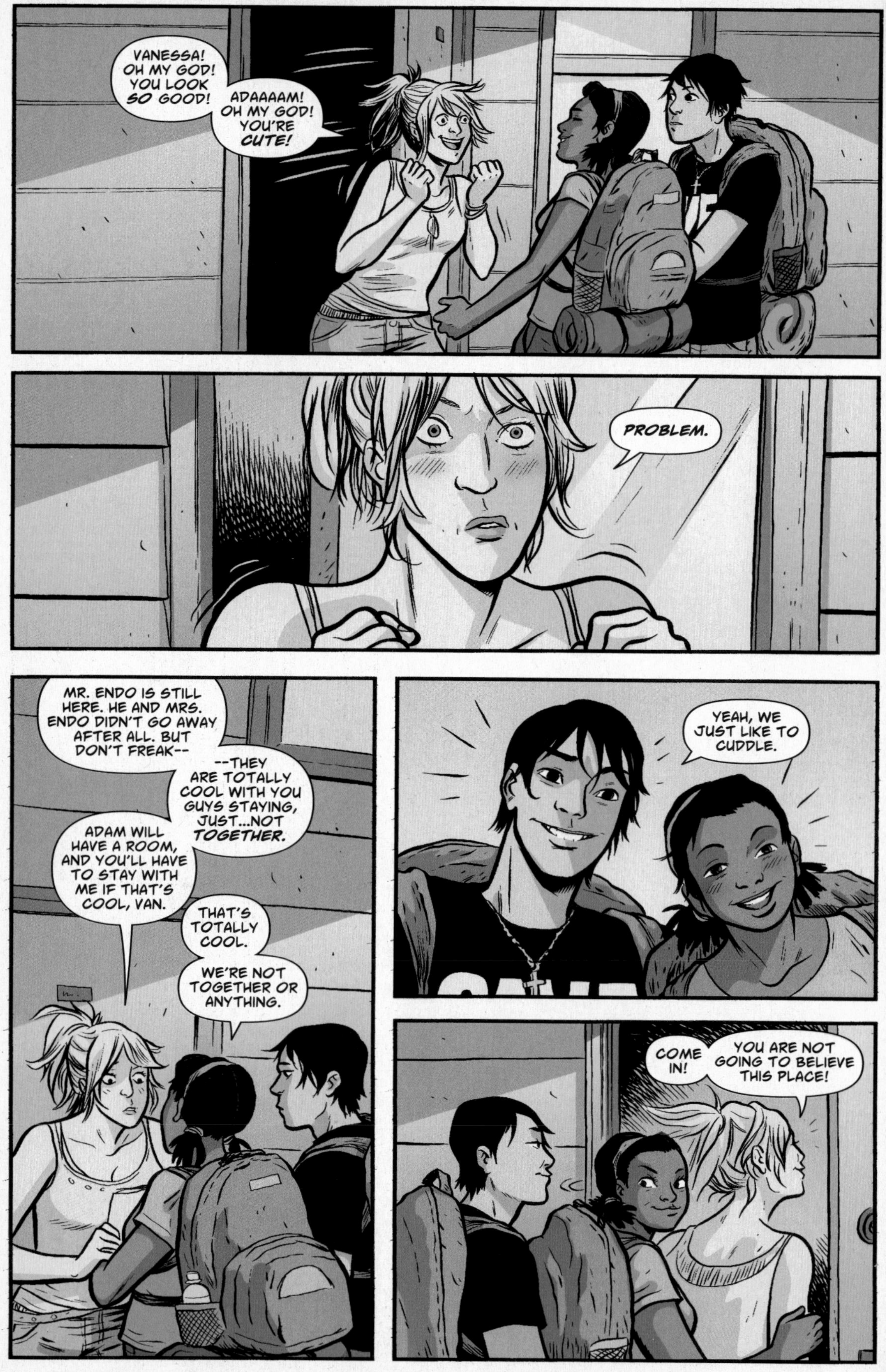
VANESSA! OH MY GOD! YOU LOOK SO GOOD!
ADAAAAM! OH MY GOD! YOU'RE CUTE!
PROBLEM.
MR. ENDO IS STILL HERE. HE AND MRS. ENDO DIDN'T GO AWAY AFTER ALL. BUT DON'T FREAK--
--THEY ARE TOTALLY COOL WITH YOU GUYS STAYING, JUST...NOT TOGETHER.
ADAM WILL HAVE A ROOM, AND YOU'LL HAVE TO STAY WITH ME IF THAT'S COOL, VAN.
THAT'S TOTALLY COOL.
WE'RE NOT TOGETHER OR ANYTHING.
YEAH, WE JUST LIKE TO CUDDLE.
COME IN!
YOU ARE NOT GOING TO BELIEVE THIS PLACE!

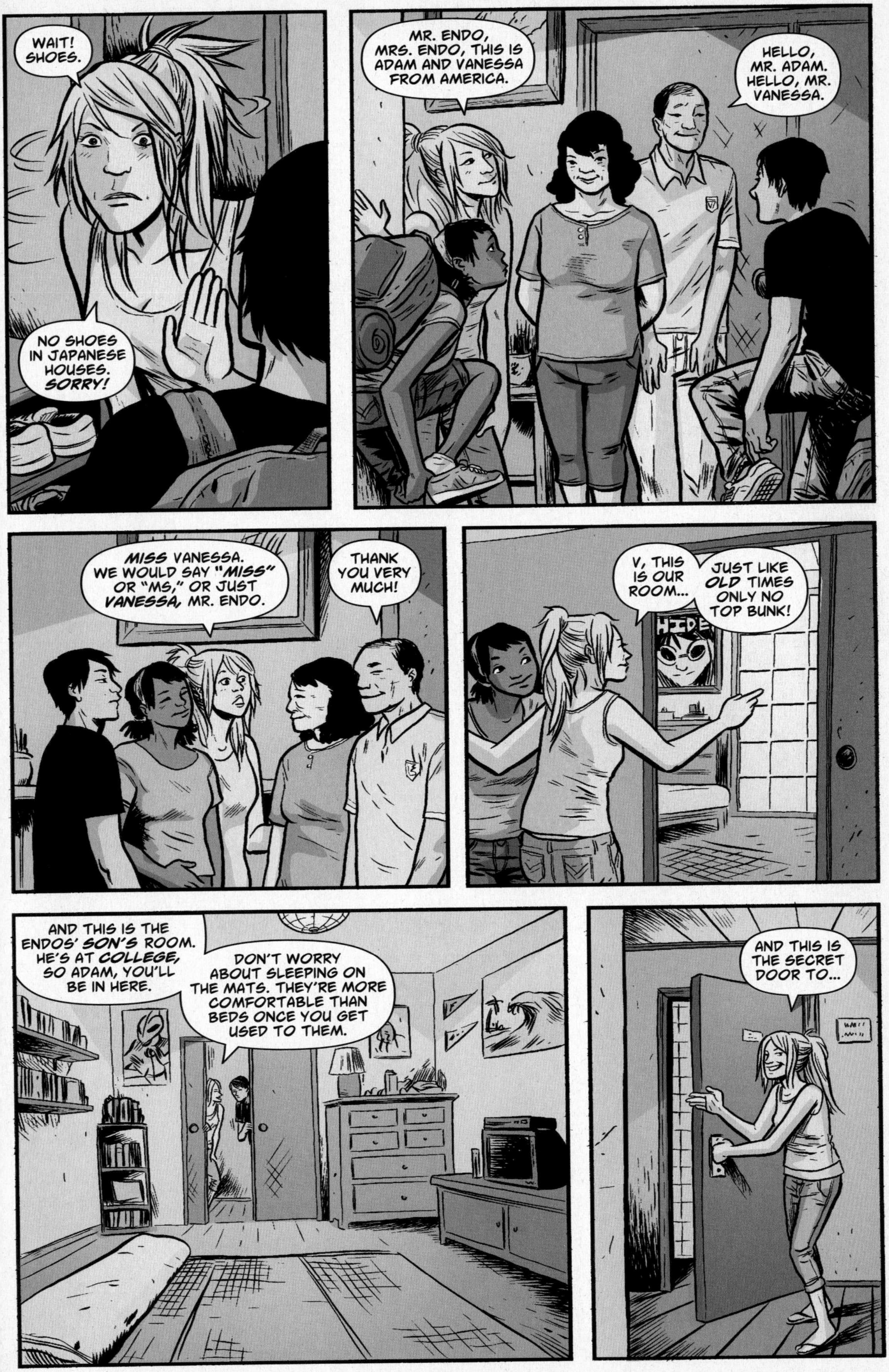
WAIT! SHOES.
NO SHOES IN JAPANESE HOUSES. *SORRY!*
MR. ENDO, MRS. ENDO, THIS IS ADAM AND VANESSA FROM AMERICA.
HELLO, MR. ADAM. HELLO, MR. VANESSA.
MISS VANESSA. WE WOULD SAY "*MISS*" OR "MS," OR JUST *VANESSA,* MR. ENDO.
THANK YOU VERY MUCH!
V, THIS IS OUR ROOM...
JUST LIKE *OLD* TIMES ONLY NO TOP BUNK!
AND THIS IS THE ENDOS' *SON'S* ROOM. HE'S AT *COLLEGE,* SO ADAM, YOU'LL BE IN HERE.
DON'T WORRY ABOUT SLEEPING ON THE MATS. THEY'RE MORE COMFORTABLE THAN BEDS ONCE YOU GET USED TO THEM.
AND THIS IS THE SECRET DOOR TO...

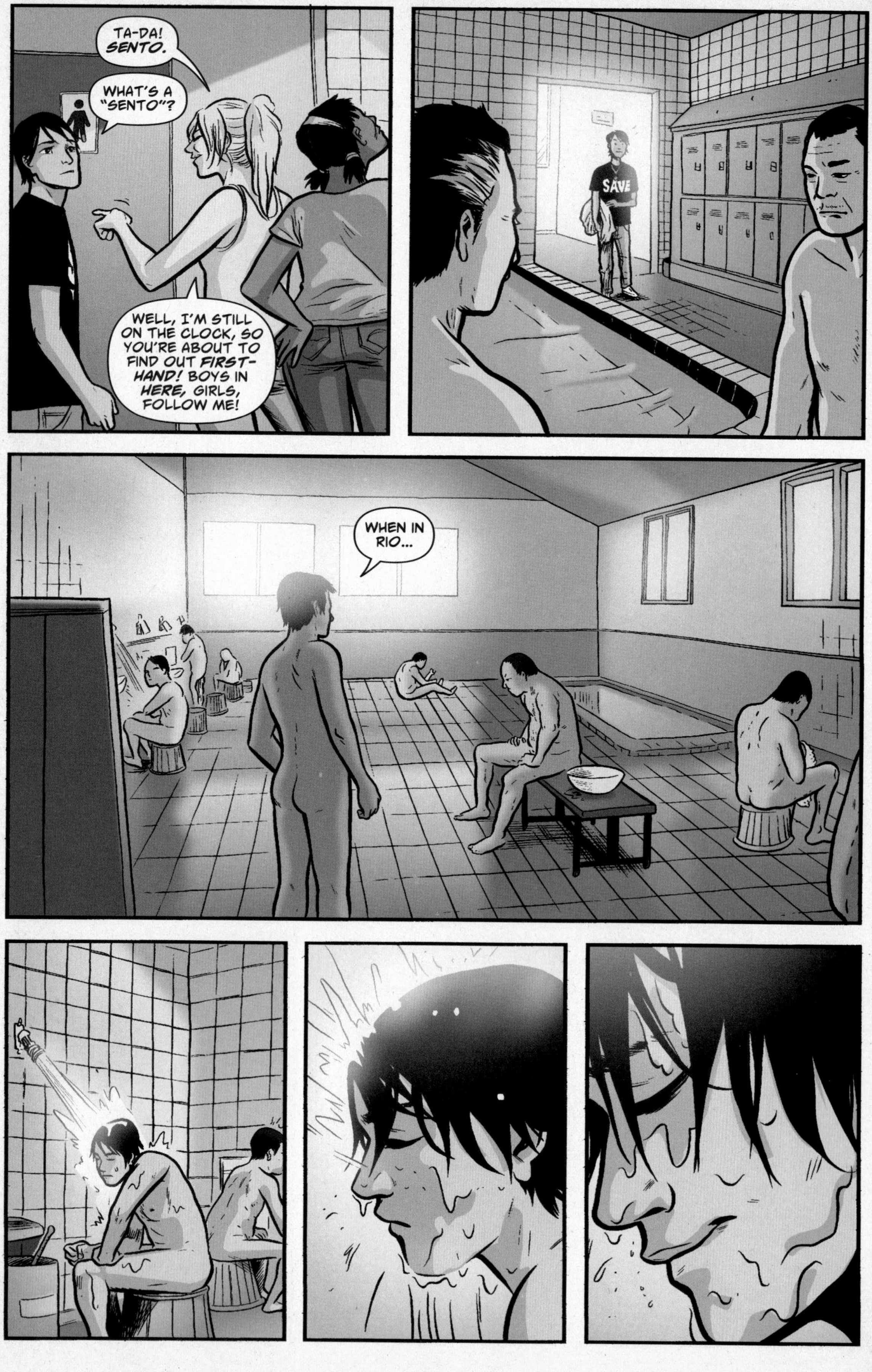
TA-DA! SENTO.
WHAT'S A "SENTO"?
WELL, I'M STILL ON THE CLOCK, SO YOU'RE ABOUT TO FIND OUT FIRST-HAND! BOYS IN HERE, GIRLS, FOLLOW ME!
SAVE
WHEN IN RIO...

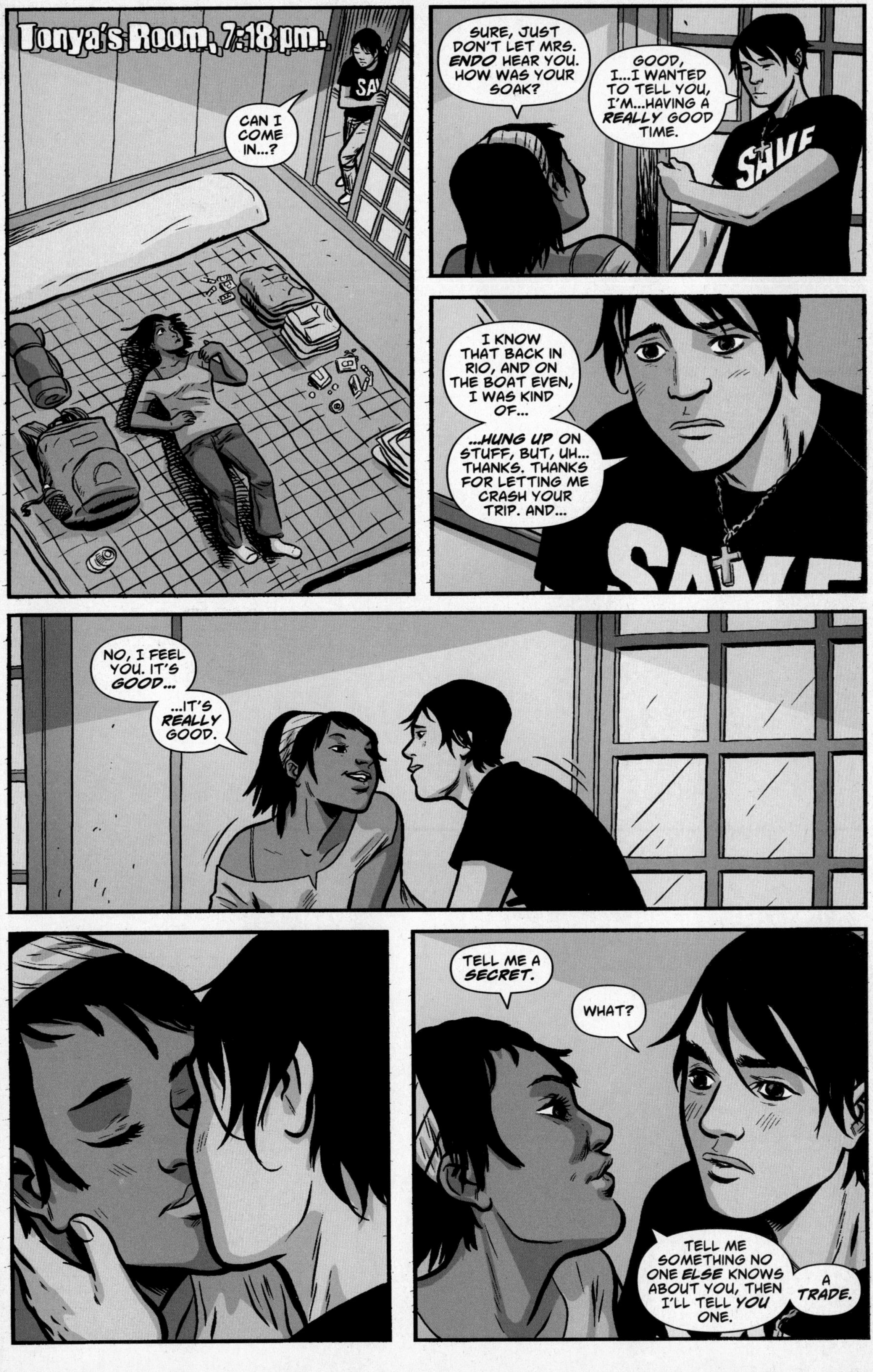
Tonya's Room, 7:18 pm.
CAN I COME IN...?
SURE, JUST DON'T LET MRS. ENDO HEAR YOU. HOW WAS YOUR SOAK?
GOOD, I...I WANTED TO TELL YOU, I'M...HAVING A REALLY GOOD TIME.
SAVE
I KNOW THAT BACK IN RIO, AND ON THE BOAT EVEN, I WAS KIND OF...
...HUNG UP ON STUFF, BUT, UH... THANKS. THANKS FOR LETTING ME CRASH YOUR TRIP. AND...
NO, I FEEL YOU. IT'S GOOD...
...IT'S REALLY GOOD.
TELL ME A SECRET.
WHAT?
TELL ME SOMETHING NO ONE ELSE KNOWS ABOUT YOU, THEN I'LL TELL YOU ONE.
A TRADE.

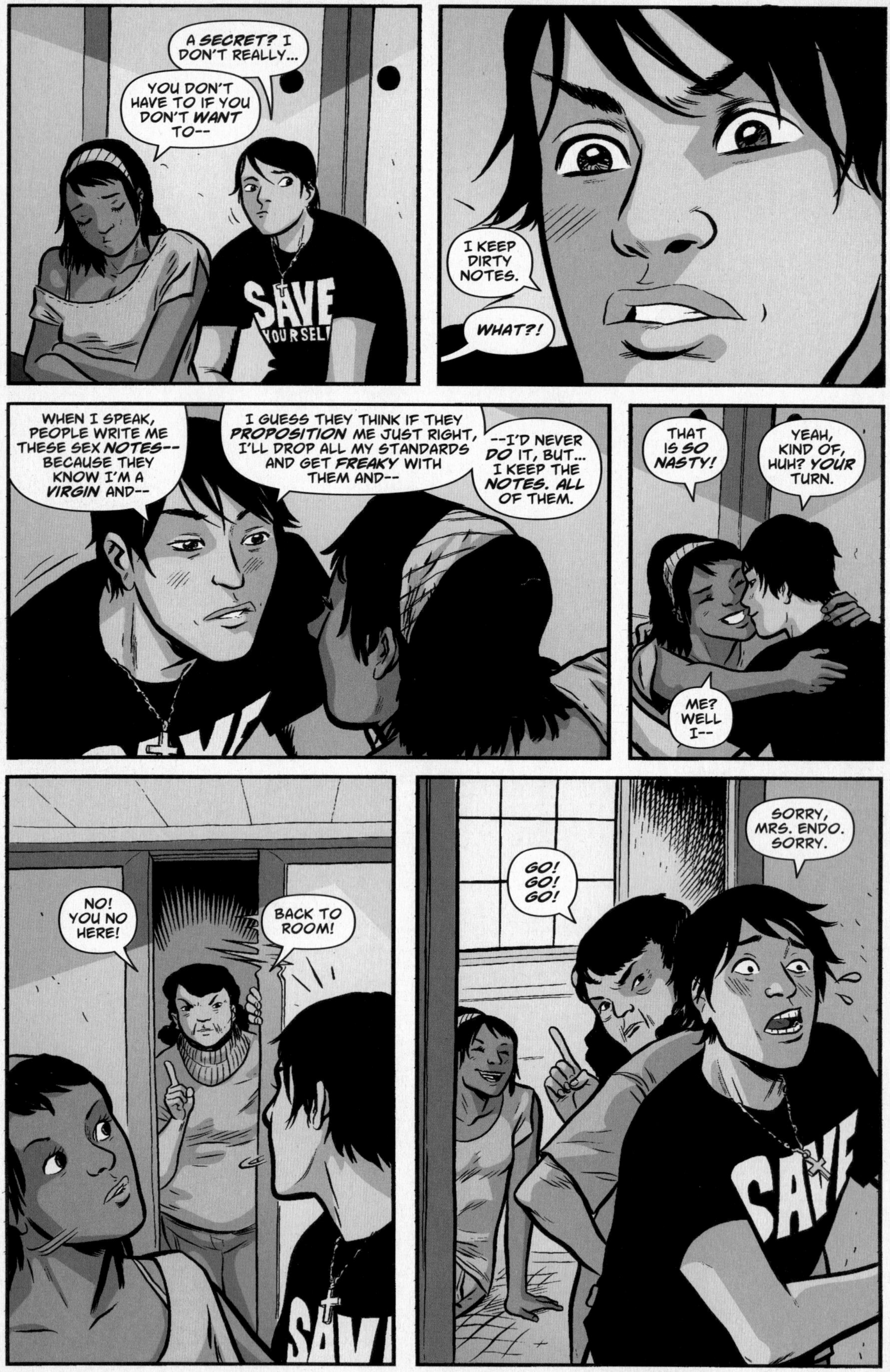
A SECRET? I DON'T REALLY...
YOU DON'T HAVE TO IF YOU DON'T WANT TO--
SAVE YOURSELF
I KEEP DIRTY NOTES.
WHAT?!
WHEN I SPEAK, PEOPLE WRITE ME THESE SEX NOTES-- BECAUSE THEY KNOW I'M A VIRGIN AND--
I GUESS THEY THINK IF THEY PROPOSITION ME JUST RIGHT, I'LL DROP ALL MY STANDARDS AND GET FREAKY WITH THEM AND--
--I'D NEVER DO IT, BUT... I KEEP THE NOTES. ALL OF THEM.
THAT IS SO NASTY!
YEAH, KIND OF, HUH? YOUR TURN.
ME? WELL I--
NO! YOU NO HERE!
BACK TO ROOM!
GO! GO! GO!
SORRY, MRS. ENDO. SORRY.

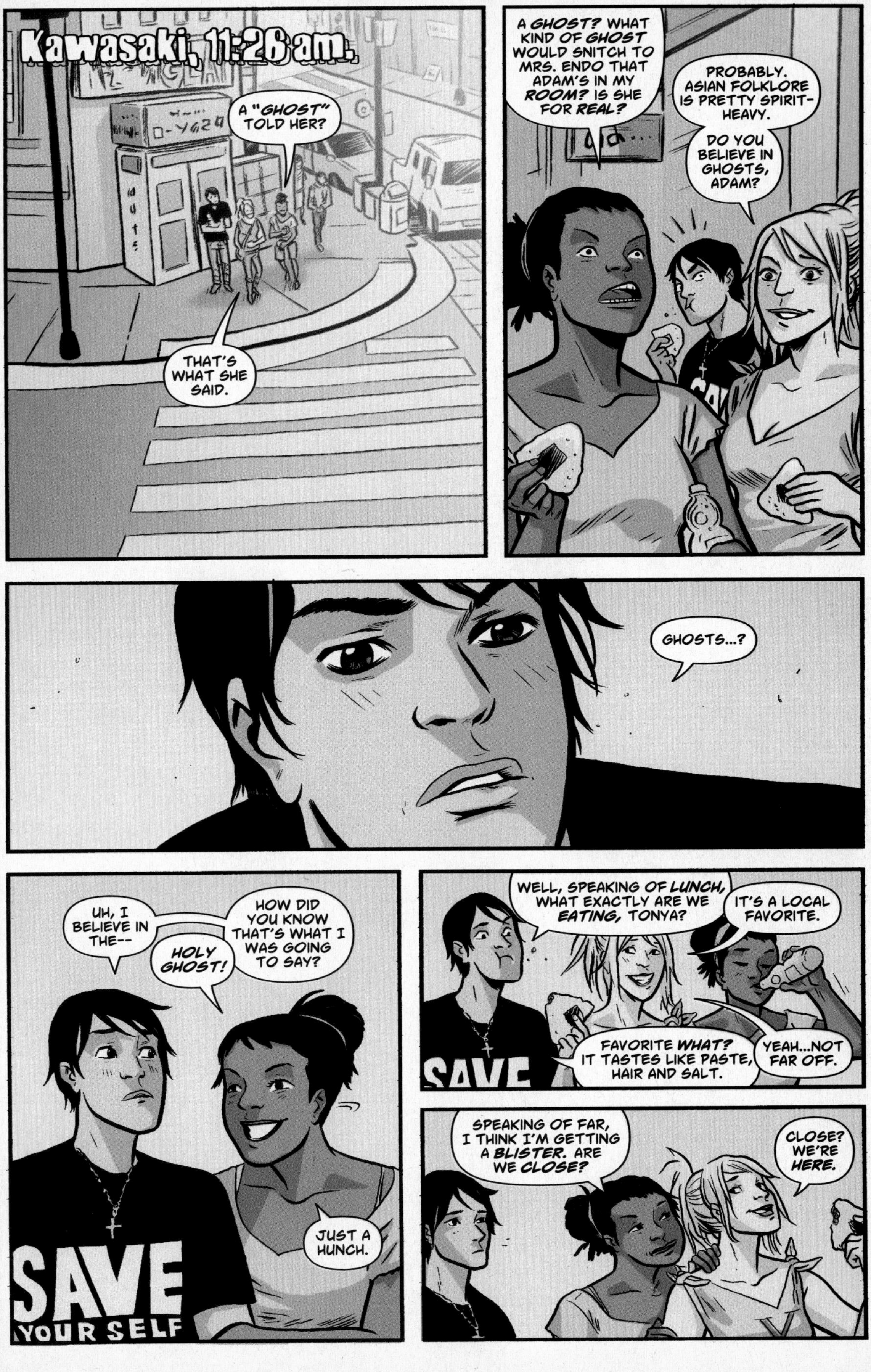
Kawasaki, 11:26 am.
A "GHOST" TOLD HER?
THAT'S WHAT SHE SAID.
A GHOST? WHAT KIND OF GHOST WOULD SNITCH TO MRS. ENDO THAT ADAM'S IN MY ROOM? IS SHE FOR REAL?
PROBABLY. ASIAN FOLKLORE IS PRETTY SPIRIT-HEAVY.
DO YOU BELIEVE IN GHOSTS, ADAM?
GHOSTS...?
UH, I BELIEVE IN THE--
HOLY GHOST!
HOW DID YOU KNOW THAT'S WHAT I WAS GOING TO SAY?
JUST A HUNCH.
SAVE YOUR SELF
WELL, SPEAKING OF LUNCH, WHAT EXACTLY ARE WE EATING, TONYA?
IT'S A LOCAL FAVORITE.
FAVORITE WHAT? IT TASTES LIKE PASTE, HAIR AND SALT.
YEAH...NOT FAR OFF.
SPEAKING OF FAR, I THINK I'M GETTING A BLISTER. ARE WE CLOSE?
CLOSE? WE'RE HERE.

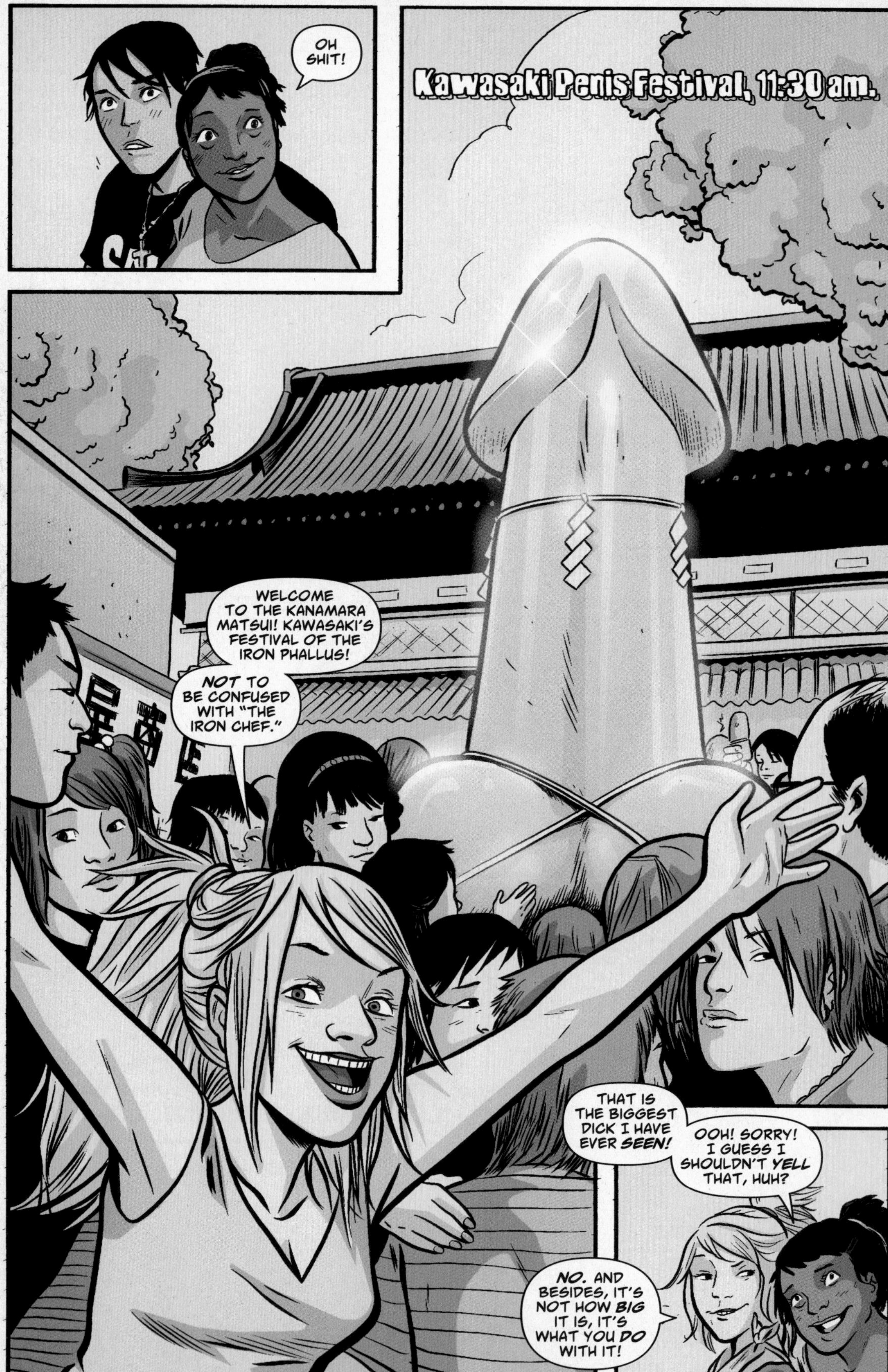
OH SHIT!
Kawasaki Penis Festival, 11:30 am.
WELCOME TO THE KANAMARA MATSUI! KAWASAKI'S FESTIVAL OF THE IRON PHALLUS!
NOT TO BE CONFUSED WITH "THE IRON CHEF."
THAT IS THE BIGGEST DICK I HAVE EVER SEEN!
OOH! SORRY! I GUESS I SHOULDN'T YELL THAT, HUH?
NO. AND BESIDES, IT'S NOT HOW BIG IT IS, IT'S WHAT YOU DO WITH IT!

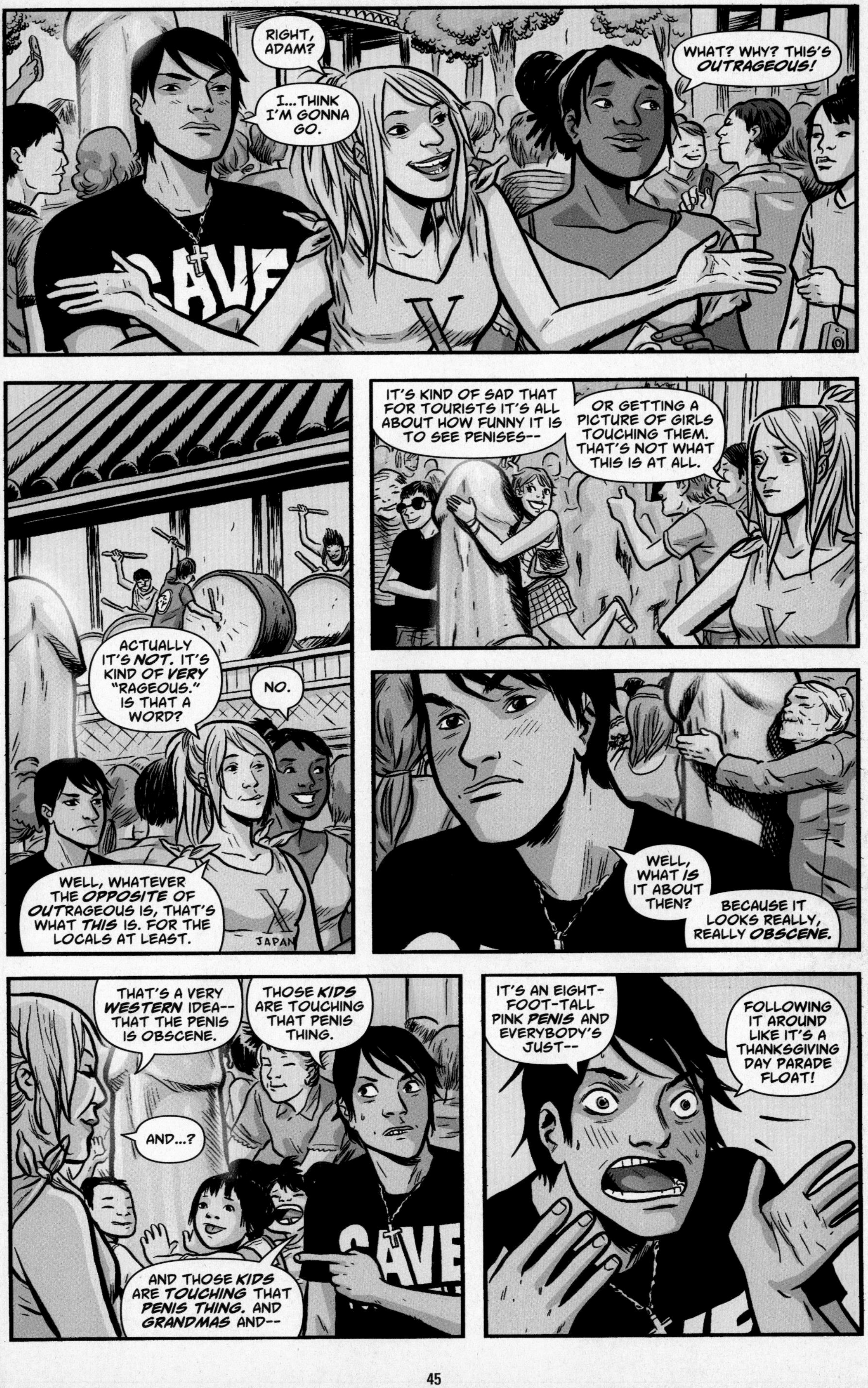
RIGHT, ADAM?
I...THINK I'M GONNA GO.
WHAT? WHY? THIS'S OUTRAGEOUS!
SAVE
X
ACTUALLY IT'S NOT. IT'S KIND OF VERY "RAGEOUS." IS THAT A WORD?
NO.
WELL, WHATEVER THE OPPOSITE OF OUTRAGEOUS IS, THAT'S WHAT THIS IS. FOR THE LOCALS AT LEAST.
JAPAN
IT'S KIND OF SAD THAT FOR TOURISTS IT'S ALL ABOUT HOW FUNNY IT IS TO SEE PENISES--
OR GETTING A PICTURE OF GIRLS TOUCHING THEM. THAT'S NOT WHAT THIS IS AT ALL.
WELL, WHAT IS IT ABOUT THEN?
BECAUSE IT LOOKS REALLY, REALLY OBSCENE.
THAT'S A VERY WESTERN IDEA-- THAT THE PENIS IS OBSCENE.
THOSE KIDS ARE TOUCHING THAT PENIS THING.
AND...?
AND THOSE KIDS ARE TOUCHING THAT PENIS THING. AND GRANDMAS AND--
SAVE
IT'S AN EIGHT-FOOT-TALL PINK PENIS AND EVERYBODY'S JUST--
FOLLOWING IT AROUND LIKE IT'S A THANKSGIVING DAY PARADE FLOAT!

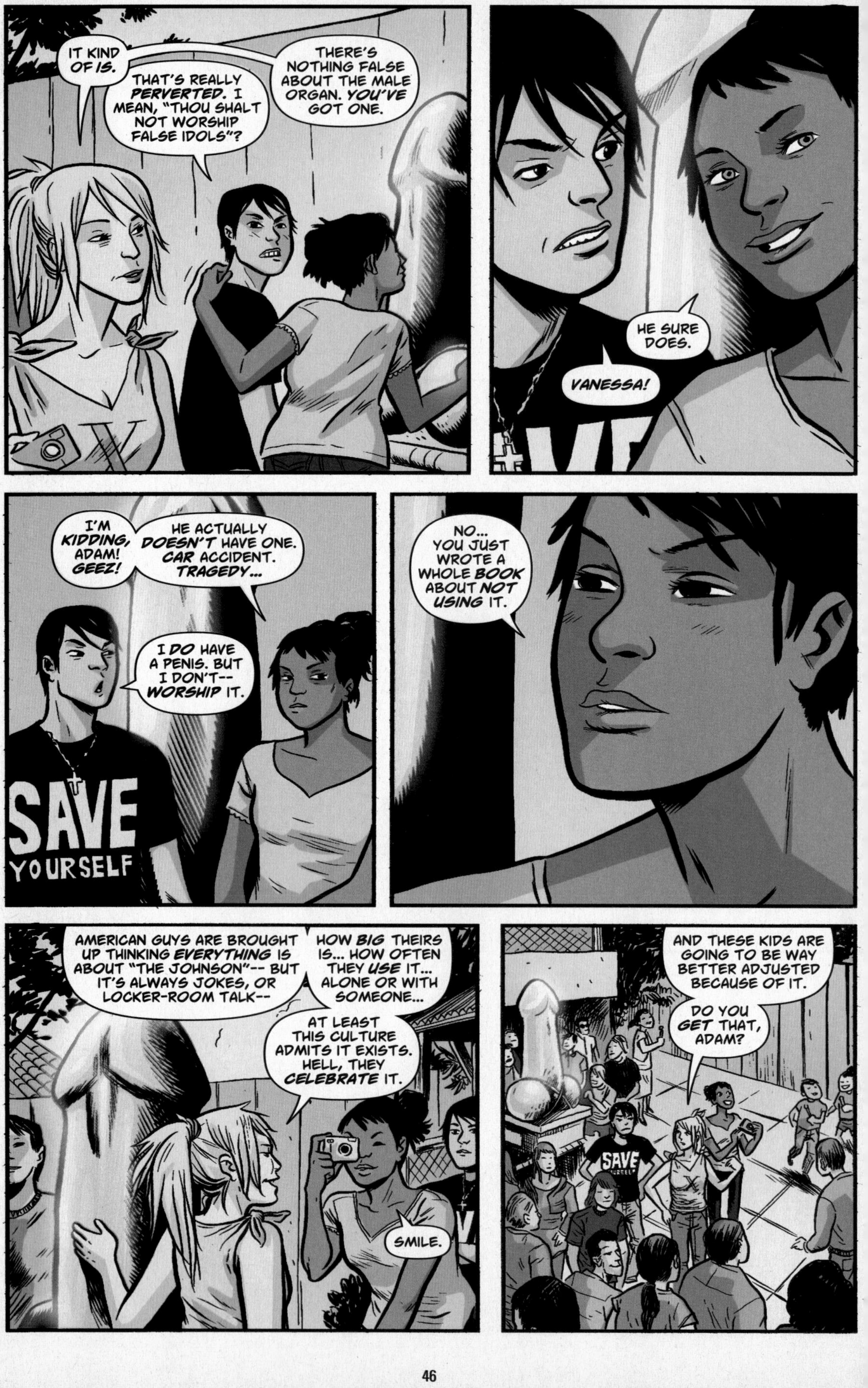

THAT'S REALLY PERVERTED. I MEAN, "THOU SHALT NOT WORSHIP FALSE IDOLS"?
IT KIND OF IS.
THERE'S NOTHING FALSE ABOUT THE MALE ORGAN. YOU'VE GOT ONE.
HE SURE DOES.
VANESSA!
I'M KIDDING, ADAM! GEEZ!
HE ACTUALLY DOESN'T HAVE ONE. CAR ACCIDENT. TRAGEDY...
I DO HAVE A PENIS. BUT I DON'T-- WORSHIP IT.
SAVE YOURSELF
NO... YOU JUST WROTE A WHOLE BOOK ABOUT NOT USING IT.
AMERICAN GUYS ARE BROUGHT UP THINKING EVERYTHING IS ABOUT "THE JOHNSON"-- BUT IT'S ALWAYS JOKES, OR LOCKER-ROOM TALK--
HOW BIG THEIRS IS... HOW OFTEN THEY USE IT... ALONE OR WITH SOMEONE...
AT LEAST THIS CULTURE ADMITS IT EXISTS. HELL, THEY CELEBRATE IT.
SMILE.
AND THESE KIDS ARE GOING TO BE WAY BETTER ADJUSTED BECAUSE OF IT.
DO YOU GET THAT, ADAM?

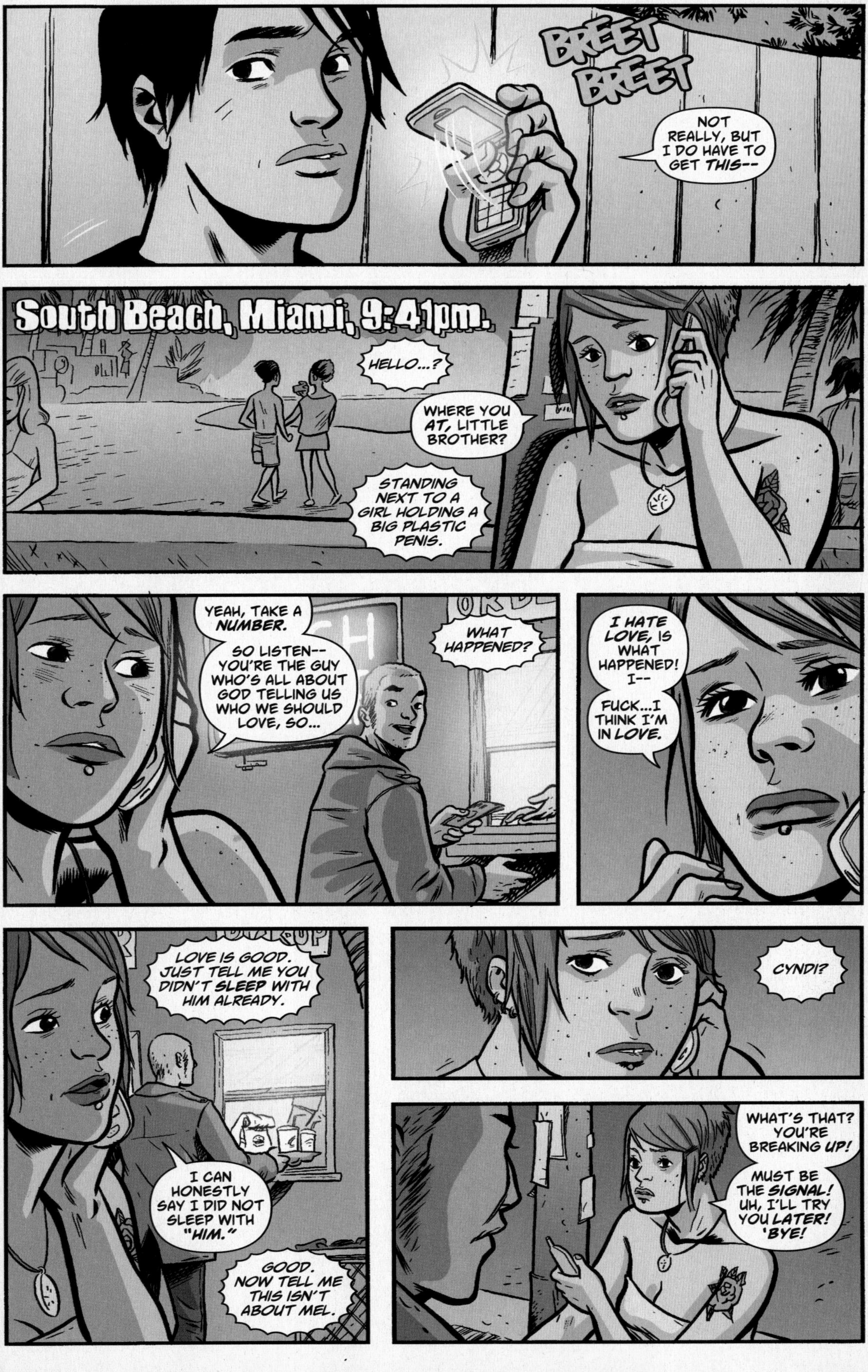
BREET BREET
NOT REALLY, BUT I DO HAVE TO GET THIS--
South Beach, Miami, 9:41pm.
HELLO...?
WHERE YOU AT, LITTLE BROTHER?
STANDING NEXT TO A GIRL HOLDING A BIG PLASTIC PENIS.
YEAH, TAKE A NUMBER.
SO LISTEN-- YOU'RE THE GUY WHO'S ALL ABOUT GOD TELLING US WHO WE SHOULD LOVE, SO...
WHAT HAPPENED?
I HATE LOVE, IS WHAT HAPPENED! I--
FUCK...I THINK I'M IN LOVE.
LOVE IS GOOD. JUST TELL ME YOU DIDN'T SLEEP WITH HIM ALREADY.
I CAN HONESTLY SAY I DID NOT SLEEP WITH "HIM."
GOOD. NOW TELL ME THIS ISN'T ABOUT MEL.
CYNDI?
WHAT'S THAT? YOU'RE BREAKING UP!
MUST BE THE SIGNAL! UH, I'LL TRY YOU LATER! 'BYE!

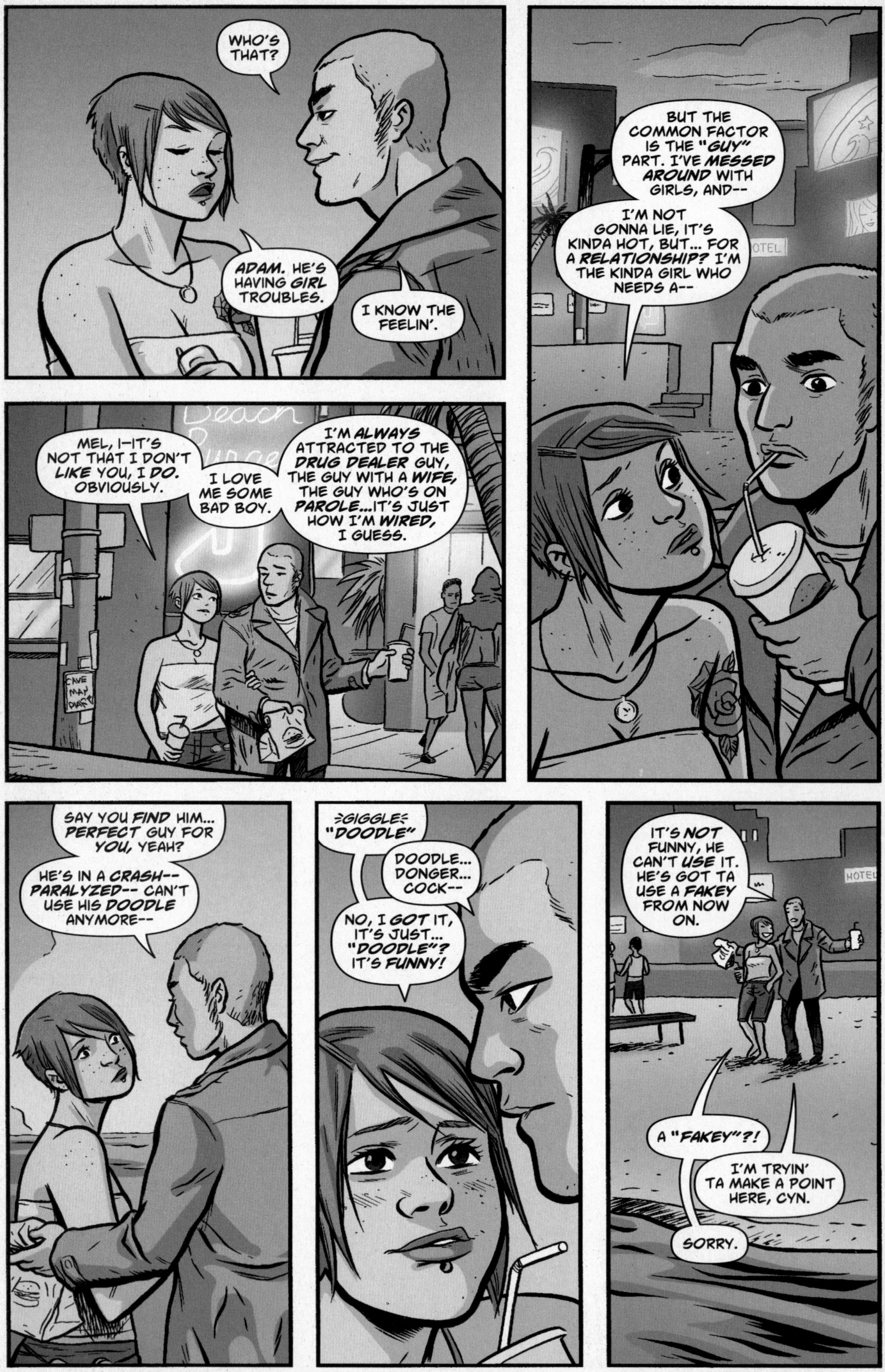
WHO'S THAT?
ADAM. HE'S HAVING GIRL TROUBLES.
I KNOW THE FEELIN'.
MEL, I-IT'S NOT THAT I DON'T LIKE YOU, I DO. OBVIOUSLY.
I LOVE ME SOME BAD BOY.
I'M ALWAYS ATTRACTED TO THE DRUG DEALER GUY, THE GUY WITH A WIFE, THE GUY WHO'S ON PAROLE...IT'S JUST HOW I'M WIRED, I GUESS.
BUT THE COMMON FACTOR IS THE "GUY" PART. I'VE MESSED AROUND WITH GIRLS, AND--
I'M NOT GONNA LIE, IT'S KINDA HOT, BUT... FOR A RELATIONSHIP? I'M THE KINDA GIRL WHO NEEDS A--
OTEL
SAY YOU FIND HIM... PERFECT GUY FOR YOU, YEAH?
HE'S IN A CRASH-- PARALYZED-- CAN'T USE HIS DOODLE ANYMORE--
GIGGLE "DOODLE"
DOODLE... DONGER... COCK--
NO, I GOT IT, IT'S JUST... "DOODLE"? IT'S FUNNY!
IT'S NOT FUNNY, HE CAN'T USE IT. HE'S GOT TA USE A FAKEY FROM NOW ON.
HOTEL
A "FAKEY"?!
I'M TRYIN' TA MAKE A POINT HERE, CYN.
SORRY.

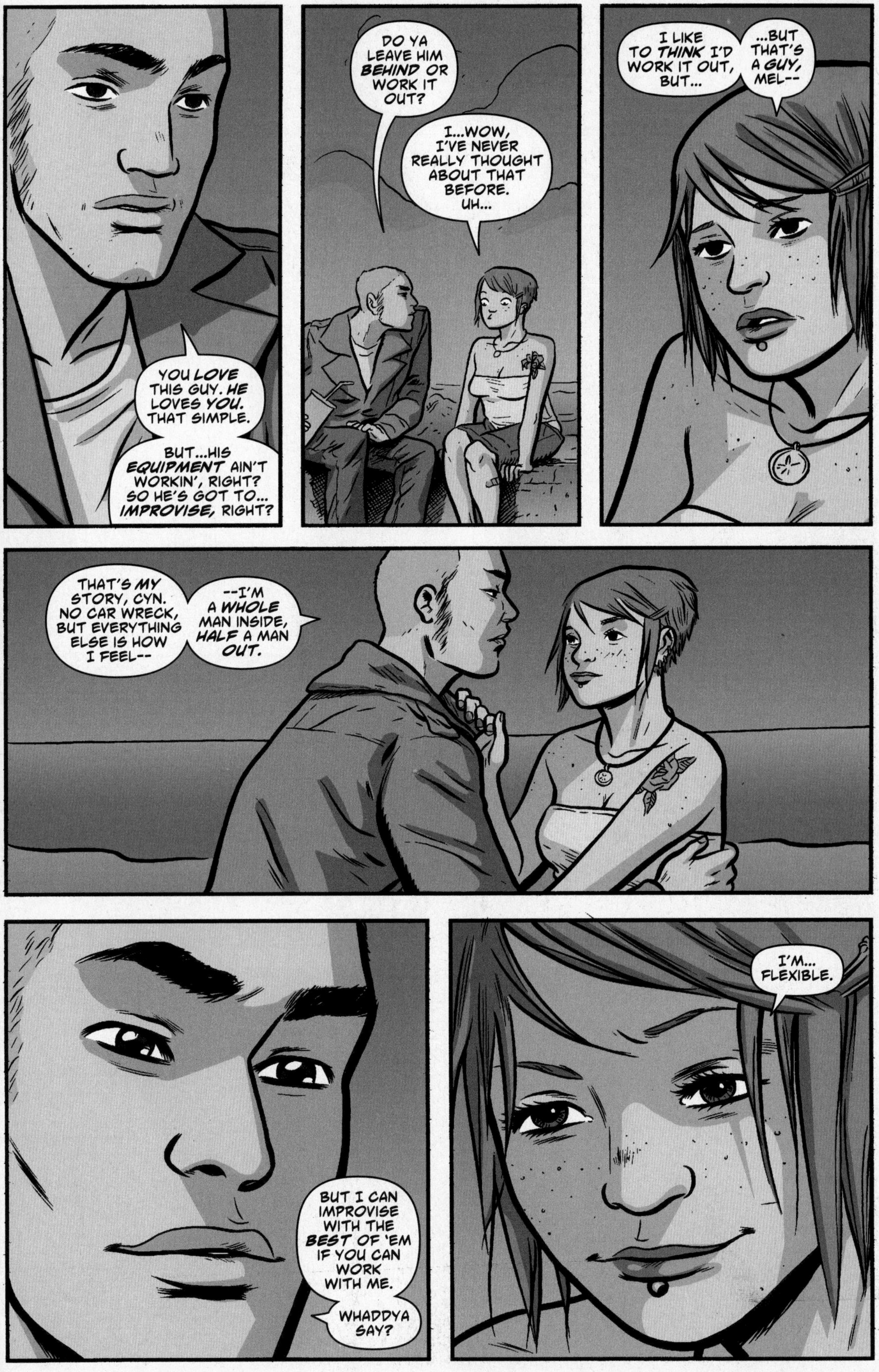

YOU LOVE THIS GUY. HE LOVES YOU. THAT SIMPLE.
BUT...HIS EQUIPMENT AIN'T WORKIN', RIGHT? SO HE'S GOT TO... IMPROVISE, RIGHT?
DO YA LEAVE HIM BEHIND OR WORK IT OUT?
I...WOW, I'VE NEVER REALLY THOUGHT ABOUT THAT BEFORE. UH...
I LIKE TO THINK I'D WORK IT OUT, BUT...
...BUT THAT'S A GUY, MEL--
THAT'S MY STORY, CYN. NO CAR WRECK, BUT EVERYTHING ELSE IS HOW I FEEL--
--I'M A WHOLE MAN INSIDE, HALF A MAN OUT.
BUT I CAN IMPROVISE WITH THE BEST OF 'EM IF YOU CAN WORK WITH ME.
WHADDYA SAY?
I'M... FLEXIBLE.

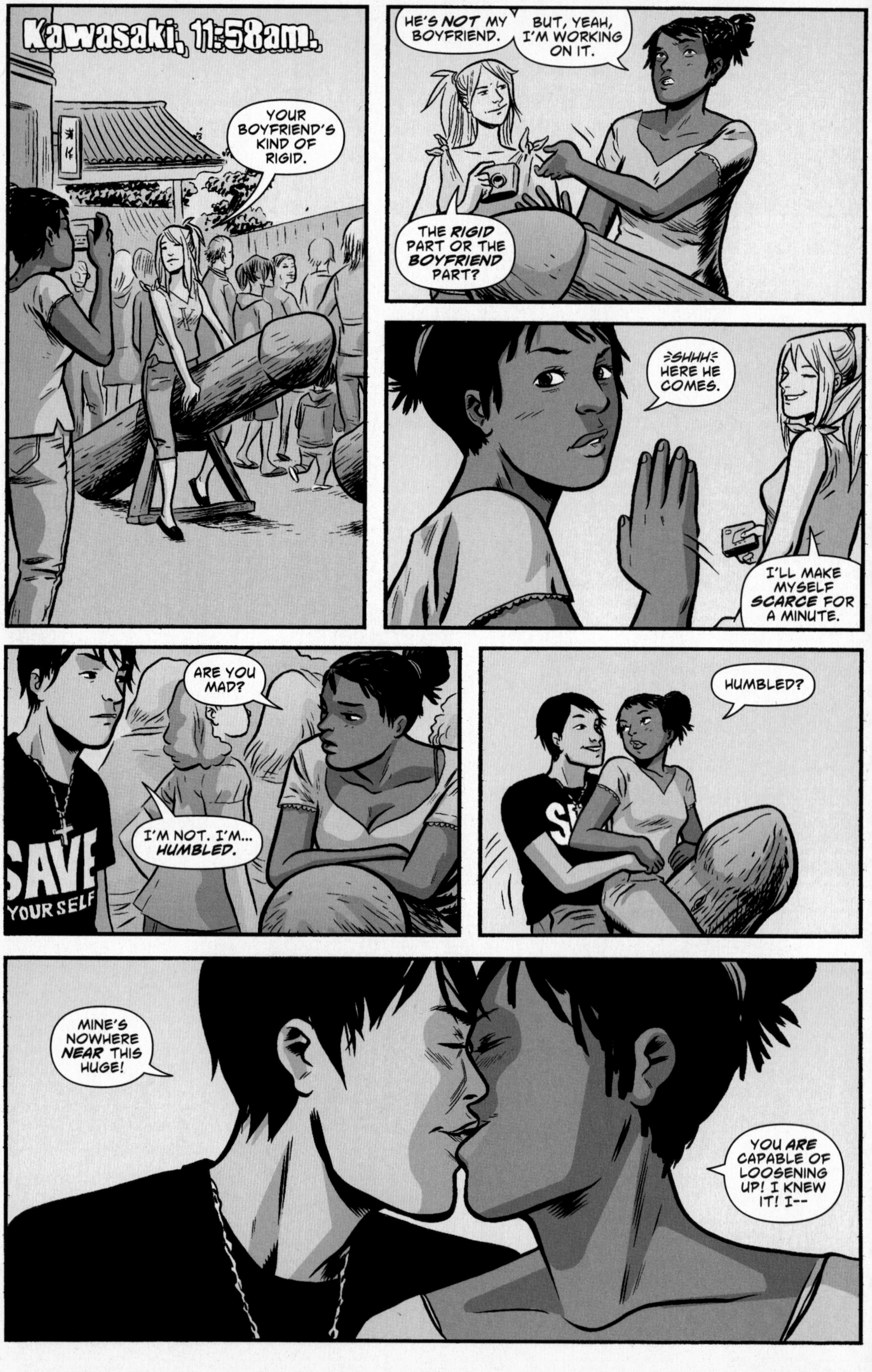
Kawasaki, 11:58am.
YOUR BOYFRIEND'S KIND OF RIGID.
HE'S NOT MY BOYFRIEND.
BUT, YEAH, I'M WORKING ON IT.
THE RIGID PART OR THE BOYFRIEND PART?
SHHH HERE HE COMES.
I'LL MAKE MYSELF SCARCE FOR A MINUTE.
ARE YOU MAD?
SAVE YOUR SELF
I'M NOT. I'M... HUMBLED.
HUMBLED?
MINE'S NOWHERE NEAR THIS HUGE!
YOU ARE CAPABLE OF LOOSENING UP! I KNEW IT! I--

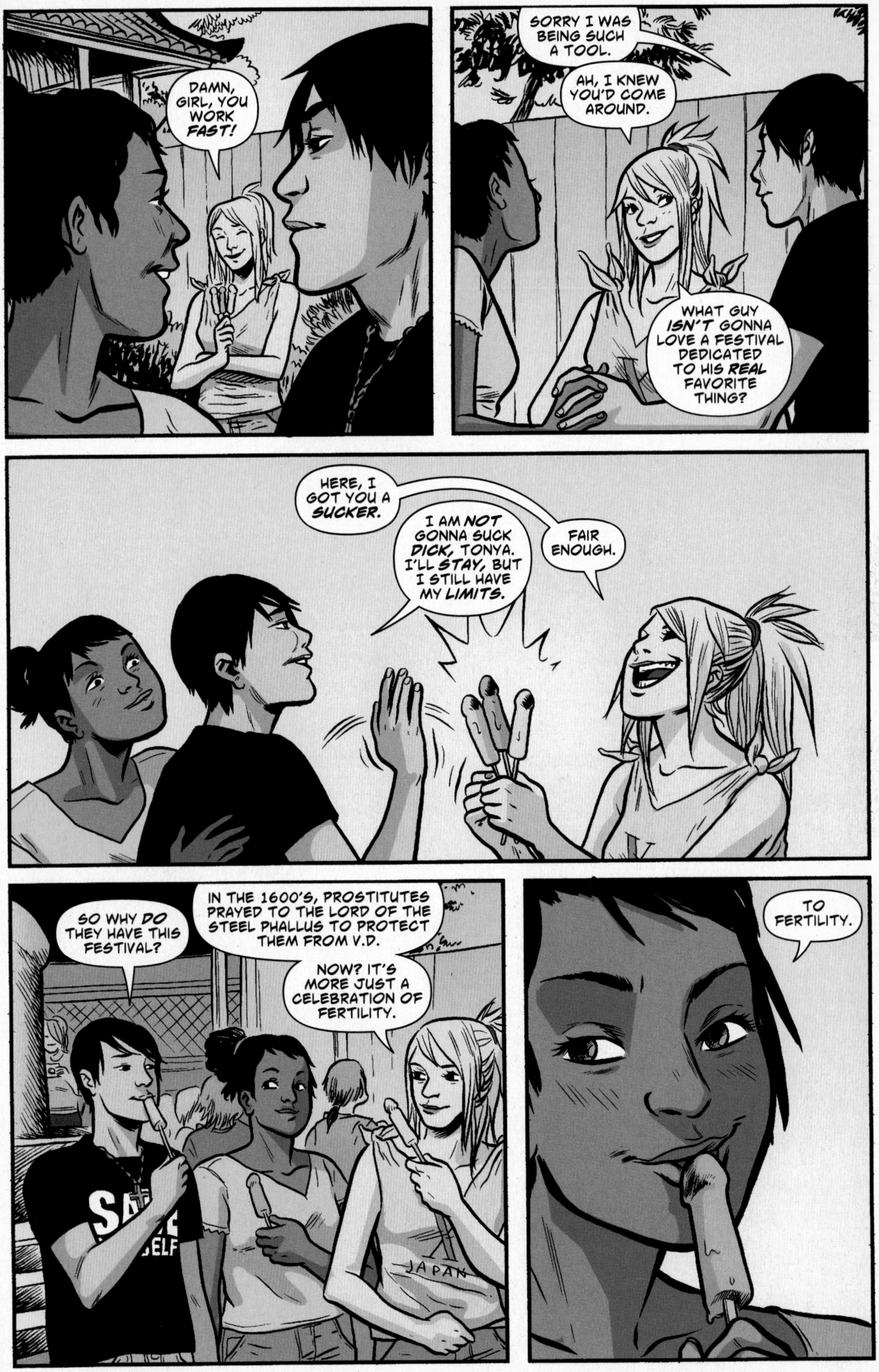
DAMN, GIRL, YOU WORK FAST!
SORRY I WAS BEING SUCH A TOOL.
AH, I KNEW YOU'D COME AROUND.
WHAT GUY ISN'T GONNA LOVE A FESTIVAL DEDICATED TO HIS REAL FAVORITE THING?
HERE, I GOT YOU A SUCKER.
I AM NOT GONNA SUCK DICK, TONYA. I'LL STAY, BUT I STILL HAVE MY LIMITS.
FAIR ENOUGH.
SO WHY DO THEY HAVE THIS FESTIVAL?
IN THE 1600'S, PROSTITUTES PRAYED TO THE LORD OF THE STEEL PHALLUS TO PROTECT THEM FROM V.D.
NOW? IT'S MORE JUST A CELEBRATION OF FERTILITY.
JAPAN
TO FERTILITY.

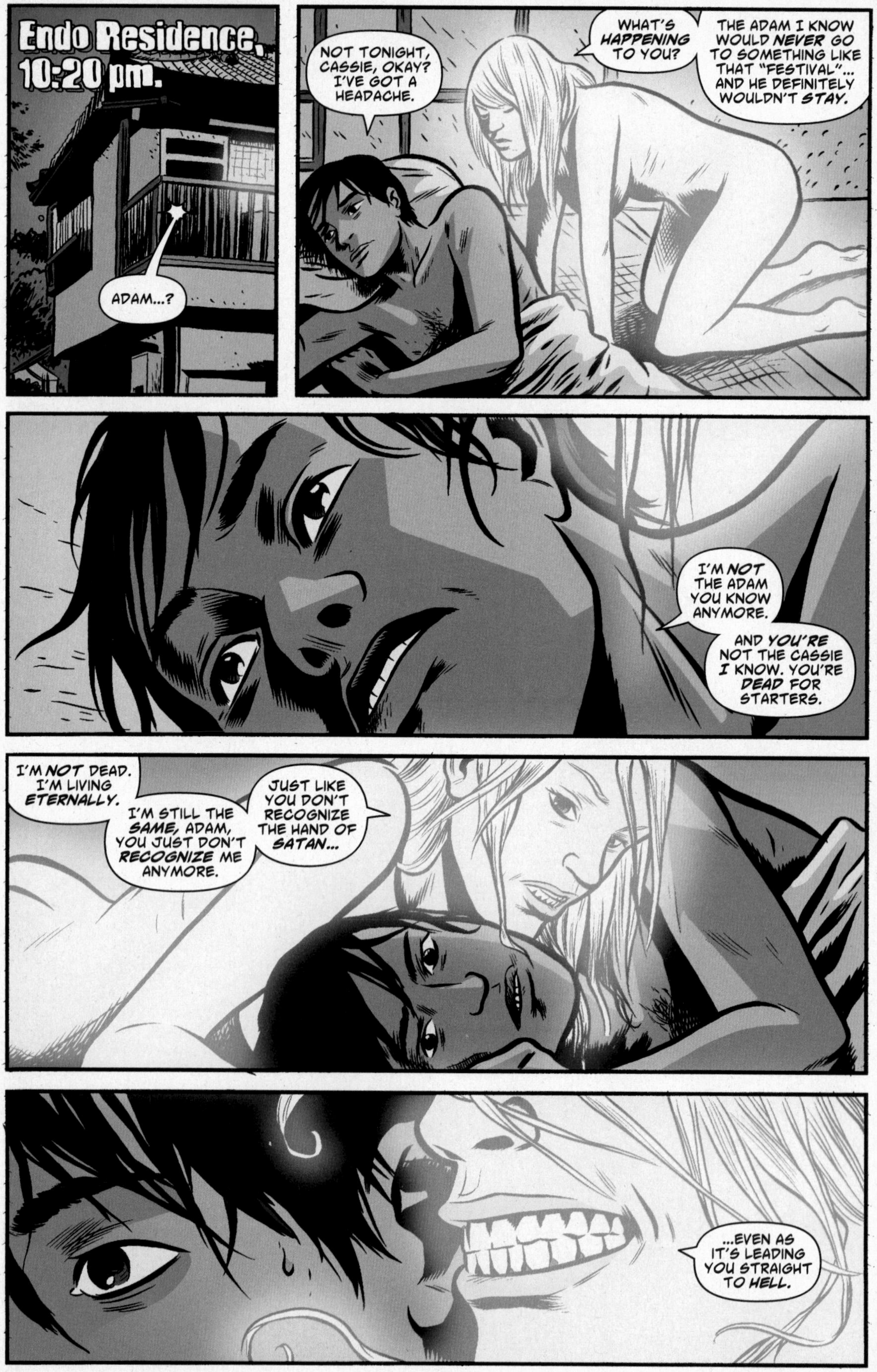
Endo Residence, 10:20 pm.
ADAM...?
NOT TONIGHT, CASSIE, OKAY? I'VE GOT A HEADACHE.
WHAT'S HAPPENING TO YOU?
THE ADAM I KNOW WOULD NEVER GO TO SOMETHING LIKE THAT "FESTIVAL"... AND HE DEFINITELY WOULDN'T STAY.
I'M NOT THE ADAM YOU KNOW ANYMORE.
AND YOU'RE NOT THE CASSIE I KNOW. YOU'RE DEAD FOR STARTERS.
I'M NOT DEAD. I'M LIVING ETERNALLY.
I'M STILL THE SAME, ADAM, YOU JUST DON'T RECOGNIZE ME ANYMORE.
JUST LIKE YOU DON'T RECOGNIZE THE HAND OF SATAN...
...EVEN AS IT'S LEADING YOU STRAIGHT TO HELL.

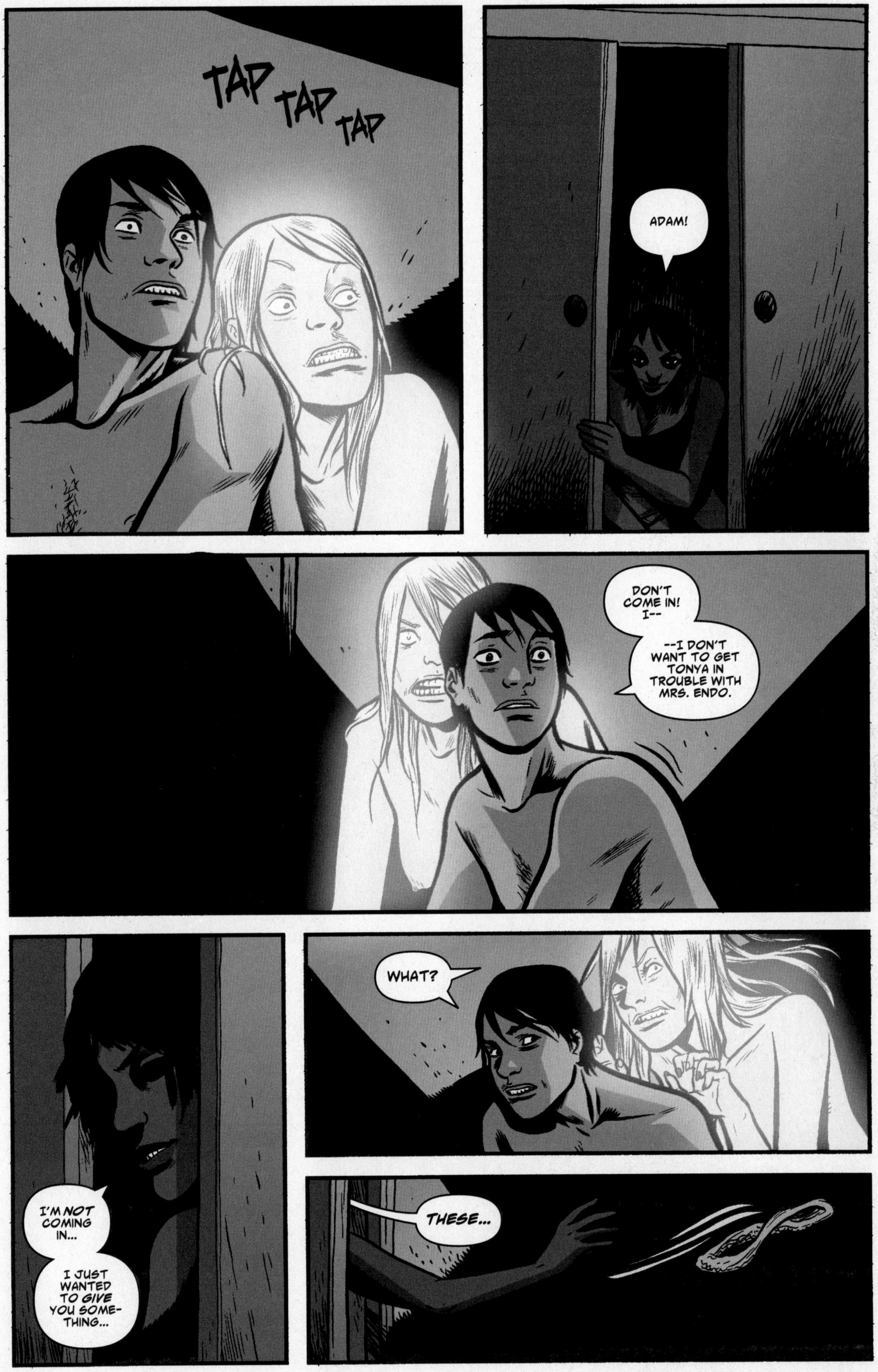
TAP TAP TAP
ADAM!
DON'T COME IN! I--
--I DON'T WANT TO GET TONYA IN TROUBLE WITH MRS. ENDO.
I'M NOT COMING IN...
I JUST WANTED TO GIVE YOU SOME-THING...
WHAT?
THESE...

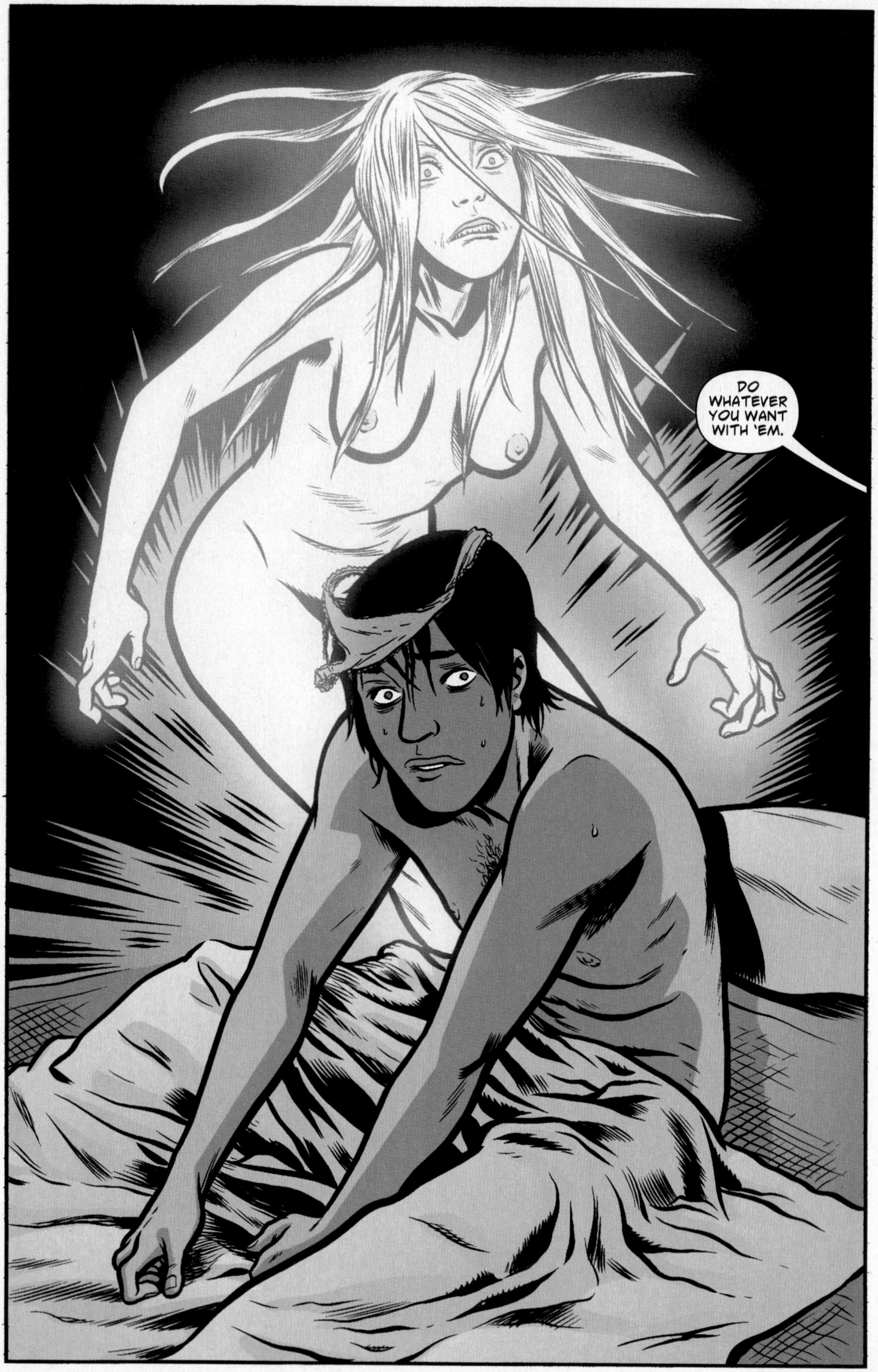
DO WHATEVER YOU WANT WITH 'EM.

CHAPTER THREE

Chapter pencils by Becky Cloonan   Chapter inks by Jim Rugg

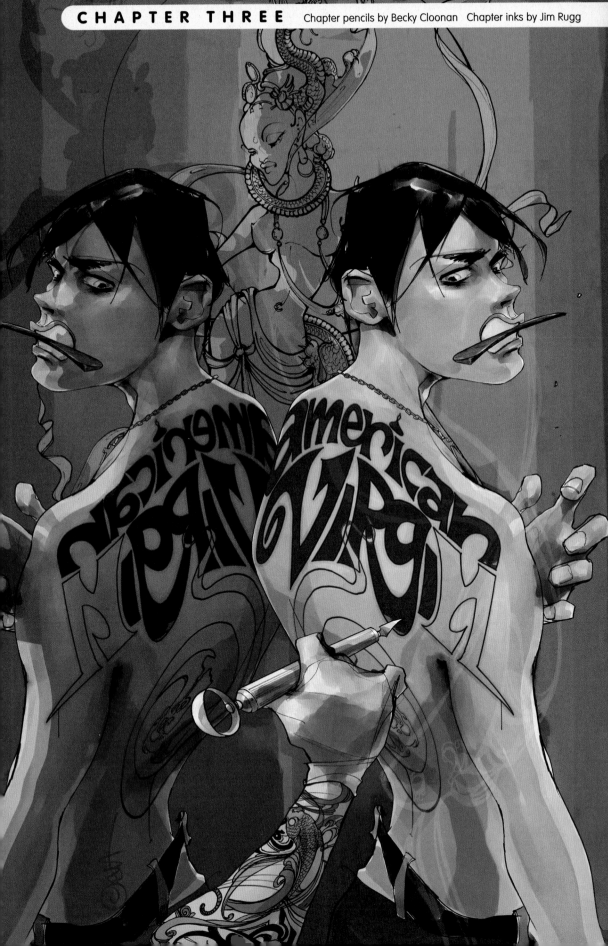

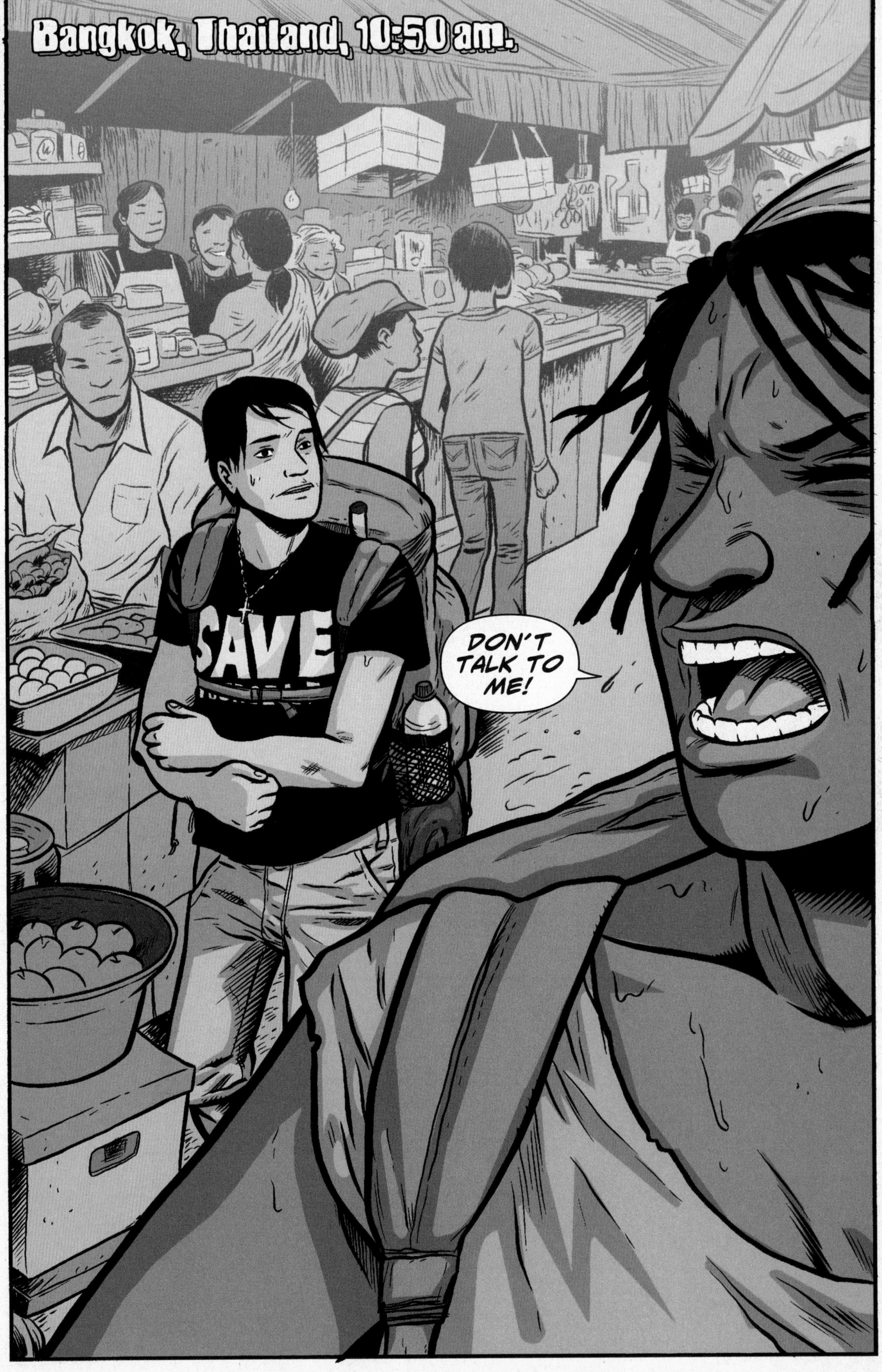
Bangkok, Thailand, 10:50 am.
SAVE
DON'T TALK TO ME!

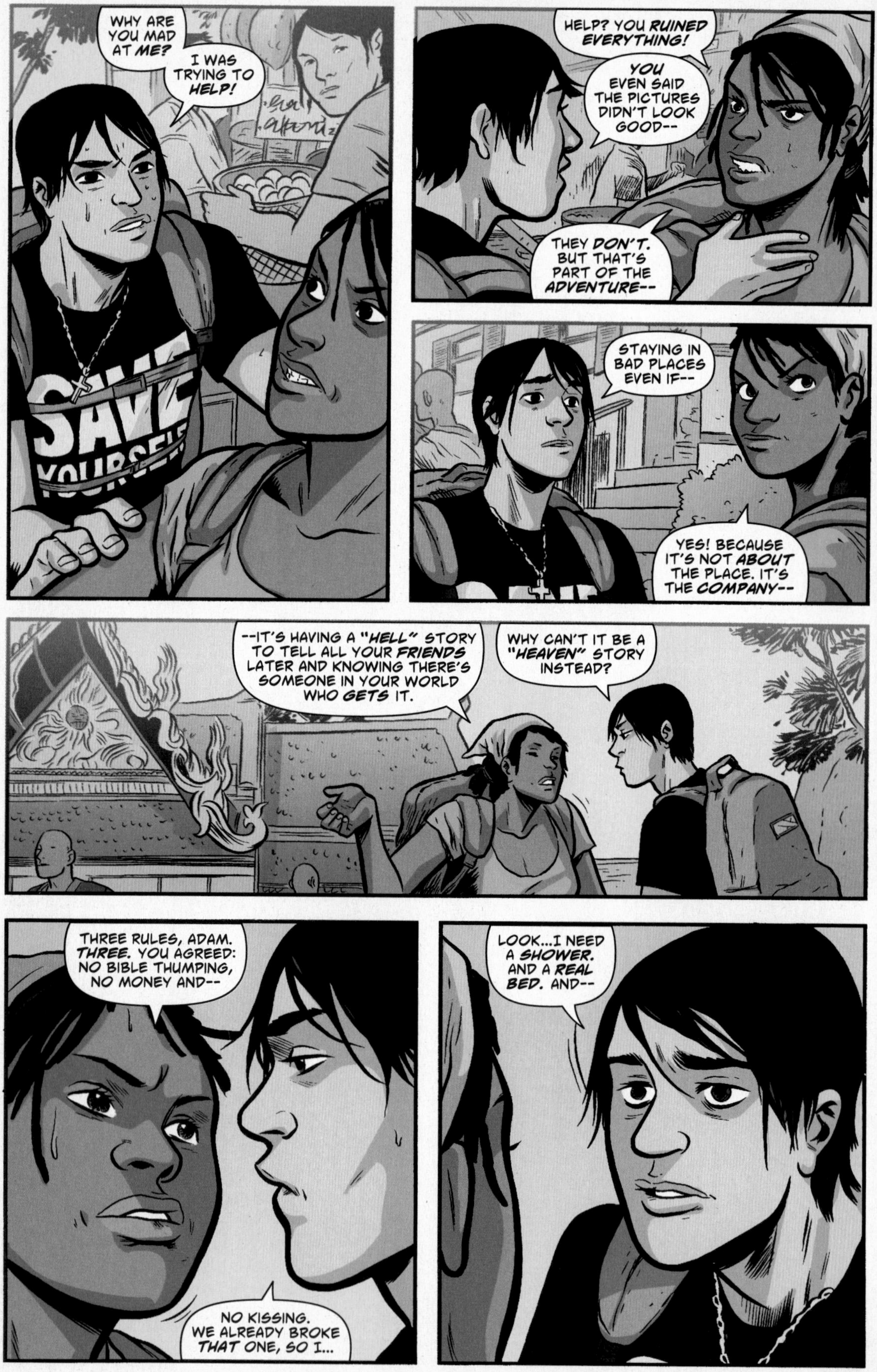
WHY ARE YOU MAD AT ME?
I WAS TRYING TO HELP!
HELP? YOU RUINED EVERYTHING!
YOU EVEN SAID THE PICTURES DIDN'T LOOK GOOD--
THEY DON'T. BUT THAT'S PART OF THE ADVENTURE--
STAYING IN BAD PLACES EVEN IF--
YES! BECAUSE IT'S NOT ABOUT THE PLACE. IT'S THE COMPANY--
--IT'S HAVING A "HELL" STORY TO TELL ALL YOUR FRIENDS LATER AND KNOWING THERE'S SOMEONE IN YOUR WORLD WHO GETS IT.
WHY CAN'T IT BE A "HEAVEN" STORY INSTEAD?
THREE RULES, ADAM. THREE. YOU AGREED: NO BIBLE THUMPING, NO MONEY AND--
NO KISSING. WE ALREADY BROKE THAT ONE, SO I...
LOOK...I NEED A SHOWER. AND A REAL BED. AND--

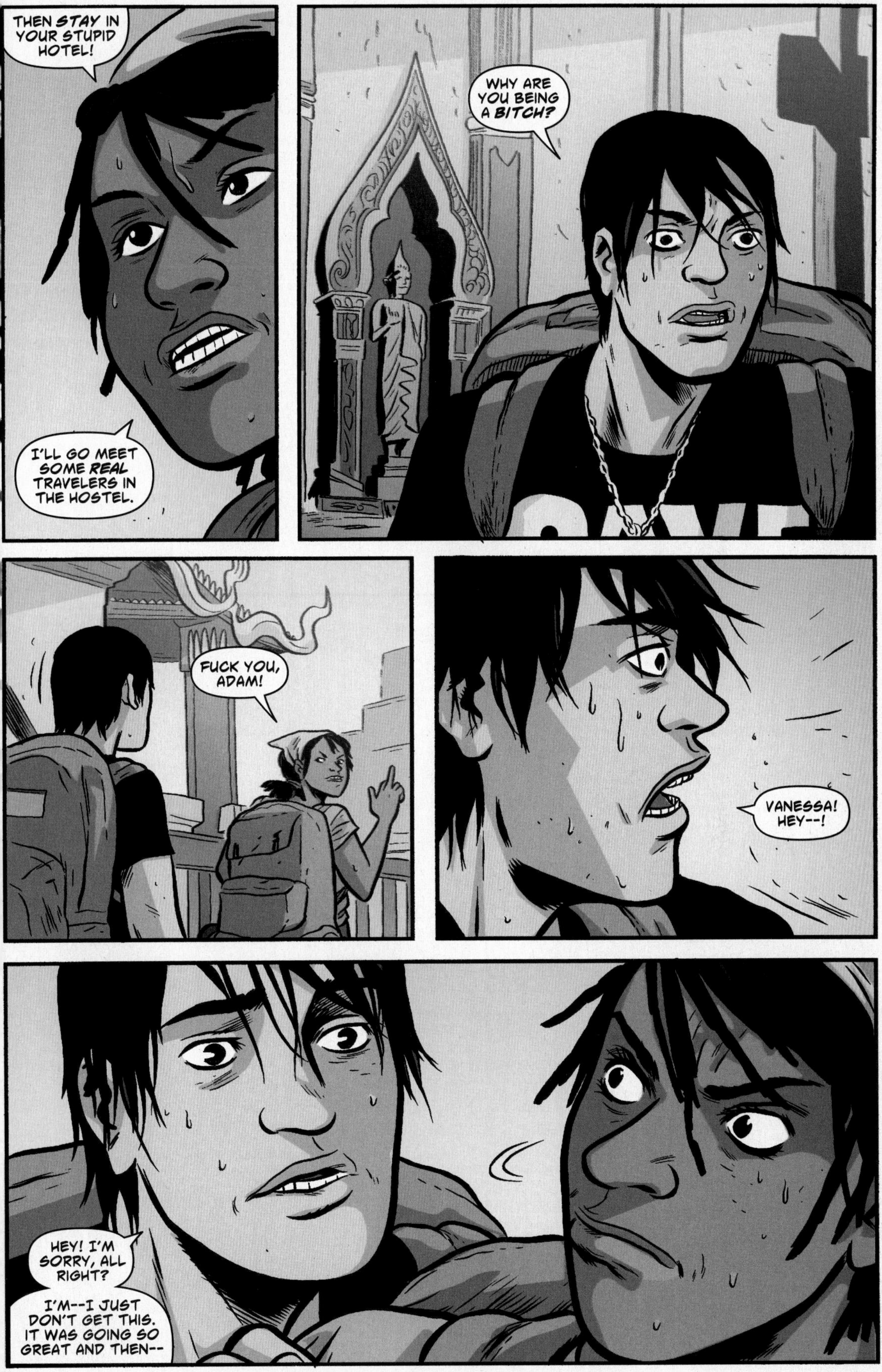
THEN STAY IN YOUR STUPID HOTEL!
I'LL GO MEET SOME REAL TRAVELERS IN THE HOSTEL.
WHY ARE YOU BEING A BITCH?
FUCK YOU, ADAM!
VANESSA! HEY--!
HEY! I'M SORRY, ALL RIGHT?
I'M--I JUST DON'T GET THIS. IT WAS GOING SO GREAT AND THEN--

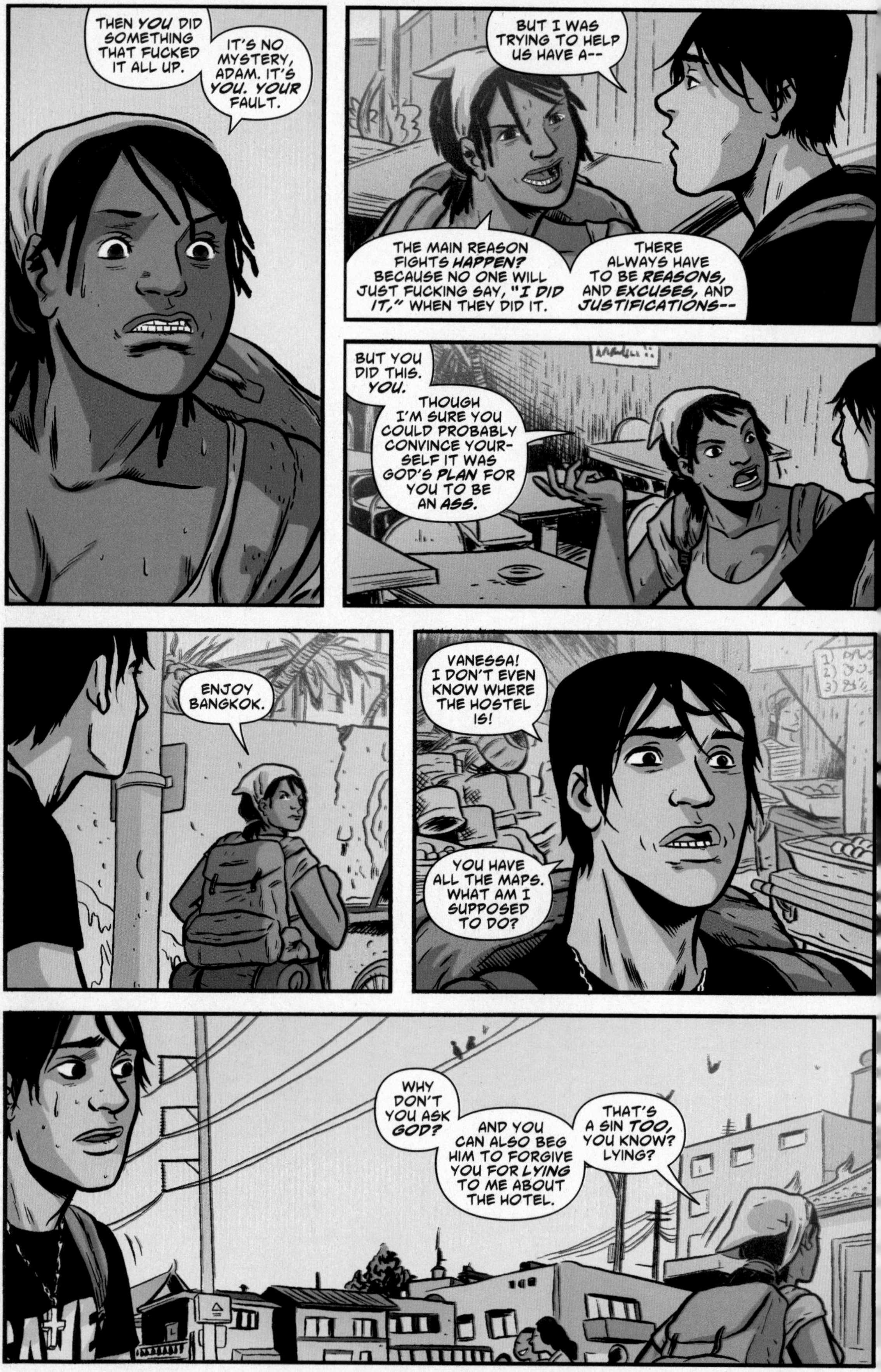
THEN YOU DID SOMETHING THAT FUCKED IT ALL UP.
IT'S NO MYSTERY, ADAM. IT'S YOU. YOUR FAULT.
BUT I WAS TRYING TO HELP US HAVE A--
THE MAIN REASON FIGHTS HAPPEN? BECAUSE NO ONE WILL JUST FUCKING SAY, "I DID IT," WHEN THEY DID IT.
THERE ALWAYS HAVE TO BE REASONS, AND EXCUSES, AND JUSTIFICATIONS--
BUT YOU DID THIS. YOU.
THOUGH I'M SURE YOU COULD PROBABLY CONVINCE YOURSELF IT WAS GOD'S PLAN FOR YOU TO BE AN ASS.
ENJOY BANGKOK.
VANESSA! I DON'T EVEN KNOW WHERE THE HOSTEL IS!
YOU HAVE ALL THE MAPS. WHAT AM I SUPPOSED TO DO?
WHY DON'T YOU ASK GOD?
AND YOU CAN ALSO BEG HIM TO FORGIVE YOU FOR LYING TO ME ABOUT THE HOTEL.
THAT'S A SIN TOO, YOU KNOW? LYING?

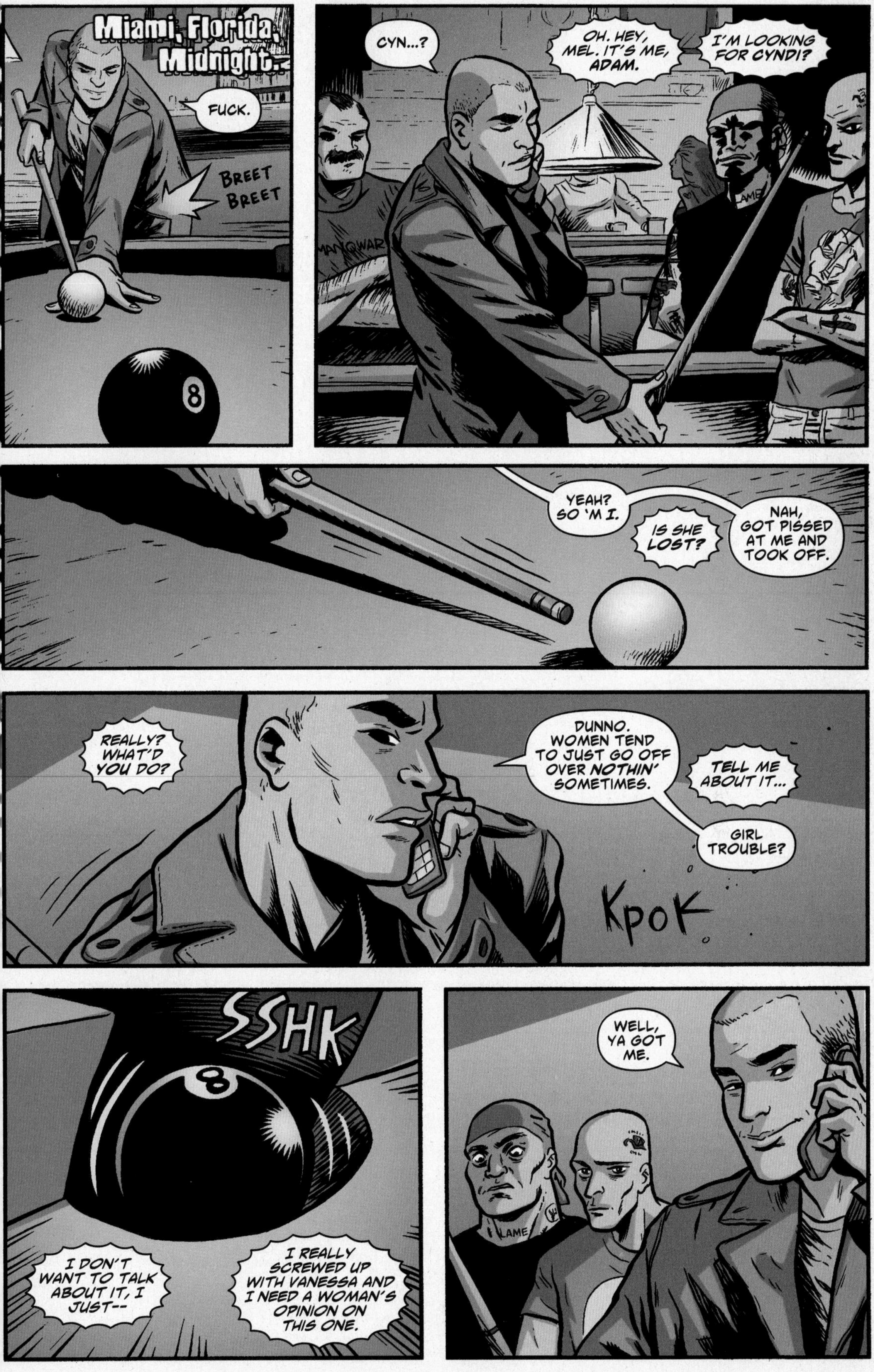
Miami, Florida, Midnight...
FUCK.
BREET BREET
CYN...?
OH. HEY, MEL. IT'S ME, ADAM.
I'M LOOKING FOR CYNDI?
MANOWAR
LAME
YEAH? SO 'M I.
IS SHE LOST?
NAH, GOT PISSED AT ME AND TOOK OFF.
REALLY? WHAT'D YOU DO?
DUNNO. WOMEN TEND TO JUST GO OFF OVER NOTHIN' SOMETIMES.
TELL ME ABOUT IT...
GIRL TROUBLE?
KPOK
SSHK
I DON'T WANT TO TALK ABOUT IT, I JUST--
I REALLY SCREWED UP WITH VANESSA AND I NEED A WOMAN'S OPINION ON THIS ONE.
WELL, YA GOT ME.
LAME

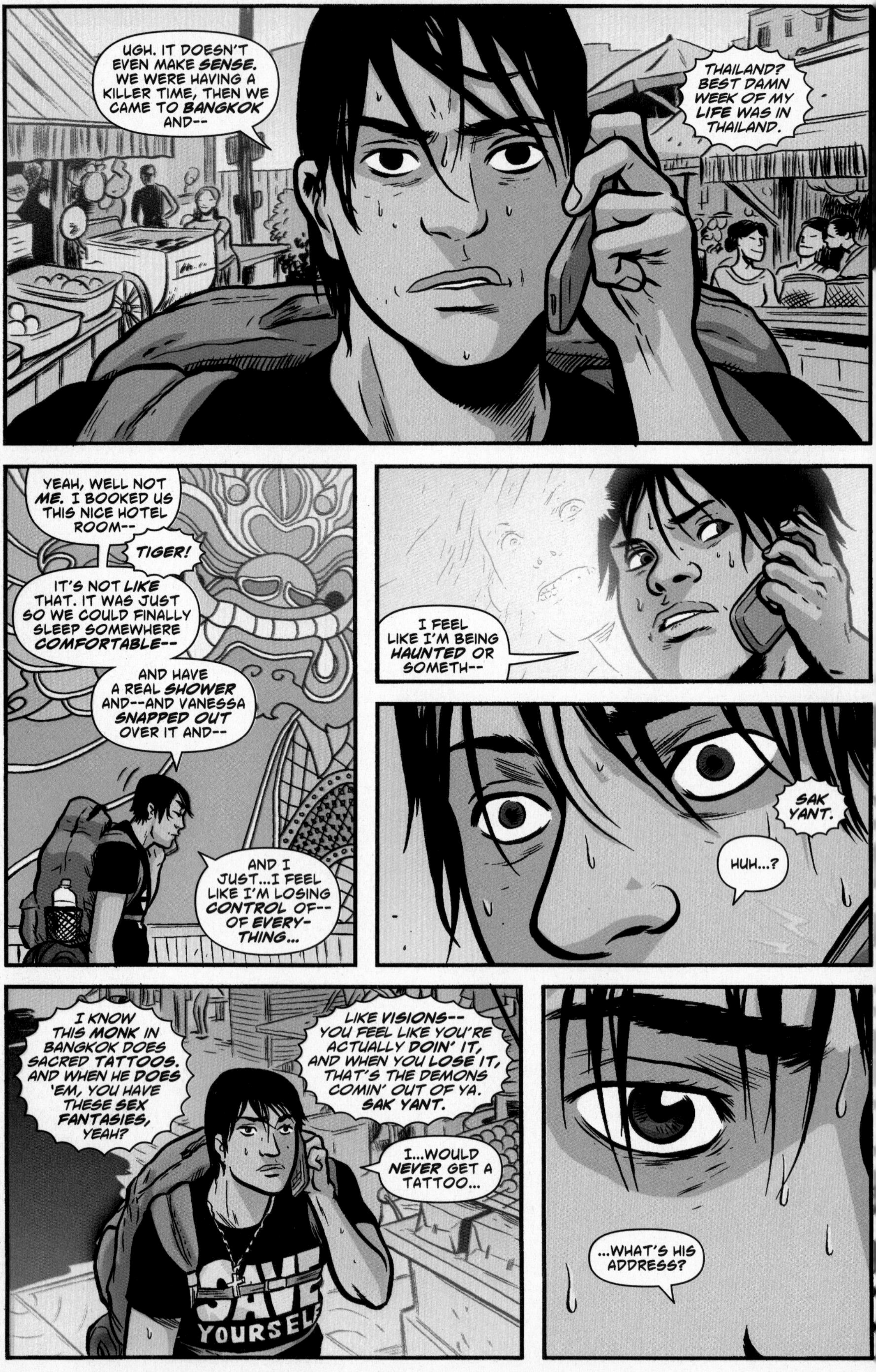
UGH. IT DOESN'T EVEN MAKE SENSE. WE WERE HAVING A KILLER TIME, THEN WE CAME TO BANGKOK AND--
THAILAND? BEST DAMN WEEK OF MY LIFE WAS IN THAILAND.
YEAH, WELL NOT ME. I BOOKED US THIS NICE HOTEL ROOM--
TIGER!
IT'S NOT LIKE THAT. IT WAS JUST SO WE COULD FINALLY SLEEP SOMEWHERE COMFORTABLE--
AND HAVE A REAL SHOWER AND--AND VANESSA SNAPPED OUT OVER IT AND--
AND I JUST...I FEEL LIKE I'M LOSING CONTROL OF--OF EVERY-THING...
I FEEL LIKE I'M BEING HAUNTED OR SOMETH--
SAK YANT.
HUH...?
I KNOW THIS MONK IN BANGKOK DOES SACRED TATTOOS. AND WHEN HE DOES 'EM, YOU HAVE THESE SEX FANTASIES, YEAH?
LIKE VISIONS--YOU FEEL LIKE YOU'RE ACTUALLY DOIN' IT, AND WHEN YOU LOSE IT, THAT'S THE DEMONS COMIN' OUT OF YA. SAK YANT.
I...WOULD NEVER GET A TATTOO...
SAVE YOURSELF
...WHAT'S HIS ADDRESS?

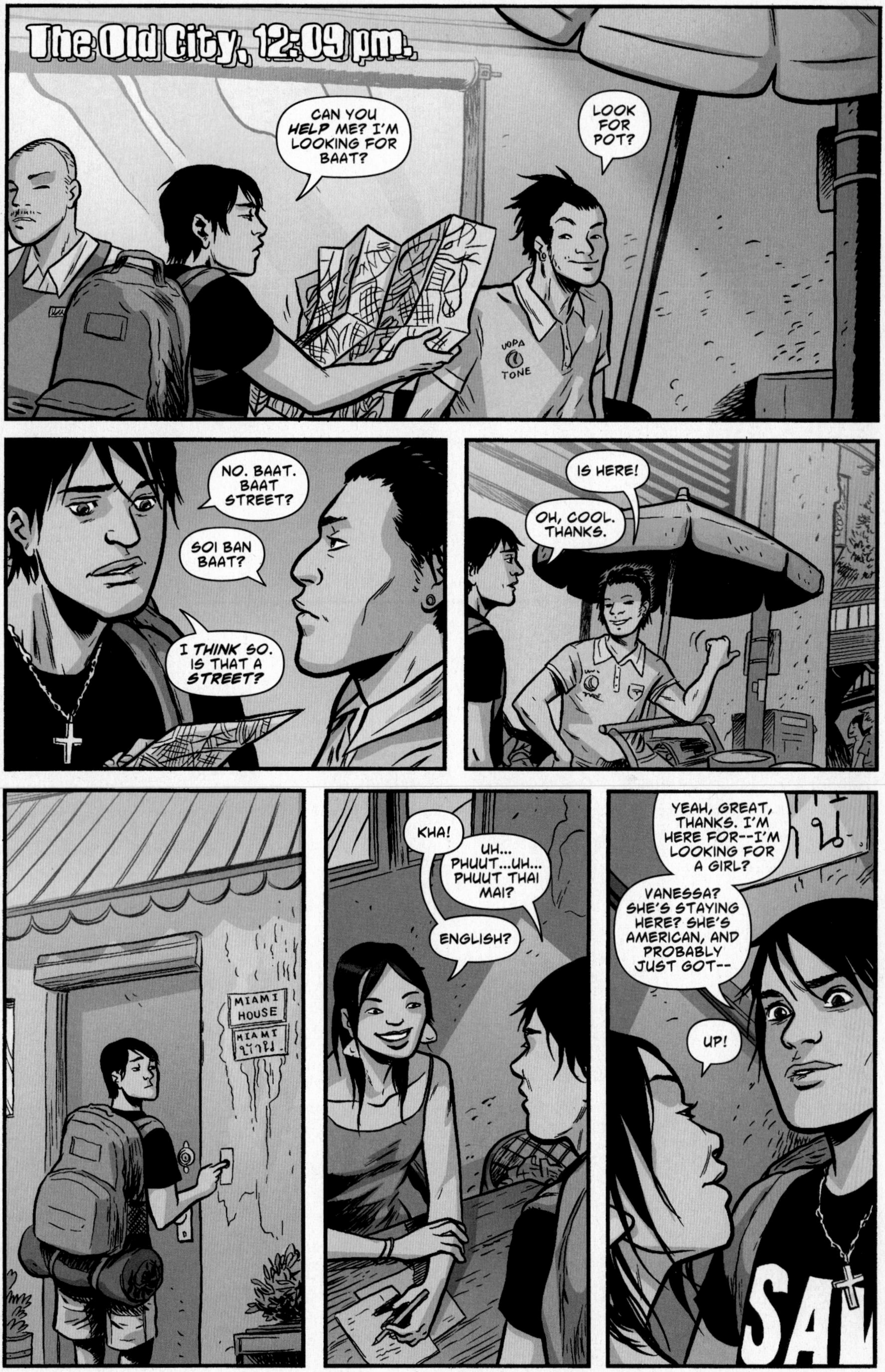
The Old City, 12:09 pm.
CAN YOU HELP ME? I'M LOOKING FOR BAAT?
LOOK FOR POT?
NO. BAAT. BAAT STREET?
SOI BAN BAAT?
I THINK SO. IS THAT A STREET?
IS HERE!
OH, COOL. THANKS.
MIAMI HOUSE
KHA!
UH... PHUUT...UH... PHUUT THAI MAI?
ENGLISH?
YEAH, GREAT, THANKS. I'M HERE FOR--I'M LOOKING FOR A GIRL?
VANESSA? SHE'S STAYING HERE? SHE'S AMERICAN, AND PROBABLY JUST GOT--
UP!

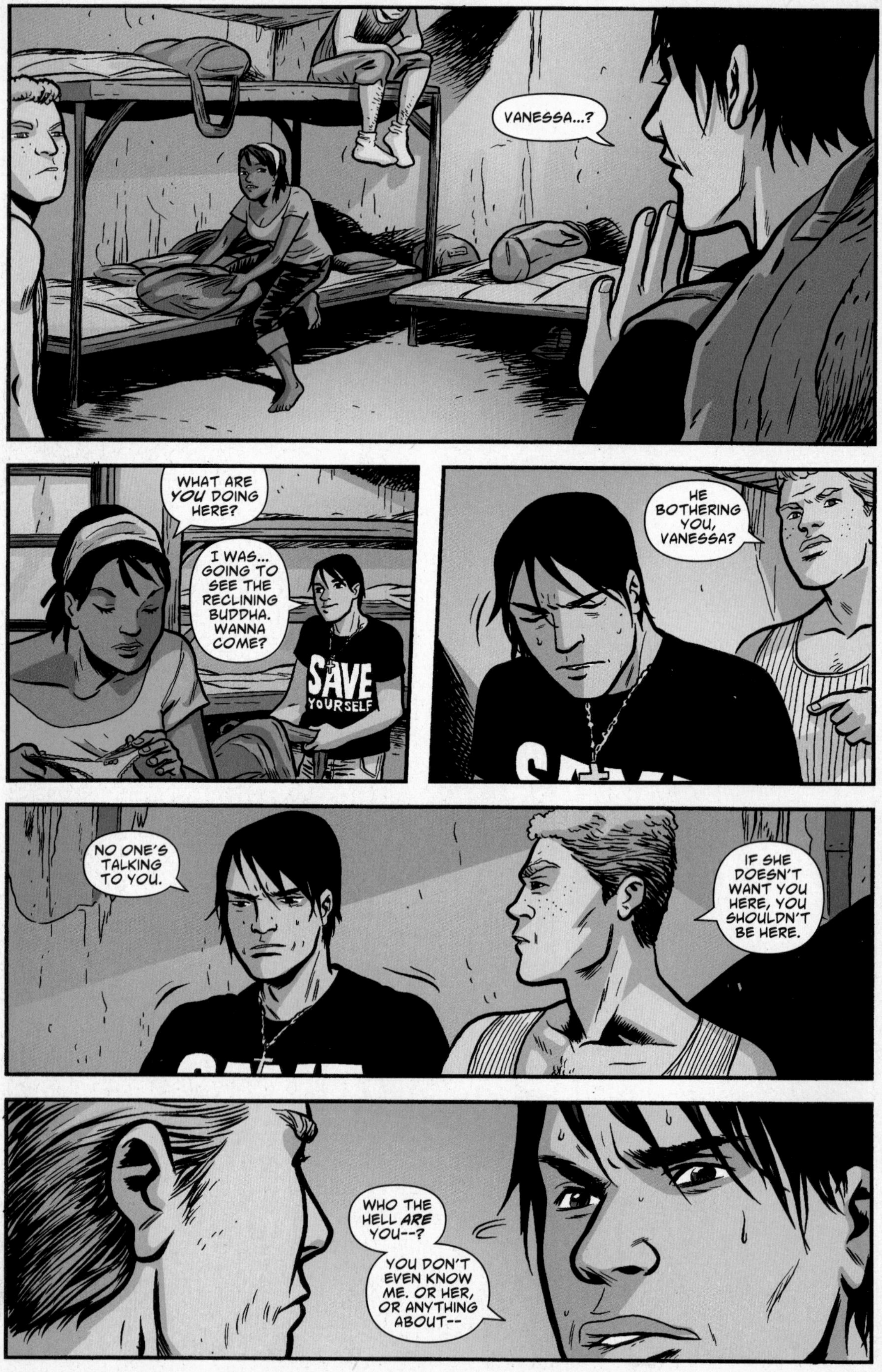
VANESSA...?
WHAT ARE YOU DOING HERE?
I WAS... GOING TO SEE THE RECLINING BUDDHA. WANNA COME?
SAVE YOURSELF
HE BOTHERING YOU, VANESSA?
NO ONE'S TALKING TO YOU.
IF SHE DOESN'T WANT YOU HERE, YOU SHOULDN'T BE HERE.
WHO THE HELL ARE YOU--?
YOU DON'T EVEN KNOW ME. OR HER, OR ANYTHING ABOUT--

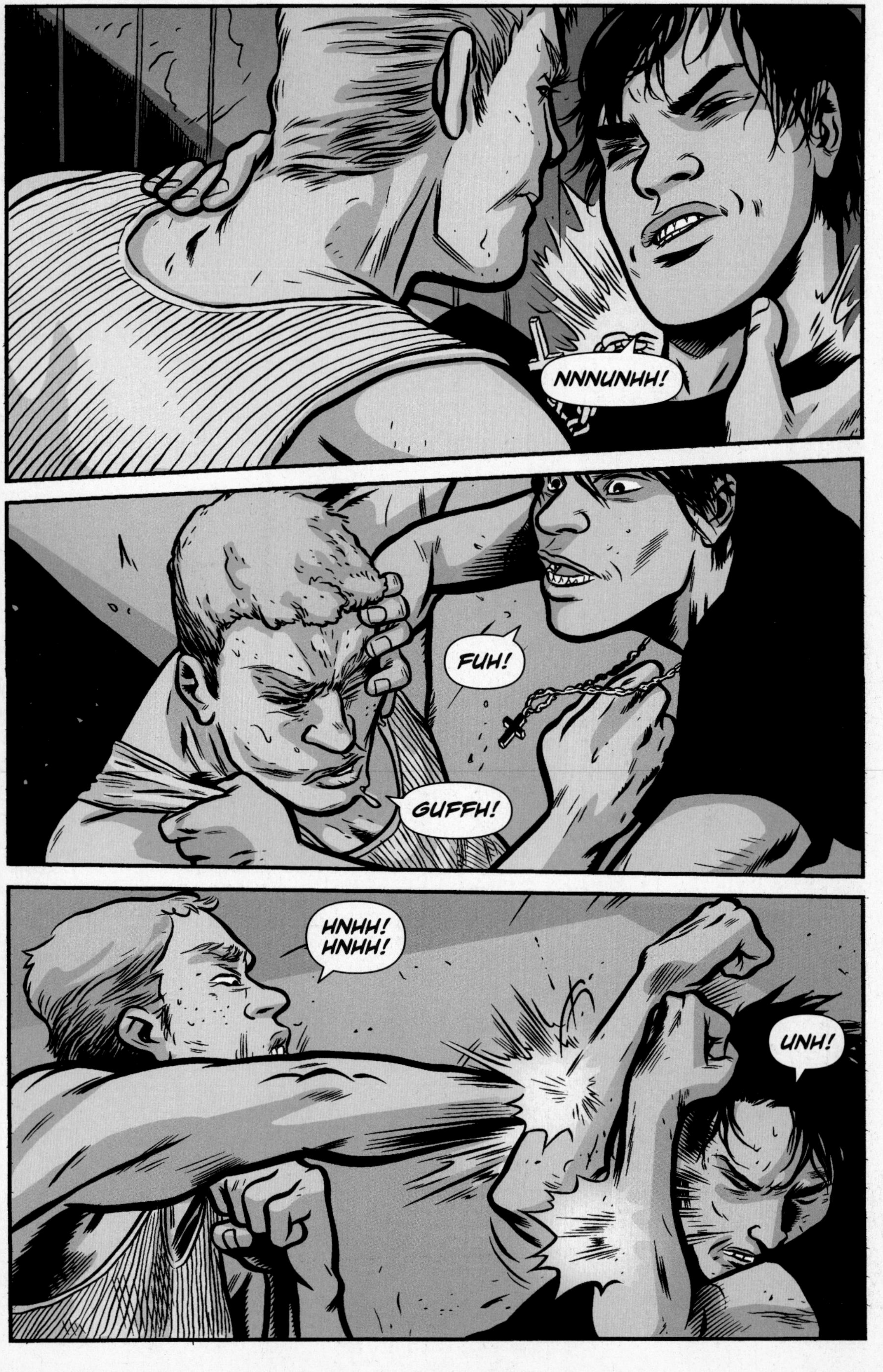
NNNUNHH!
FUH!
GUFFH!
HNHH! HNHH!
UNH!

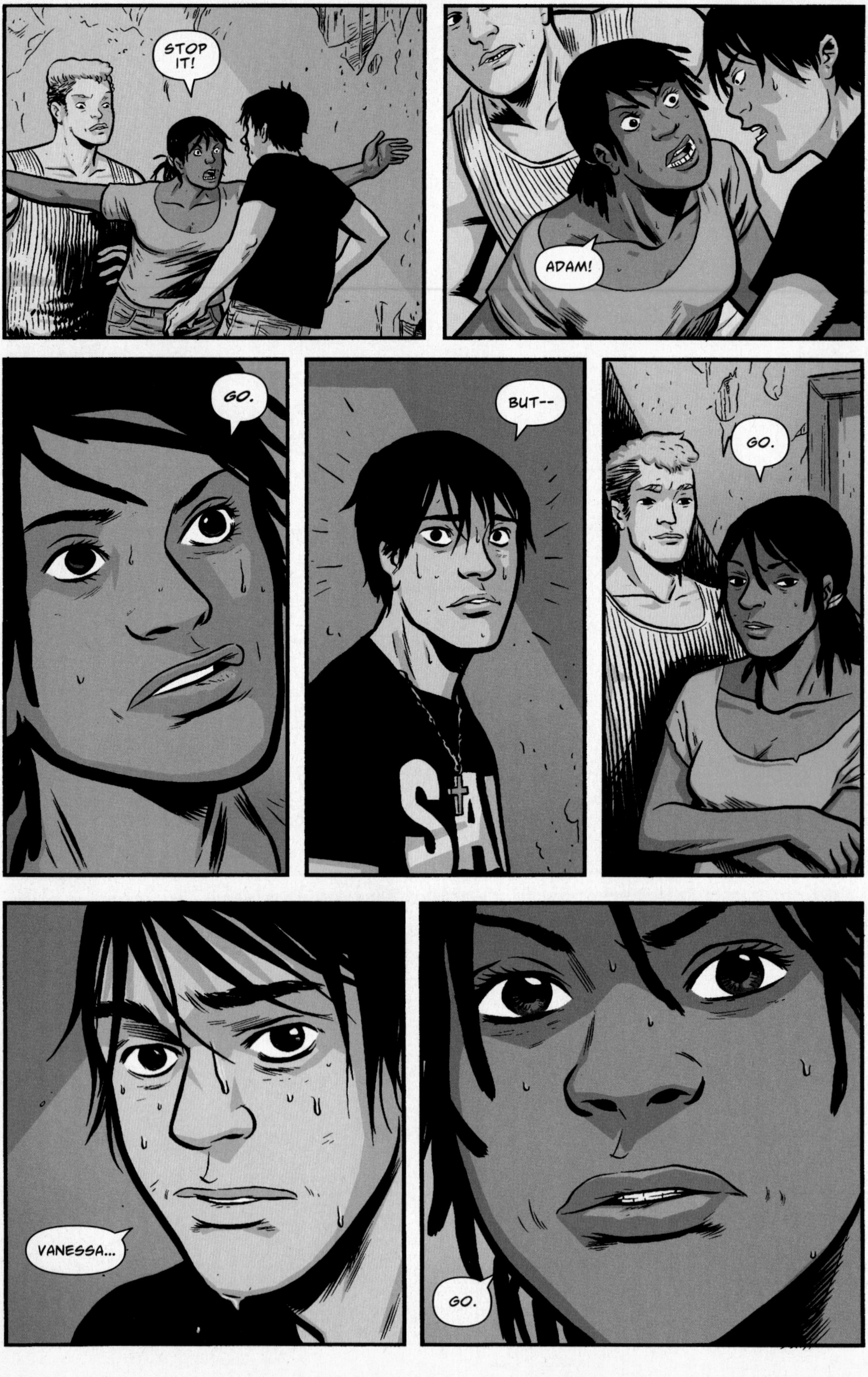
STOP IT!
ADAM!
GO.
BUT--
GO.
VANESSA...
GO.

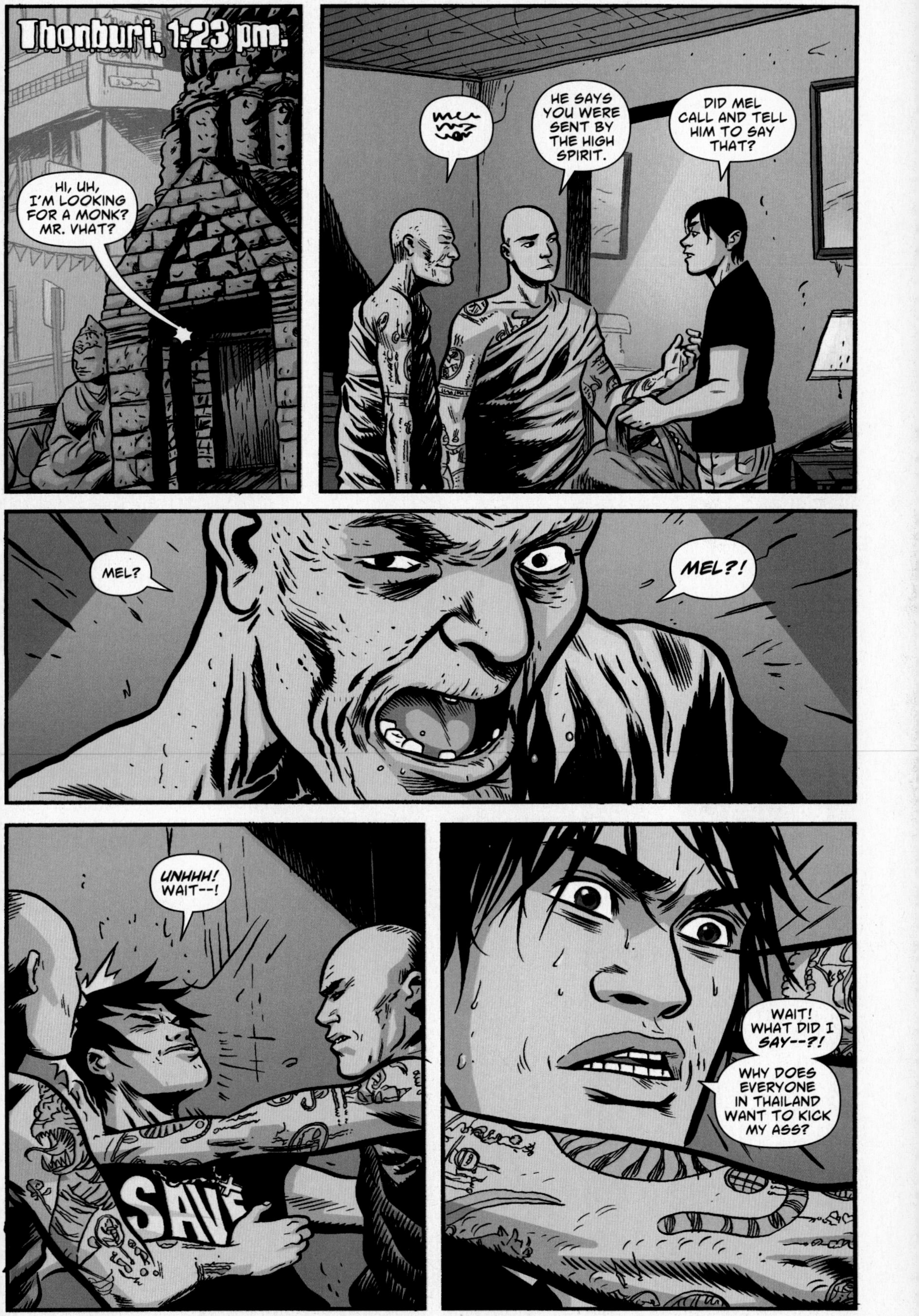
Thonburi, 1:23 pm.
HI, UH, I'M LOOKING FOR A MONK? MR. VHAT?
HE SAYS YOU WERE SENT BY THE HIGH SPIRIT.
DID MEL CALL AND TELL HIM TO SAY THAT?
MEL?
MEL?!
UNHHH! WAIT--!
SAVE
WAIT! WHAT DID I SAY--?!
WHY DOES EVERYONE IN THAILAND WANT TO KICK MY ASS?

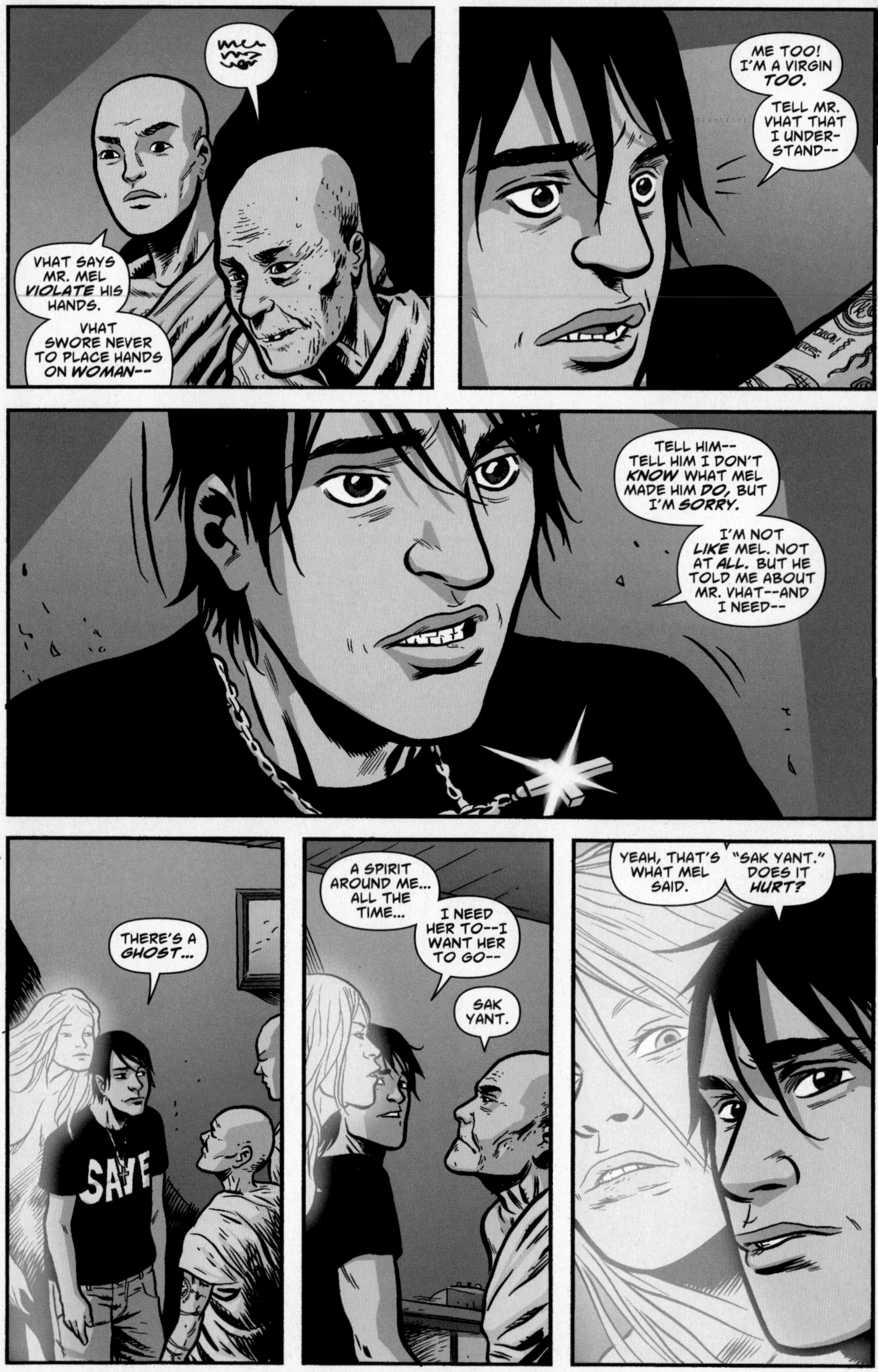
VHAT SAYS MR. MEL VIOLATE HIS HANDS.
VHAT SWORE NEVER TO PLACE HANDS ON WOMAN--
ME TOO! I'M A VIRGIN TOO.
TELL MR. VHAT THAT I UNDER-STAND--
TELL HIM-- TELL HIM I DON'T KNOW WHAT MEL MADE HIM DO, BUT I'M SORRY.
I'M NOT LIKE MEL. NOT AT ALL. BUT HE TOLD ME ABOUT MR. VHAT--AND I NEED--
THERE'S A GHOST...
A SPIRIT AROUND ME... ALL THE TIME...
I NEED HER TO--I WANT HER TO GO--
SAK YANT.
YEAH, THAT'S WHAT MEL SAID.
"SAK YANT." DOES IT HURT?
SAVE

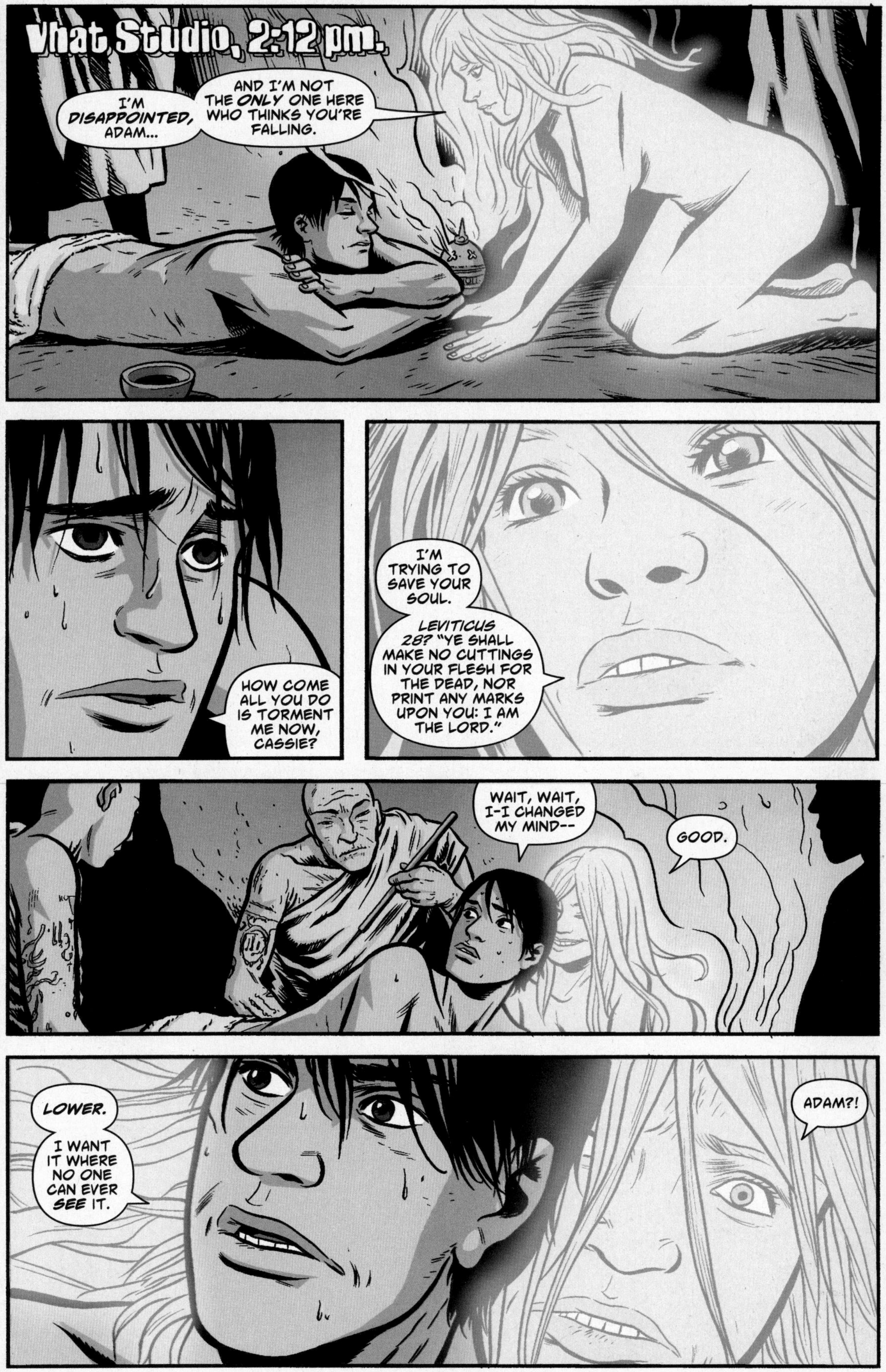
Vhat Studio, 2:12 pm.
I'M DISAPPOINTED, ADAM...
AND I'M NOT THE ONLY ONE HERE WHO THINKS YOU'RE FALLING.
HOW COME ALL YOU DO IS TORMENT ME NOW, CASSIE?
I'M TRYING TO SAVE YOUR SOUL.
LEVITICUS 28? "YE SHALL MAKE NO CUTTINGS IN YOUR FLESH FOR THE DEAD, NOR PRINT ANY MARKS UPON YOU: I AM THE LORD."
WAIT, WAIT, I-I CHANGED MY MIND--
GOOD.
LOWER.
I WANT IT WHERE NO ONE CAN EVER SEE IT.
ADAM?!

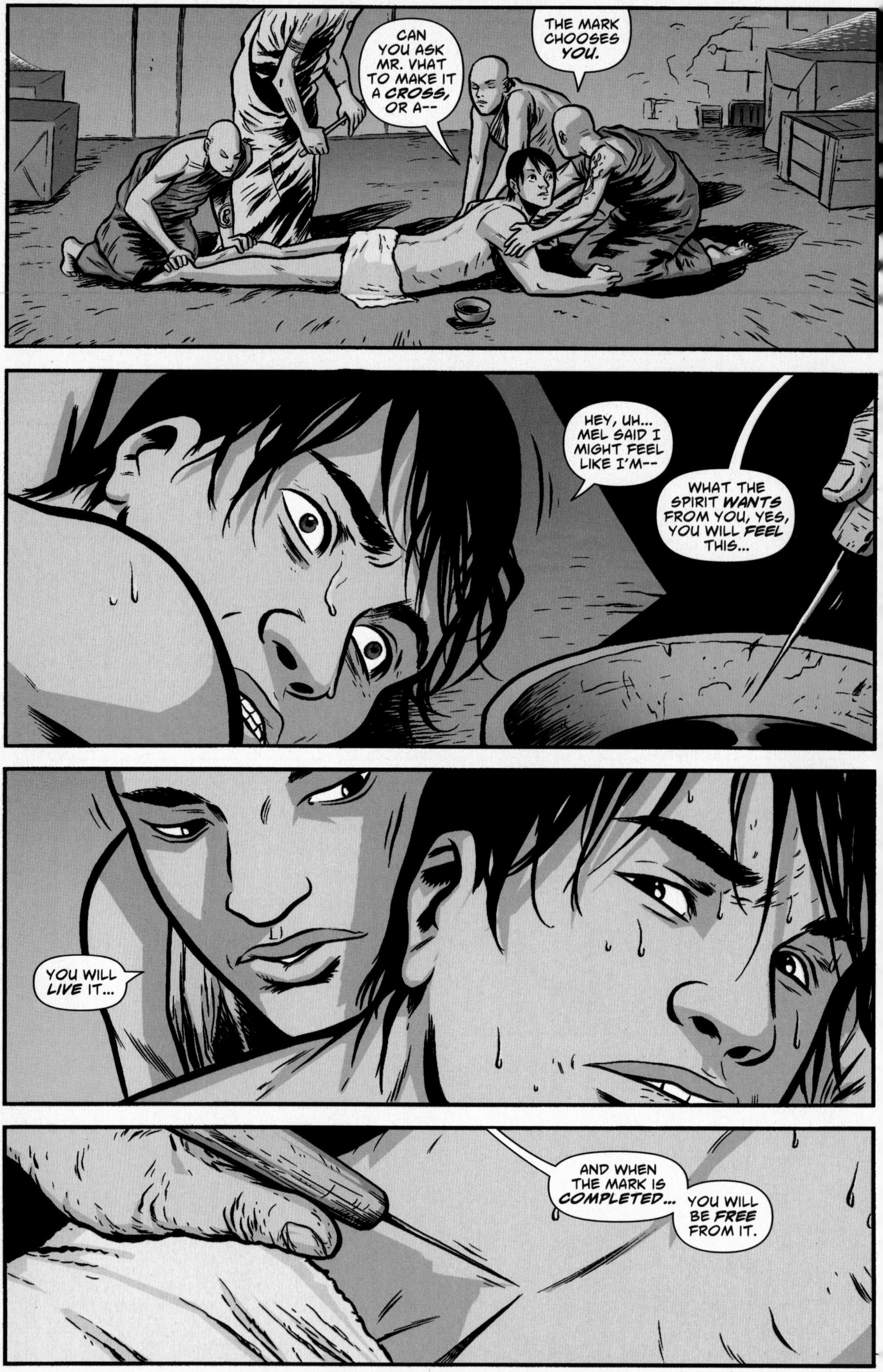
CAN YOU ASK MR. VHAT TO MAKE IT A CROSS, OR A--
THE MARK CHOOSES YOU.
HEY, UH... MEL SAID I MIGHT FEEL LIKE I'M--
WHAT THE SPIRIT WANTS FROM YOU, YES, YOU WILL FEEL THIS...
YOU WILL LIVE IT...
AND WHEN THE MARK IS COMPLETED...
YOU WILL BE FREE FROM IT.

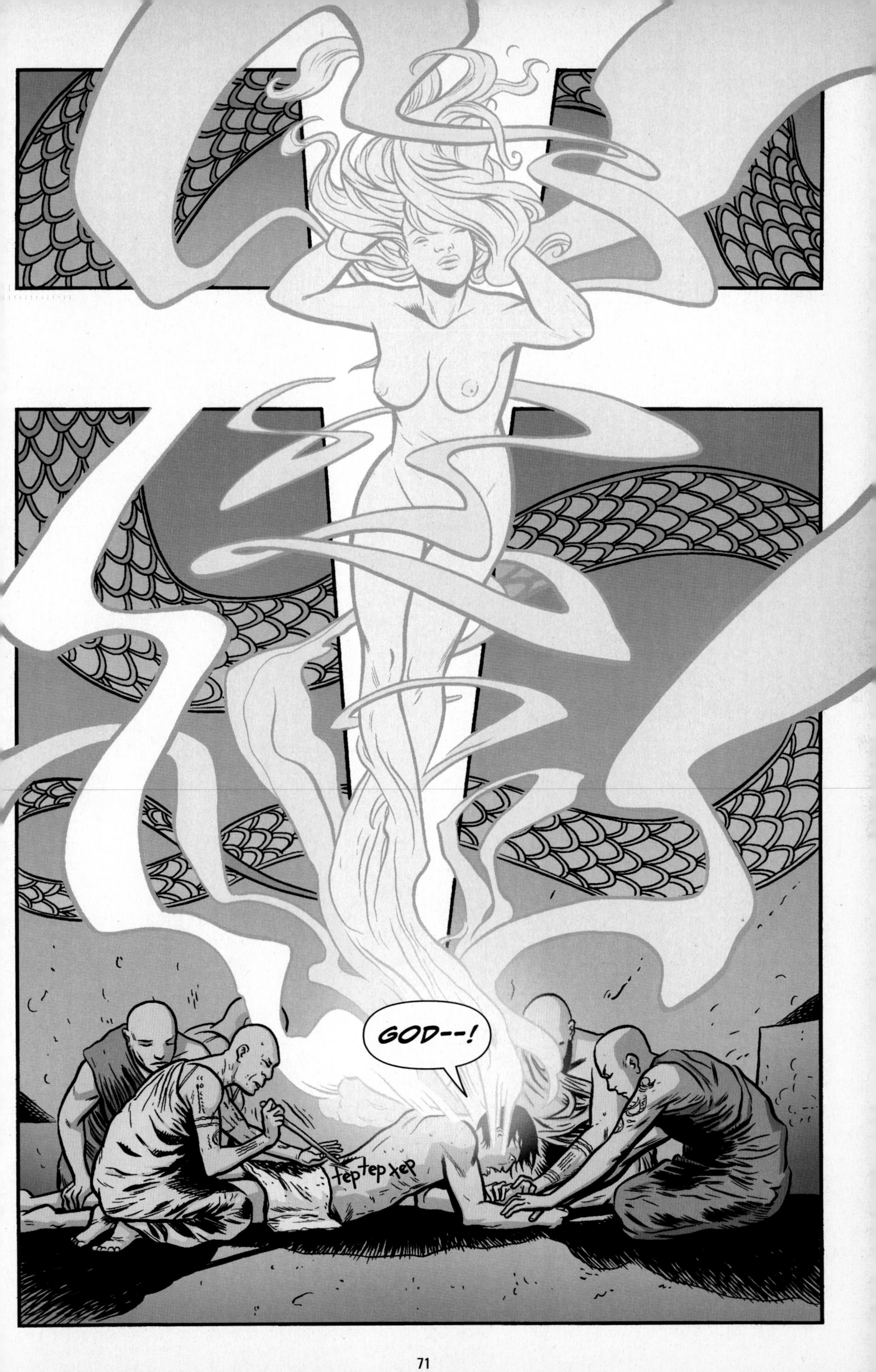
GOD--!
tep tep xep

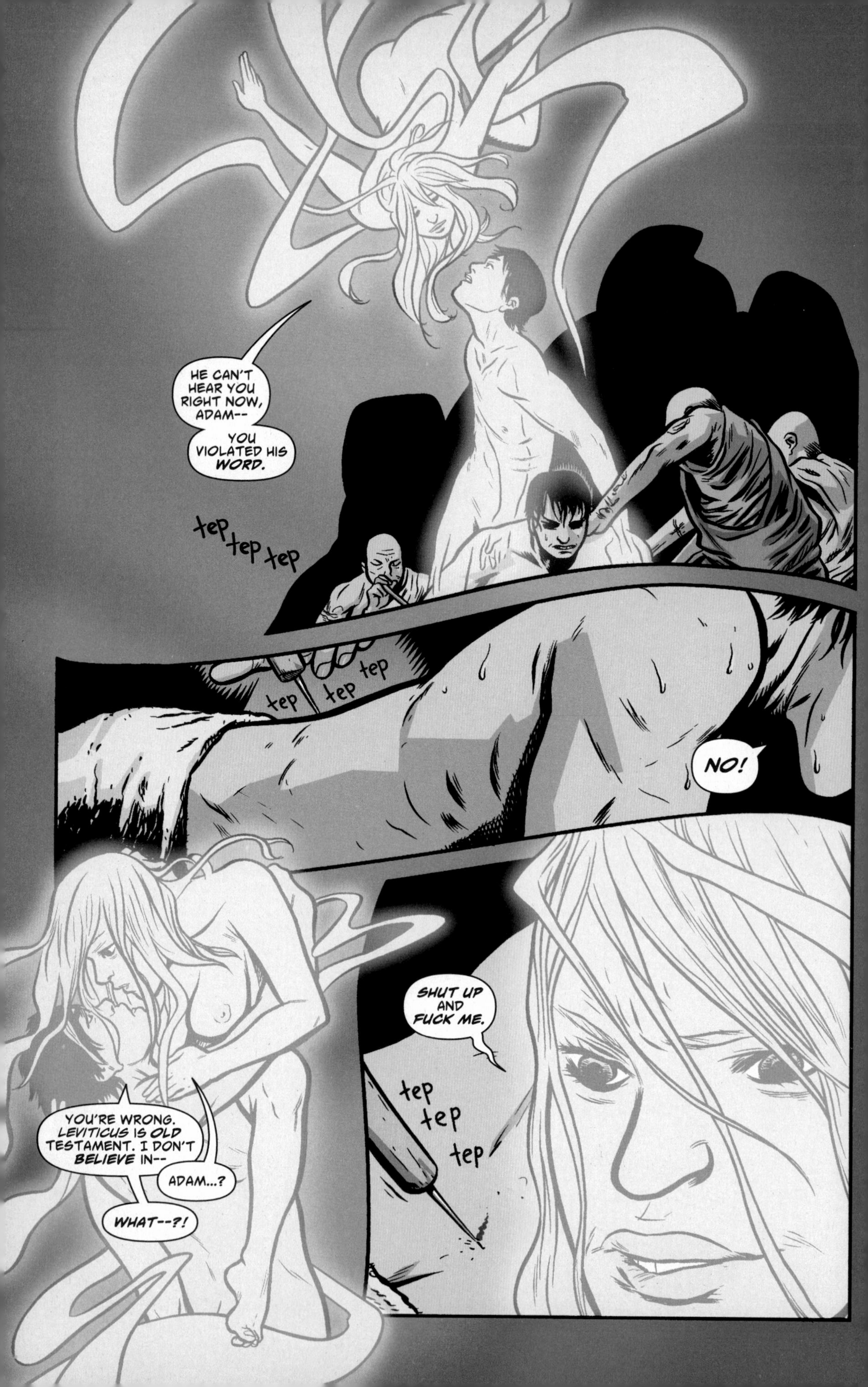

HE CAN'T HEAR YOU RIGHT NOW, ADAM--
YOU VIOLATED HIS WORD.
tep tep tep
tep tep tep
NO!
SHUT UP AND FUCK ME.
tep tep tep
YOU'RE WRONG. LEVITICUS IS OLD TESTAMENT. I DON'T BELIEVE IN--
ADAM...?
WHAT--?!

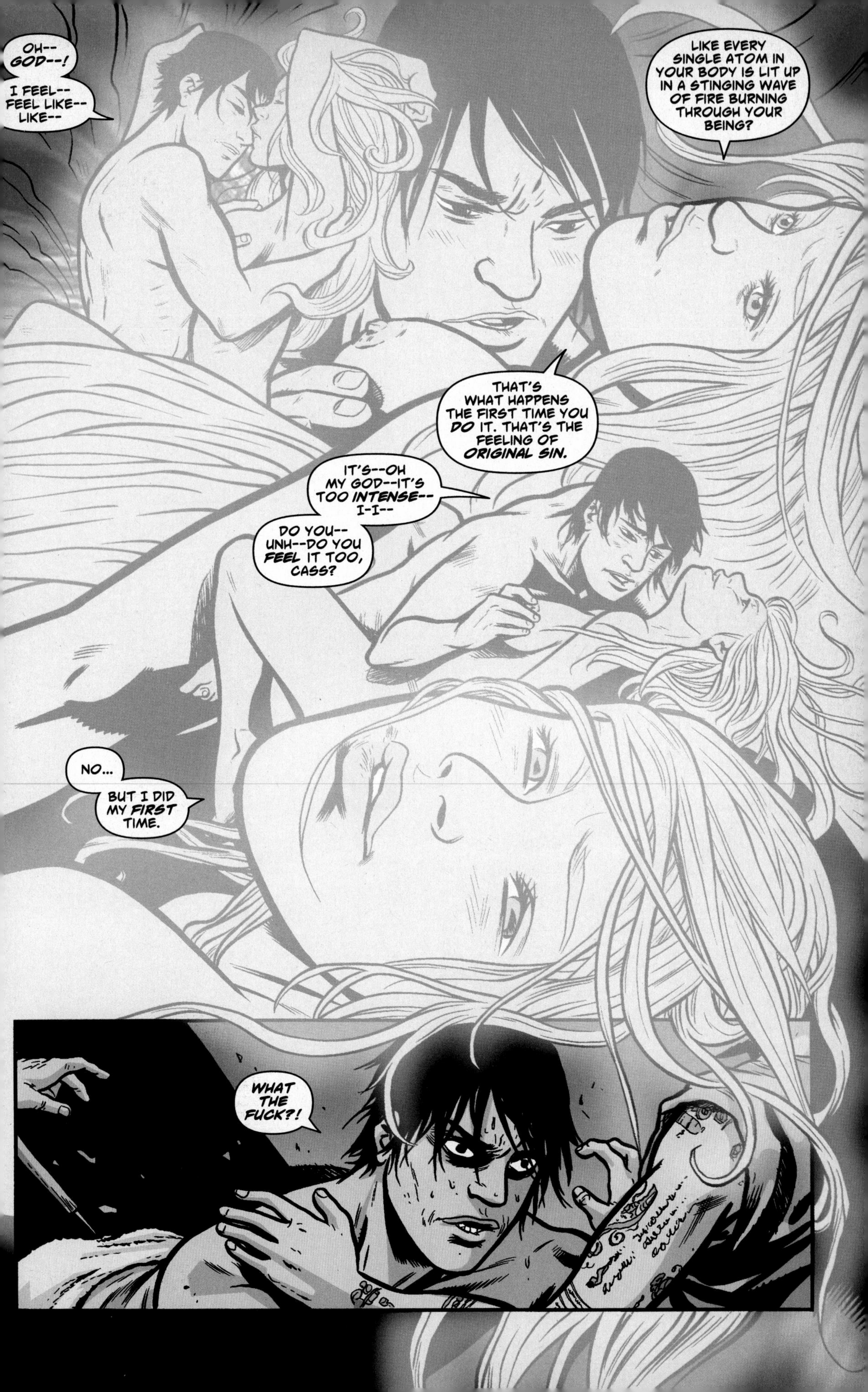
OH-- GOD--!
I FEEL-- FEEL LIKE-- LIKE--
LIKE EVERY SINGLE ATOM IN YOUR BODY IS LIT UP IN A STINGING WAVE OF FIRE BURNING THROUGH YOUR BEING?
THAT'S WHAT HAPPENS THE FIRST TIME YOU DO IT. THAT'S THE FEELING OF ORIGINAL SIN.
IT'S--OH MY GOD--IT'S TOO INTENSE-- I-I--
DO YOU-- UNH--DO YOU FEEL IT TOO, CASS?
NO...
BUT I DID MY FIRST TIME.
WHAT THE FUCK?!

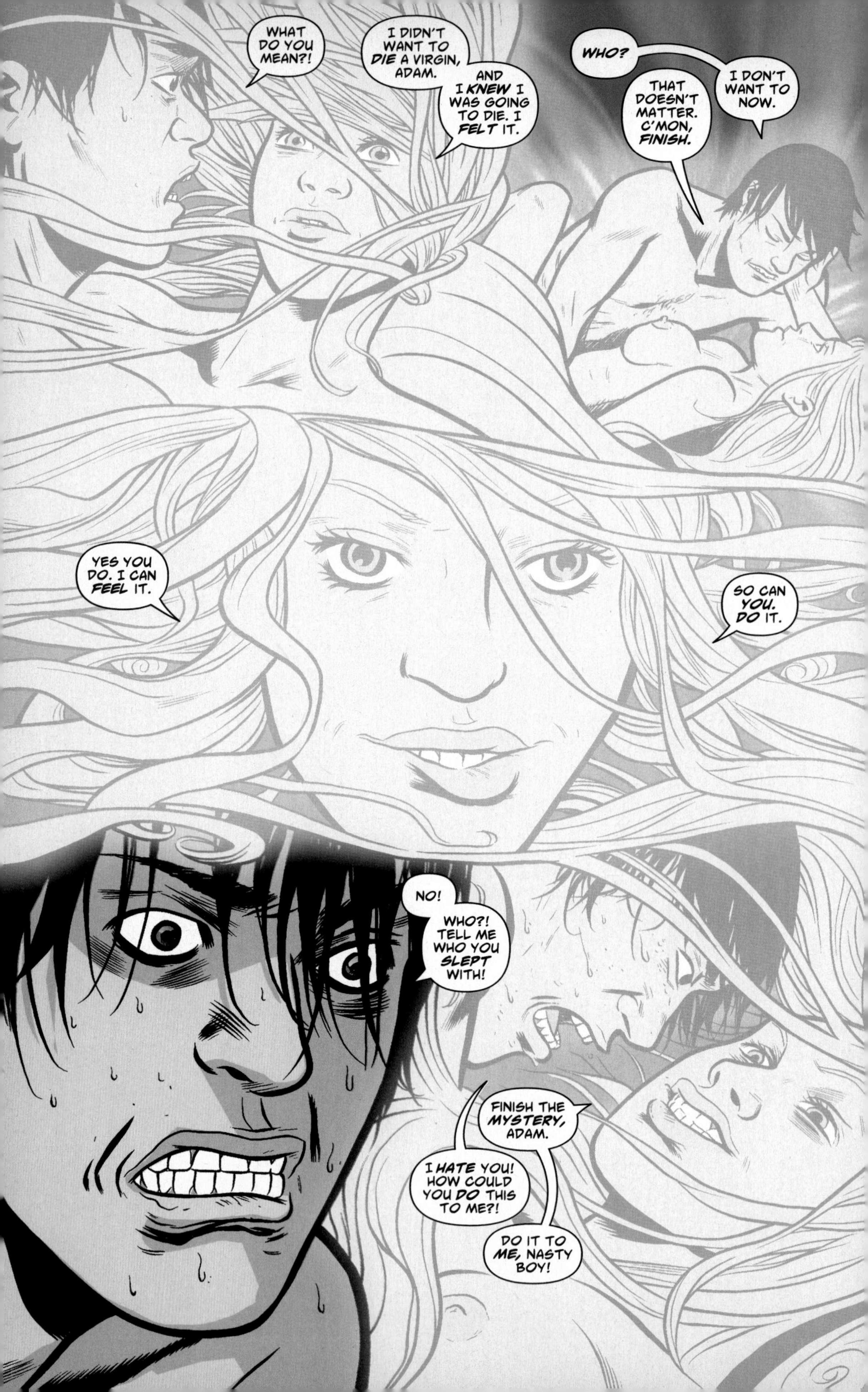
WHAT DO YOU MEAN?!
I DIDN'T WANT TO DIE A VIRGIN, ADAM.
AND I KNEW I WAS GOING TO DIE. I FELT IT.
WHO?
THAT DOESN'T MATTER. C'MON, FINISH.
I DON'T WANT TO NOW.
YES YOU DO. I CAN FEEL IT.
SO CAN YOU. DO IT.
NO!
WHO?! TELL ME WHO YOU SLEPT WITH!
FINISH THE MYSTERY, ADAM.
I HATE YOU! HOW COULD YOU DO THIS TO ME?!
DO IT TO ME, NASTY BOY!

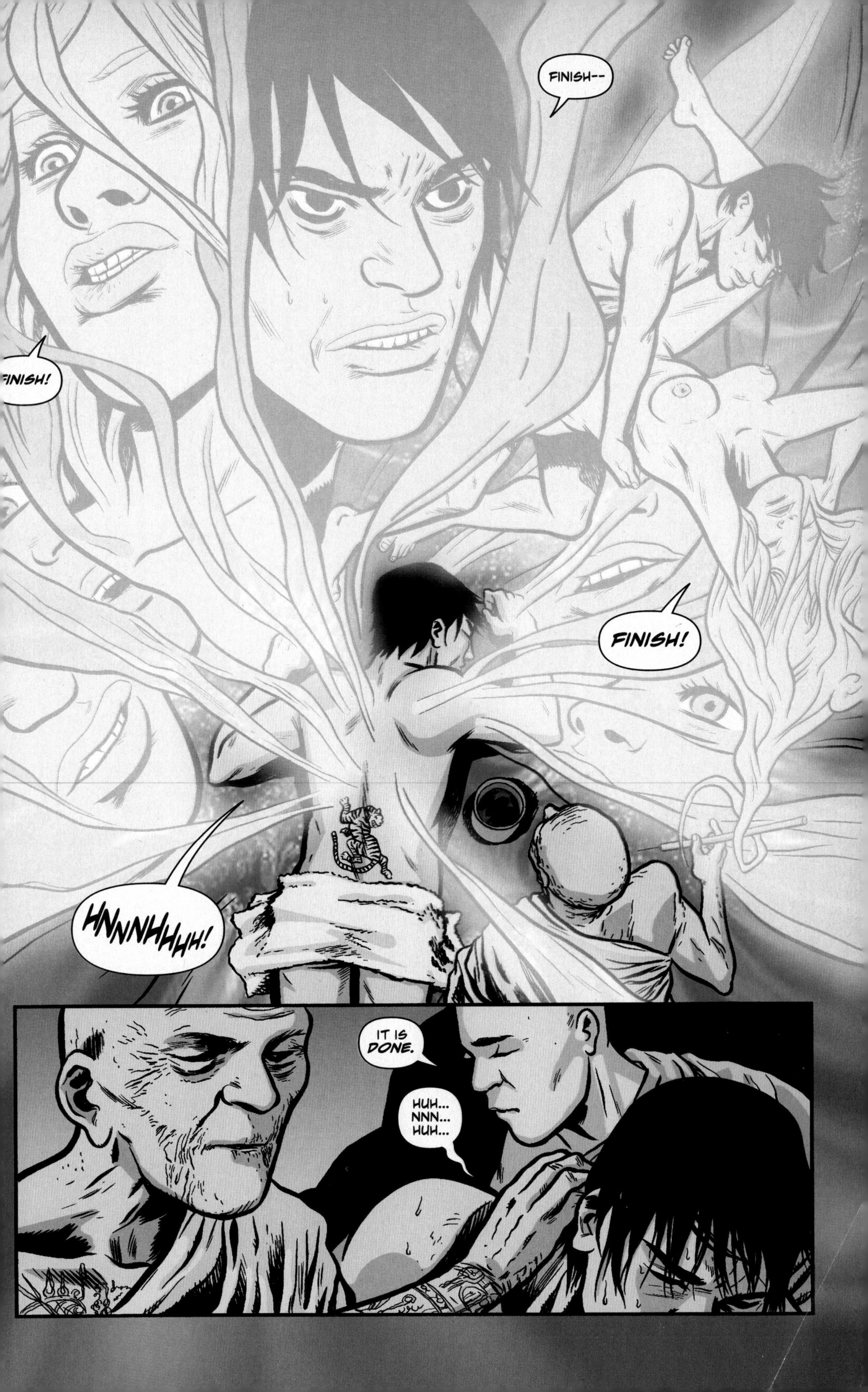
FINISH--
FINISH!
FINISH!
HNNNHHHH!
IT IS DONE.
HUH... NNN... HUH...

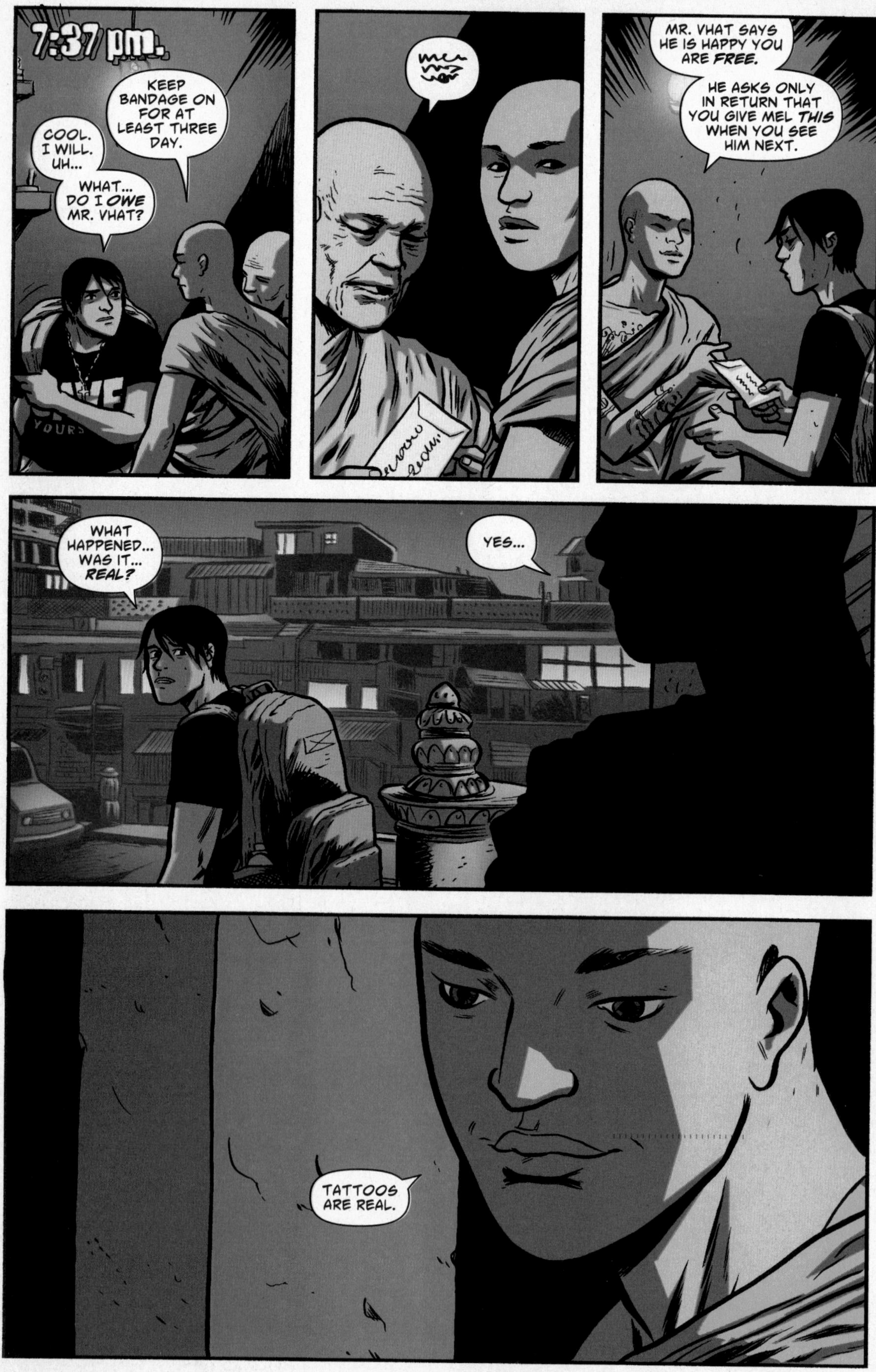
7:37 pm.
KEEP BANDAGE ON FOR AT LEAST THREE DAY.
COOL. I WILL. UH...
WHAT... DO I *OWE* MR. VHAT?
MR. VHAT SAYS HE IS HAPPY YOU ARE *FREE.*
HE ASKS ONLY IN RETURN THAT YOU GIVE MEL *THIS* WHEN YOU SEE HIM NEXT.
WHAT HAPPENED... WAS IT... *REAL?*
YES...
TATTOOS ARE REAL.

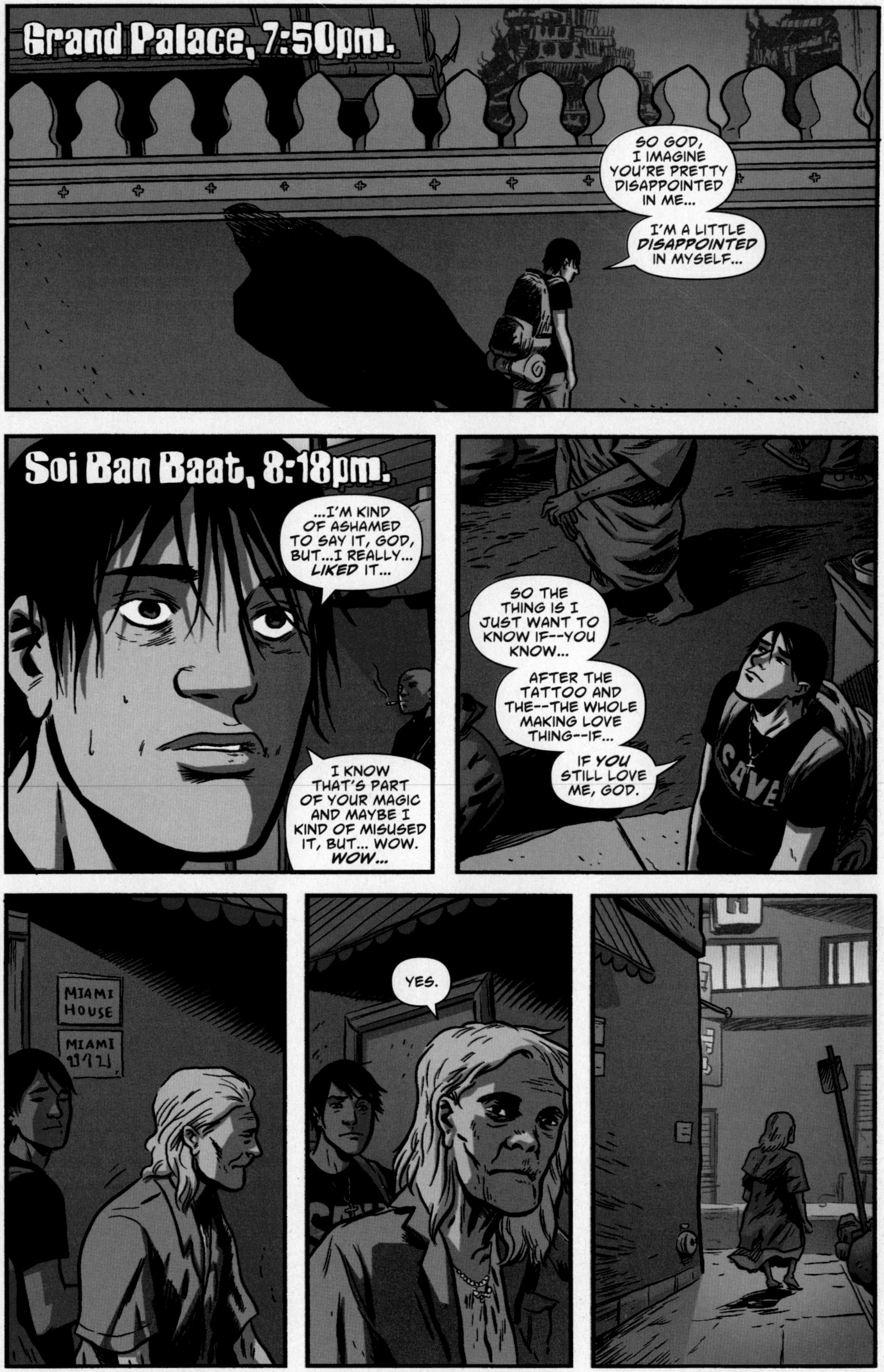

Grand Palace, 7:50pm.
SO GOD, I IMAGINE YOU'RE PRETTY DISAPPOINTED IN ME...
I'M A LITTLE DISAPPOINTED IN MYSELF...
Soi Ban Baat, 8:18pm.
...I'M KIND OF ASHAMED TO SAY IT, GOD, BUT...I REALLY... LIKED IT...
I KNOW THAT'S PART OF YOUR MAGIC AND MAYBE I KIND OF MISUSED IT, BUT... WOW. WOW...
SO THE THING IS I JUST WANT TO KNOW IF--YOU KNOW...
AFTER THE TATTOO AND THE--THE WHOLE MAKING LOVE THING--IF...
IF YOU STILL LOVE ME, GOD.
SAVE
MIAMI HOUSE
MIAMI
YES.

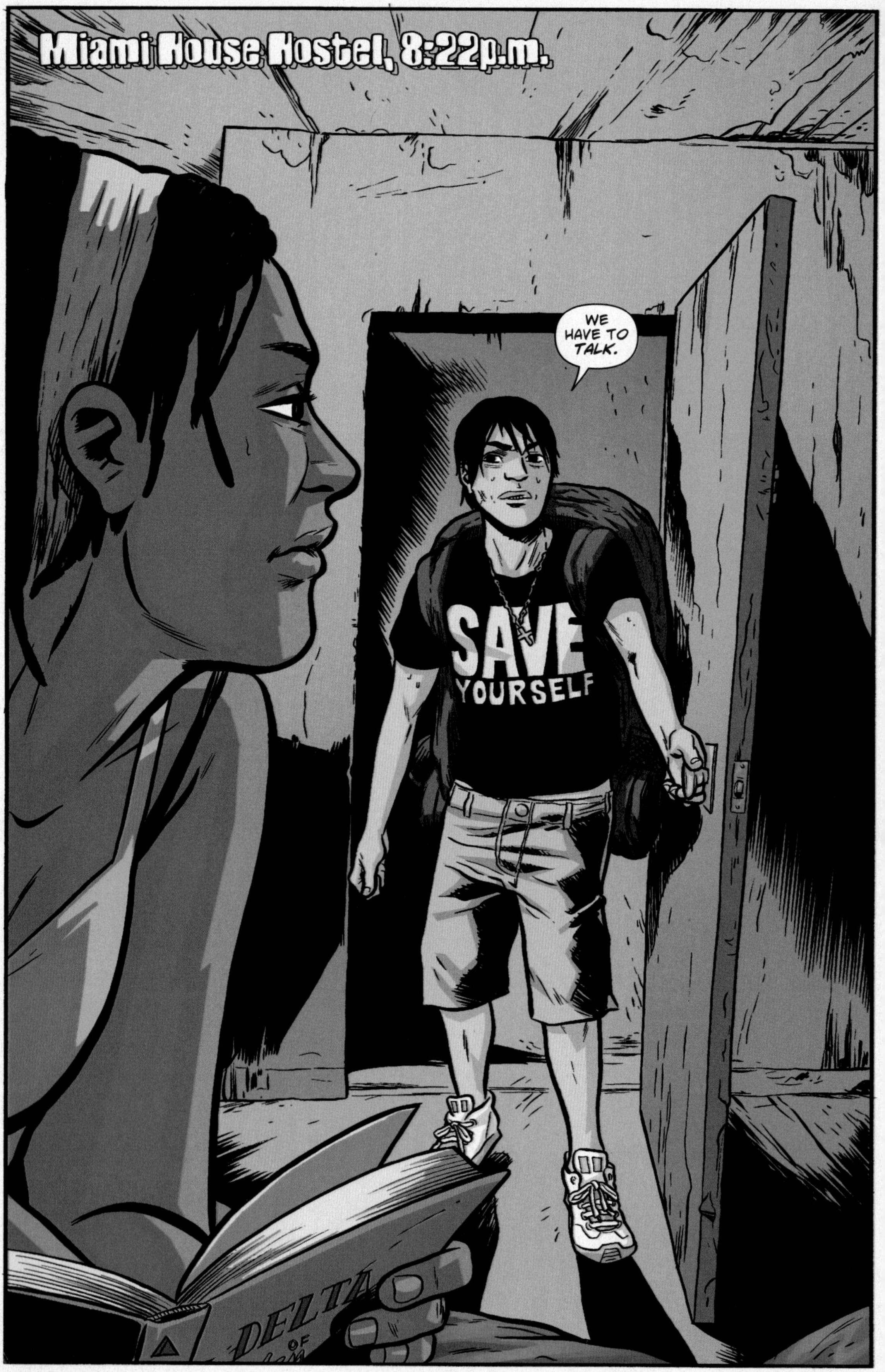
Miami House Hostel, 8:22p.m.
WE HAVE TO TALK.
SAVE YOURSELF
DELTA OF

AROUND THE WORLD :: DELHI

CHAPTER FOUR

Chapter pencils by Ryan Kelly Chapter inks by Jim Rugg and Jasen Lex

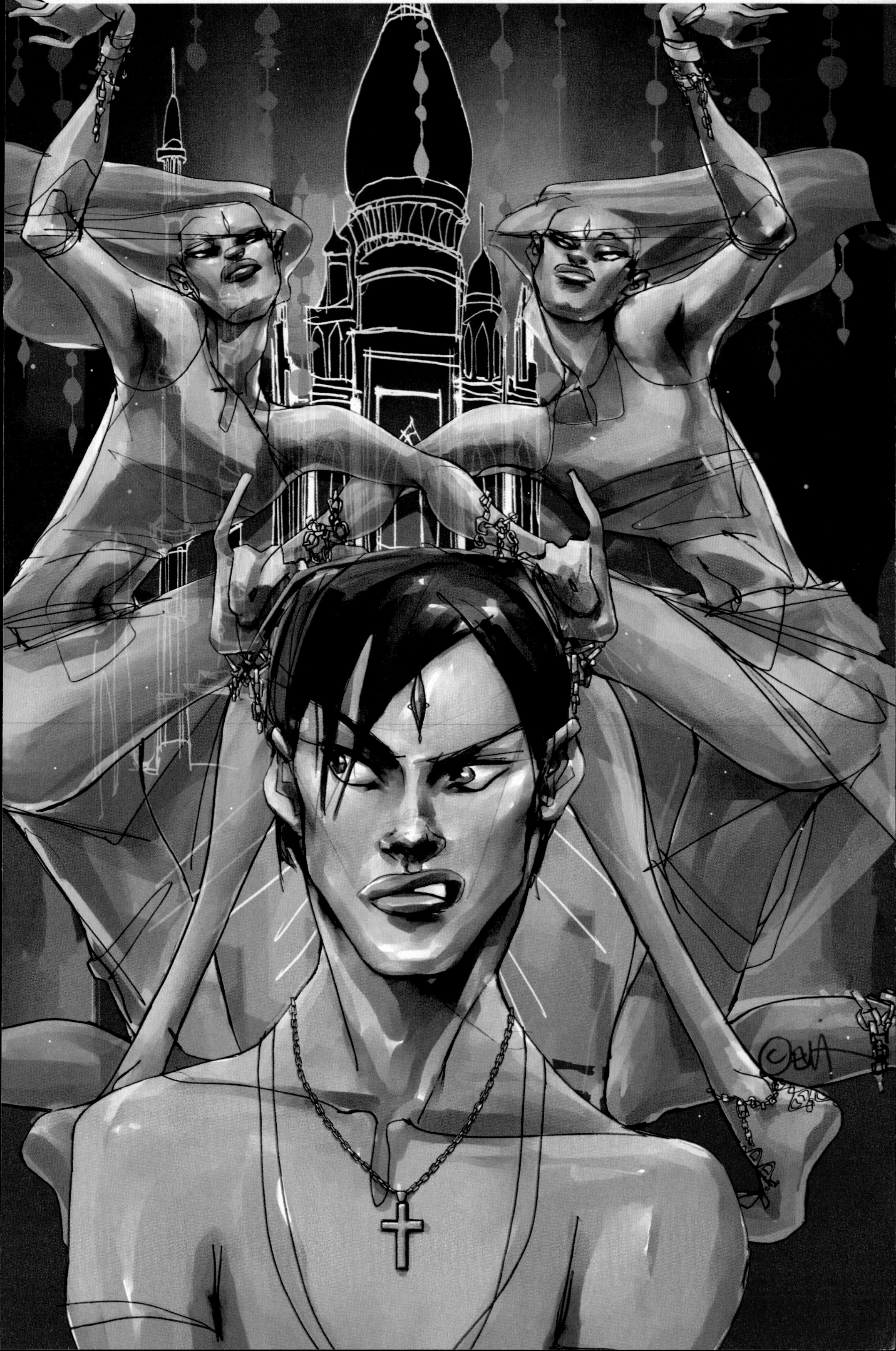

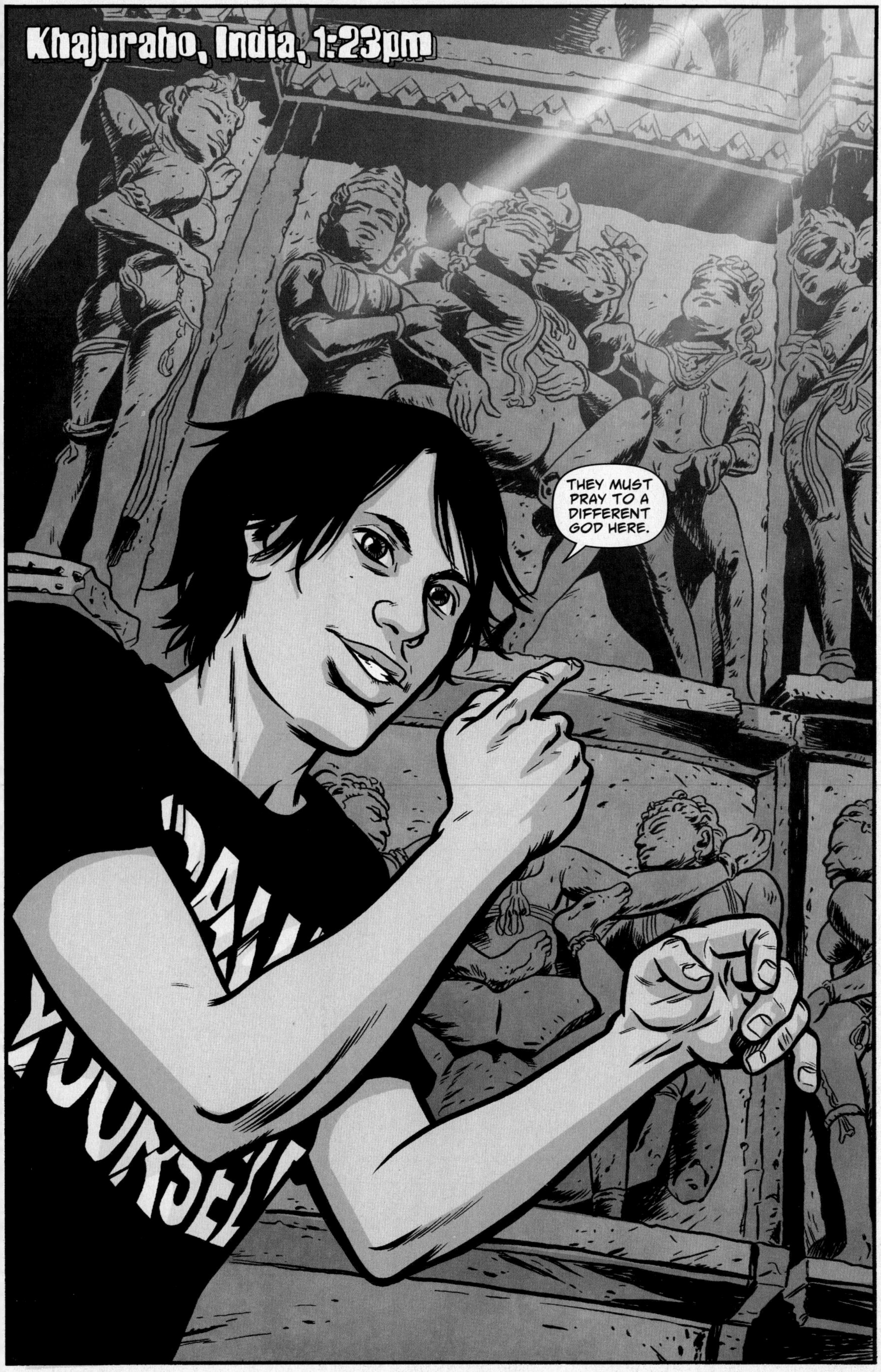
Khajuraho, India, 1:23pm
THEY MUST PRAY TO A DIFFERENT GOD HERE.
YOURSELF

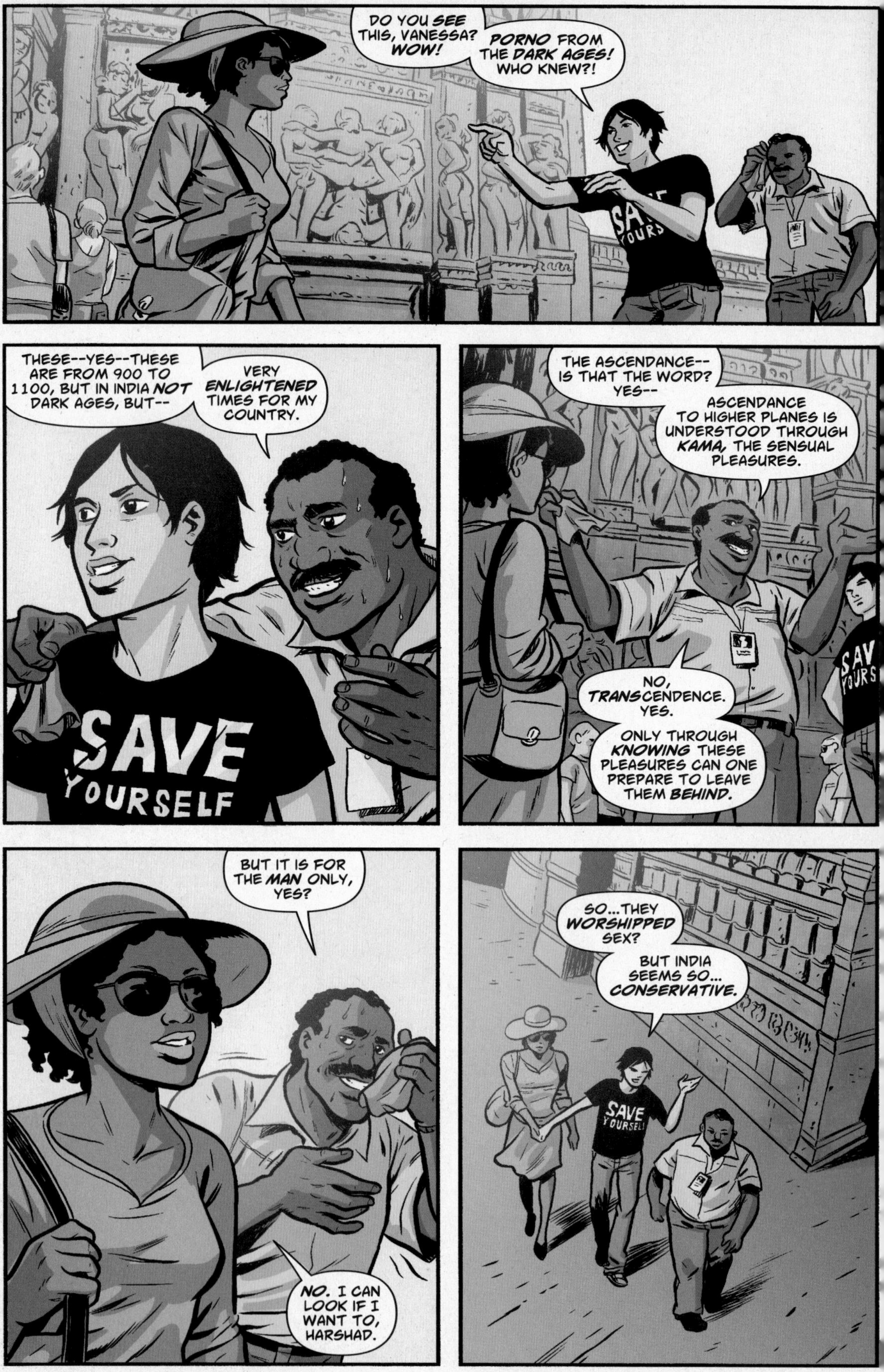
DO YOU SEE THIS, VANESSA? WOW!
PORNO FROM THE DARK AGES! WHO KNEW?!
THESE--YES--THESE ARE FROM 900 TO 1100, BUT IN INDIA NOT DARK AGES, BUT--
VERY ENLIGHTENED TIMES FOR MY COUNTRY.
SAVE YOURSELF
THE ASCENDANCE-- IS THAT THE WORD? YES--
ASCENDANCE TO HIGHER PLANES IS UNDERSTOOD THROUGH KAMA, THE SENSUAL PLEASURES.
NO, TRANSCENDENCE. YES.
ONLY THROUGH KNOWING THESE PLEASURES CAN ONE PREPARE TO LEAVE THEM BEHIND.
BUT IT IS FOR THE MAN ONLY, YES?
NO. I CAN LOOK IF I WANT TO, HARSHAD.
SO...THEY WORSHIPPED SEX?
BUT INDIA SEEMS SO... CONSERVATIVE.

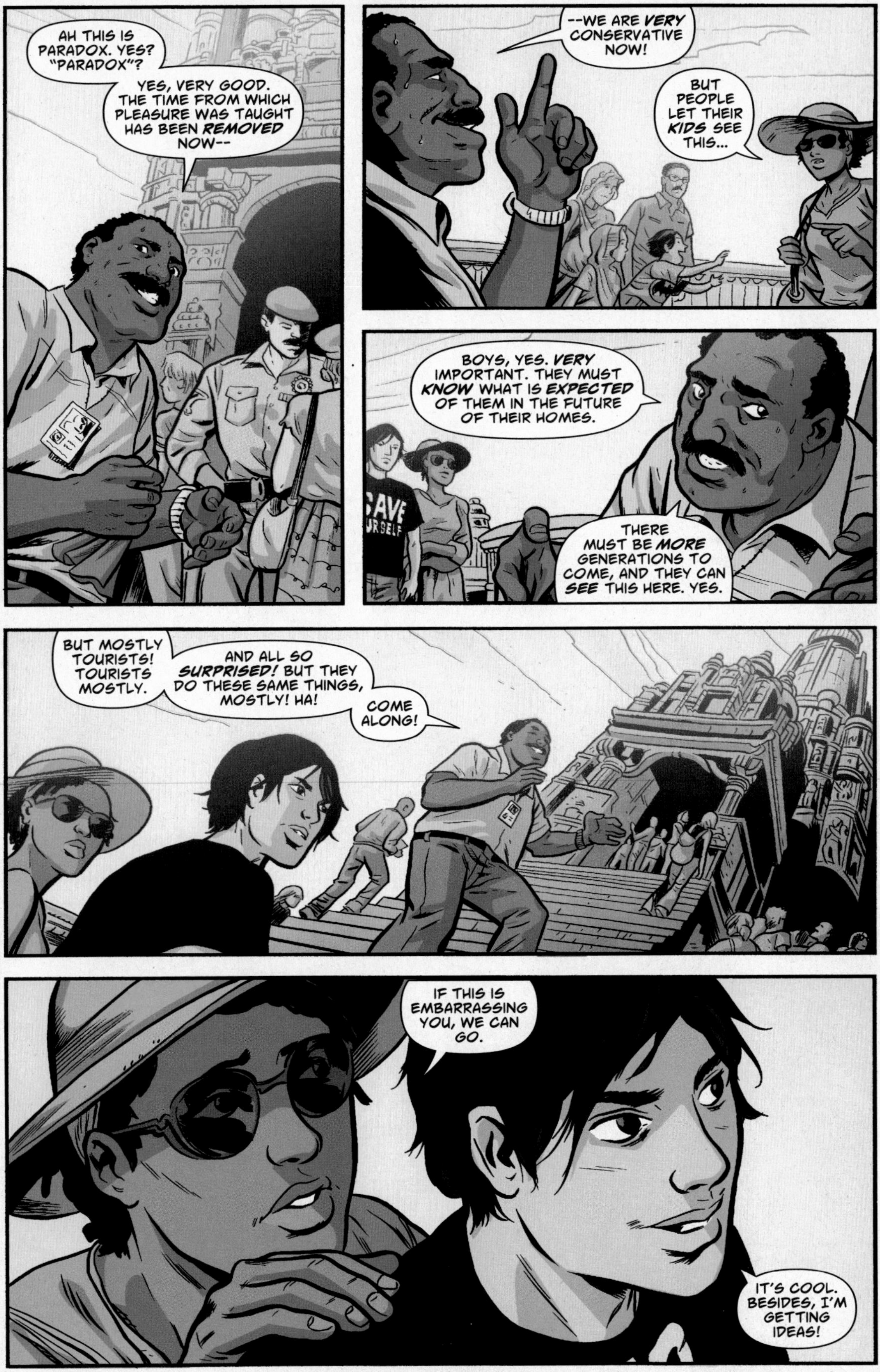
AH THIS IS PARADOX. YES? "PARADOX"?
YES, VERY GOOD. THE TIME FROM WHICH PLEASURE WAS TAUGHT HAS BEEN REMOVED NOW--
--WE ARE VERY CONSERVATIVE NOW!
BUT PEOPLE LET THEIR KIDS SEE THIS...
BOYS, YES. VERY IMPORTANT. THEY MUST KNOW WHAT IS EXPECTED OF THEM IN THE FUTURE OF THEIR HOMES.
SAVE YOURSELF
THERE MUST BE MORE GENERATIONS TO COME, AND THEY CAN SEE THIS HERE. YES.
BUT MOSTLY TOURISTS! TOURISTS MOSTLY.
AND ALL SO SURPRISED! BUT THEY DO THESE SAME THINGS, MOSTLY! HA!
COME ALONG!
IF THIS IS EMBARRASSING YOU, WE CAN GO.
IT'S COOL. BESIDES, I'M GETTING IDEAS!

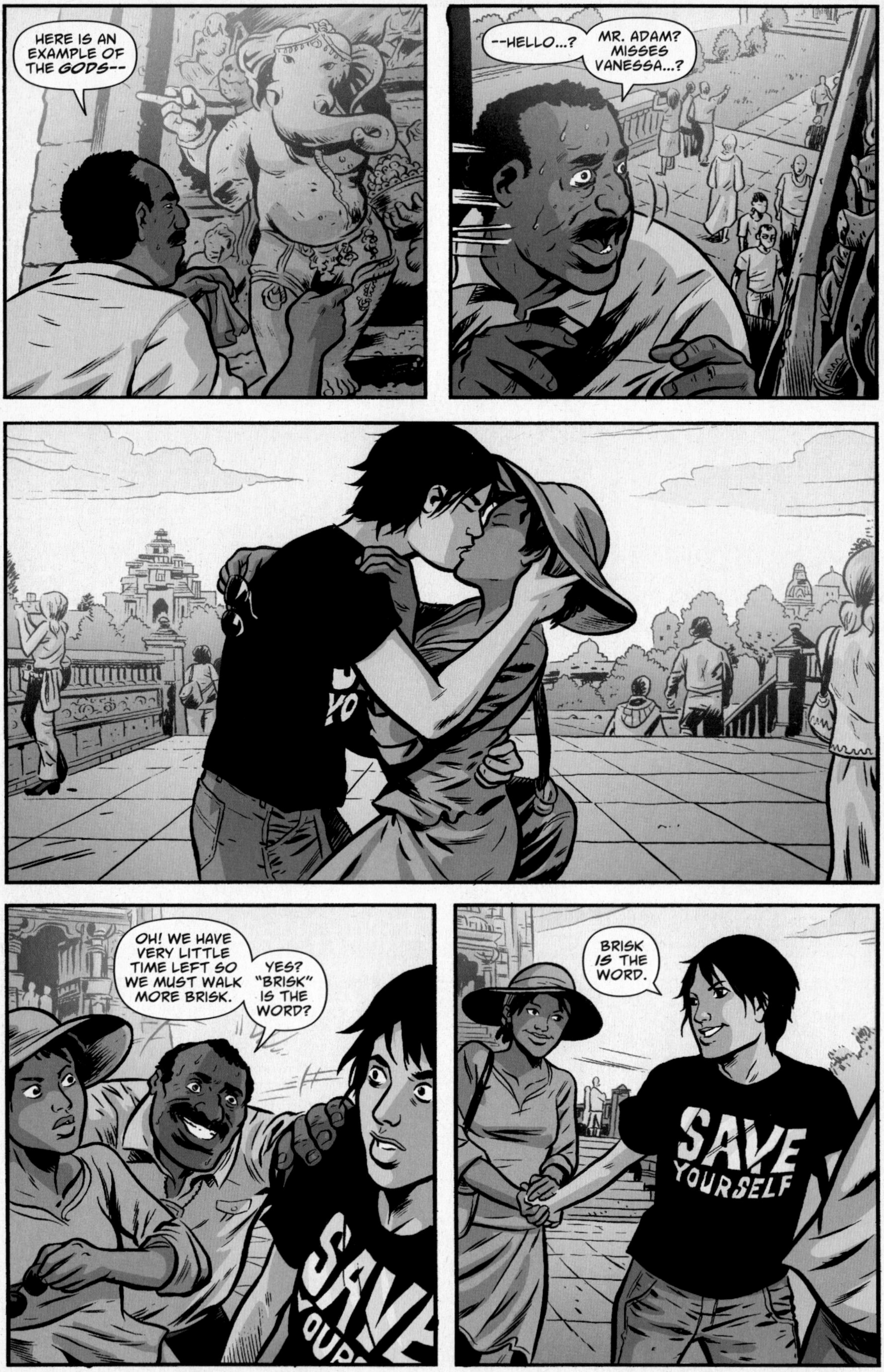
HERE IS AN EXAMPLE OF THE *GODS*--
--HELLO...?
MR. ADAM? MISSES VANESSA...?
OH! WE HAVE VERY LITTLE TIME LEFT SO WE MUST WALK MORE BRISK.
YES? "BRISK" IS THE WORD?
SAVE YOUR
BRISK *IS* THE WORD.
SAVE YOURSELF

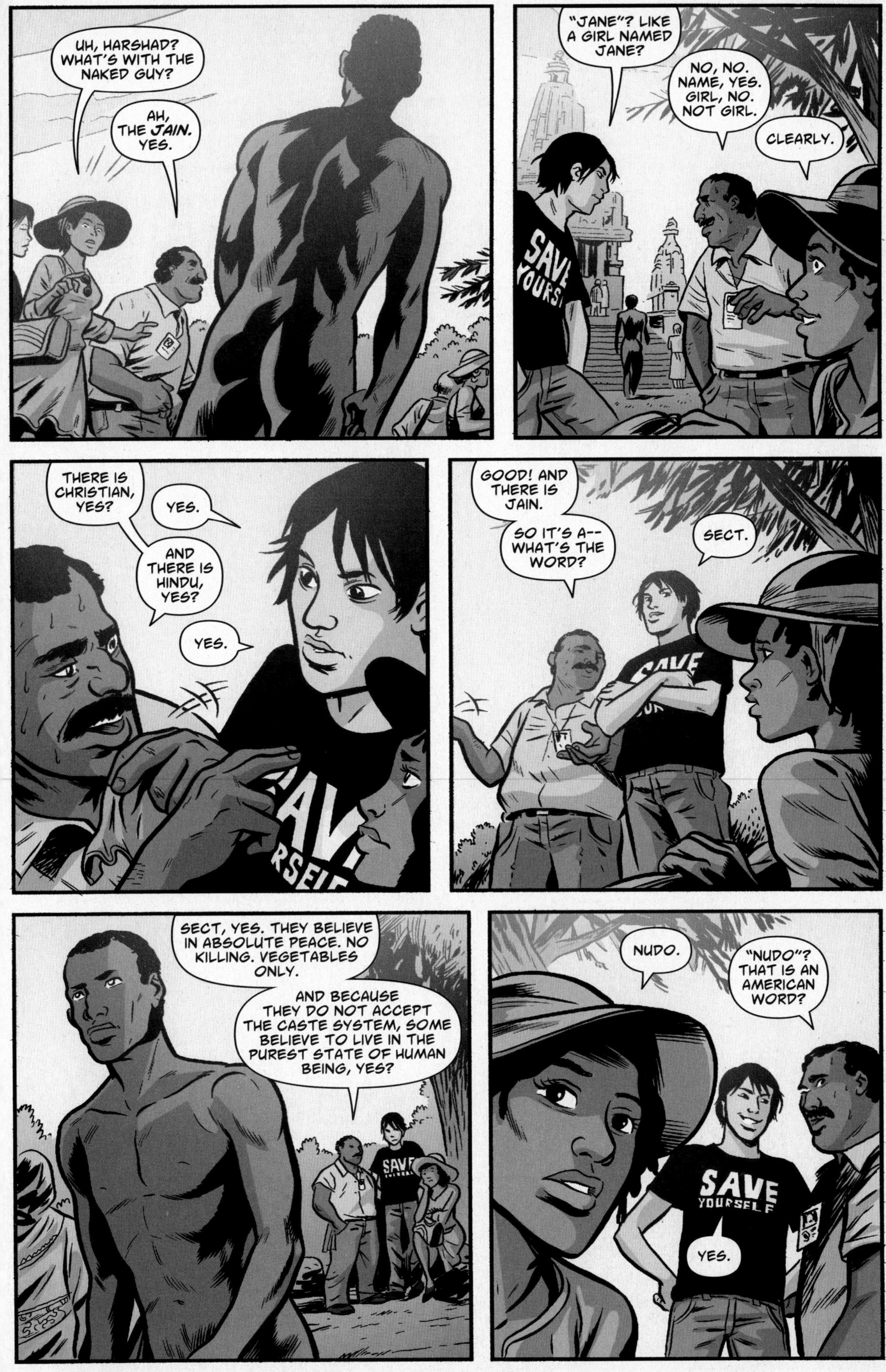
UH, HARSHAD? WHAT'S WITH THE NAKED GUY?
AH, THE JAIN. YES.
"JANE"? LIKE A GIRL NAMED JANE?
NO, NO. NAME, YES. GIRL, NO. NOT GIRL.
CLEARLY.
SAVE YOURS
THERE IS CHRISTIAN, YES?
YES.
AND THERE IS HINDU, YES?
YES.
GOOD! AND THERE IS JAIN.
SO IT'S A-- WHAT'S THE WORD?
SECT.
SECT, YES. THEY BELIEVE IN ABSOLUTE PEACE. NO KILLING. VEGETABLES ONLY.
AND BECAUSE THEY DO NOT ACCEPT THE CASTE SYSTEM, SOME BELIEVE TO LIVE IN THE PUREST STATE OF HUMAN BEING, YES?
NUDO.
"NUDO"? THAT IS AN AMERICAN WORD?
SAVE YOURSELF
YES.

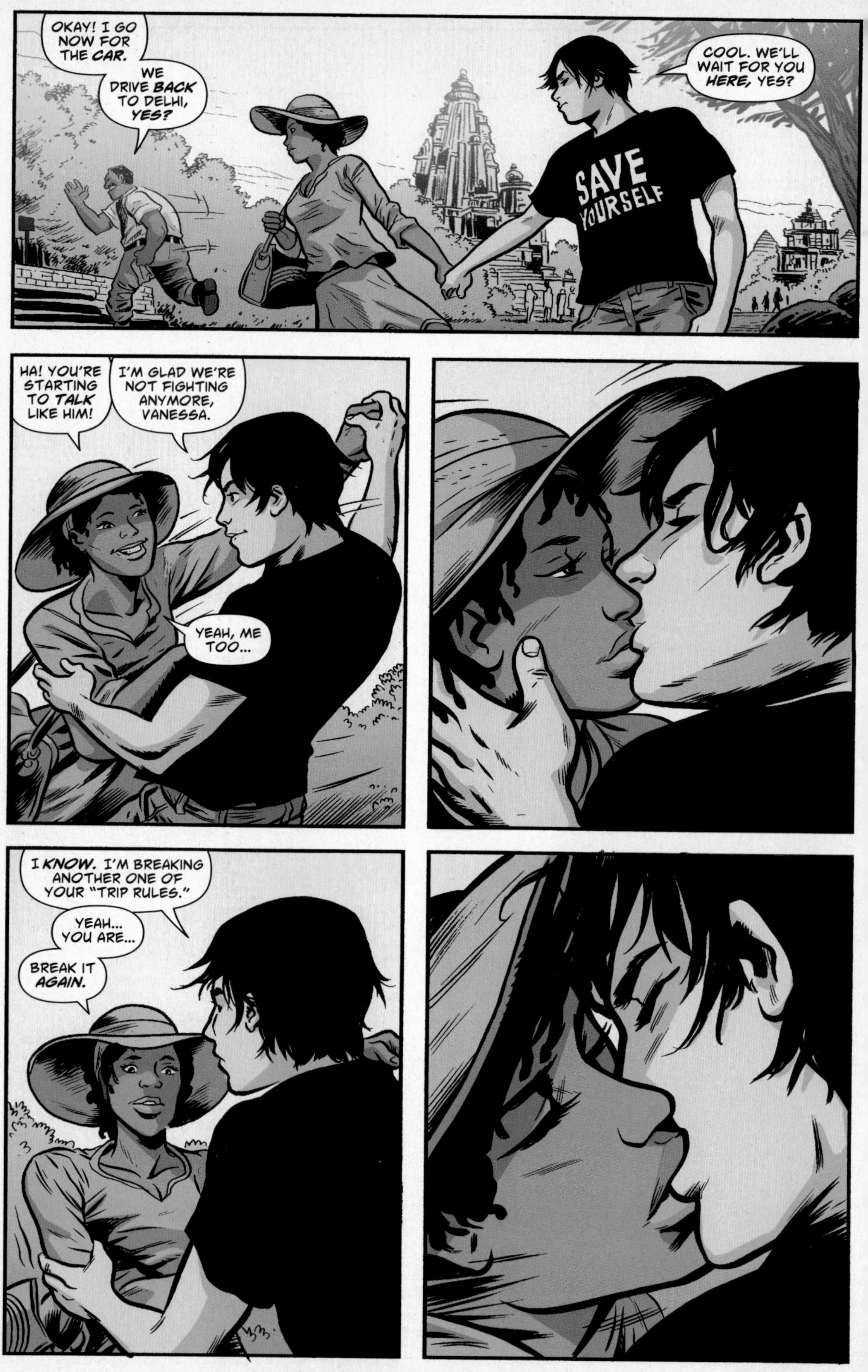
OKAY! I GO NOW FOR THE CAR.
WE DRIVE BACK TO DELHI, YES?
COOL. WE'LL WAIT FOR YOU HERE, YES?
SAVE YOURSELF
HA! YOU'RE STARTING TO TALK LIKE HIM!
I'M GLAD WE'RE NOT FIGHTING ANYMORE, VANESSA.
YEAH, ME TOO...
I KNOW. I'M BREAKING ANOTHER ONE OF YOUR "TRIP RULES."
YEAH... YOU ARE...
BREAK IT AGAIN.

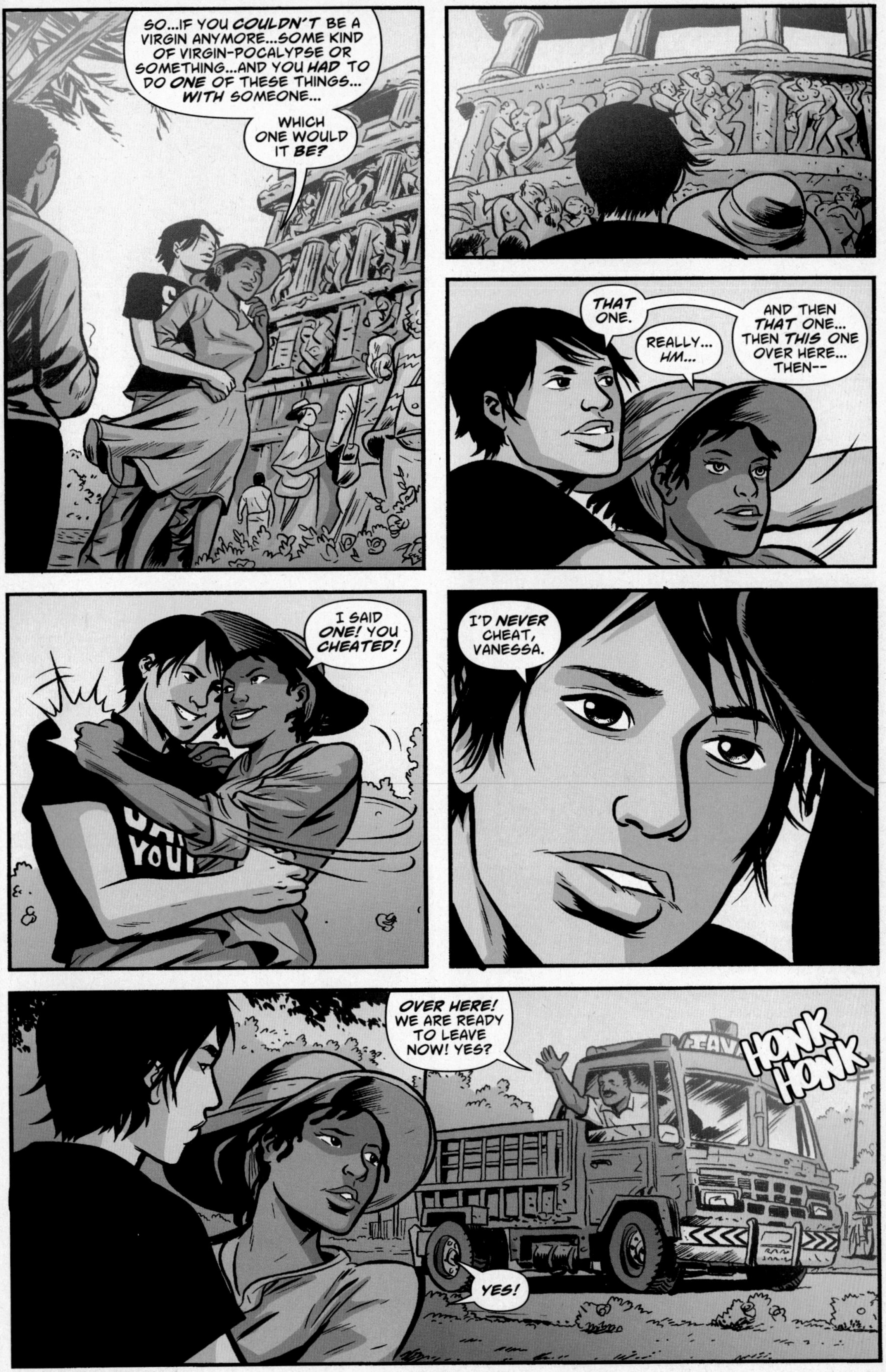
SO...IF YOU COULDN'T BE A VIRGIN ANYMORE...SOME KIND OF VIRGIN-POCALYPSE OR SOMETHING...AND YOU HAD TO DO ONE OF THESE THINGS... WITH SOMEONE...
WHICH ONE WOULD IT BE?
THAT ONE.
REALLY... HM...
AND THEN THAT ONE... THEN THIS ONE OVER HERE... THEN--
I SAID ONE! YOU CHEATED!
I'D NEVER CHEAT, VANESSA.
OVER HERE! WE ARE READY TO LEAVE NOW! YES?
HONK HONK
YES!

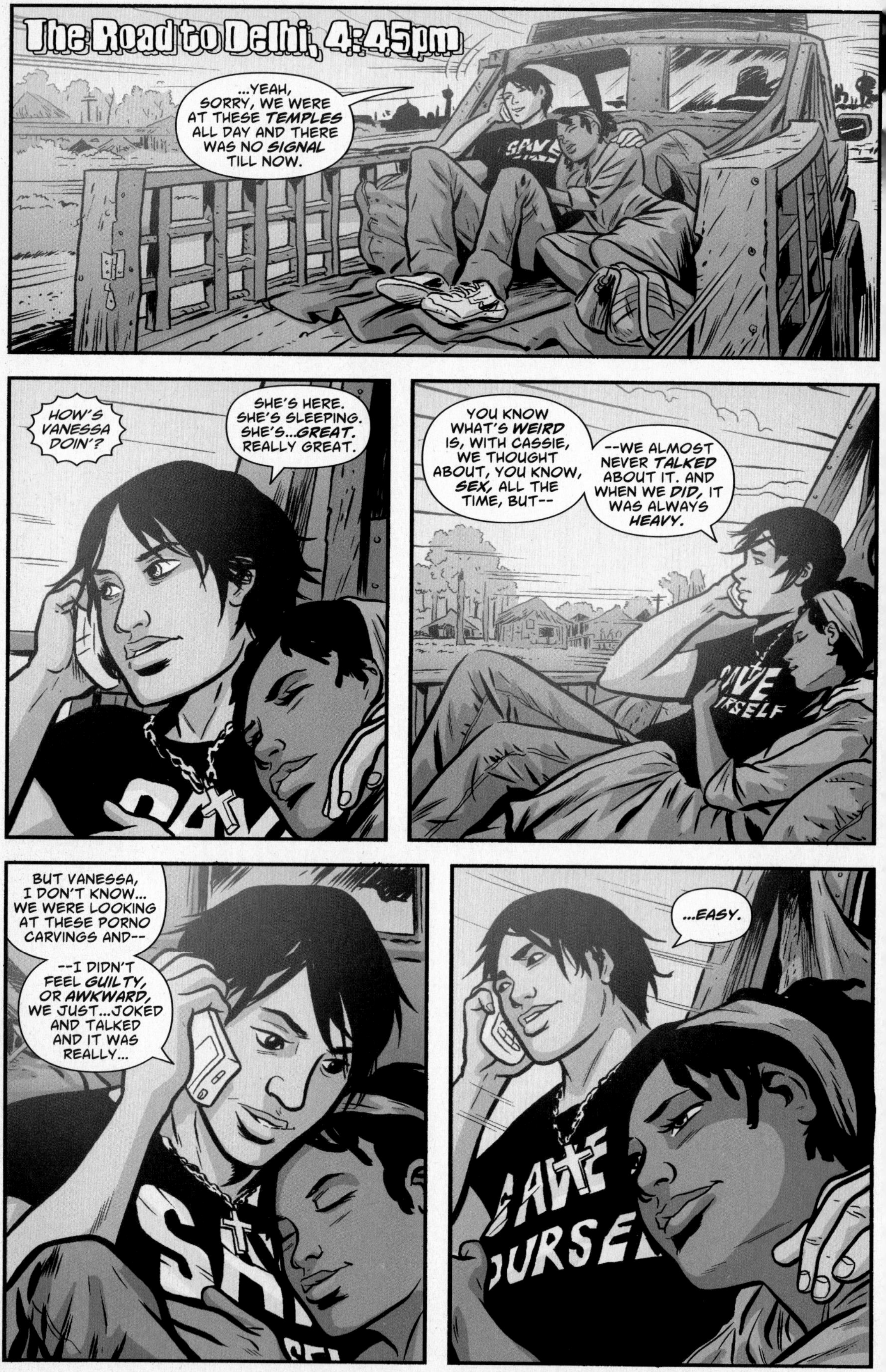
The Road to Delhi, 4:45pm
...YEAH, SORRY, WE WERE AT THESE TEMPLES ALL DAY AND THERE WAS NO SIGNAL TILL NOW.
HOW'S VANESSA DOIN'?
SHE'S HERE. SHE'S SLEEPING. SHE'S...GREAT. REALLY GREAT.
YOU KNOW WHAT'S WEIRD IS, WITH CASSIE, WE THOUGHT ABOUT, YOU KNOW, SEX, ALL THE TIME, BUT--
--WE ALMOST NEVER TALKED ABOUT IT. AND WHEN WE DID, IT WAS ALWAYS HEAVY.
BUT VANESSA, I DON'T KNOW... WE WERE LOOKING AT THESE PORNO CARVINGS AND--
--I DIDN'T FEEL GUILTY, OR AWKWARD, WE JUST...JOKED AND TALKED AND IT WAS REALLY...
...EASY.

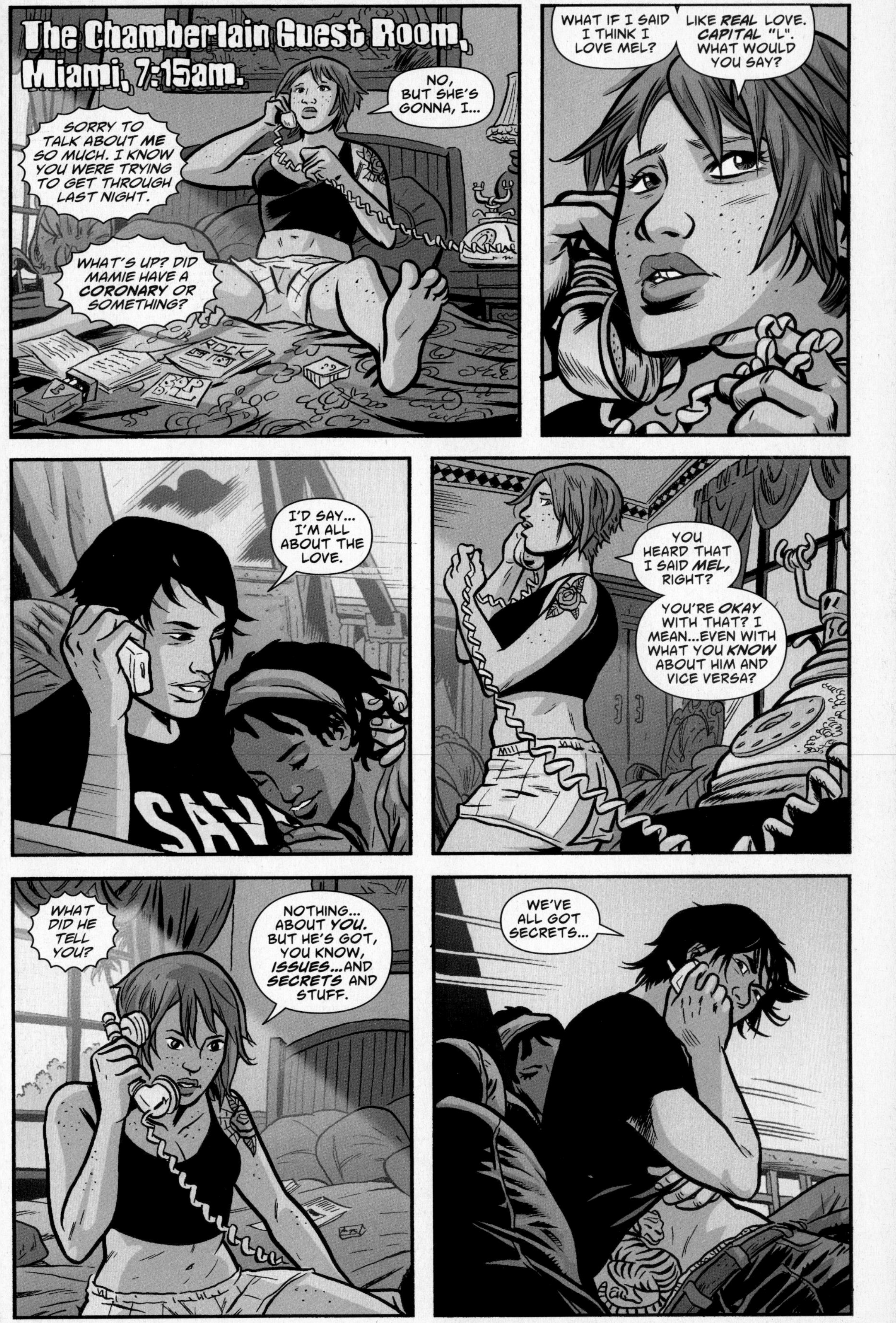
The Chamberlain Guest Room, Miami, 7:15am.
SORRY TO TALK ABOUT ME SO MUCH. I KNOW YOU WERE TRYING TO GET THROUGH LAST NIGHT.
WHAT'S UP? DID MAMIE HAVE A CORONARY OR SOMETHING?
NO, BUT SHE'S GONNA, I...
WHAT IF I SAID I THINK I LOVE MEL?
LIKE REAL LOVE. CAPITAL "L". WHAT WOULD YOU SAY?
I'D SAY... I'M ALL ABOUT THE LOVE.
YOU HEARD THAT I SAID MEL, RIGHT?
YOU'RE OKAY WITH THAT? I MEAN...EVEN WITH WHAT YOU KNOW ABOUT HIM AND VICE VERSA?
WHAT DID HE TELL YOU?
NOTHING... ABOUT YOU. BUT HE'S GOT, YOU KNOW, ISSUES...AND SECRETS AND STUFF.
WE'VE ALL GOT SECRETS...

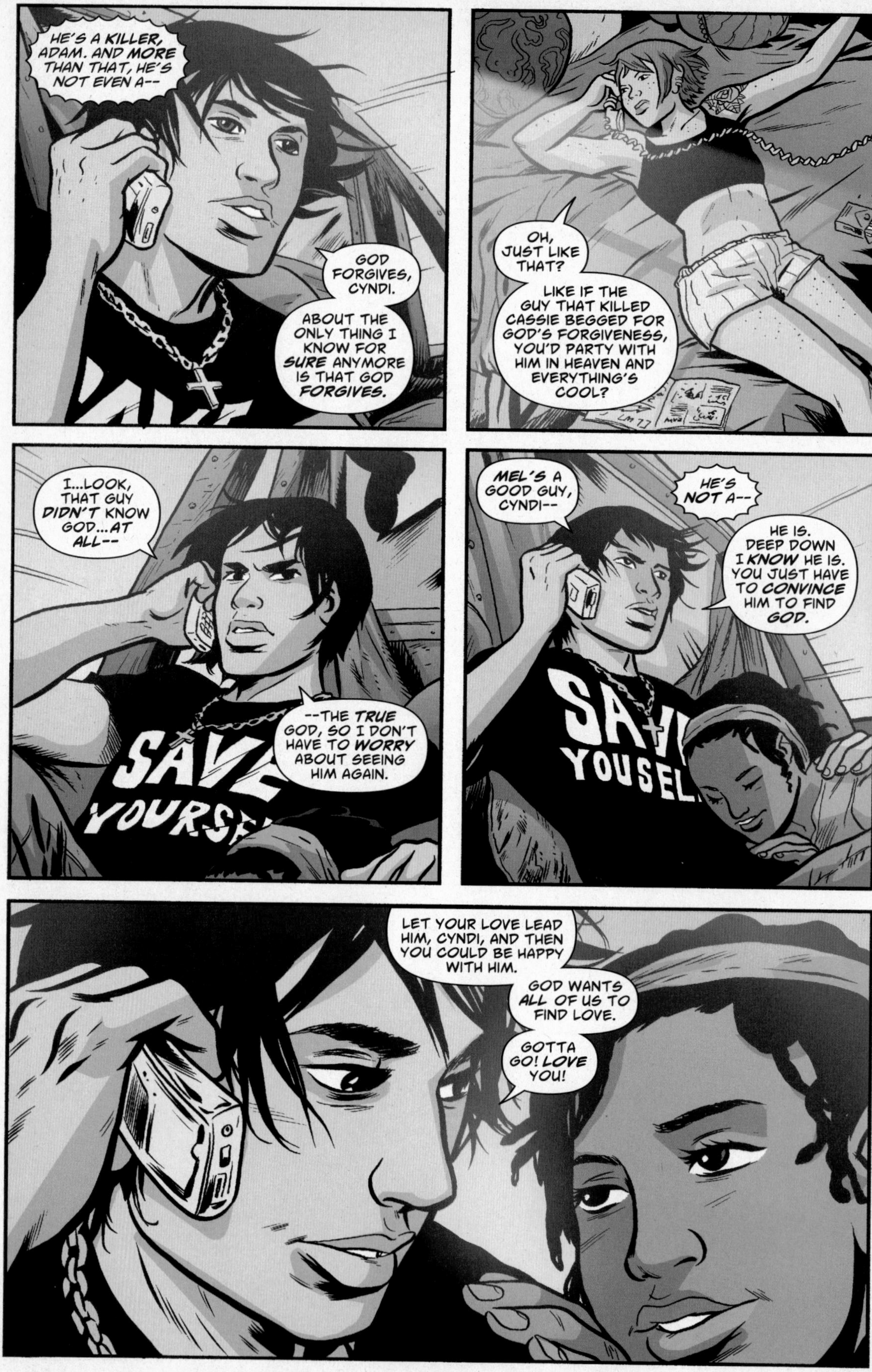
HE'S A KILLER, ADAM. AND MORE THAN THAT, HE'S NOT EVEN A--
GOD FORGIVES, CYNDI.
ABOUT THE ONLY THING I KNOW FOR SURE ANYMORE IS THAT GOD FORGIVES.
OH, JUST LIKE THAT?
LIKE IF THE GUY THAT KILLED CASSIE BEGGED FOR GOD'S FORGIVENESS, YOU'D PARTY WITH HIM IN HEAVEN AND EVERYTHING'S COOL?
I...LOOK, THAT GUY DIDN'T KNOW GOD...AT ALL--
--THE TRUE GOD, SO I DON'T HAVE TO WORRY ABOUT SEEING HIM AGAIN.
SAVE YOURSE
MEL'S A GOOD GUY, CYNDI--
HE'S NOT A--
HE IS. DEEP DOWN I KNOW HE IS. YOU JUST HAVE TO CONVINCE HIM TO FIND GOD.
SAV YOUSEL
LET YOUR LOVE LEAD HIM, CYNDI, AND THEN YOU COULD BE HAPPY WITH HIM.
GOD WANTS ALL OF US TO FIND LOVE.
GOTTA GO! LOVE YOU!

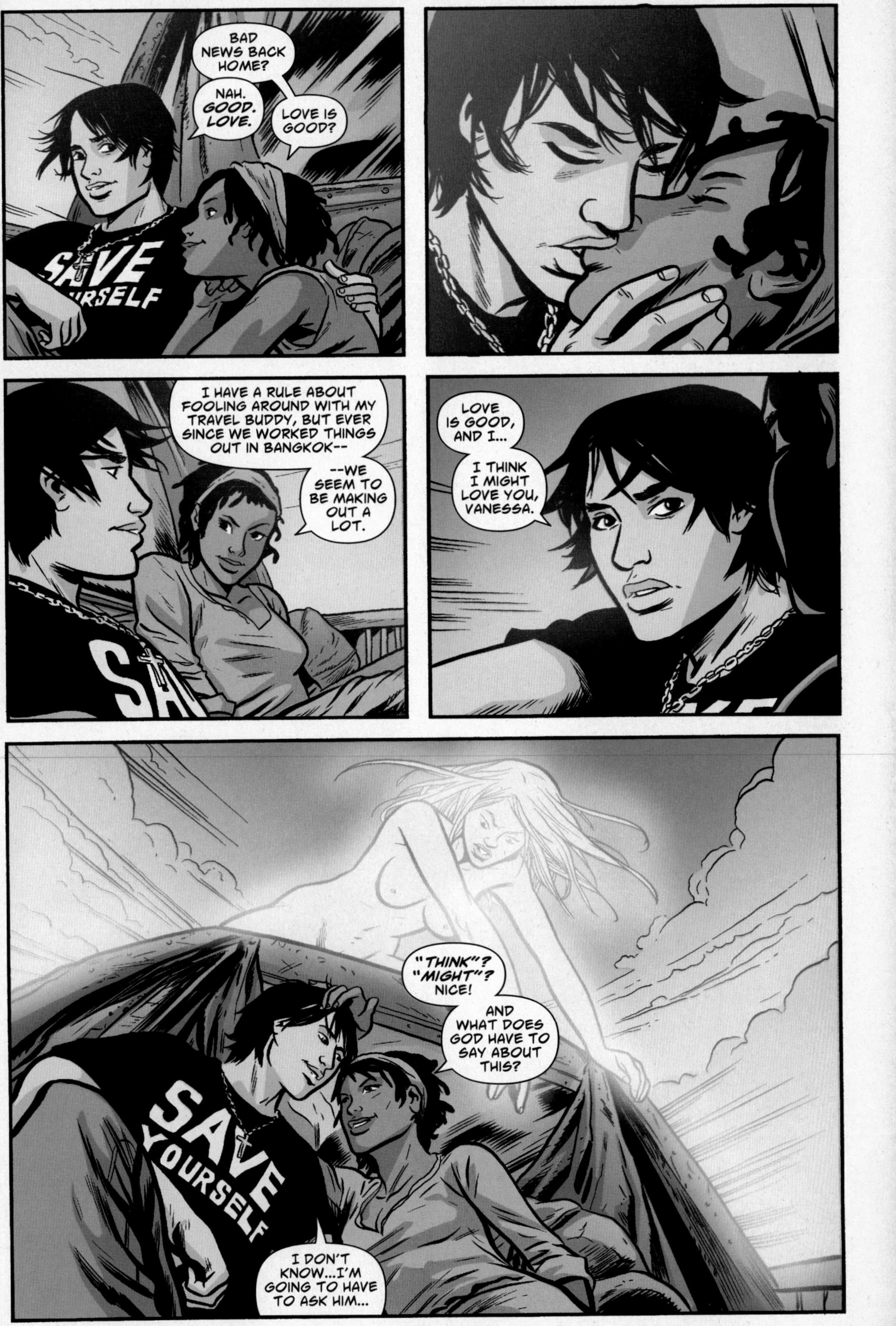
BAD NEWS BACK HOME?
NAH. GOOD. LOVE.
LOVE IS GOOD?
SAVE YOURSELF
I HAVE A RULE ABOUT FOOLING AROUND WITH MY TRAVEL BUDDY, BUT EVER SINCE WE WORKED THINGS OUT IN BANGKOK--
--WE SEEM TO BE MAKING OUT A LOT.
LOVE IS GOOD, AND I...
I THINK I MIGHT LOVE YOU, VANESSA.
"THINK"? "MIGHT"? NICE!
AND WHAT DOES GOD HAVE TO SAY ABOUT THIS?
SAVE YOURSELF
I DON'T KNOW...I'M GOING TO HAVE TO ASK HIM...

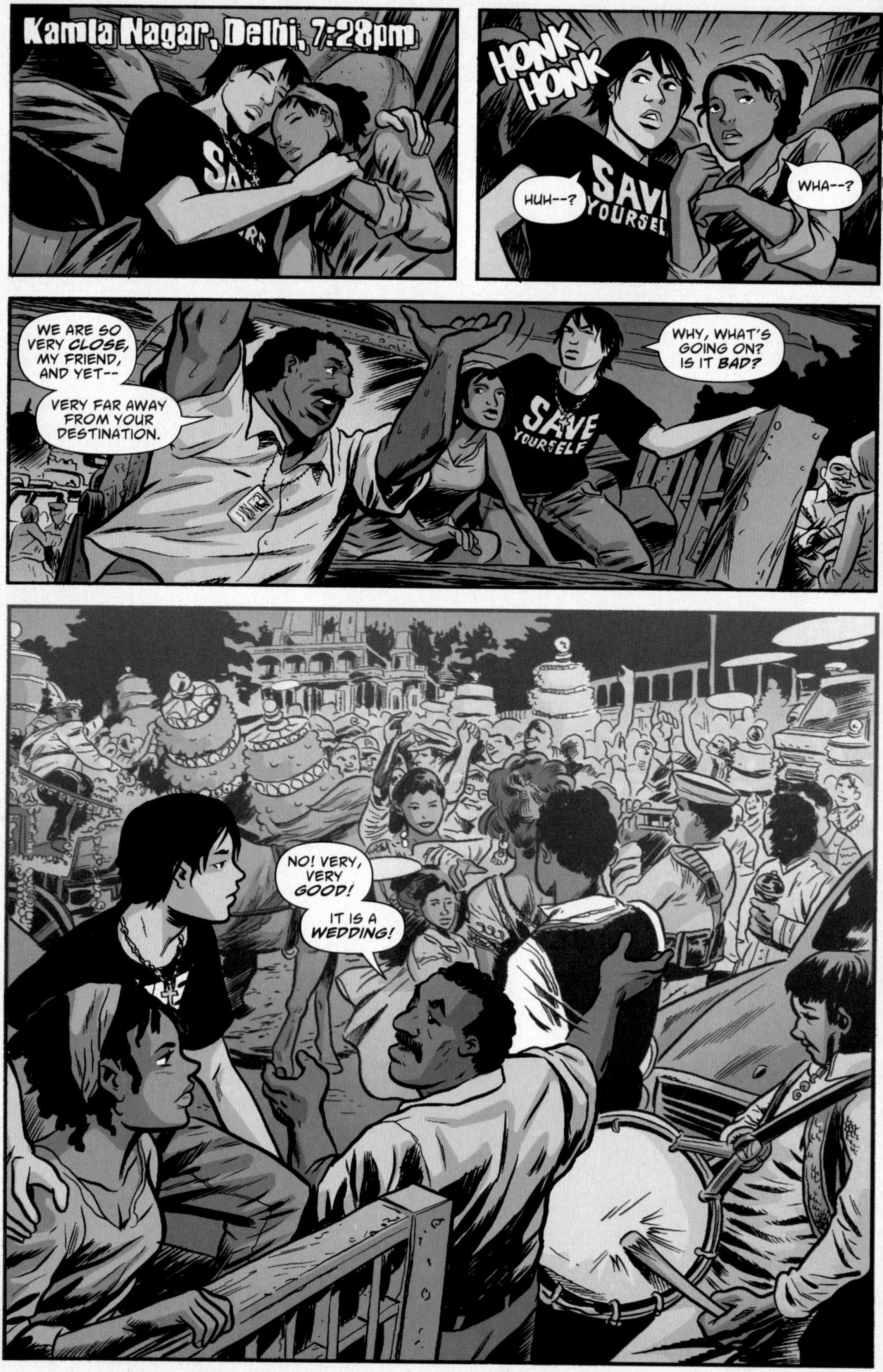
Kamla Nagar, Delhi, 7:28pm
HONK HONK
HUH--?
WHA--?
WE ARE SO VERY CLOSE, MY FRIEND, AND YET--
VERY FAR AWAY FROM YOUR DESTINATION.
WHY, WHAT'S GOING ON? IS IT BAD?
NO! VERY, VERY GOOD!
IT IS A WEDDING!

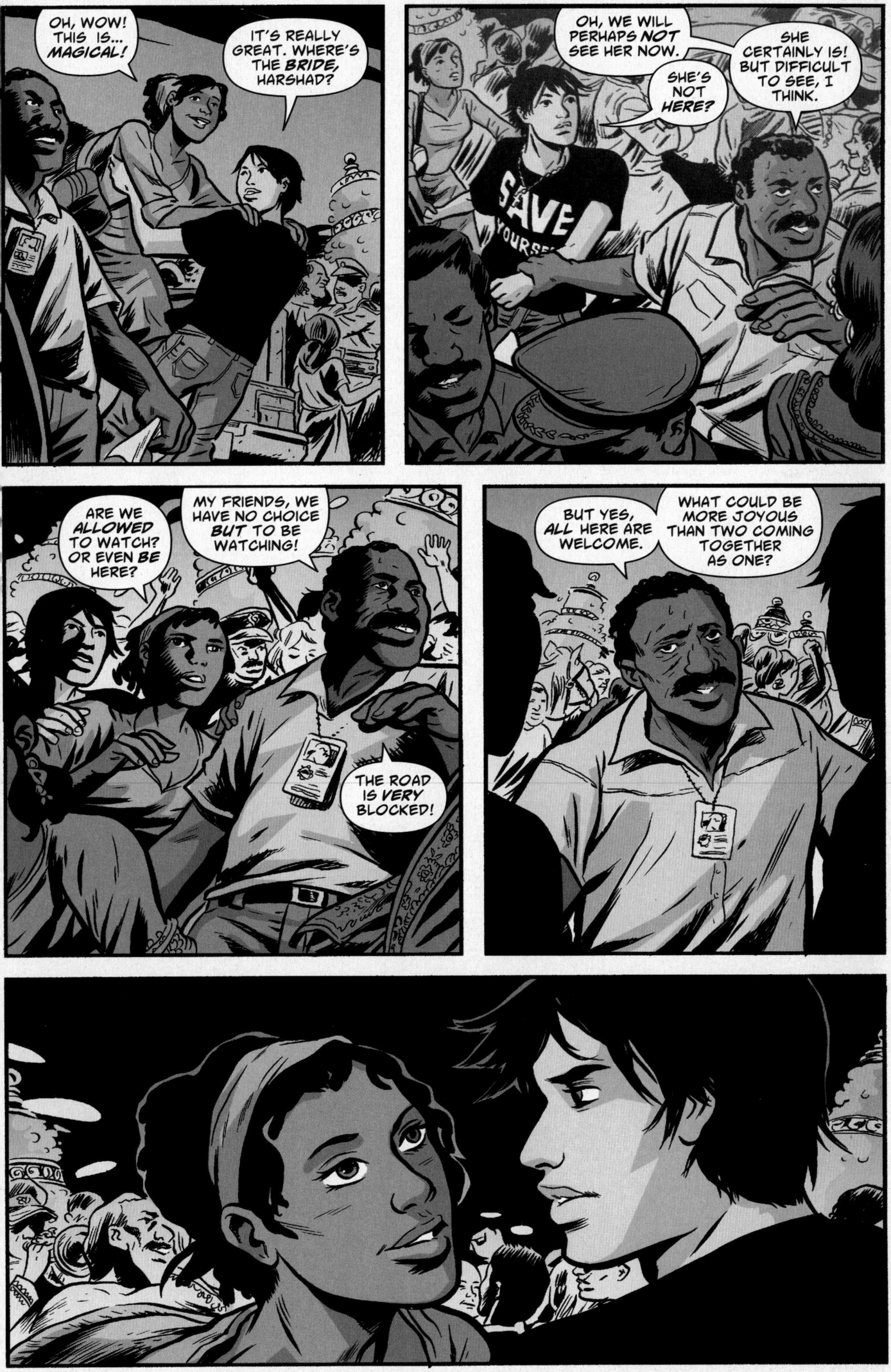
OH, WOW! THIS IS... MAGICAL!
IT'S REALLY GREAT. WHERE'S THE BRIDE, HARSHAD?
OH, WE WILL PERHAPS NOT SEE HER NOW.
SHE'S NOT HERE?
SHE CERTAINLY IS! BUT DIFFICULT TO SEE, I THINK.
SAVE YOURSE
ARE WE ALLOWED TO WATCH? OR EVEN BE HERE?
MY FRIENDS, WE HAVE NO CHOICE BUT TO BE WATCHING!
THE ROAD IS VERY BLOCKED!
BUT YES, ALL HERE ARE WELCOME.
WHAT COULD BE MORE JOYOUS THAN TWO COMING TOGETHER AS ONE?

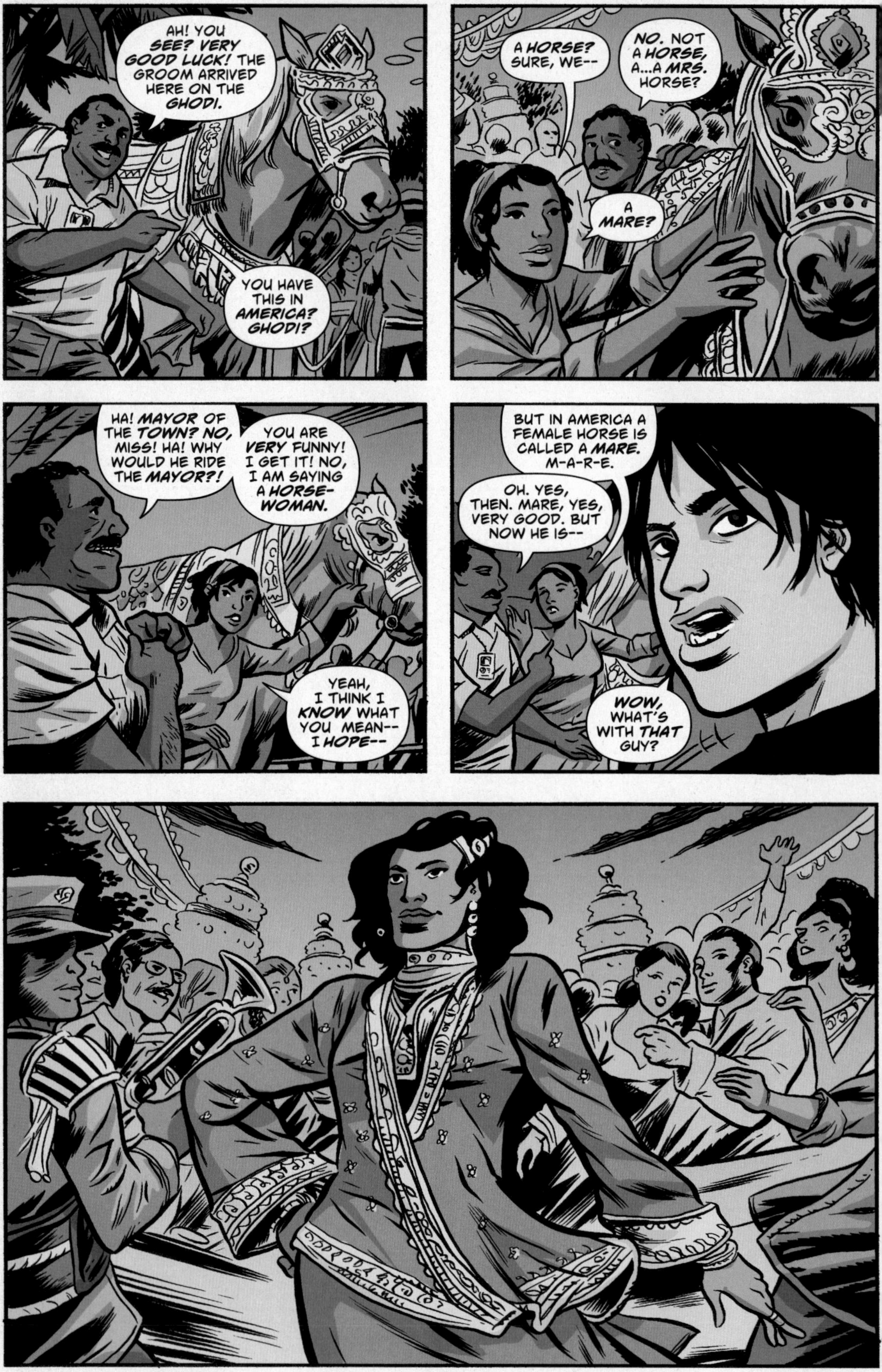
AH! YOU SEE? VERY GOOD LUCK! THE GROOM ARRIVED HERE ON THE GHODI.
YOU HAVE THIS IN AMERICA? GHODI?
A HORSE? SURE, WE--
NO. NOT A HORSE, A...A MRS. HORSE?
A MARE?
HA! MAYOR OF THE TOWN? NO, MISS! HA! WHY WOULD HE RIDE THE MAYOR?!
YOU ARE VERY FUNNY! I GET IT! NO, I AM SAYING A HORSE-WOMAN.
YEAH, I THINK I KNOW WHAT YOU MEAN-- I HOPE--
BUT IN AMERICA A FEMALE HORSE IS CALLED A MARE. M-A-R-E.
OH. YES, THEN. MARE, YES, VERY GOOD. BUT NOW HE IS--
WOW, WHAT'S WITH THAT GUY?

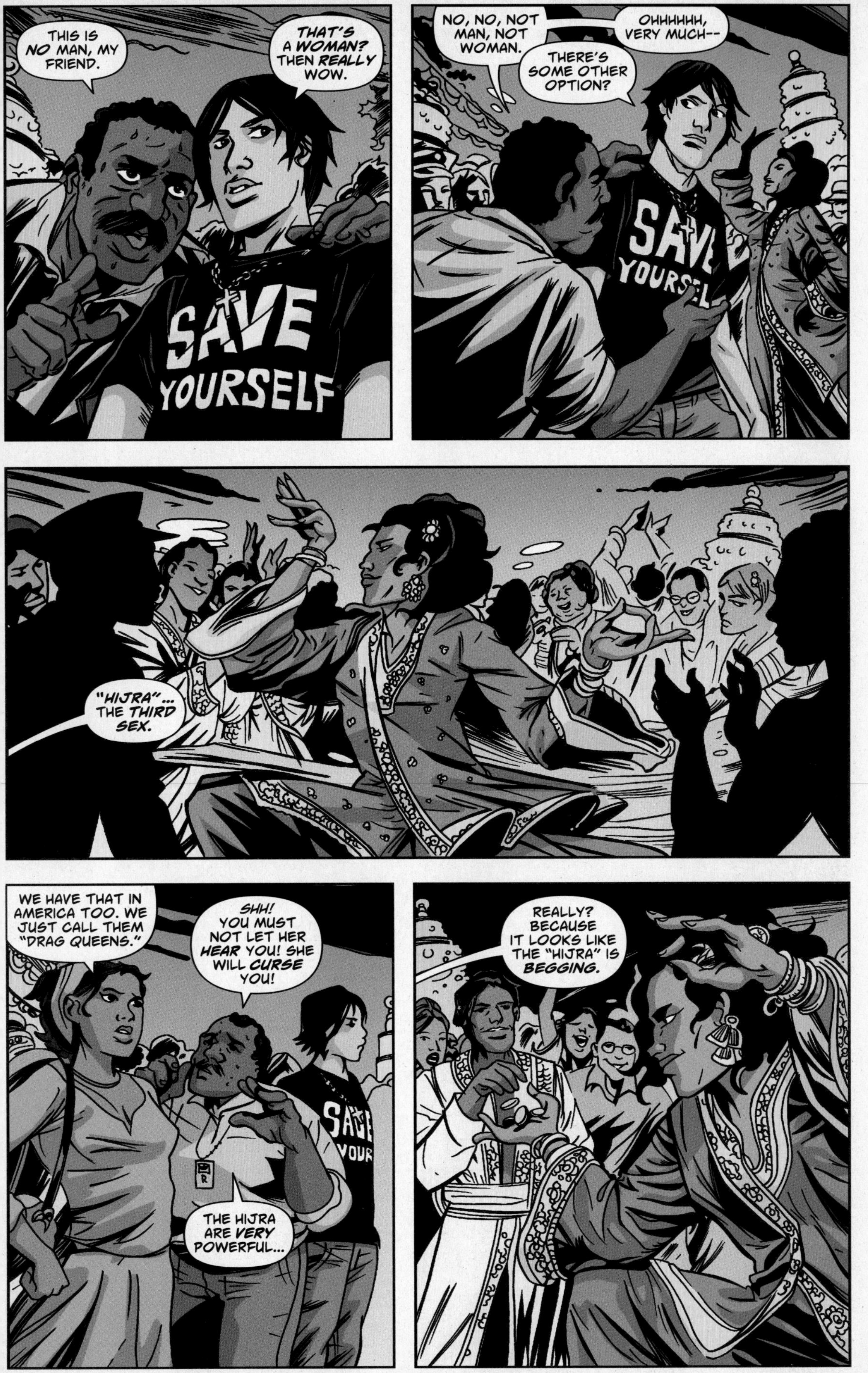
THIS IS NO MAN, MY FRIEND.
THAT'S A WOMAN? THEN REALLY WOW.
SAVE YOURSELF
NO, NO, NOT MAN, NOT WOMAN.
OHHHHHH, VERY MUCH--
THERE'S SOME OTHER OPTION?
SAVE YOURSELF
"HIJRA"... THE THIRD SEX.
WE HAVE THAT IN AMERICA TOO. WE JUST CALL THEM "DRAG QUEENS."
SHH! YOU MUST NOT LET HER HEAR YOU! SHE WILL CURSE YOU!
THE HIJRA ARE VERY POWERFUL...
REALLY? BECAUSE IT LOOKS LIKE THE "HIJRA" IS BEGGING.

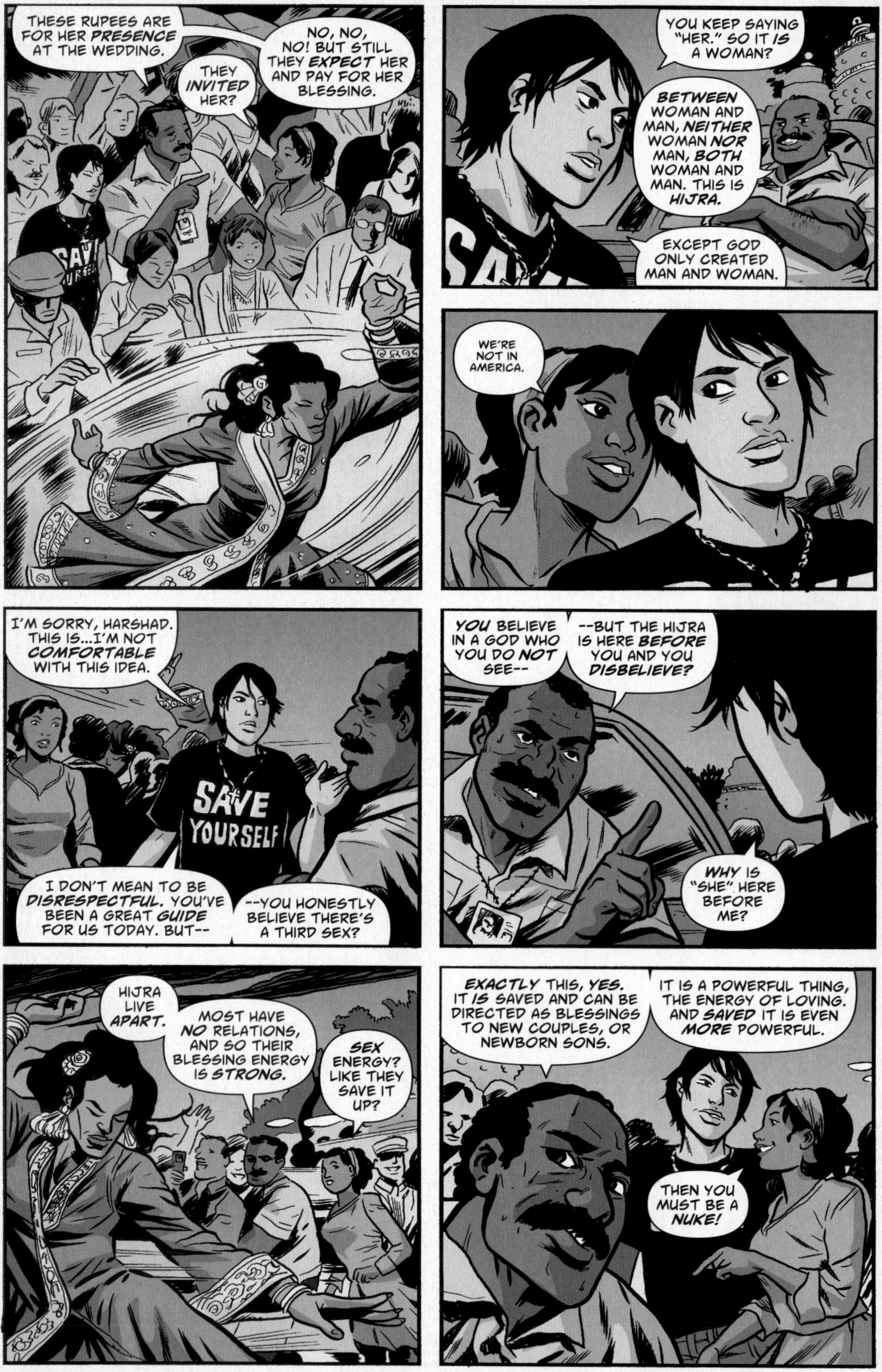
THESE RUPEES ARE FOR HER PRESENCE AT THE WEDDING.
THEY INVITED HER?
NO, NO, NO! BUT STILL THEY EXPECT HER AND PAY FOR HER BLESSING.
YOU KEEP SAYING "HER." SO IT IS A WOMAN?
BETWEEN WOMAN AND MAN, NEITHER WOMAN NOR MAN, BOTH WOMAN AND MAN. THIS IS HIJRA.
EXCEPT GOD ONLY CREATED MAN AND WOMAN.
WE'RE NOT IN AMERICA.
I'M SORRY, HARSHAD. THIS IS...I'M NOT COMFORTABLE WITH THIS IDEA.
SAVE YOURSELF
I DON'T MEAN TO BE DISRESPECTFUL. YOU'VE BEEN A GREAT GUIDE FOR US TODAY. BUT--
--YOU HONESTLY BELIEVE THERE'S A THIRD SEX?
YOU BELIEVE IN A GOD WHO YOU DO NOT SEE--
--BUT THE HIJRA IS HERE BEFORE YOU AND YOU DISBELIEVE?
WHY IS "SHE" HERE BEFORE ME?
HIJRA LIVE APART.
MOST HAVE NO RELATIONS, AND SO THEIR BLESSING ENERGY IS STRONG.
SEX ENERGY? LIKE THEY SAVE IT UP?
EXACTLY THIS, YES. IT IS SAVED AND CAN BE DIRECTED AS BLESSINGS TO NEW COUPLES, OR NEWBORN SONS.
IT IS A POWERFUL THING, THE ENERGY OF LOVING. AND SAVED IT IS EVEN MORE POWERFUL.
THEN YOU MUST BE A NUKE!

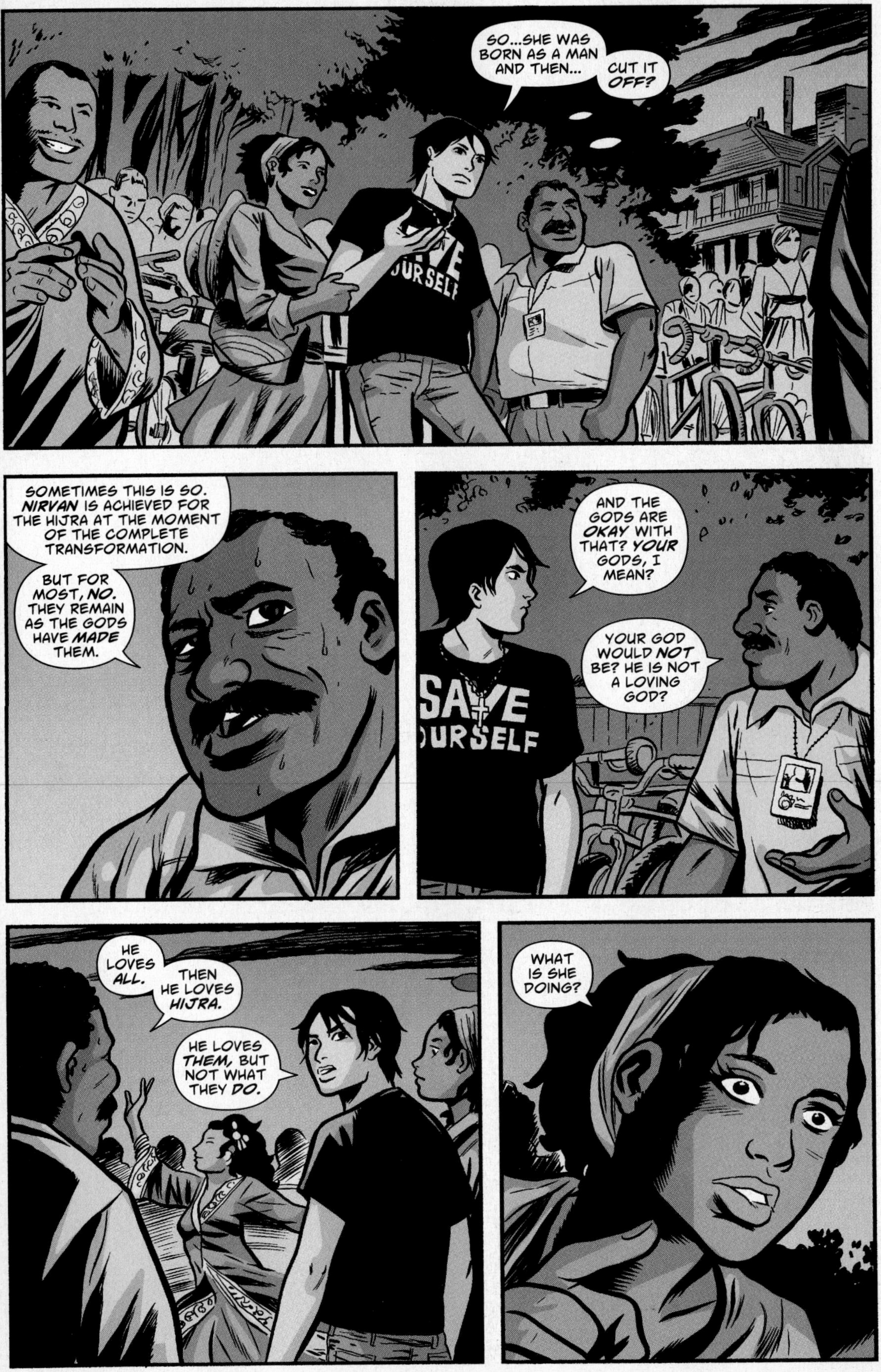
SO...SHE WAS BORN AS A MAN AND THEN...
CUT IT OFF?
SAVE YOURSELF
SOMETIMES THIS IS SO. NIRVAN IS ACHIEVED FOR THE HIJRA AT THE MOMENT OF THE COMPLETE TRANSFORMATION.
BUT FOR MOST, NO. THEY REMAIN AS THE GODS HAVE MADE THEM.
AND THE GODS ARE OKAY WITH THAT? YOUR GODS, I MEAN?
YOUR GOD WOULD NOT BE? HE IS NOT A LOVING GOD?
SAVE YOURSELF
HE LOVES ALL.
THEN HE LOVES HIJRA.
HE LOVES THEM, BUT NOT WHAT THEY DO.
WHAT IS SHE DOING?

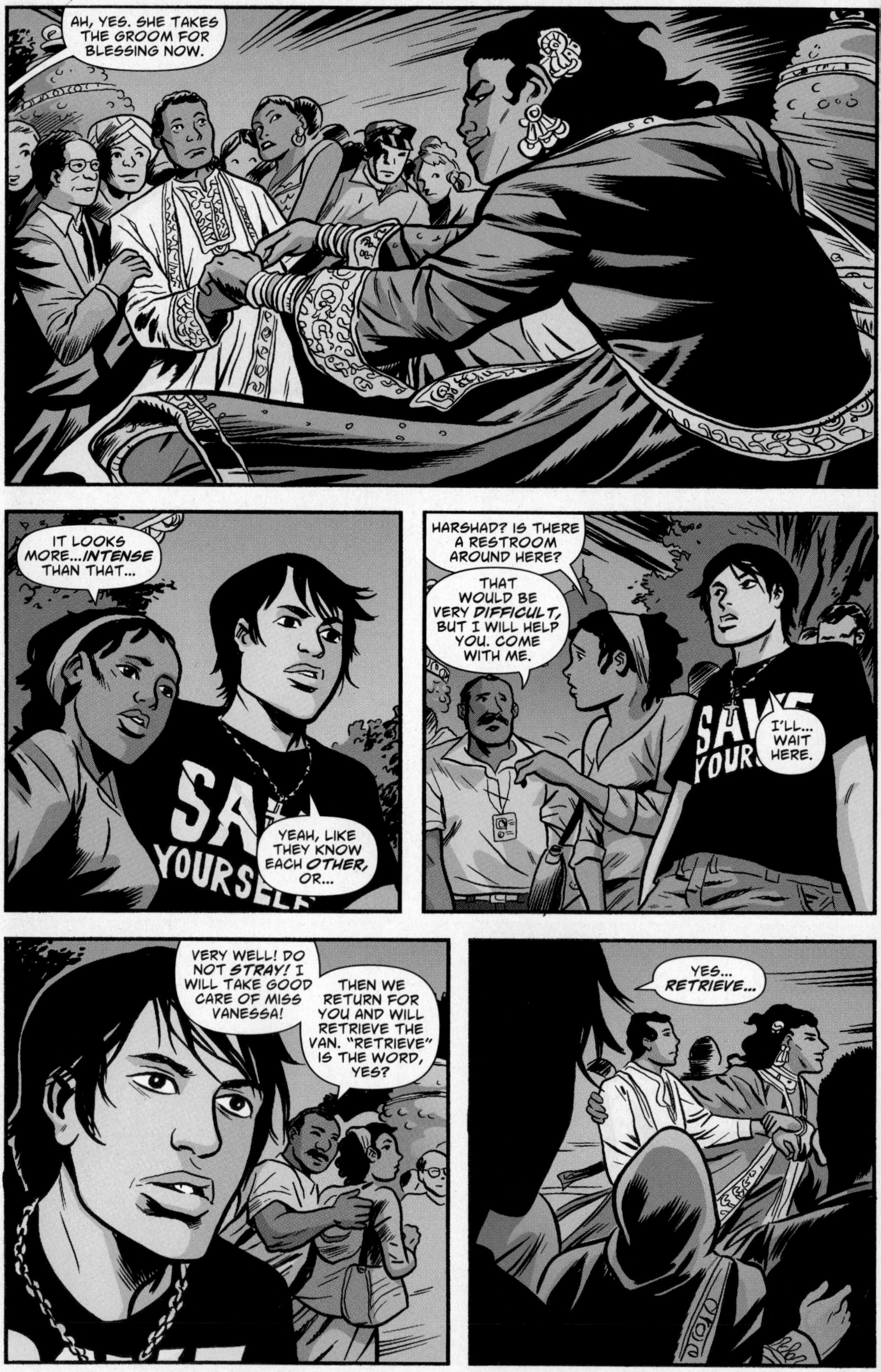
AH, YES. SHE TAKES THE GROOM FOR BLESSING NOW.
IT LOOKS MORE...INTENSE THAN THAT...
SAVE YOURSELF
YEAH, LIKE THEY KNOW EACH OTHER, OR...
HARSHAD? IS THERE A RESTROOM AROUND HERE?
THAT WOULD BE VERY DIFFICULT, BUT I WILL HELP YOU. COME WITH ME.
I'LL... WAIT HERE.
VERY WELL! DO NOT STRAY! I WILL TAKE GOOD CARE OF MISS VANESSA!
THEN WE RETURN FOR YOU AND WILL RETRIEVE THE VAN. "RETRIEVE" IS THE WORD, YES?
YES... RETRIEVE...

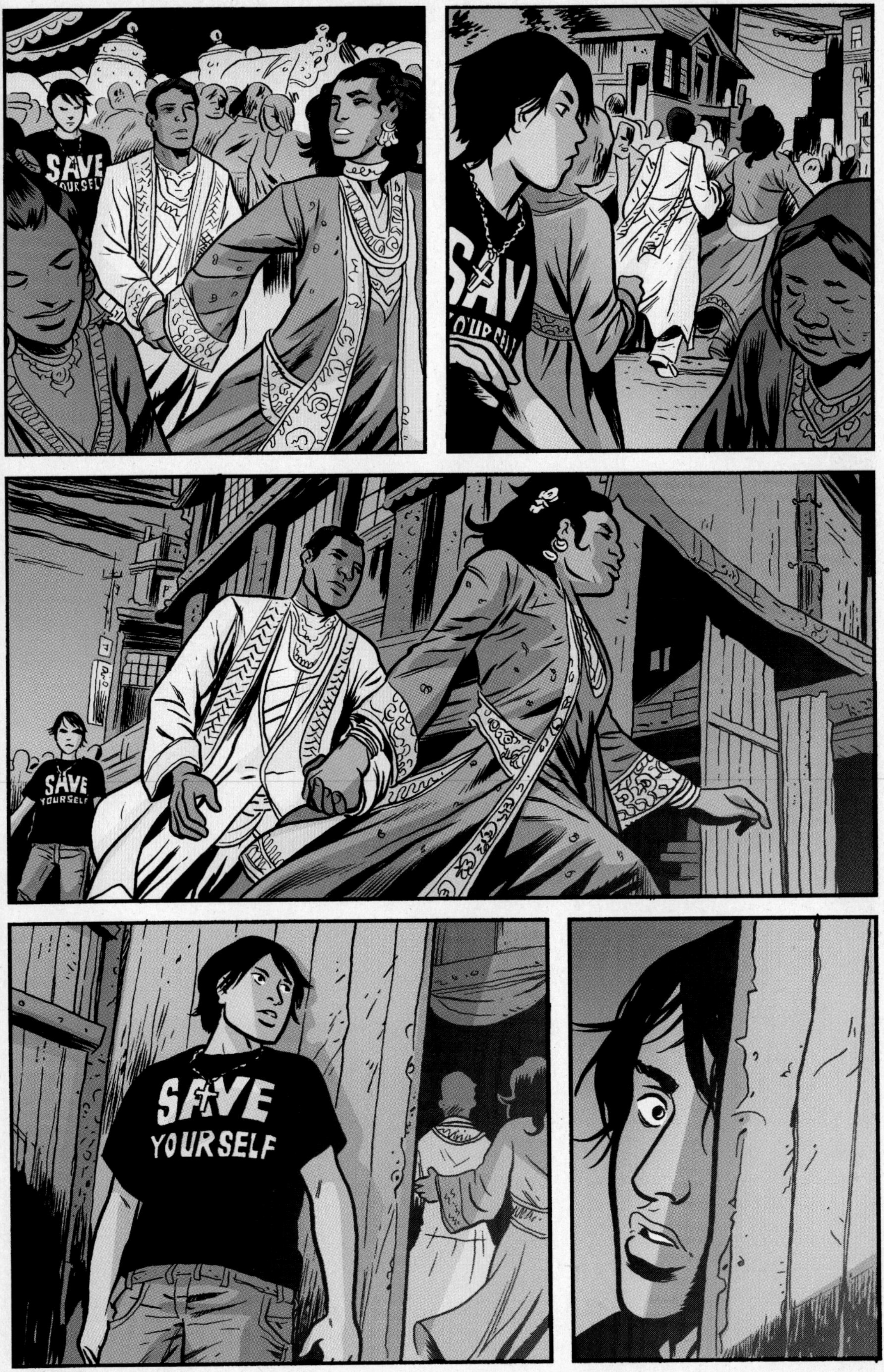
SAVE YOURSELF
SAVE YOURSELF
SAVE YOURSELF

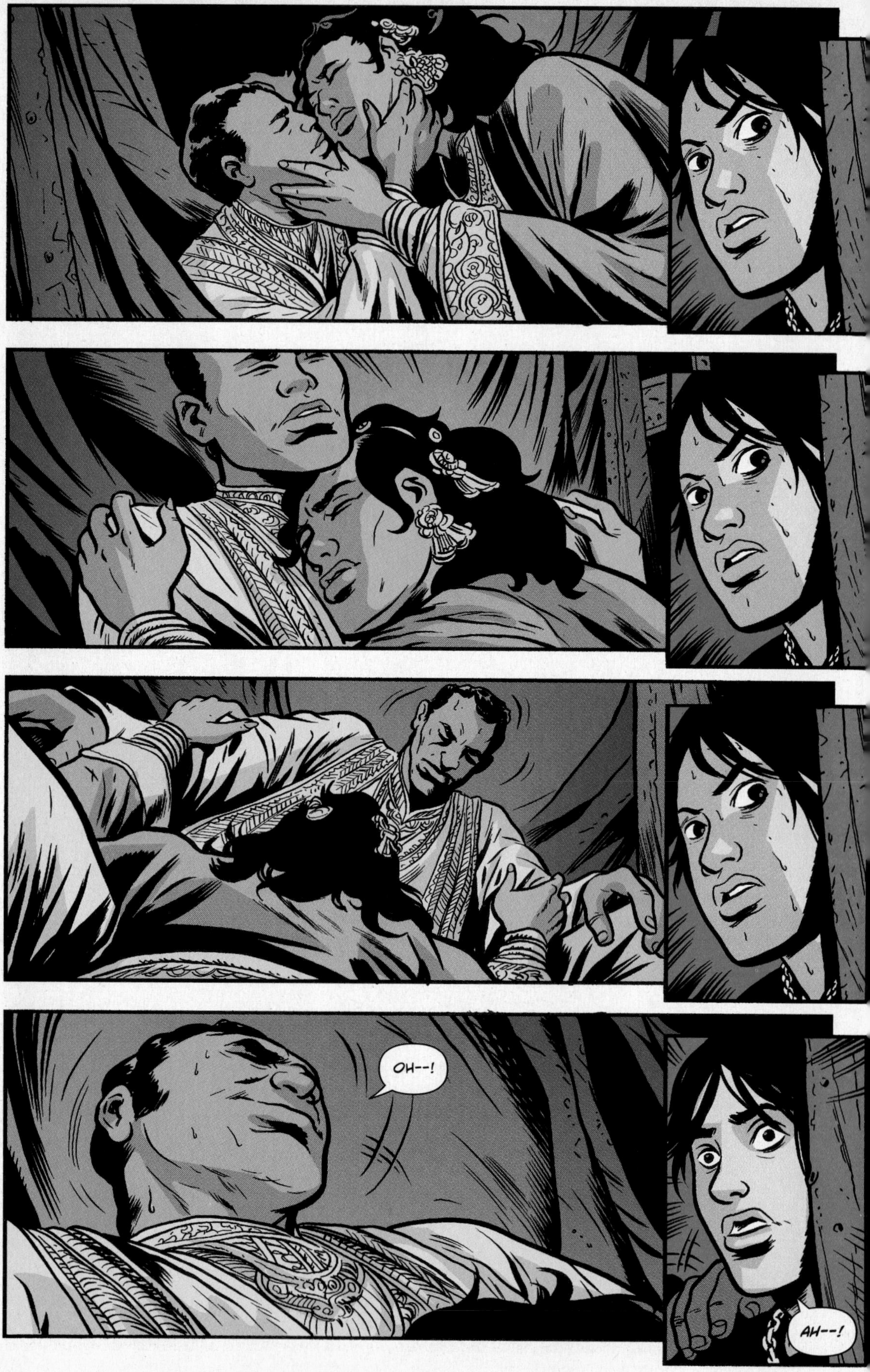
OH--!
AH--!

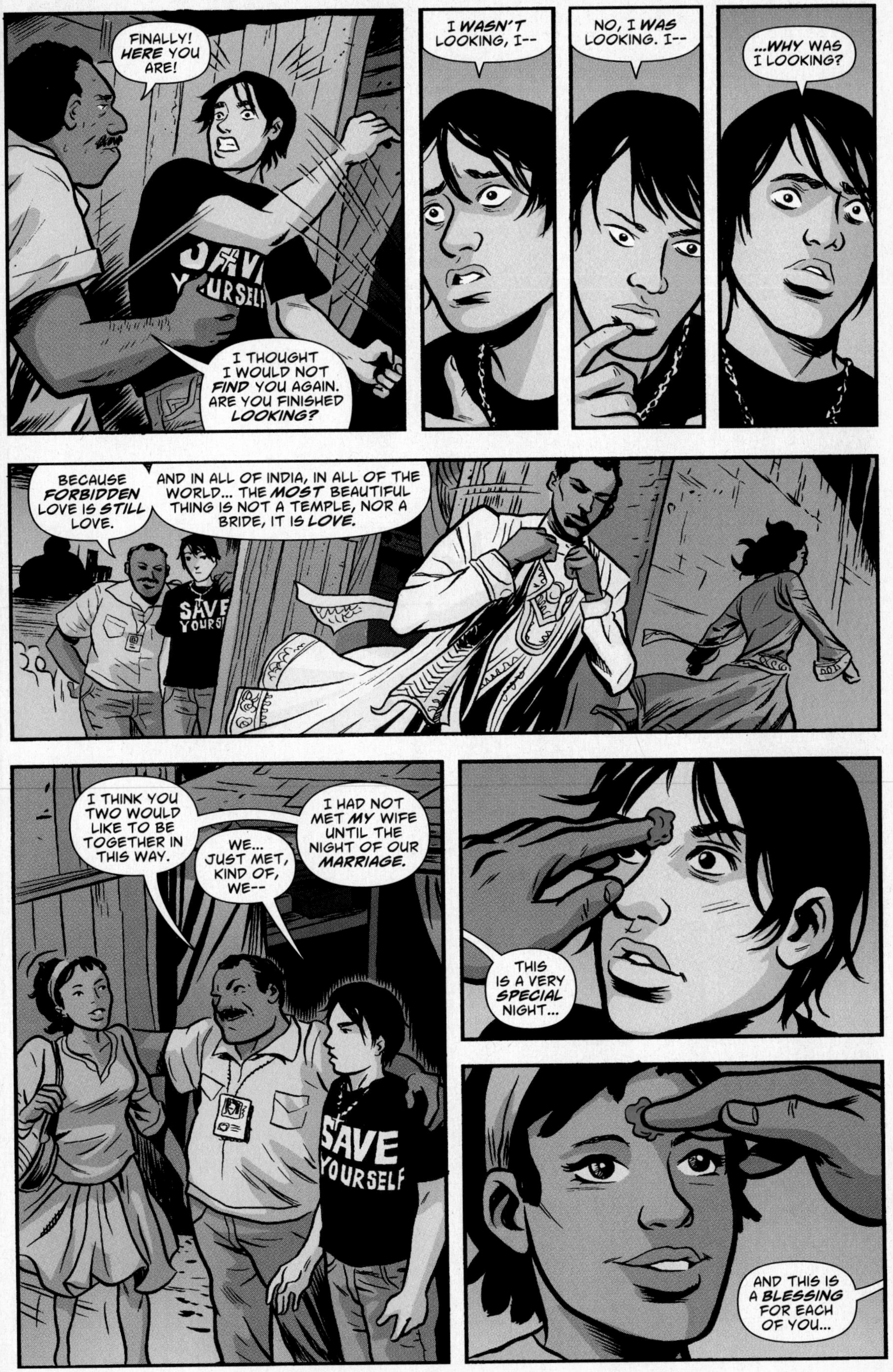
FINALLY! HERE YOU ARE!
SAVE YOURSELF
I THOUGHT I WOULD NOT FIND YOU AGAIN. ARE YOU FINISHED LOOKING?
I WASN'T LOOKING, I--
NO, I WAS LOOKING. I--
...WHY WAS I LOOKING?
BECAUSE FORBIDDEN LOVE IS STILL LOVE.
AND IN ALL OF INDIA, IN ALL OF THE WORLD... THE MOST BEAUTIFUL THING IS NOT A TEMPLE, NOR A BRIDE, IT IS LOVE.
SAVE YOURSELF
I THINK YOU TWO WOULD LIKE TO BE TOGETHER IN THIS WAY.
WE... JUST MET, KIND OF, WE--
I HAD NOT MET MY WIFE UNTIL THE NIGHT OF OUR MARRIAGE.
SAVE YOURSELF
THIS IS A VERY SPECIAL NIGHT...
AND THIS IS A BLESSING FOR EACH OF YOU...

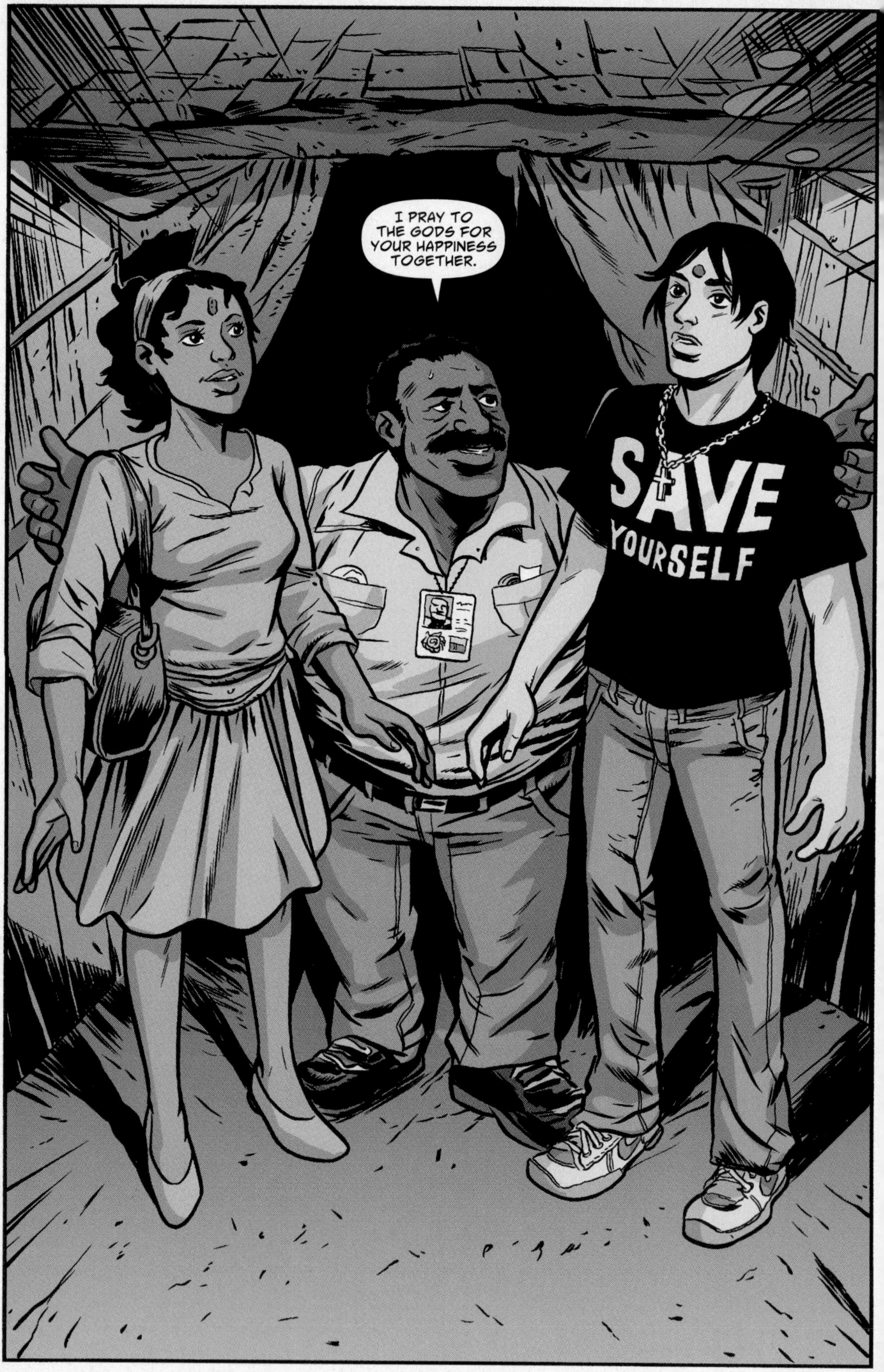
I PRAY TO THE GODS FOR YOUR HAPPINESS TOGETHER.
SAVE YOURSELF

CHAPTER FIVE

Chapter pencils by Ryan Kelly Chapter inks by Jim Rugg

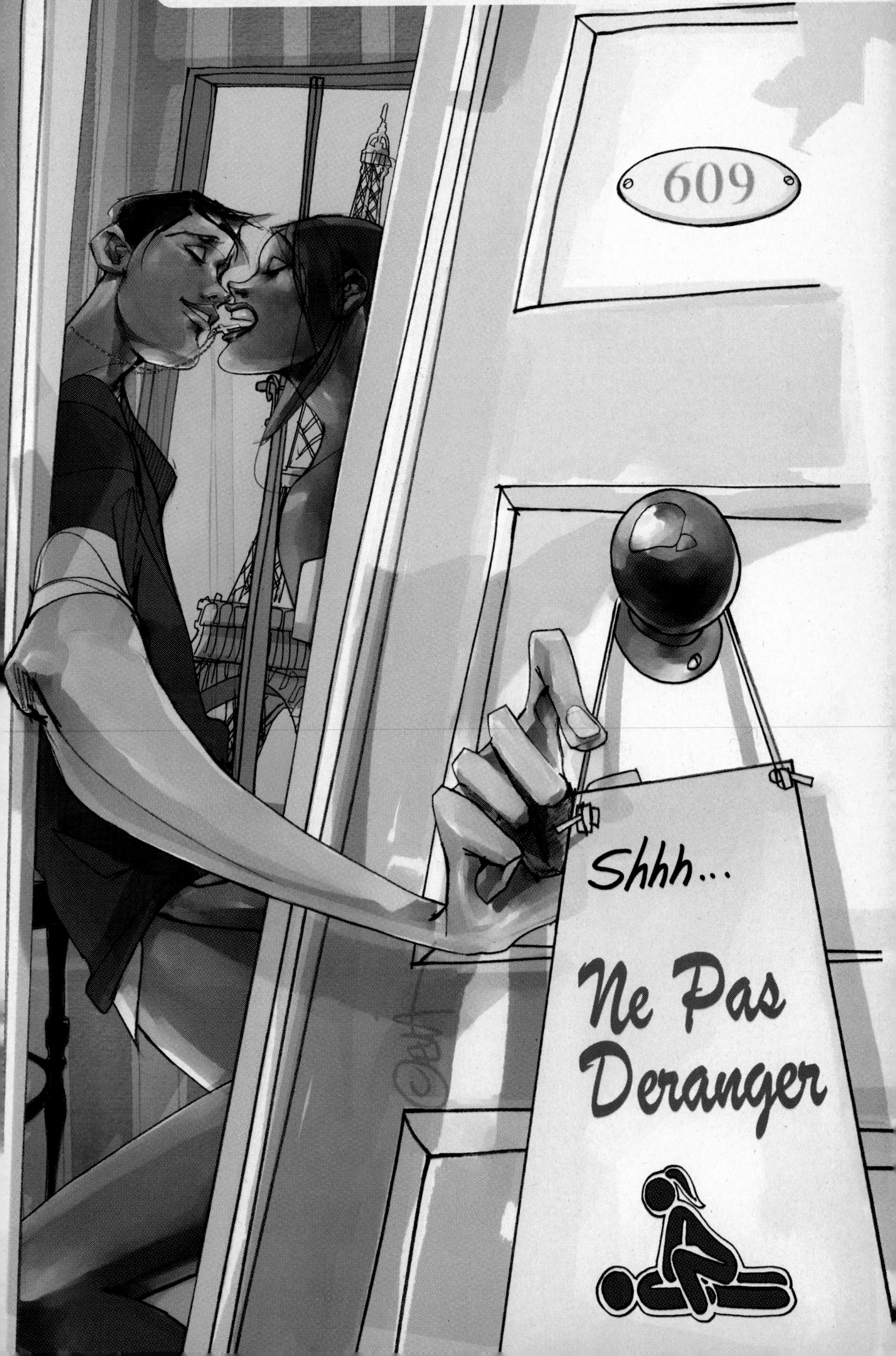
609
Shhh...
Ne Pas Deranger

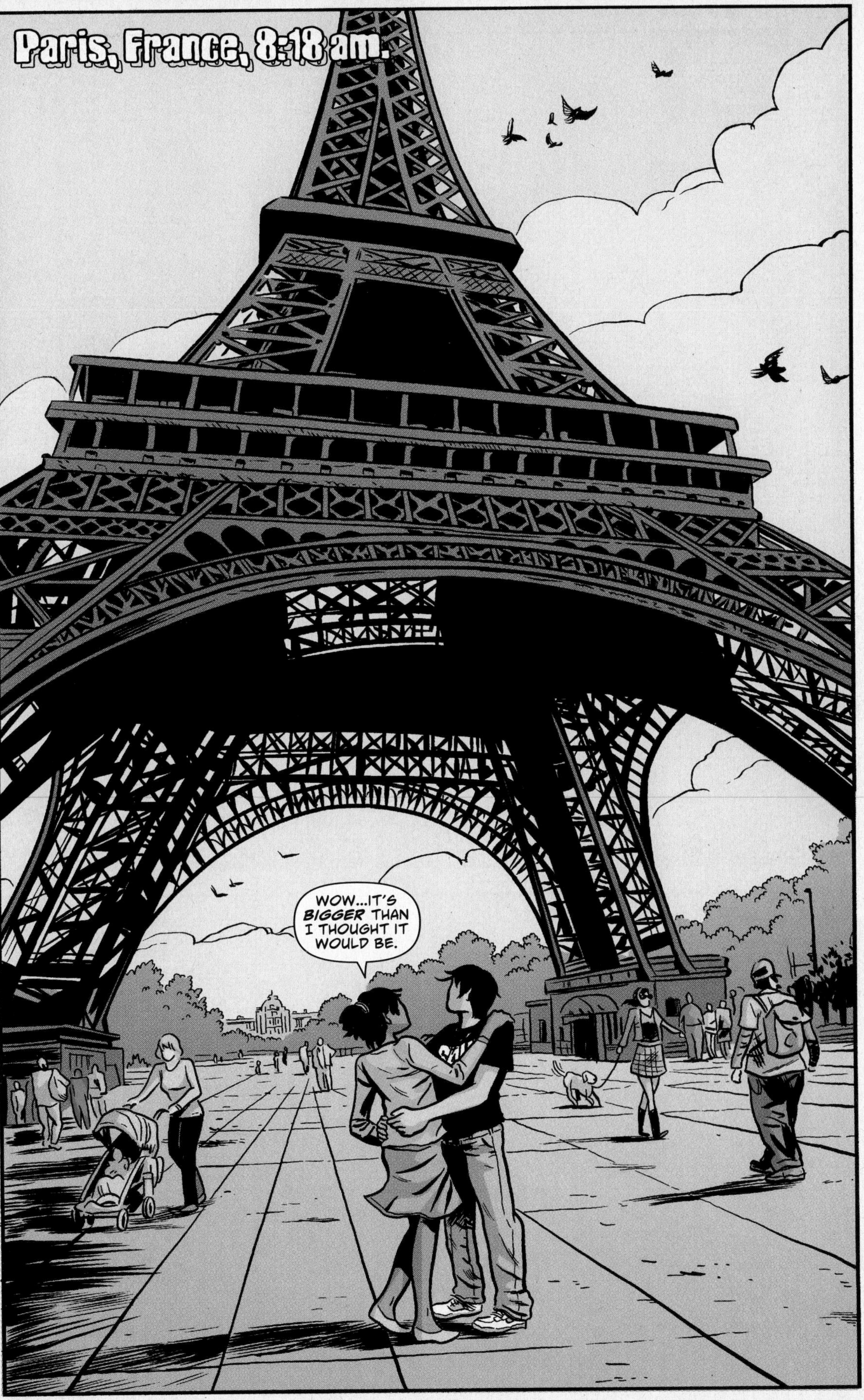
Paris, France, 8:18 am.
WOW...IT'S BIGGER THAN I THOUGHT IT WOULD BE.

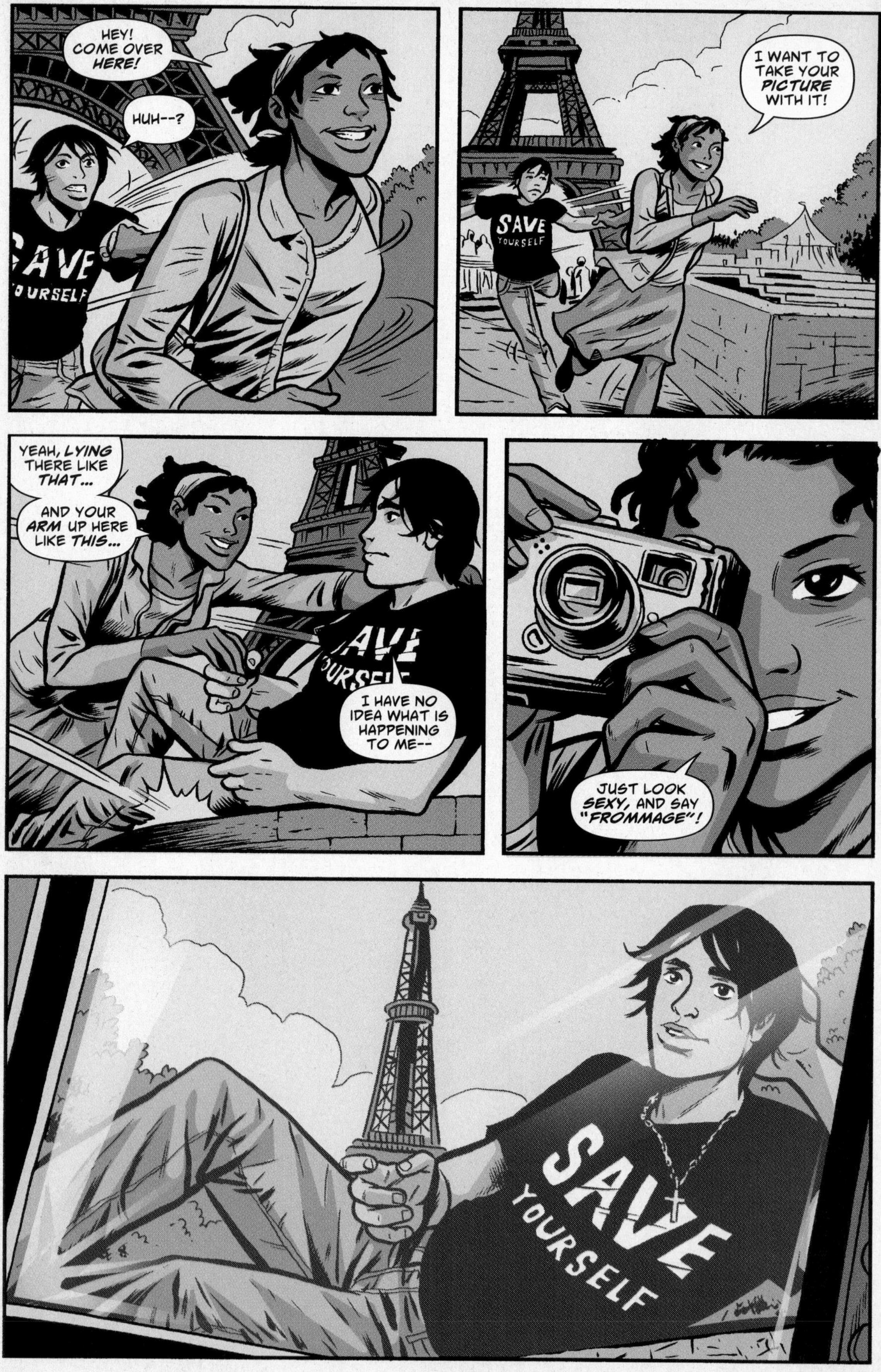
HEY! COME OVER HERE!
HUH--?
SAVE YOURSELF
I WANT TO TAKE YOUR PICTURE WITH IT!
SAVE YOURSELF
YEAH, LYING THERE LIKE THAT...
AND YOUR ARM UP HERE LIKE THIS...
I HAVE NO IDEA WHAT IS HAPPENING TO ME--
JUST LOOK SEXY, AND SAY "FROMMAGE"!
SAVE YOURSELF

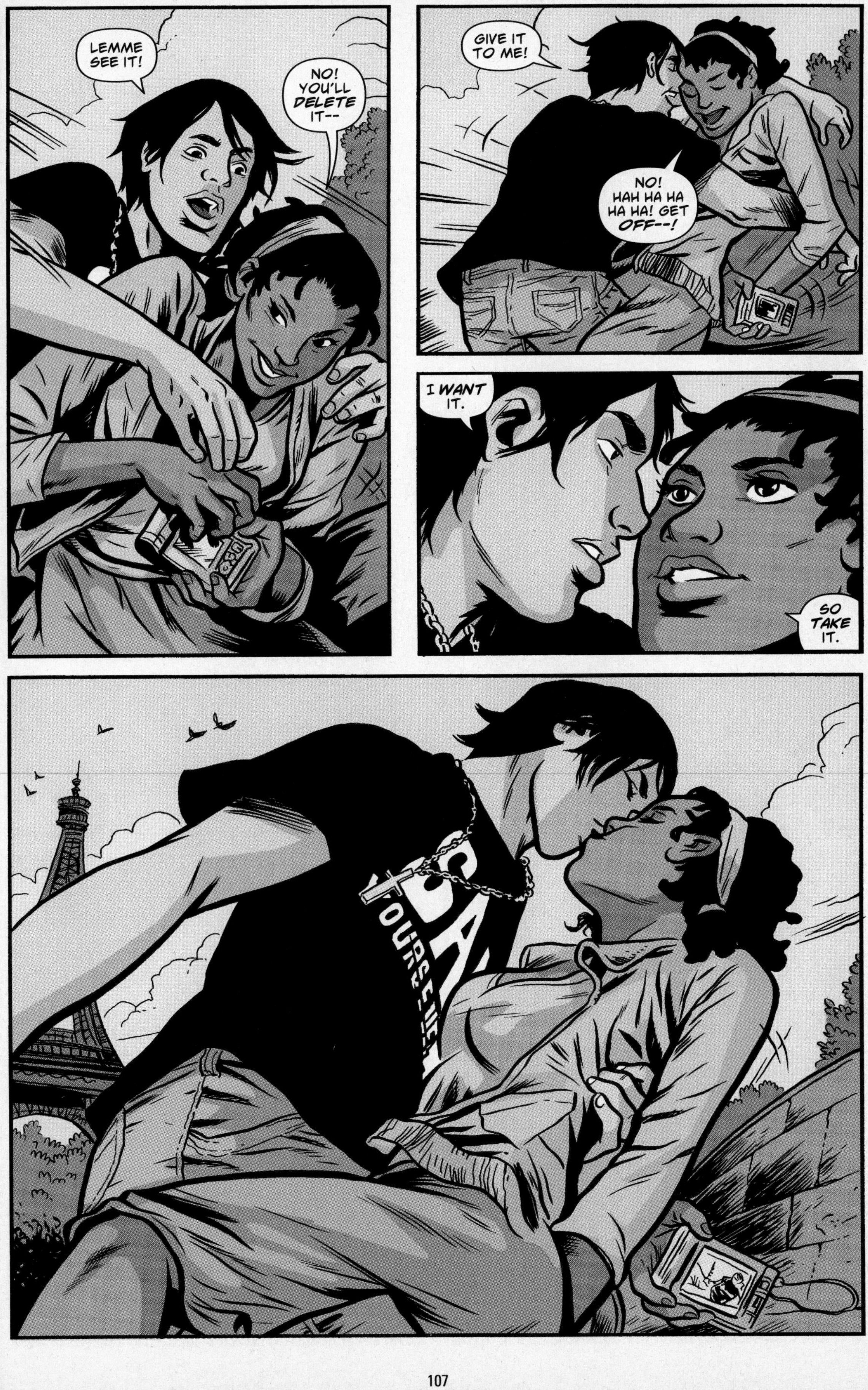
LEMME SEE IT!
NO! YOU'LL DELETE IT--
GIVE IT TO ME!
NO! HAH HA HA HA HA! GET OFF--!
I WANT IT.
SO TAKE IT.

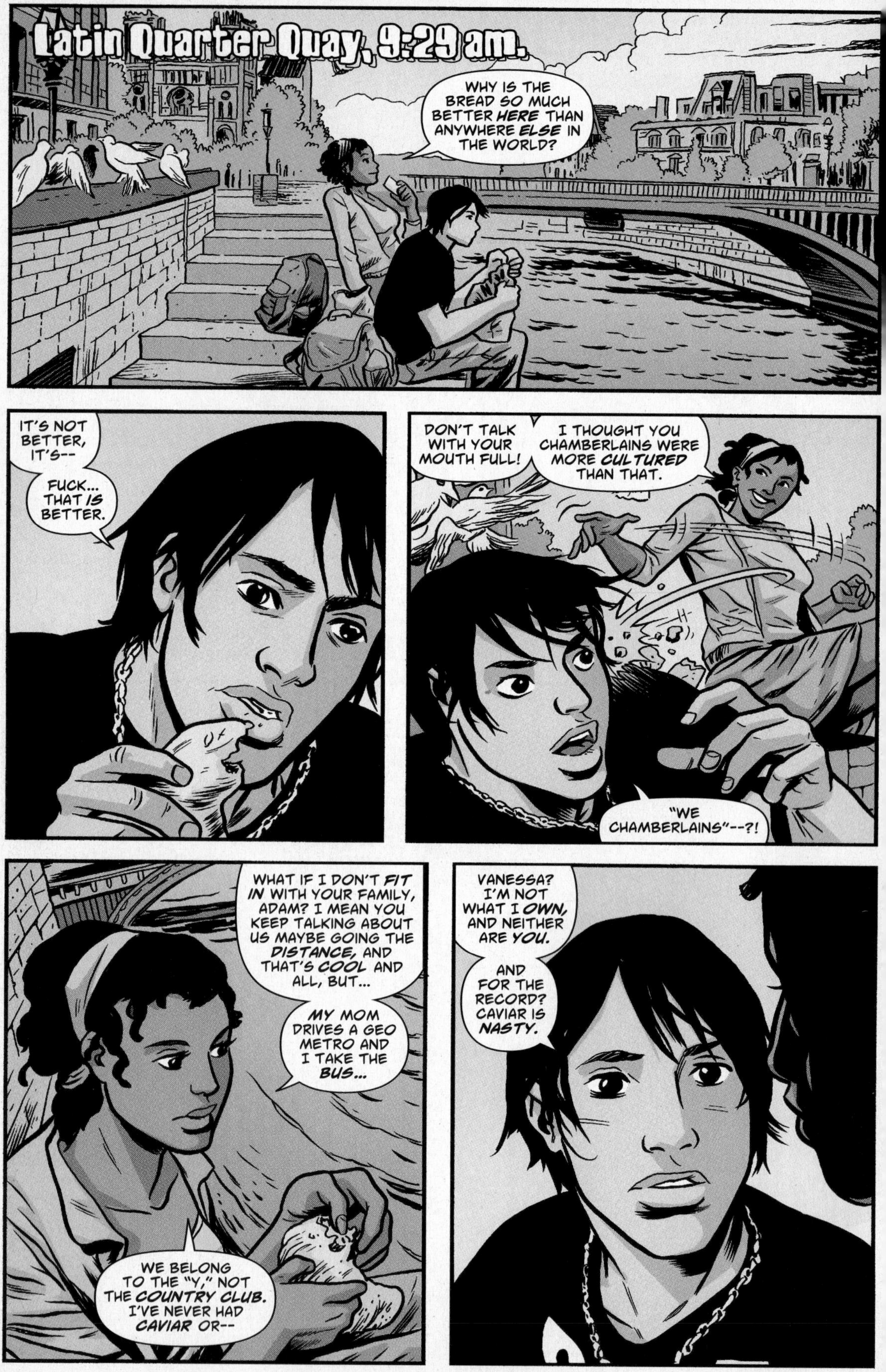
Latin Quarter Quay, 9:29 am.
WHY IS THE BREAD SO MUCH BETTER HERE THAN ANYWHERE ELSE IN THE WORLD?
IT'S NOT BETTER, IT'S--
FUCK... THAT IS BETTER.
DON'T TALK WITH YOUR MOUTH FULL!
I THOUGHT YOU CHAMBERLAINS WERE MORE CULTURED THAN THAT.
"WE CHAMBERLAINS"--?!
WHAT IF I DON'T FIT IN WITH YOUR FAMILY, ADAM? I MEAN YOU KEEP TALKING ABOUT US MAYBE GOING THE DISTANCE, AND THAT'S COOL AND ALL, BUT...
MY MOM DRIVES A GEO METRO AND I TAKE THE BUS...
WE BELONG TO THE "Y," NOT THE COUNTRY CLUB. I'VE NEVER HAD CAVIAR OR--
VANESSA? I'M NOT WHAT I OWN, AND NEITHER ARE YOU.
AND FOR THE RECORD? CAVIAR IS NASTY.

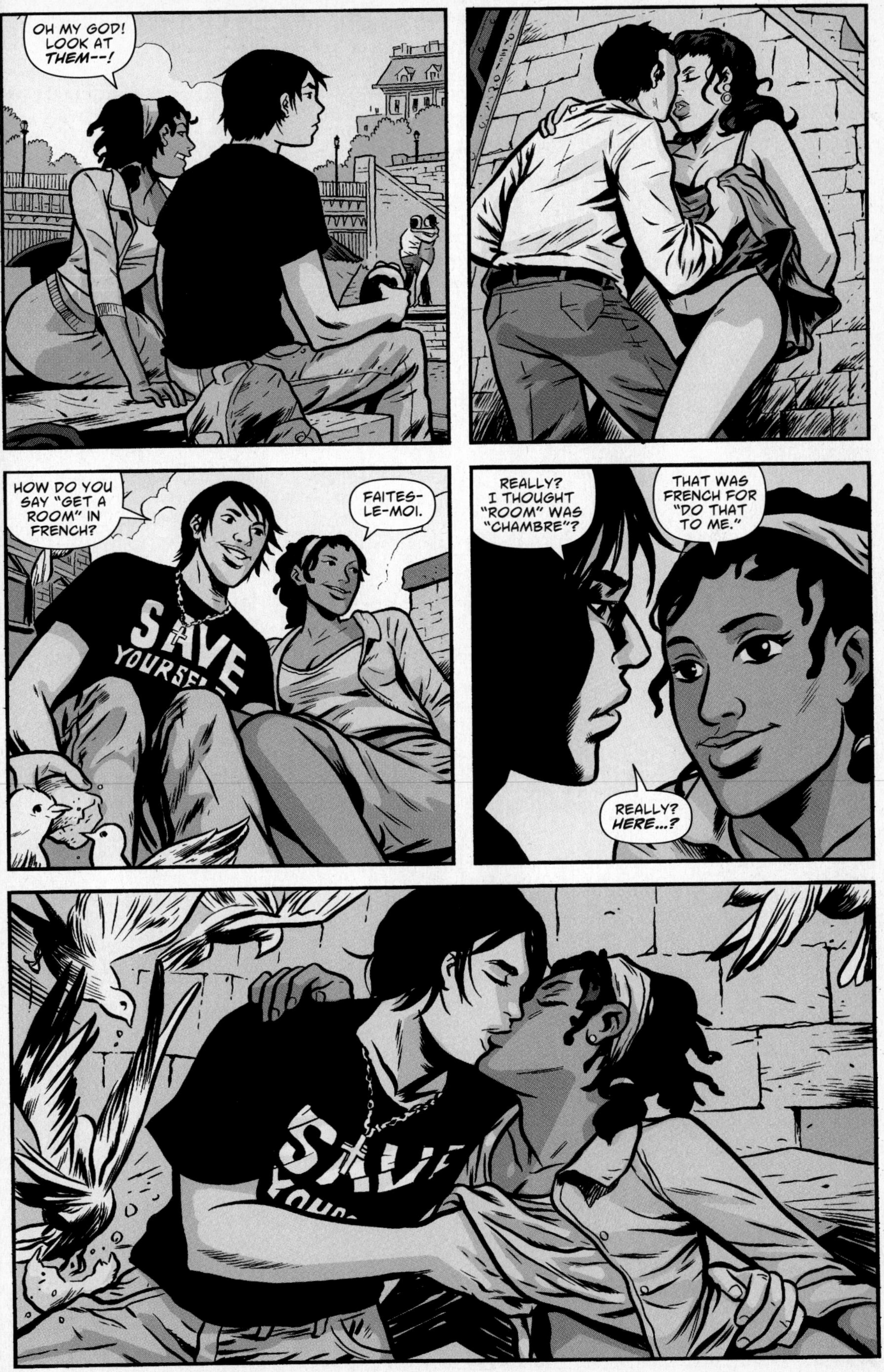
OH MY GOD! LOOK AT *THEM--!*
HOW DO YOU SAY "GET A ROOM" IN FRENCH?
FAITES-LE-MOI.
SAVE YOURSELF
REALLY? I THOUGHT "ROOM" WAS "CHAMBRE"?
THAT WAS FRENCH FOR "DO THAT TO ME."
REALLY? *HERE...?*
SAVE

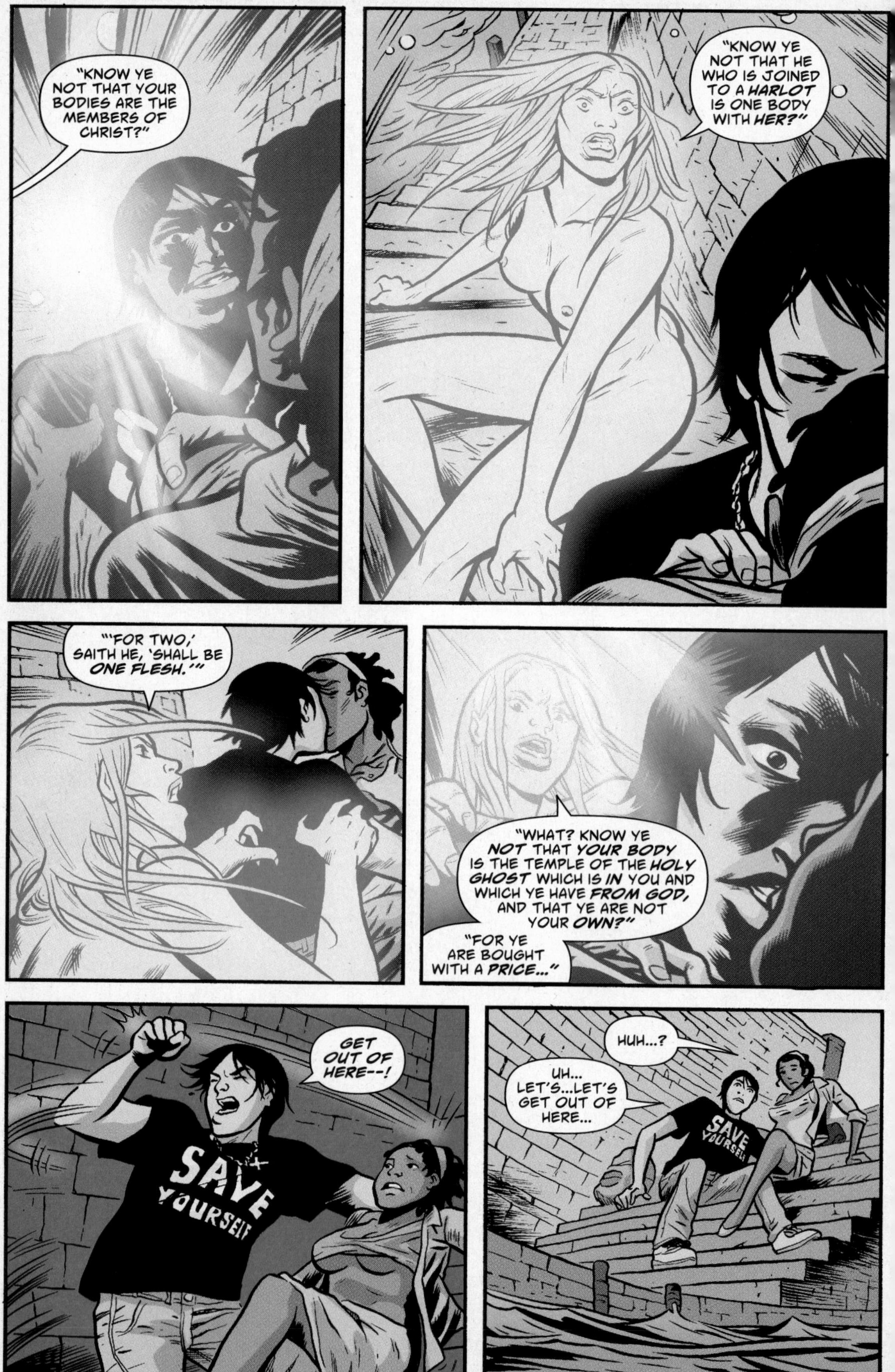
"KNOW YE NOT THAT YOUR BODIES ARE THE MEMBERS OF CHRIST?"
"KNOW YE NOT THAT HE WHO IS JOINED TO A *HARLOT* IS ONE BODY WITH *HER?"*
"'FOR TWO,' SAITH HE, 'SHALL BE *ONE FLESH.'"*
"WHAT? KNOW YE *NOT* THAT *YOUR BODY* IS THE TEMPLE OF THE *HOLY GHOST* WHICH IS *IN* YOU AND WHICH YE HAVE *FROM GOD,* AND THAT YE ARE NOT YOUR *OWN?"*
"FOR YE ARE BOUGHT WITH A *PRICE..."*
GET OUT OF HERE--!
SAVE YOURSELF
HUH...?
UH... LET'S...LET'S GET OUT OF HERE...
SAVE YOURSELF

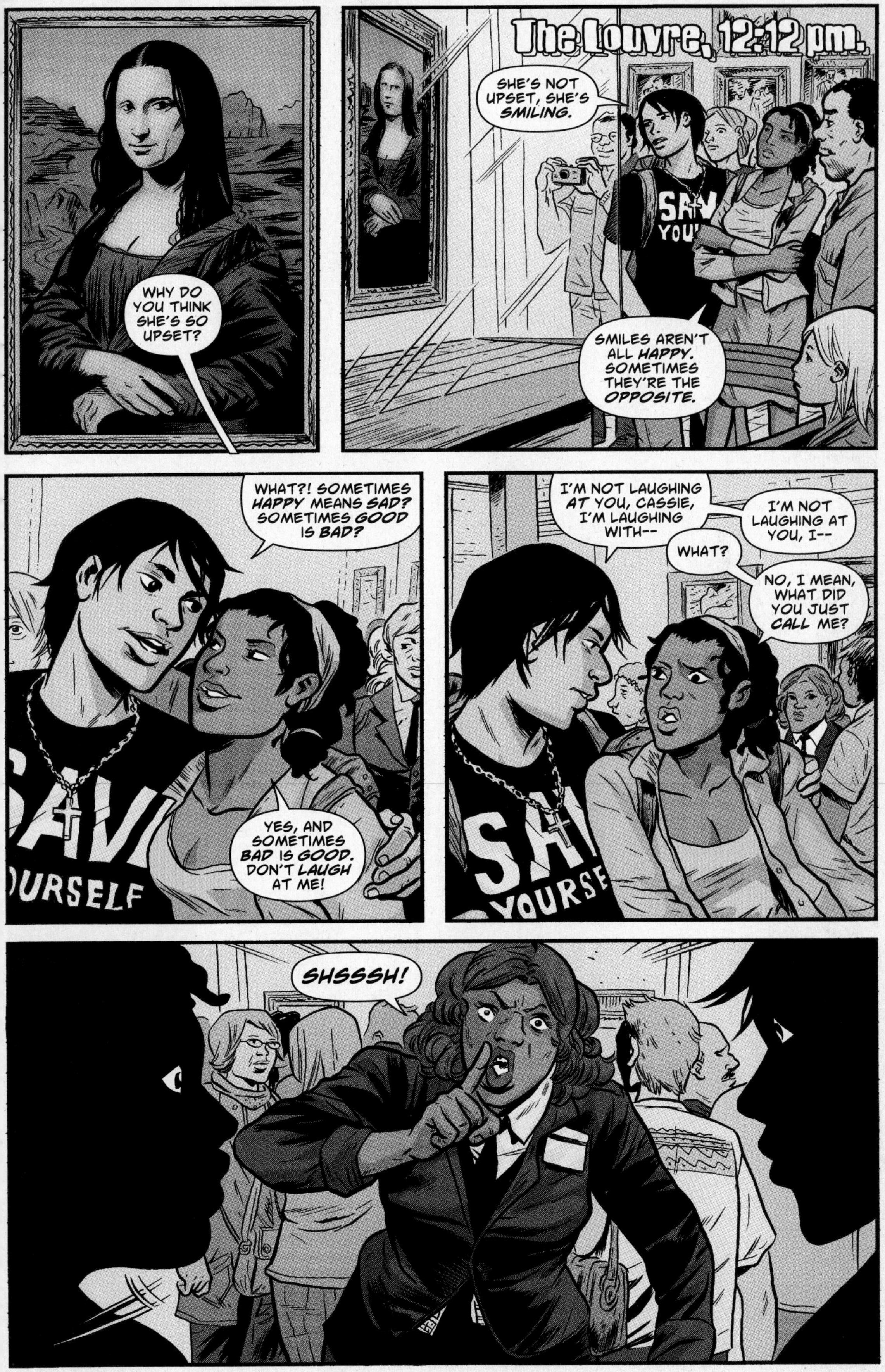
WHY DO YOU THINK SHE'S SO UPSET?
The Louvre, 12:12 pm.
SHE'S NOT UPSET, SHE'S SMILING.
SMILES AREN'T ALL HAPPY. SOMETIMES THEY'RE THE OPPOSITE.
WHAT?! SOMETIMES HAPPY MEANS SAD? SOMETIMES GOOD IS BAD?
YES, AND SOMETIMES BAD IS GOOD. DON'T LAUGH AT ME!
I'M NOT LAUGHING AT YOU, CASSIE, I'M LAUGHING WITH--
I'M NOT LAUGHING AT YOU, I--
WHAT?
NO, I MEAN, WHAT DID YOU JUST CALL ME?
SHSSSH!

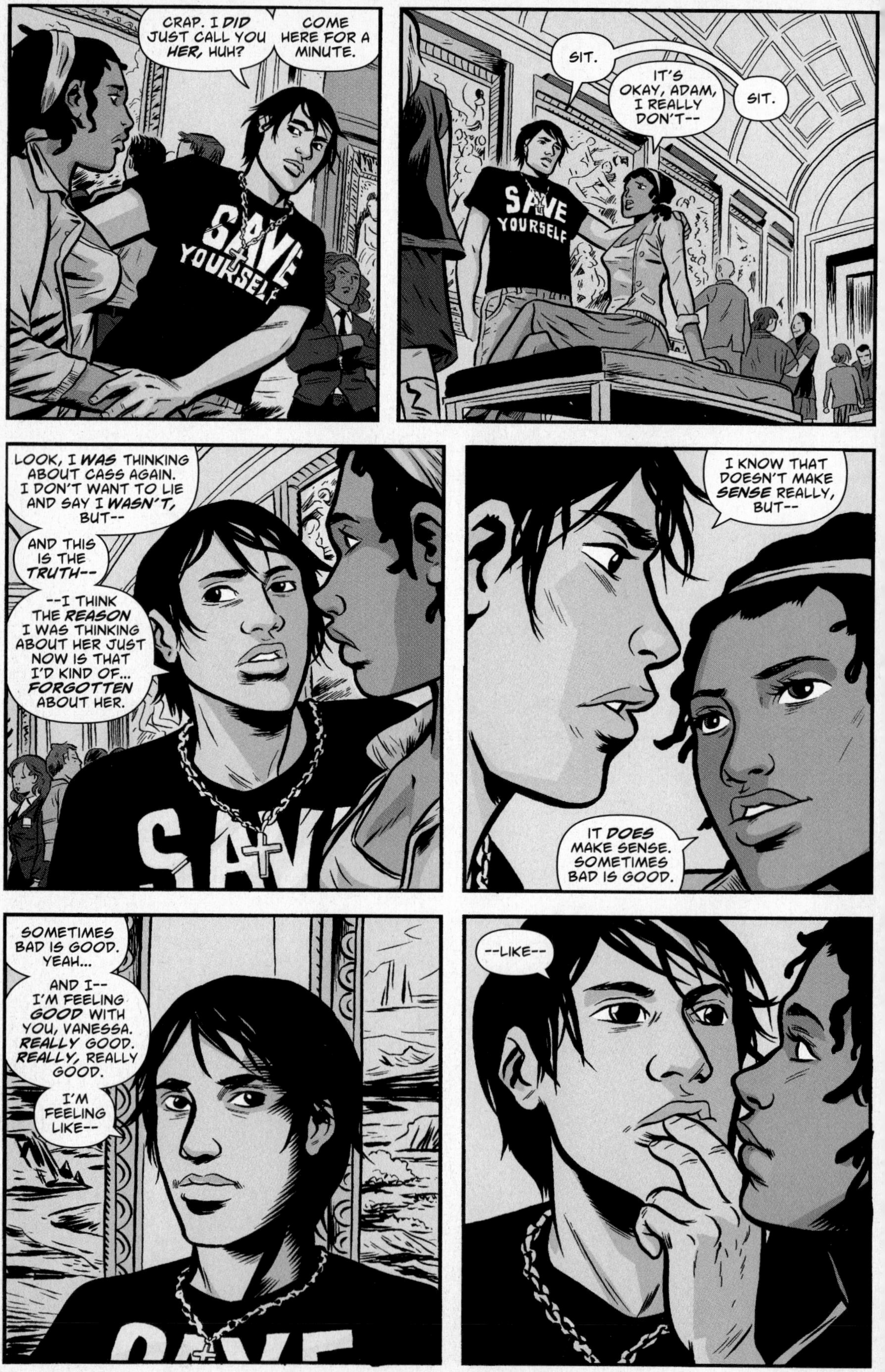
CRAP. I DID JUST CALL YOU HER, HUH?
COME HERE FOR A MINUTE.
SIT.
IT'S OKAY, ADAM, I REALLY DON'T--
SIT.
LOOK, I WAS THINKING ABOUT CASS AGAIN. I DON'T WANT TO LIE AND SAY I WASN'T, BUT--
AND THIS IS THE TRUTH--
--I THINK THE REASON I WAS THINKING ABOUT HER JUST NOW IS THAT I'D KIND OF... FORGOTTEN ABOUT HER.
I KNOW THAT DOESN'T MAKE SENSE REALLY, BUT--
IT DOES MAKE SENSE. SOMETIMES BAD IS GOOD.
SOMETIMES BAD IS GOOD. YEAH...
AND I-- I'M FEELING GOOD WITH YOU, VANESSA. REALLY GOOD. REALLY, REALLY GOOD.
I'M FEELING LIKE--
--LIKE--

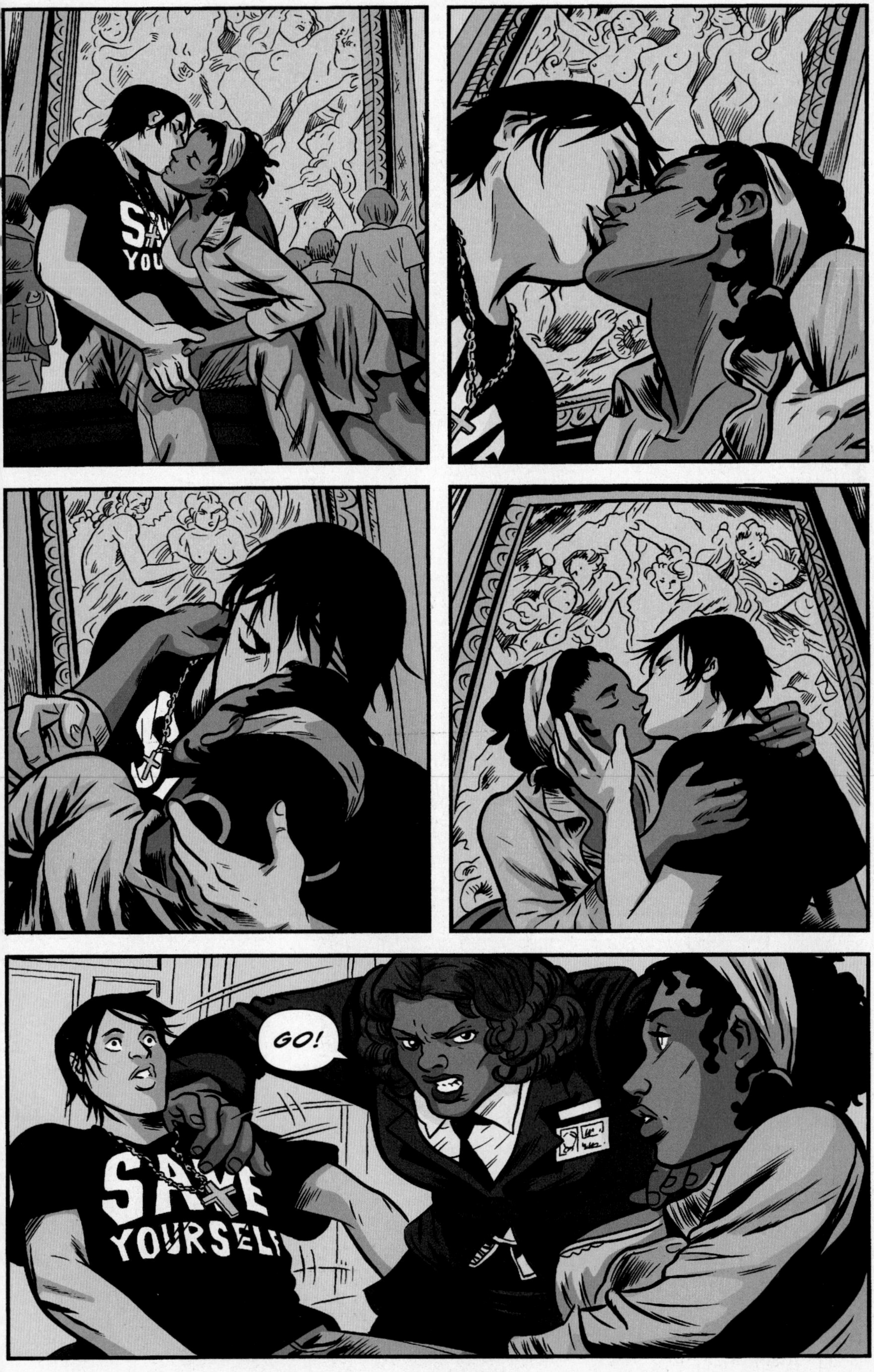
GO!
YOURSELF

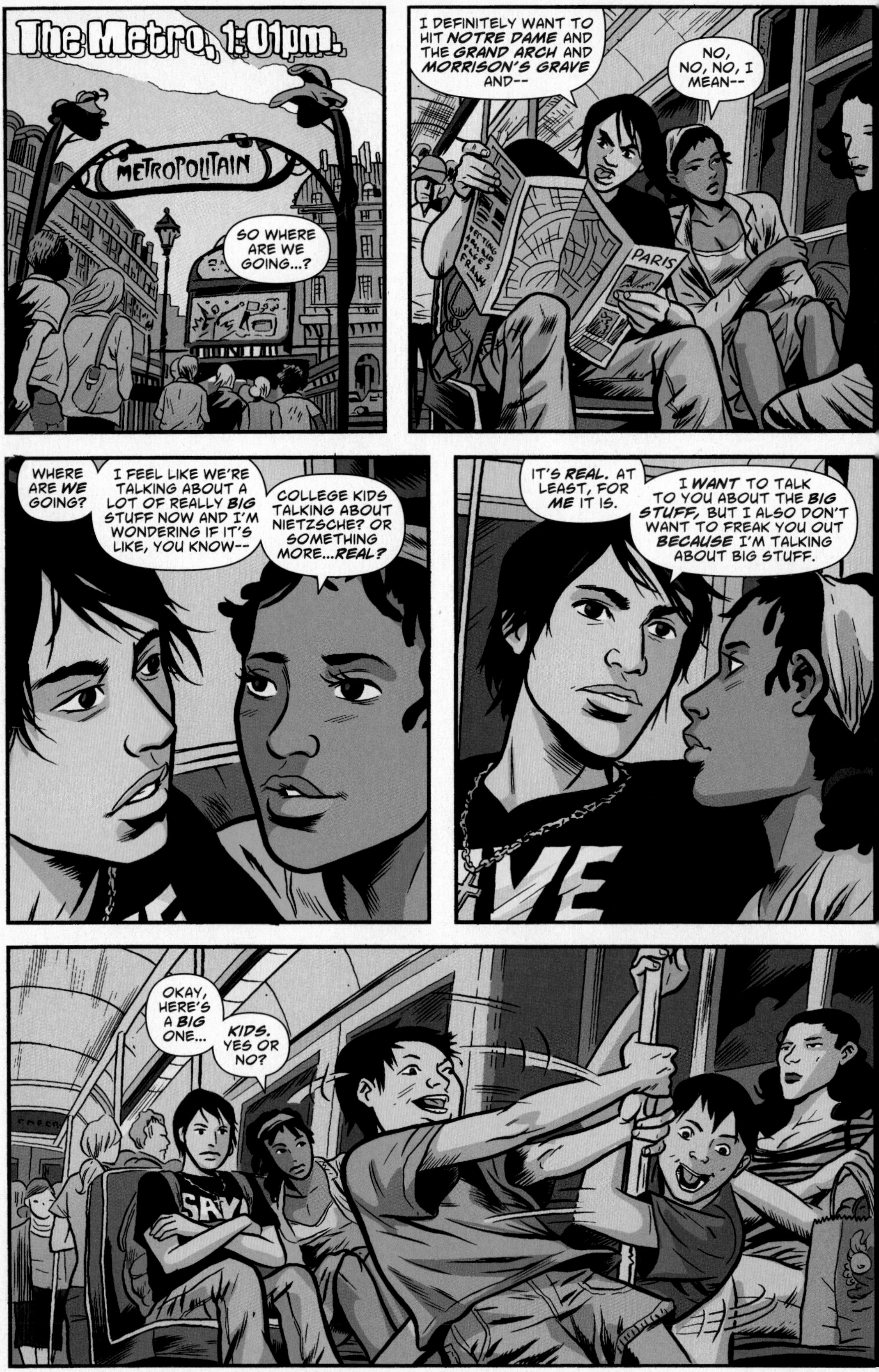
The Metro, 1:01pm.
METROPOLITAIN
SO WHERE ARE WE GOING...?
I DEFINITELY WANT TO HIT NOTRE DAME AND THE GRAND ARCH AND MORRISON'S GRAVE AND--
NO, NO, NO, I MEAN--
PARIS
WHERE ARE WE GOING?
I FEEL LIKE WE'RE TALKING ABOUT A LOT OF REALLY BIG STUFF NOW AND I'M WONDERING IF IT'S LIKE, YOU KNOW--
COLLEGE KIDS TALKING ABOUT NIETZSCHE? OR SOMETHING MORE...REAL?
IT'S REAL. AT LEAST, FOR ME IT IS.
I WANT TO TALK TO YOU ABOUT THE BIG STUFF, BUT I ALSO DON'T WANT TO FREAK YOU OUT BECAUSE I'M TALKING ABOUT BIG STUFF.
OKAY, HERE'S A BIG ONE...
KIDS. YES OR NO?

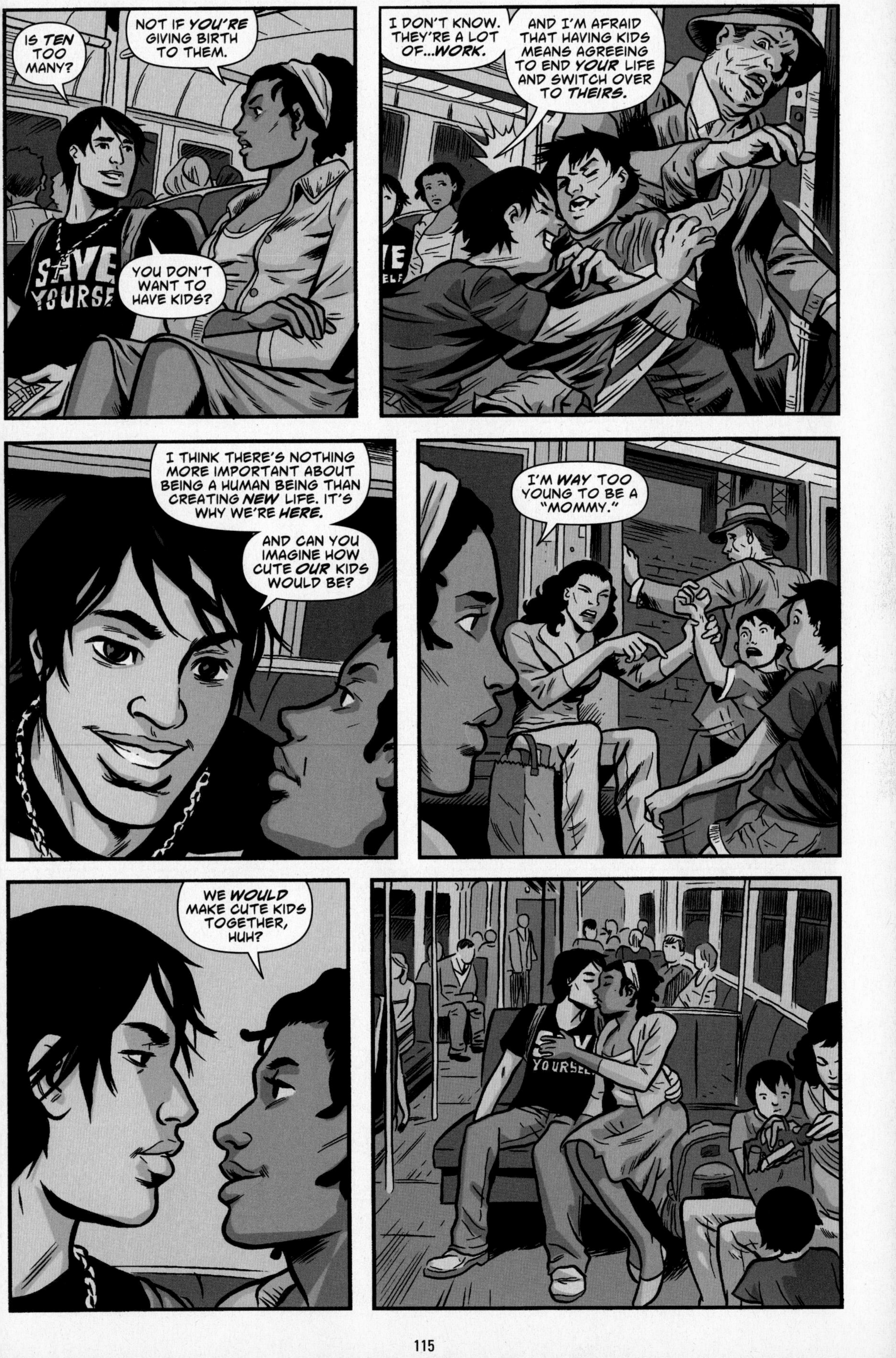
IS TEN TOO MANY?
NOT IF YOU'RE GIVING BIRTH TO THEM.
SAVE YOURSE
YOU DON'T WANT TO HAVE KIDS?
I DON'T KNOW. THEY'RE A LOT OF...WORK.
AND I'M AFRAID THAT HAVING KIDS MEANS AGREEING TO END YOUR LIFE AND SWITCH OVER TO THEIRS.
I THINK THERE'S NOTHING MORE IMPORTANT ABOUT BEING A HUMAN BEING THAN CREATING NEW LIFE. IT'S WHY WE'RE HERE.
AND CAN YOU IMAGINE HOW CUTE OUR KIDS WOULD BE?
I'M WAY TOO YOUNG TO BE A "MOMMY."
WE WOULD MAKE CUTE KIDS TOGETHER, HUH?

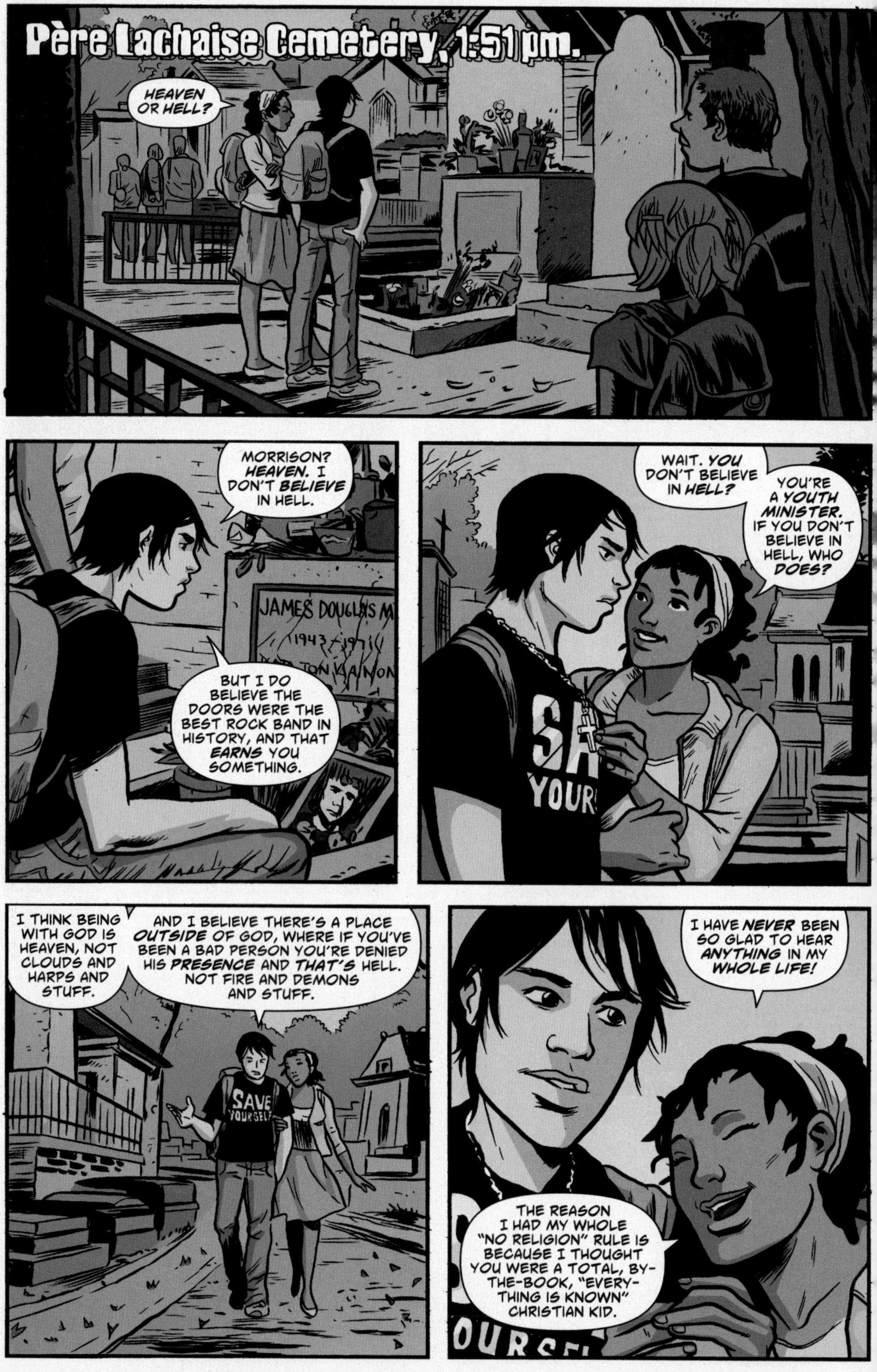
Père Lachaise Cemetery, 1:51 pm.
HEAVEN OR HELL?
MORRISON? HEAVEN. I DON'T BELIEVE IN HELL.
JAMES DOUGLAS M
1943 1971
BUT I DO BELIEVE THE DOORS WERE THE BEST ROCK BAND IN HISTORY, AND THAT EARNS YOU SOMETHING.
WAIT. YOU DON'T BELIEVE IN HELL?
YOU'RE A YOUTH MINISTER. IF YOU DON'T BELIEVE IN HELL, WHO DOES?
I THINK BEING WITH GOD IS HEAVEN, NOT CLOUDS AND HARPS AND STUFF.
AND I BELIEVE THERE'S A PLACE OUTSIDE OF GOD, WHERE IF YOU'VE BEEN A BAD PERSON YOU'RE DENIED HIS PRESENCE AND THAT'S HELL. NOT FIRE AND DEMONS AND STUFF.
SAVE YOURSELF
I HAVE NEVER BEEN SO GLAD TO HEAR ANYTHING IN MY WHOLE LIFE!
THE REASON I HAD MY WHOLE "NO RELIGION" RULE IS BECAUSE I THOUGHT YOU WERE A TOTAL, BY-THE-BOOK, "EVERYTHING IS KNOWN" CHRISTIAN KID.

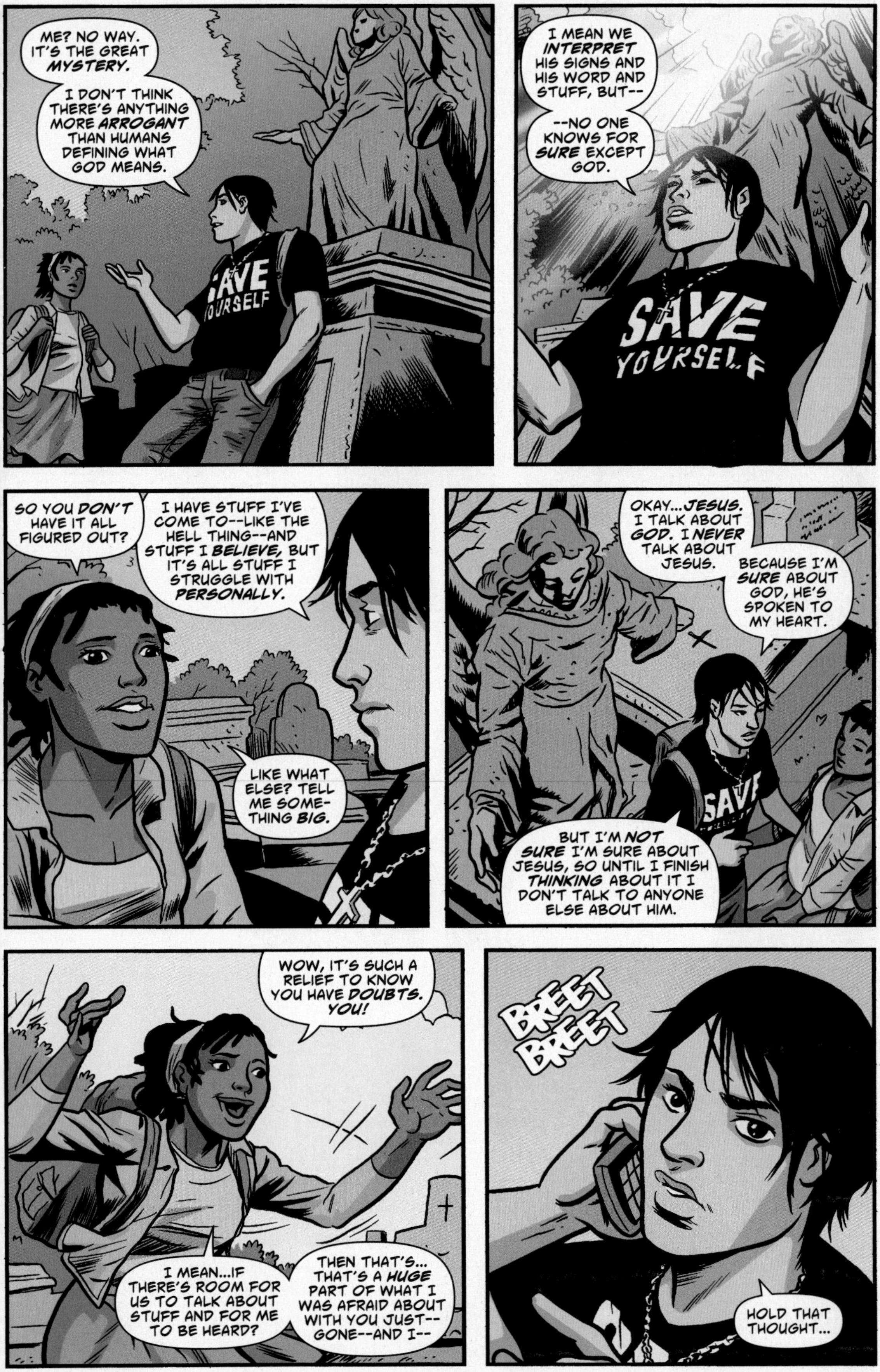
ME? NO WAY. IT'S THE GREAT MYSTERY.
I DON'T THINK THERE'S ANYTHING MORE ARROGANT THAN HUMANS DEFINING WHAT GOD MEANS.
SAVE YOURSELF
I MEAN WE INTERPRET HIS SIGNS AND HIS WORD AND STUFF, BUT--
--NO ONE KNOWS FOR SURE EXCEPT GOD.
SAVE YOURSELF
SO YOU DON'T HAVE IT ALL FIGURED OUT?
I HAVE STUFF I'VE COME TO--LIKE THE HELL THING--AND STUFF I BELIEVE, BUT IT'S ALL STUFF I STRUGGLE WITH PERSONALLY.
LIKE WHAT ELSE? TELL ME SOMETHING BIG.
OKAY...JESUS. I TALK ABOUT GOD. I NEVER TALK ABOUT JESUS.
BECAUSE I'M SURE ABOUT GOD, HE'S SPOKEN TO MY HEART.
BUT I'M NOT SURE I'M SURE ABOUT JESUS, SO UNTIL I FINISH THINKING ABOUT IT I DON'T TALK TO ANYONE ELSE ABOUT HIM.
WOW, IT'S SUCH A RELIEF TO KNOW YOU HAVE DOUBTS. YOU!
I MEAN...IF THERE'S ROOM FOR US TO TALK ABOUT STUFF AND FOR ME TO BE HEARD?
THEN THAT'S... THAT'S A HUGE PART OF WHAT I WAS AFRAID ABOUT WITH YOU JUST--GONE--AND I--
BREET BREET
HOLD THAT THOUGHT...

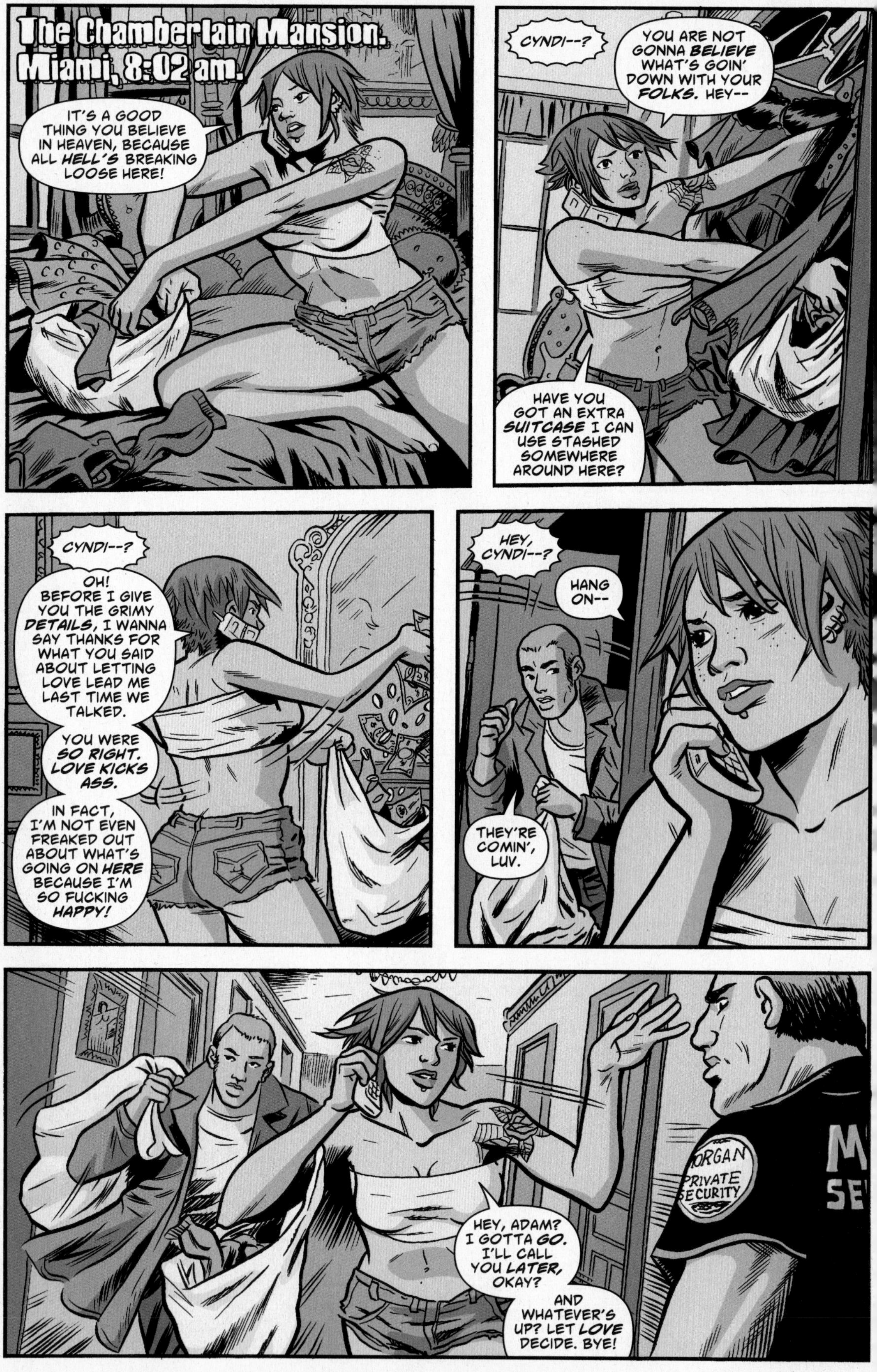
The Chamberlain Mansion. Miami, 8:02 am.
IT'S A GOOD THING YOU BELIEVE IN HEAVEN, BECAUSE ALL HELL'S BREAKING LOOSE HERE!
CYNDI--?
YOU ARE NOT GONNA BELIEVE WHAT'S GOIN' DOWN WITH YOUR FOLKS. HEY--
HAVE YOU GOT AN EXTRA SUITCASE I CAN USE STASHED SOMEWHERE AROUND HERE?
CYNDI--?
OH! BEFORE I GIVE YOU THE GRIMY DETAILS, I WANNA SAY THANKS FOR WHAT YOU SAID ABOUT LETTING LOVE LEAD ME LAST TIME WE TALKED.
YOU WERE SO RIGHT. LOVE KICKS ASS.
IN FACT, I'M NOT EVEN FREAKED OUT ABOUT WHAT'S GOING ON HERE BECAUSE I'M SO FUCKING HAPPY!
HEY, CYNDI--?
HANG ON--
THEY'RE COMIN', LUV.
MORGAN PRIVATE SECURITY
HEY, ADAM? I GOTTA GO. I'LL CALL YOU LATER, OKAY?
AND WHATEVER'S UP? LET LOVE DECIDE. BYE!

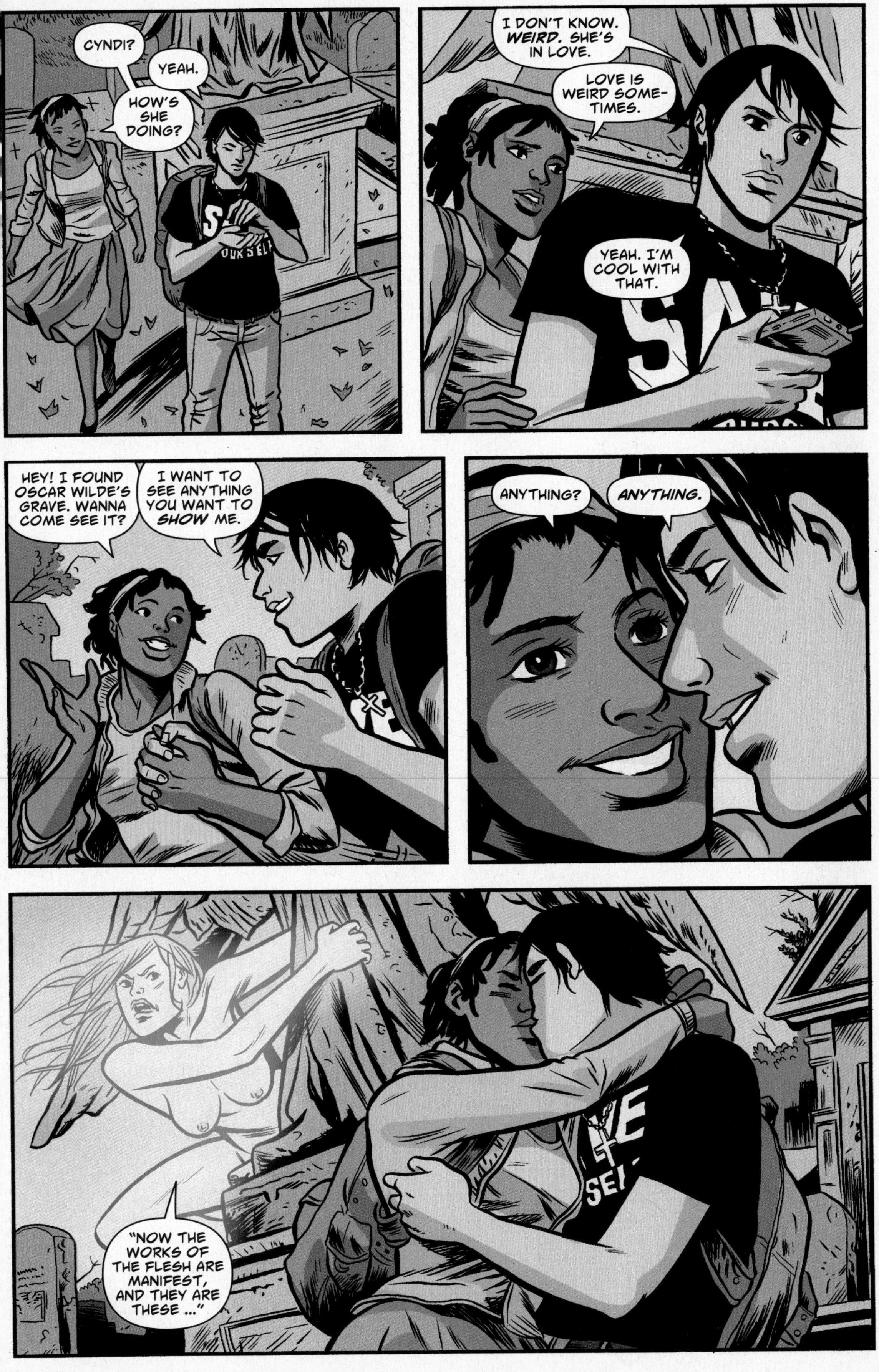

CYNDI?
YEAH.
HOW'S SHE DOING?
I DON'T KNOW. WEIRD. SHE'S IN LOVE.
LOVE IS WEIRD SOME-TIMES.
YEAH. I'M COOL WITH THAT.
HEY! I FOUND OSCAR WILDE'S GRAVE. WANNA COME SEE IT?
I WANT TO SEE ANYTHING YOU WANT TO SHOW ME.
ANYTHING?
ANYTHING.
"NOW THE WORKS OF THE FLESH ARE MANIFEST, AND THEY ARE THESE ..."

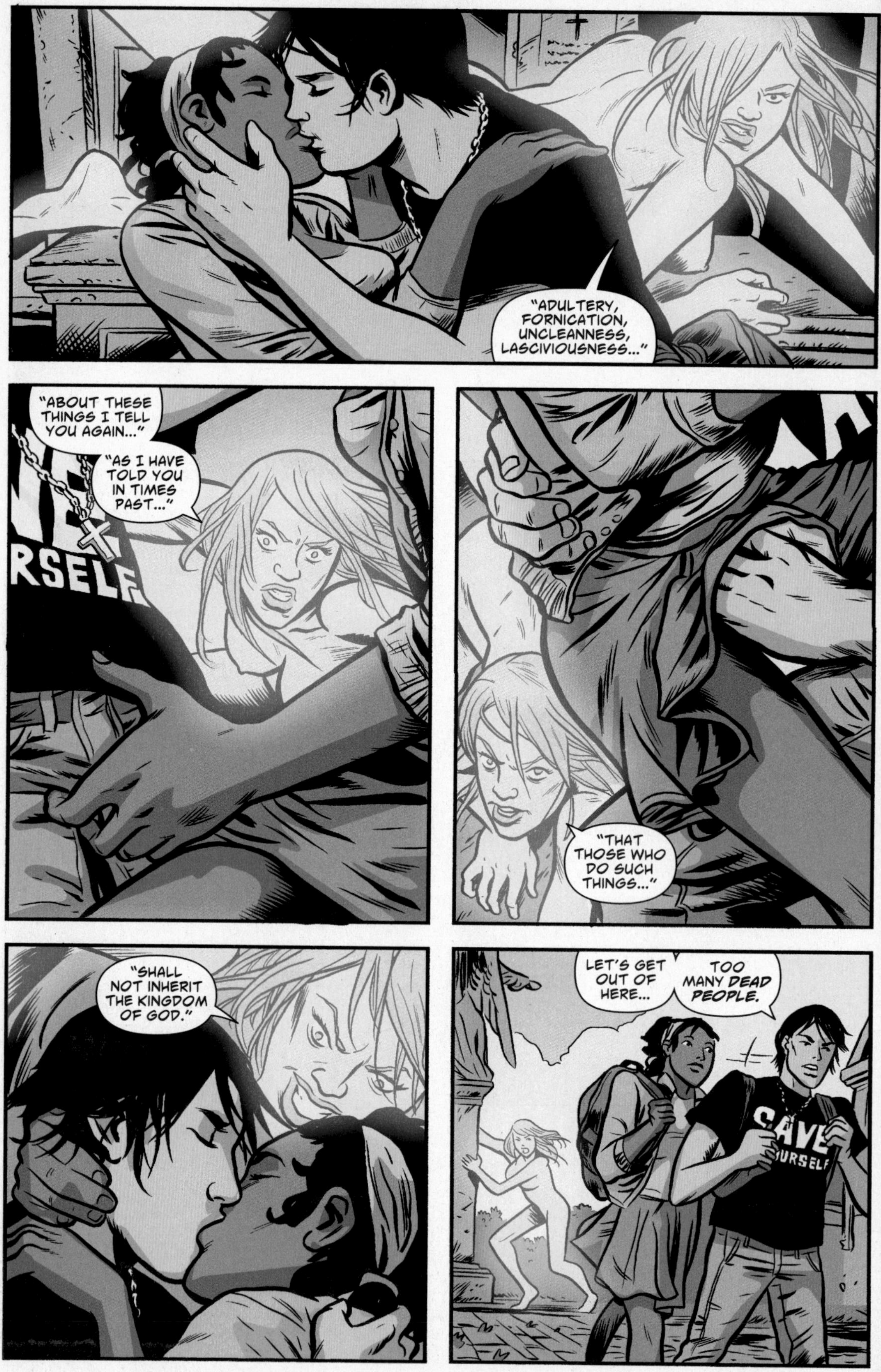
"ADULTERY, FORNICATION, UNCLEANNESS, LASCIVIOUSNESS..."
"ABOUT THESE THINGS I TELL YOU AGAIN..."
"AS I HAVE TOLD YOU IN TIMES PAST..."
RSELF
"THAT THOSE WHO DO SUCH THINGS..."
"SHALL NOT INHERIT THE KINGDOM OF GOD."
LET'S GET OUT OF HERE...
TOO MANY DEAD PEOPLE.

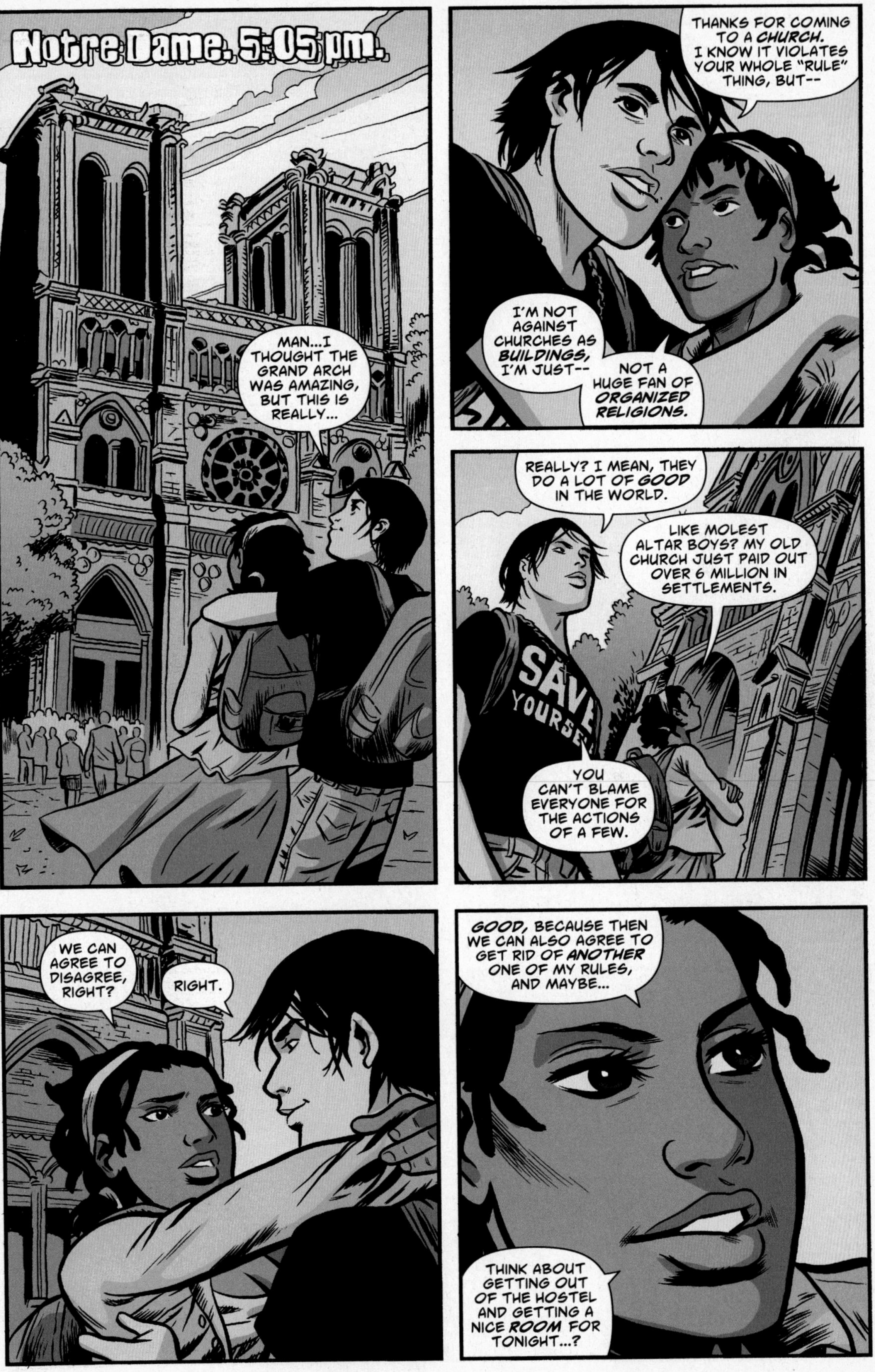
Notre Dame. 5:05 pm.
MAN...I THOUGHT THE GRAND ARCH WAS AMAZING, BUT THIS IS REALLY...
THANKS FOR COMING TO A CHURCH. I KNOW IT VIOLATES YOUR WHOLE "RULE" THING, BUT--
I'M NOT AGAINST CHURCHES AS BUILDINGS, I'M JUST--
NOT A HUGE FAN OF ORGANIZED RELIGIONS.
REALLY? I MEAN, THEY DO A LOT OF GOOD IN THE WORLD.
LIKE MOLEST ALTAR BOYS? MY OLD CHURCH JUST PAID OUT OVER 6 MILLION IN SETTLEMENTS.
YOU CAN'T BLAME EVERYONE FOR THE ACTIONS OF A FEW.
WE CAN AGREE TO DISAGREE, RIGHT?
RIGHT.
GOOD, BECAUSE THEN WE CAN ALSO AGREE TO GET RID OF ANOTHER ONE OF MY RULES, AND MAYBE...
THINK ABOUT GETTING OUT OF THE HOSTEL AND GETTING A NICE ROOM FOR TONIGHT...?

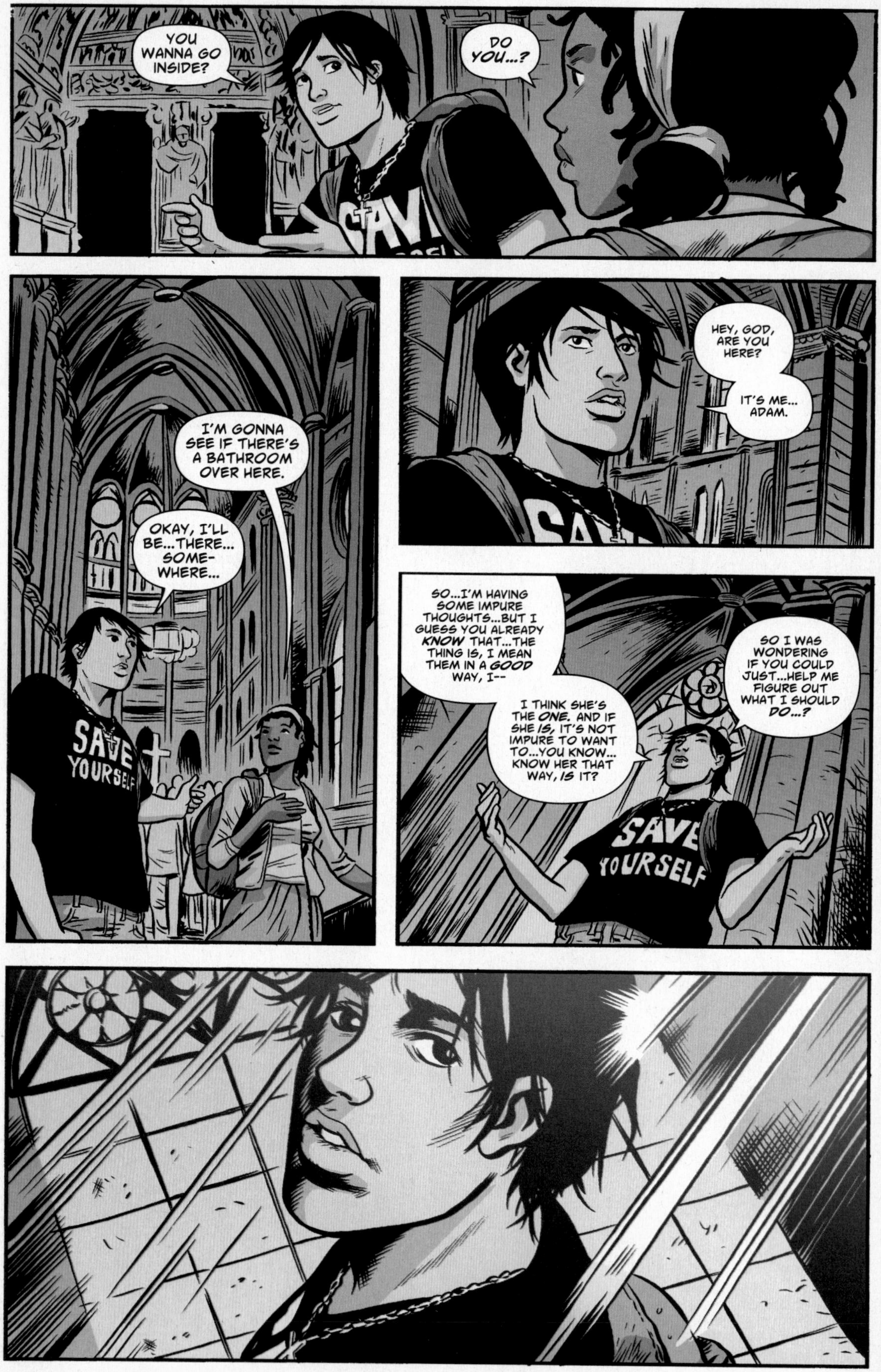
YOU WANNA GO INSIDE?
DO YOU...?
I'M GONNA SEE IF THERE'S A BATHROOM OVER HERE.
OKAY, I'LL BE...THERE... SOME-WHERE...
SAVE YOURSELF
HEY, GOD, ARE YOU HERE?
IT'S ME... ADAM.
SO...I'M HAVING SOME IMPURE THOUGHTS...BUT I GUESS YOU ALREADY KNOW THAT...THE THING IS, I MEAN THEM IN A GOOD WAY, I--
I THINK SHE'S THE ONE. AND IF SHE IS, IT'S NOT IMPURE TO WANT TO...YOU KNOW... KNOW HER THAT WAY, IS IT?
SO I WAS WONDERING IF YOU COULD JUST...HELP ME FIGURE OUT WHAT I SHOULD DO...?
SAVE YOURSELF

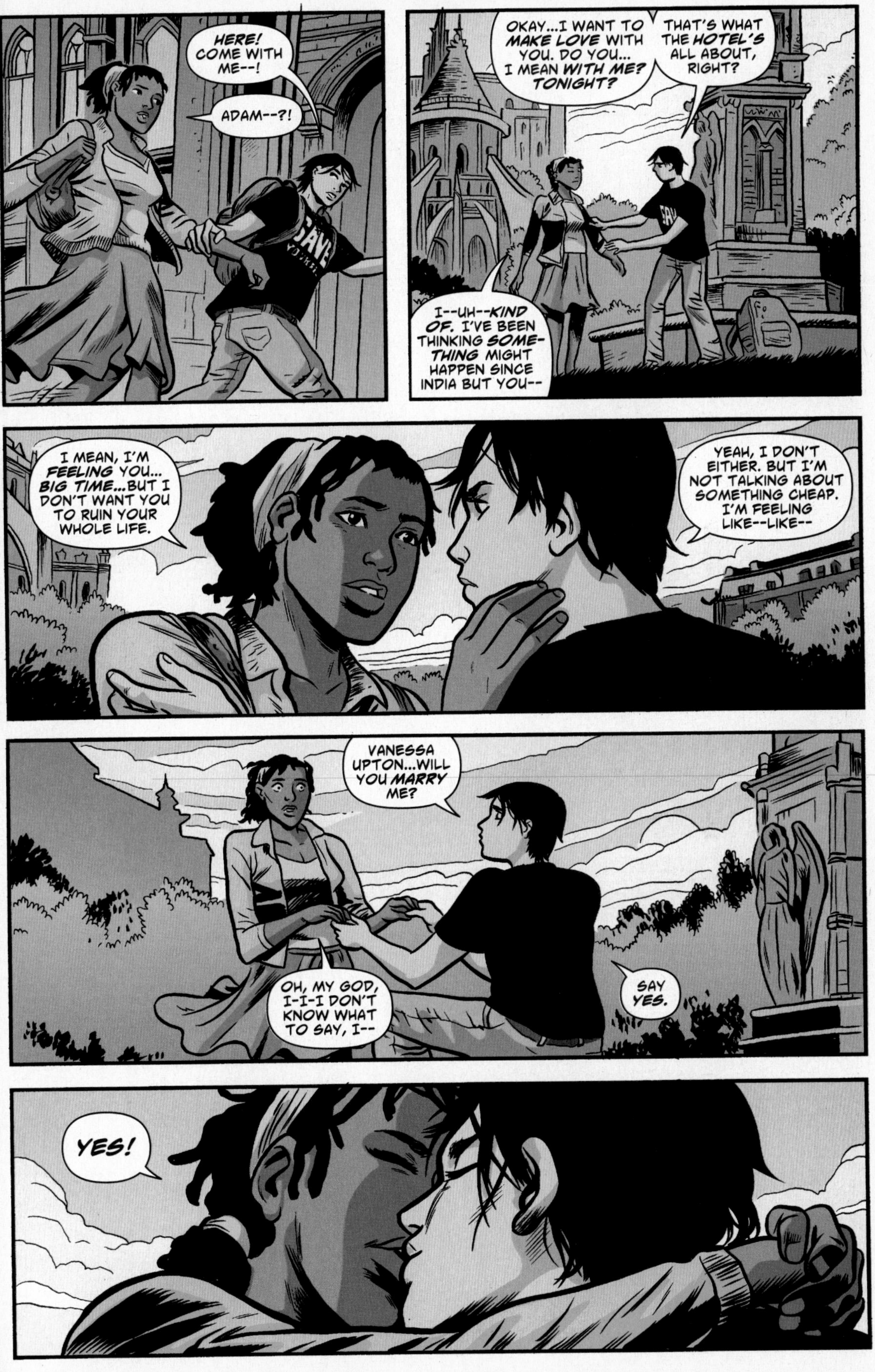
HERE! COME WITH ME--!
ADAM--?!
OKAY...I WANT TO MAKE LOVE WITH YOU. DO YOU... I MEAN WITH ME? TONIGHT?
THAT'S WHAT THE HOTEL'S ALL ABOUT, RIGHT?
I--UH--KIND OF. I'VE BEEN THINKING SOMETHING MIGHT HAPPEN SINCE INDIA BUT YOU--
I MEAN, I'M FEELING YOU... BIG TIME...BUT I DON'T WANT YOU TO RUIN YOUR WHOLE LIFE.
YEAH, I DON'T EITHER. BUT I'M NOT TALKING ABOUT SOMETHING CHEAP. I'M FEELING LIKE--LIKE--
VANESSA UPTON...WILL YOU MARRY ME?
OH, MY GOD, I-I-I DON'T KNOW WHAT TO SAY, I--
SAY YES.
YES!

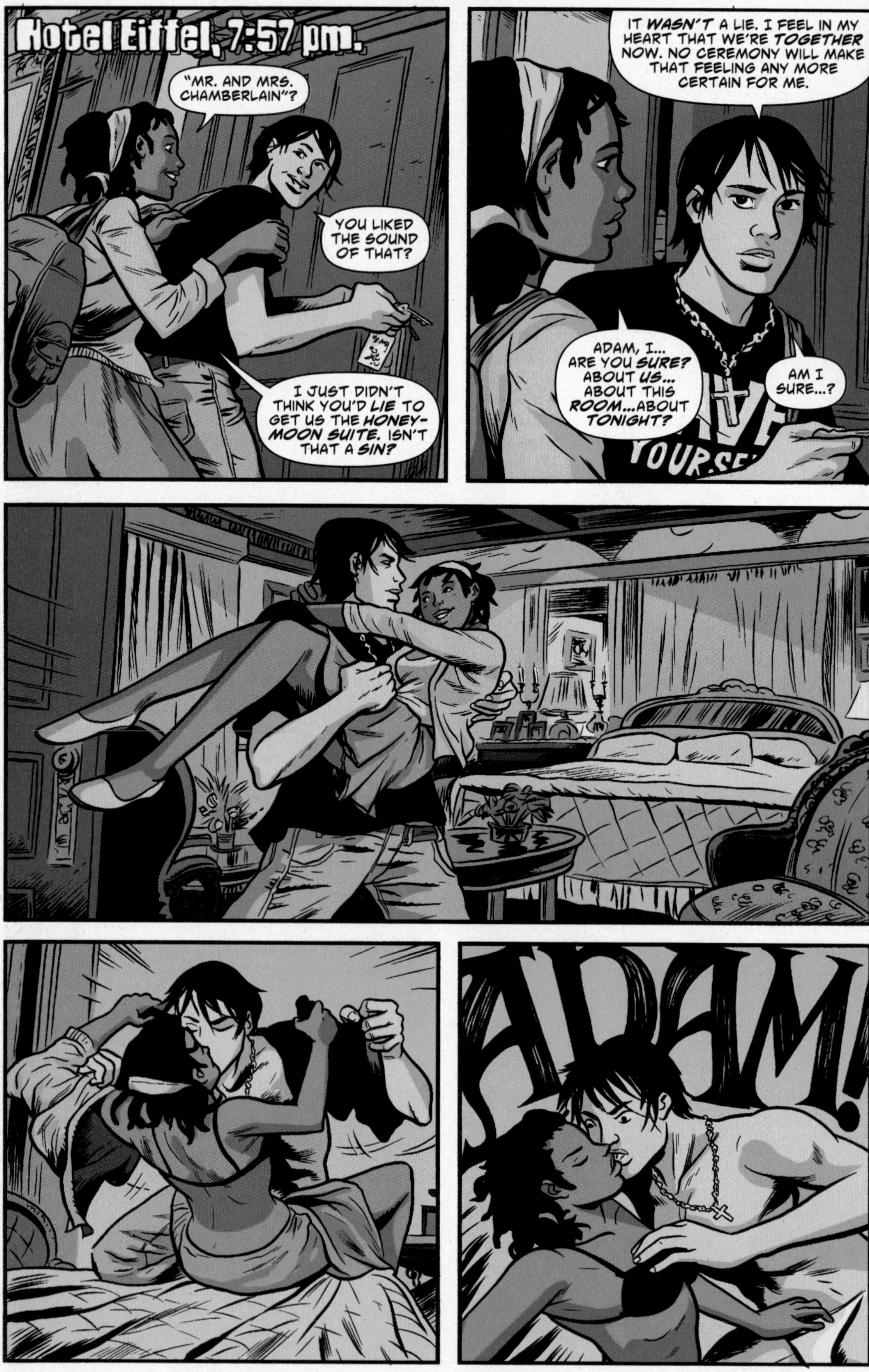
Hotel Eiffel, 7:57 pm.
"MR. AND MRS. CHAMBERLAIN"?
YOU LIKED THE SOUND OF THAT?
I JUST DIDN'T THINK YOU'D LIE TO GET US THE HONEY-MOON SUITE. ISN'T THAT A SIN?
IT WASN'T A LIE. I FEEL IN MY HEART THAT WE'RE TOGETHER NOW. NO CEREMONY WILL MAKE THAT FEELING ANY MORE CERTAIN FOR ME.
ADAM, I... ARE YOU SURE? ABOUT US... ABOUT THIS ROOM...ABOUT TONIGHT?
AM I SURE...?
YOURSE
ADAM!

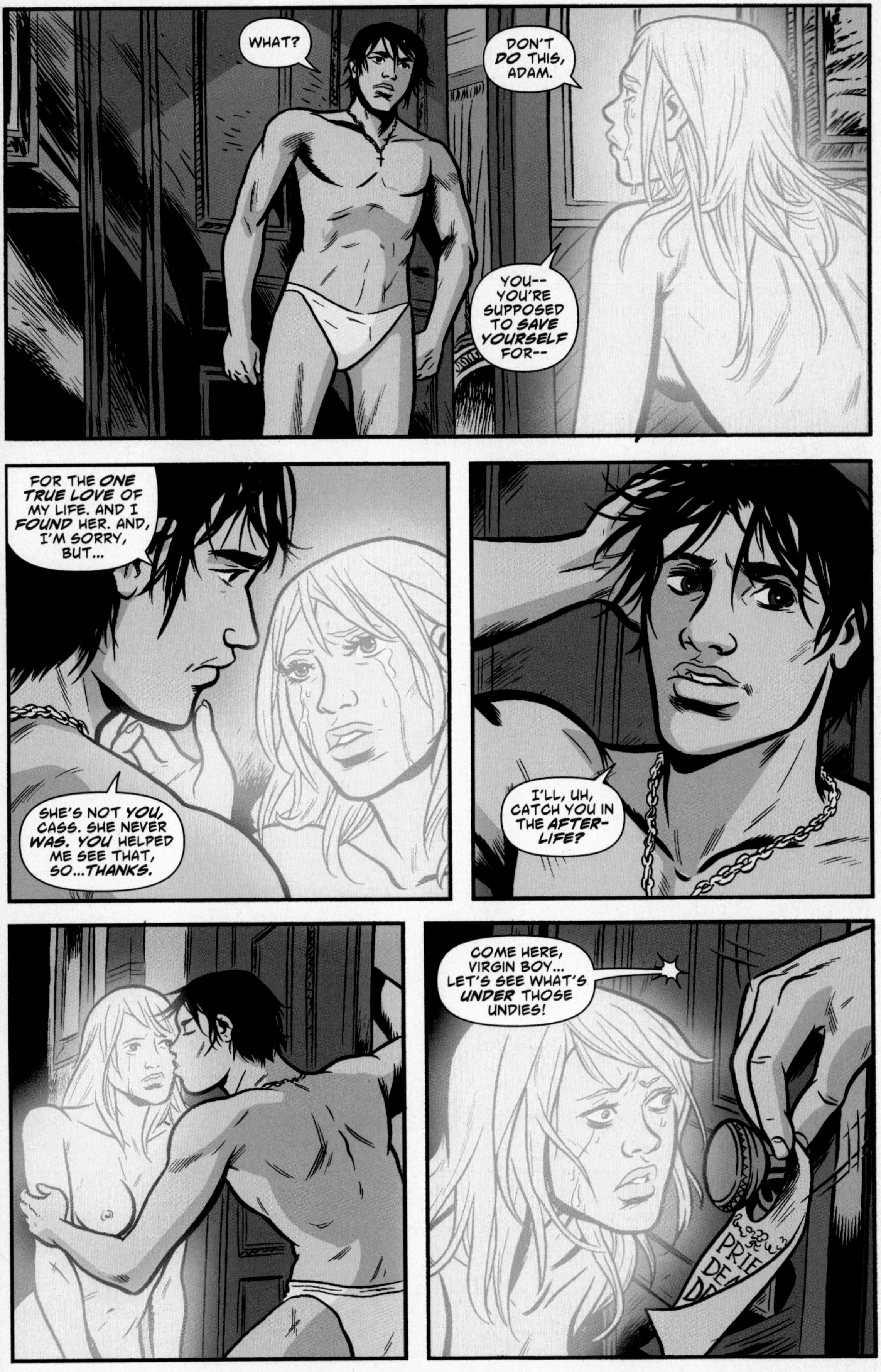

WHAT?
DON'T DO THIS, ADAM.
YOU-- YOU'RE SUPPOSED TO SAVE YOURSELF FOR--
FOR THE ONE TRUE LOVE OF MY LIFE. AND I FOUND HER. AND, I'M SORRY, BUT...
SHE'S NOT YOU, CASS. SHE NEVER WAS. YOU HELPED ME SEE THAT, SO...THANKS.
I'LL, UH, CATCH YOU IN THE AFTER-LIFE?
COME HERE, VIRGIN BOY... LET'S SEE WHAT'S UNDER THOSE UNDIES!

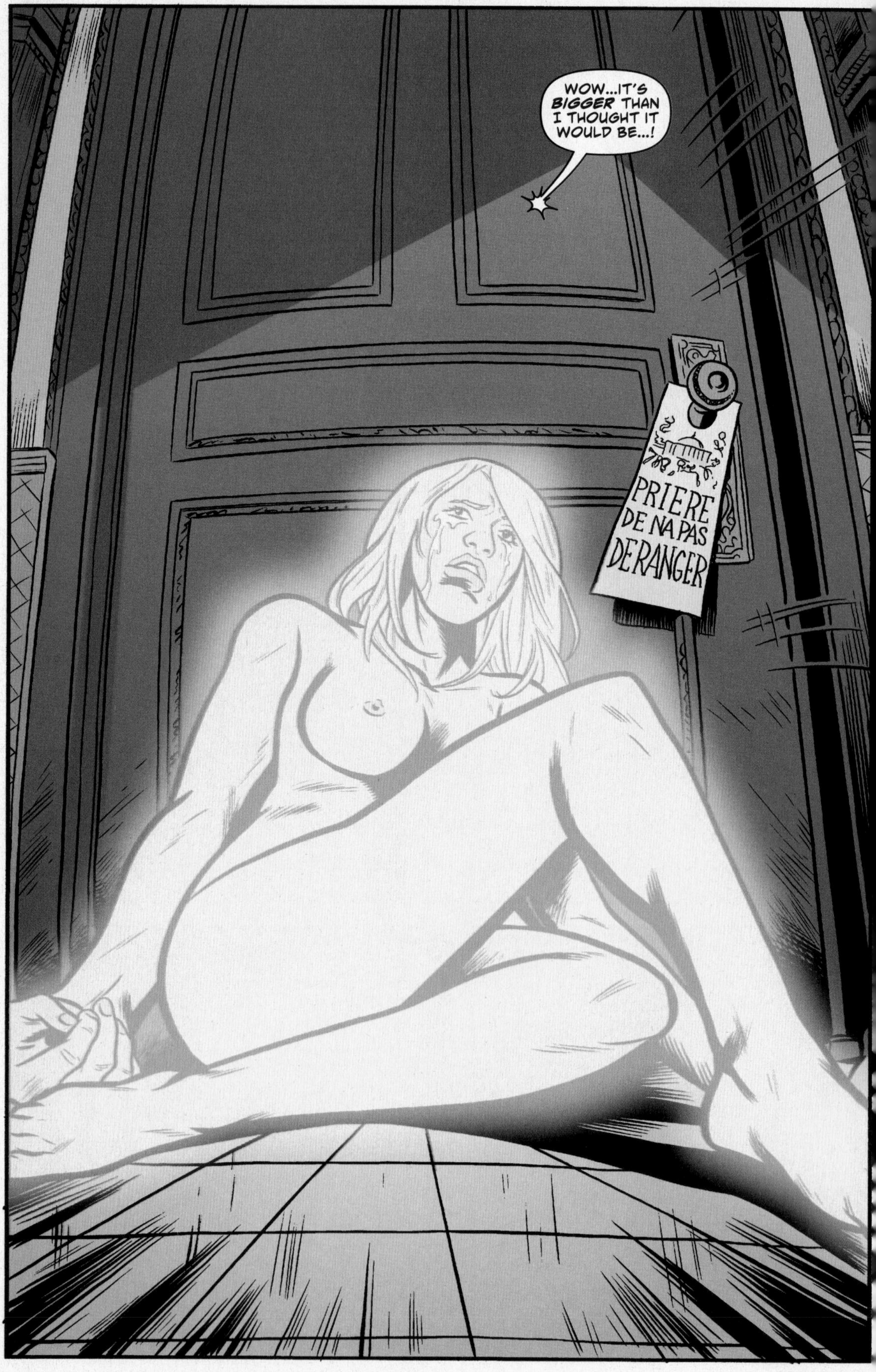
WOW...IT'S *BIGGER* THAN I THOUGHT IT WOULD BE...!
PRIERE DE NA PAS DERANGER

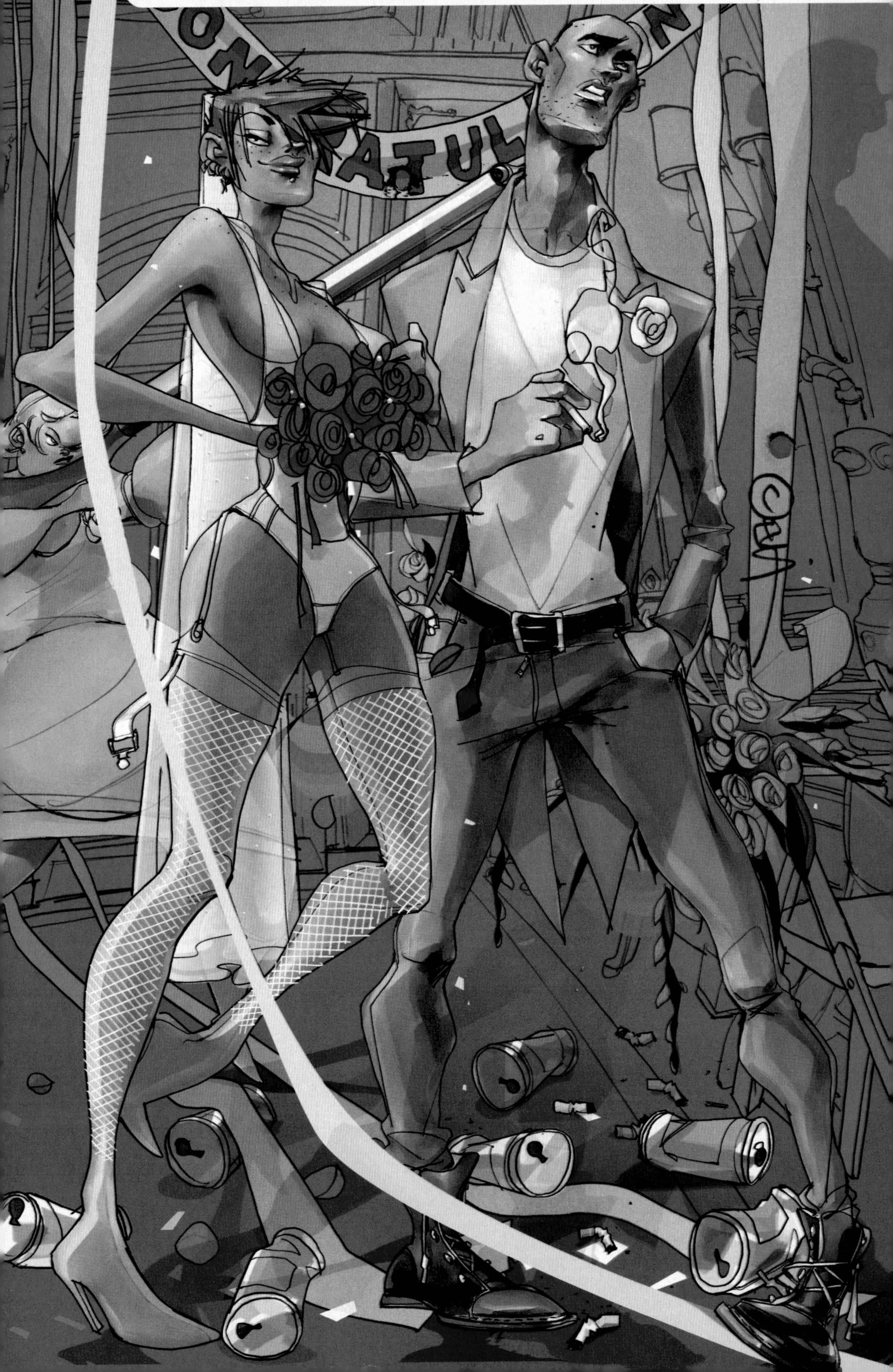

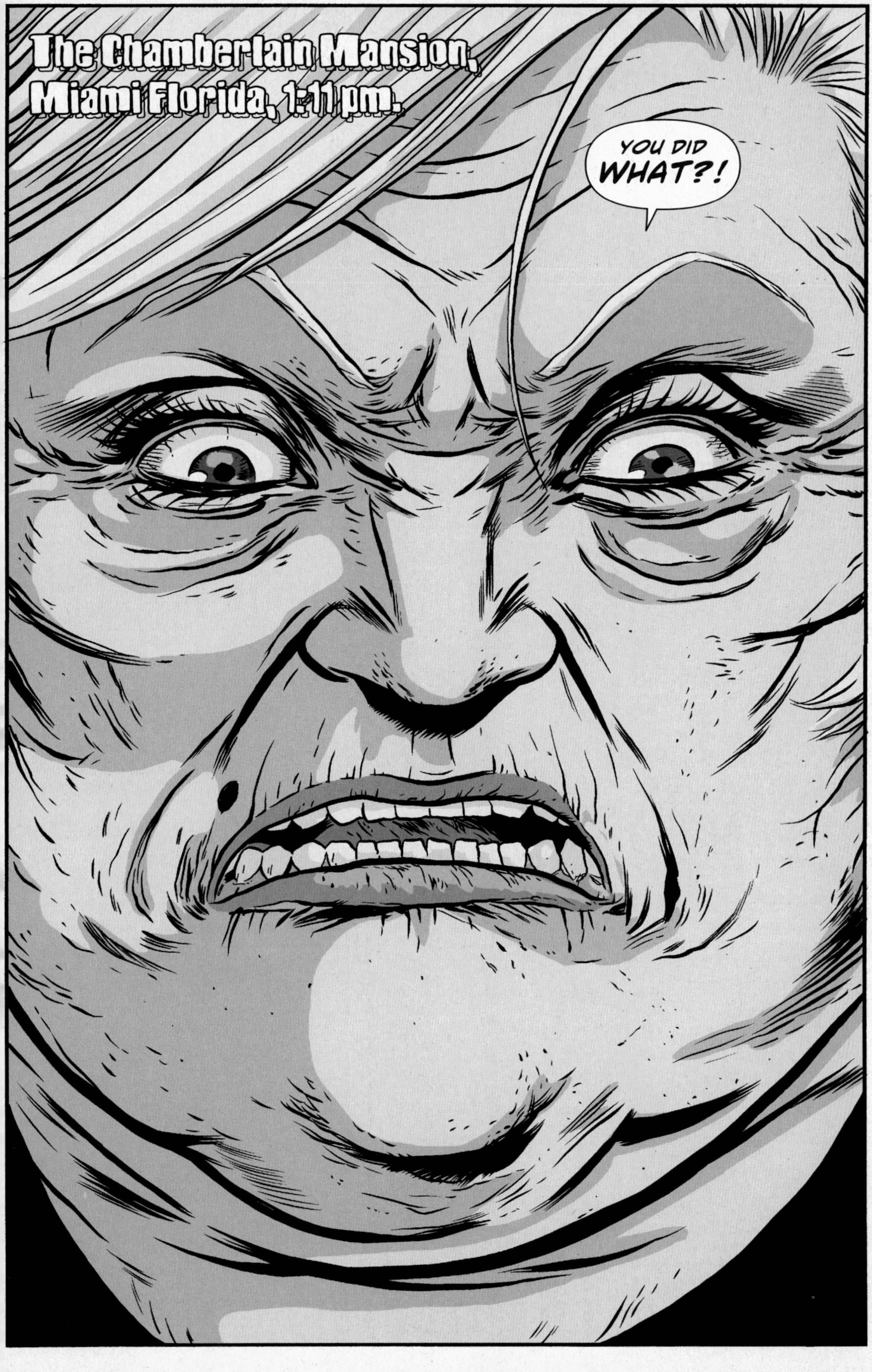
The Chamberlain Mansion, Miami Florida, 1:11 pm.
YOU DID WHAT?!

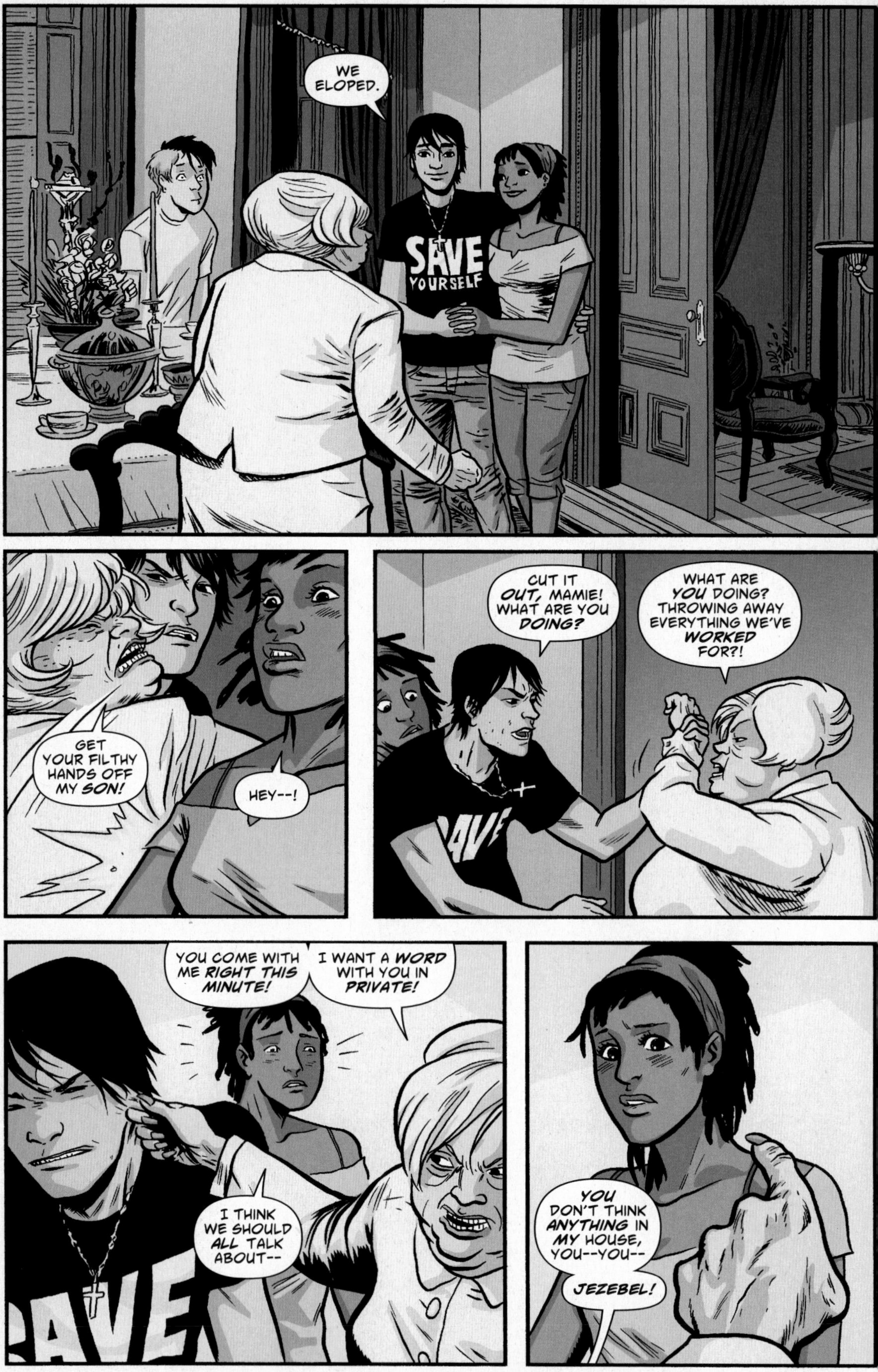
WE ELOPED.
SAVE YOURSELF
GET YOUR FILTHY HANDS OFF MY SON!
HEY--!
CUT IT OUT, MAMIE! WHAT ARE YOU DOING?
WHAT ARE YOU DOING? THROWING AWAY EVERYTHING WE'VE WORKED FOR?!
YOU COME WITH ME RIGHT THIS MINUTE!
I WANT A WORD WITH YOU IN PRIVATE!
I THINK WE SHOULD ALL TALK ABOUT--
YOU DON'T THINK ANYTHING IN MY HOUSE, YOU--YOU--
JEZEBEL!

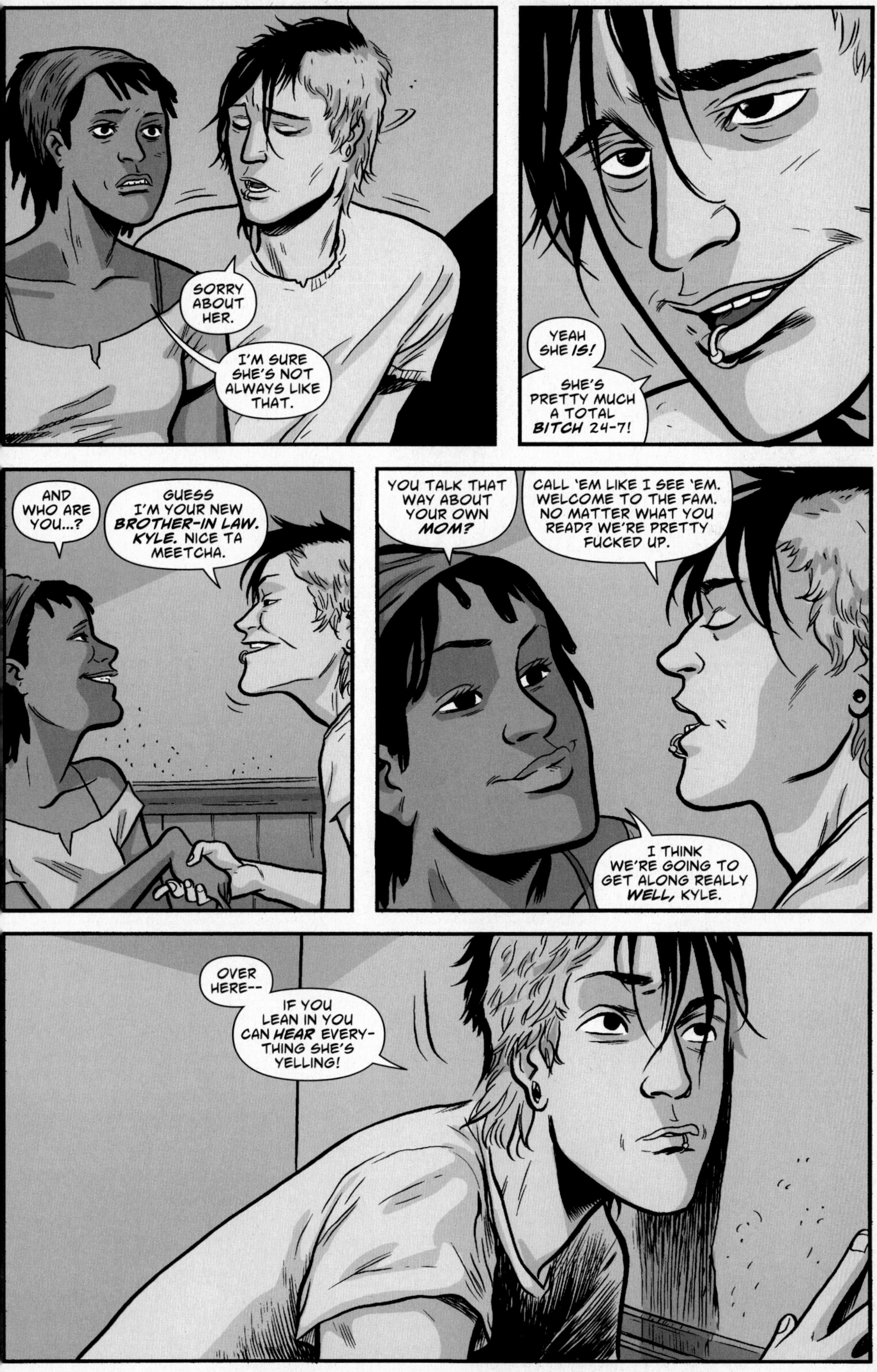
SORRY ABOUT HER.
I'M SURE SHE'S NOT ALWAYS LIKE THAT.
YEAH SHE IS!
SHE'S PRETTY MUCH A TOTAL BITCH 24-7!
AND WHO ARE YOU...?
GUESS I'M YOUR NEW BROTHER-IN LAW. KYLE. NICE TA MEETCHA.
YOU TALK THAT WAY ABOUT YOUR OWN MOM?
CALL 'EM LIKE I SEE 'EM. WELCOME TO THE FAM. NO MATTER WHAT YOU READ? WE'RE PRETTY FUCKED UP.
I THINK WE'RE GOING TO GET ALONG REALLY WELL, KYLE.
OVER HERE--
IF YOU LEAN IN YOU CAN HEAR EVERY-THING SHE'S YELLING!

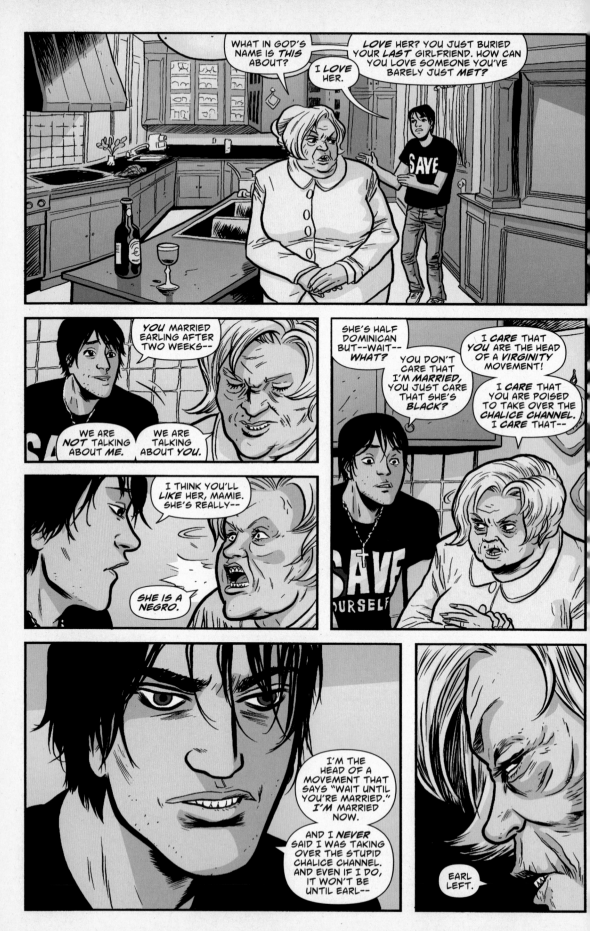

WHAT IN GOD'S NAME IS *THIS* ABOUT?

I *LOVE* HER.

LOVE HER? YOU JUST BURIED YOUR *LAST* GIRLFRIEND. HOW CAN YOU LOVE SOMEONE YOU'VE BARELY JUST *MET*?

YOU MARRIED EARLING AFTER TWO WEEKS--

WE ARE *NOT* TALKING ABOUT *ME*.

WE ARE TALKING ABOUT *YOU*.

SHE'S HALF DOMINICAN BUT--WAIT-- *WHAT*?

YOU DON'T CARE THAT I'M *MARRIED*, YOU JUST CARE THAT SHE'S *BLACK*?

I *CARE* THAT *YOU* ARE THE HEAD OF A *VIRGINITY* MOVEMENT!

I *CARE* THAT YOU ARE POISED TO TAKE OVER THE *CHALICE CHANNEL*. I *CARE* THAT--

I THINK YOU'LL *LIKE* HER, MAMIE. SHE'S REALLY--

SHE IS A NEGRO.

I'M THE HEAD OF A MOVEMENT THAT SAYS "WAIT UNTIL YOU'RE MARRIED." I'M MARRIED NOW.

AND I *NEVER* SAID I WAS TAKING OVER THE STUPID CHALICE CHANNEL. AND EVEN IF I DO, IT WON'T BE UNTIL EARL--

EARL LEFT.

SAVE

SAVE OURSELF

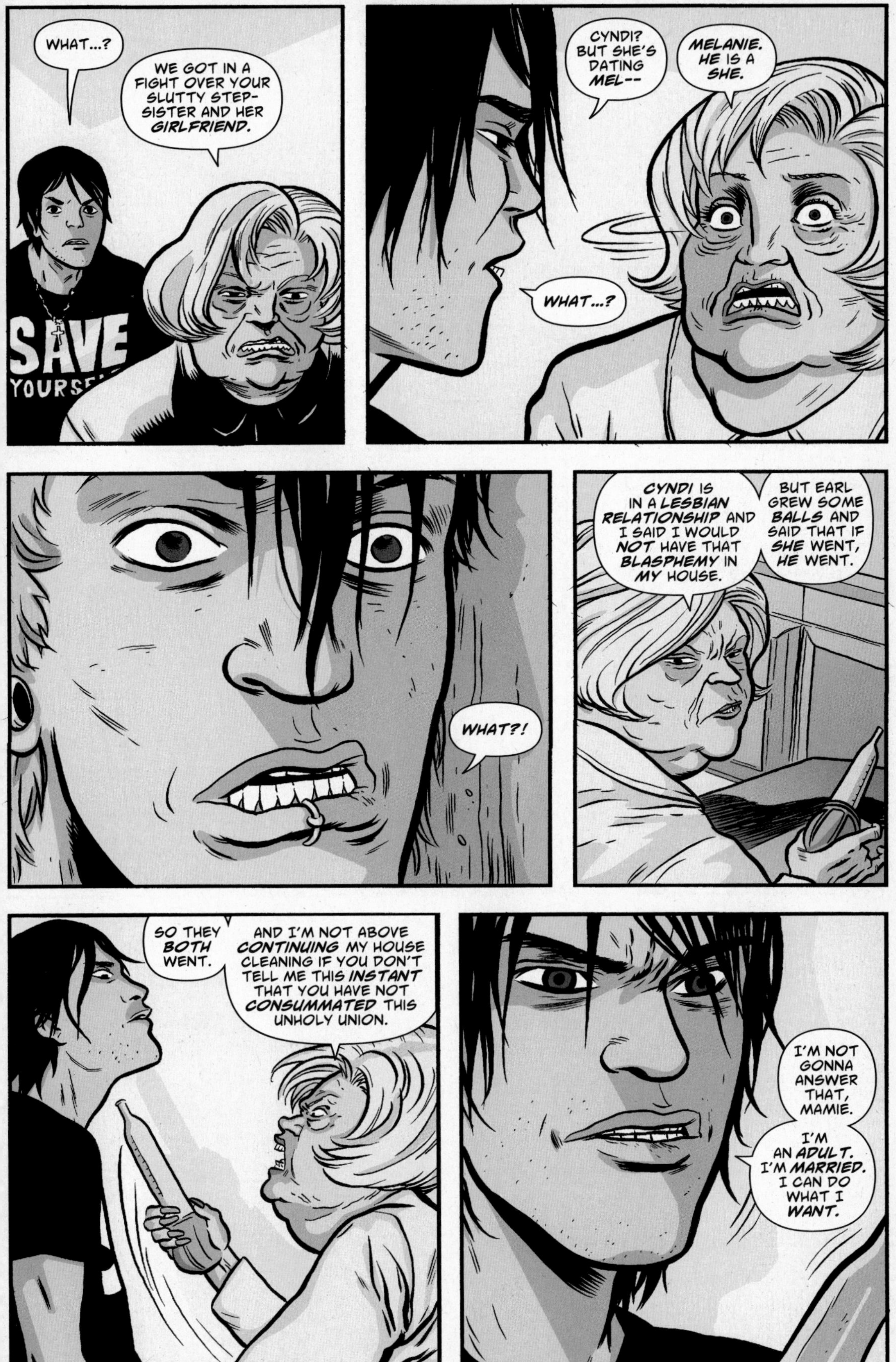
WHAT...?
WE GOT IN A FIGHT OVER YOUR SLUTTY STEP-SISTER AND HER GIRLFRIEND.
SAVE YOURSE
CYNDI? BUT SHE'S DATING MEL--
MELANIE. HE IS A SHE.
WHAT...?
WHAT?!
CYNDI IS IN A LESBIAN RELATIONSHIP AND I SAID I WOULD NOT HAVE THAT BLASPHEMY IN MY HOUSE.
BUT EARL GREW SOME BALLS AND SAID THAT IF SHE WENT, HE WENT.
SO THEY BOTH WENT.
AND I'M NOT ABOVE CONTINUING MY HOUSE CLEANING IF YOU DON'T TELL ME THIS INSTANT THAT YOU HAVE NOT CONSUMMATED THIS UNHOLY UNION.
I'M NOT GONNA ANSWER THAT, MAMIE.
I'M AN ADULT. I'M MARRIED. I CAN DO WHAT I WANT.

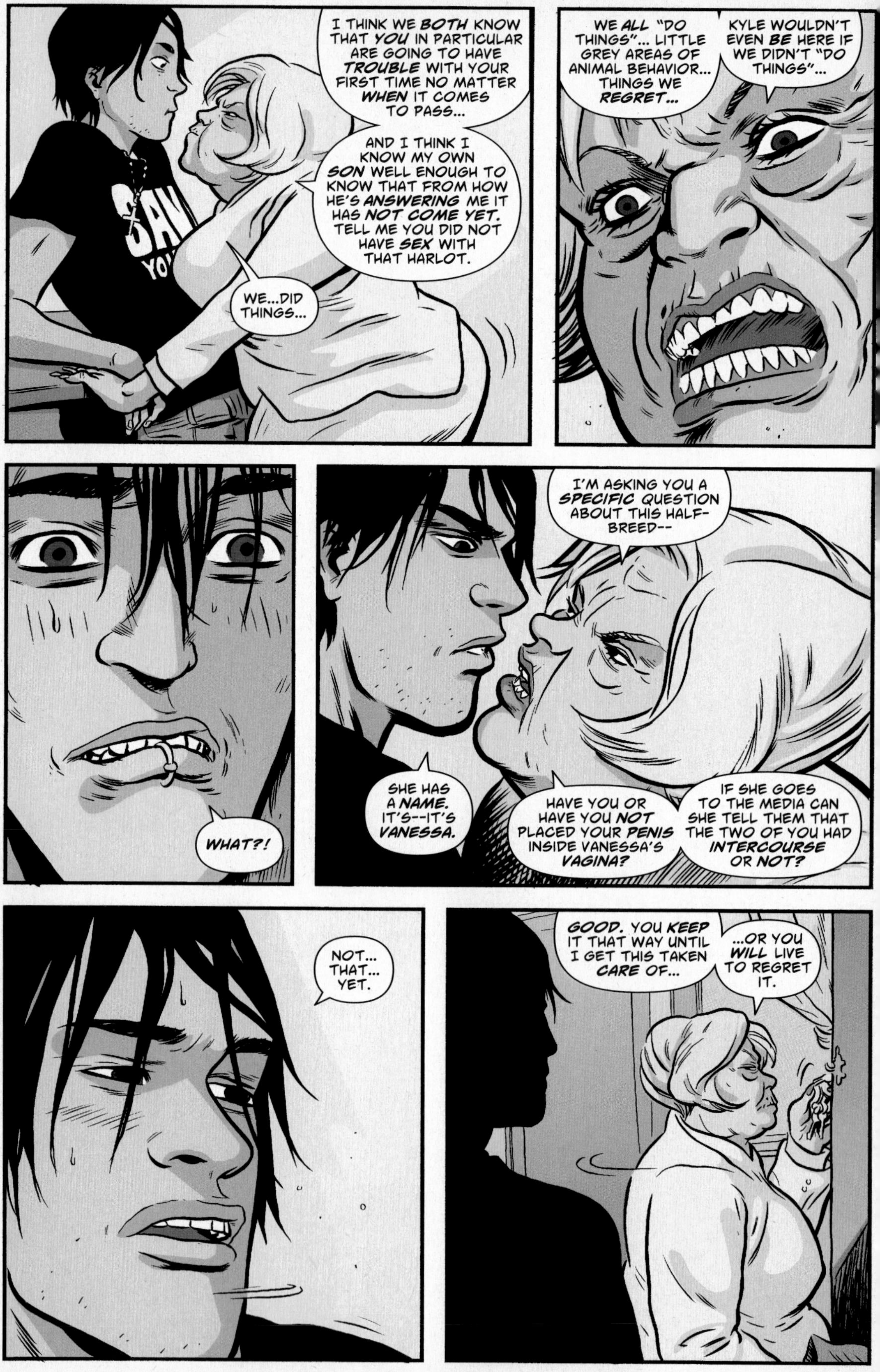
I THINK WE BOTH KNOW THAT YOU IN PARTICULAR ARE GOING TO HAVE TROUBLE WITH YOUR FIRST TIME NO MATTER WHEN IT COMES TO PASS...
AND I THINK I KNOW MY OWN SON WELL ENOUGH TO KNOW THAT FROM HOW HE'S ANSWERING ME IT HAS NOT COME YET. TELL ME YOU DID NOT HAVE SEX WITH THAT HARLOT.
WE...DID THINGS...
WE ALL "DO THINGS"... LITTLE GREY AREAS OF ANIMAL BEHAVIOR... THINGS WE REGRET...
KYLE WOULDN'T EVEN BE HERE IF WE DIDN'T "DO THINGS"...
WHAT?!
I'M ASKING YOU A SPECIFIC QUESTION ABOUT THIS HALF-BREED--
SHE HAS A NAME. IT'S--IT'S VANESSA.
HAVE YOU OR HAVE YOU NOT PLACED YOUR PENIS INSIDE VANESSA'S VAGINA?
IF SHE GOES TO THE MEDIA CAN SHE TELL THEM THAT THE TWO OF YOU HAD INTERCOURSE OR NOT?
NOT... THAT... YET.
GOOD. YOU KEEP IT THAT WAY UNTIL I GET THIS TAKEN CARE OF...
...OR YOU WILL LIVE TO REGRET IT.

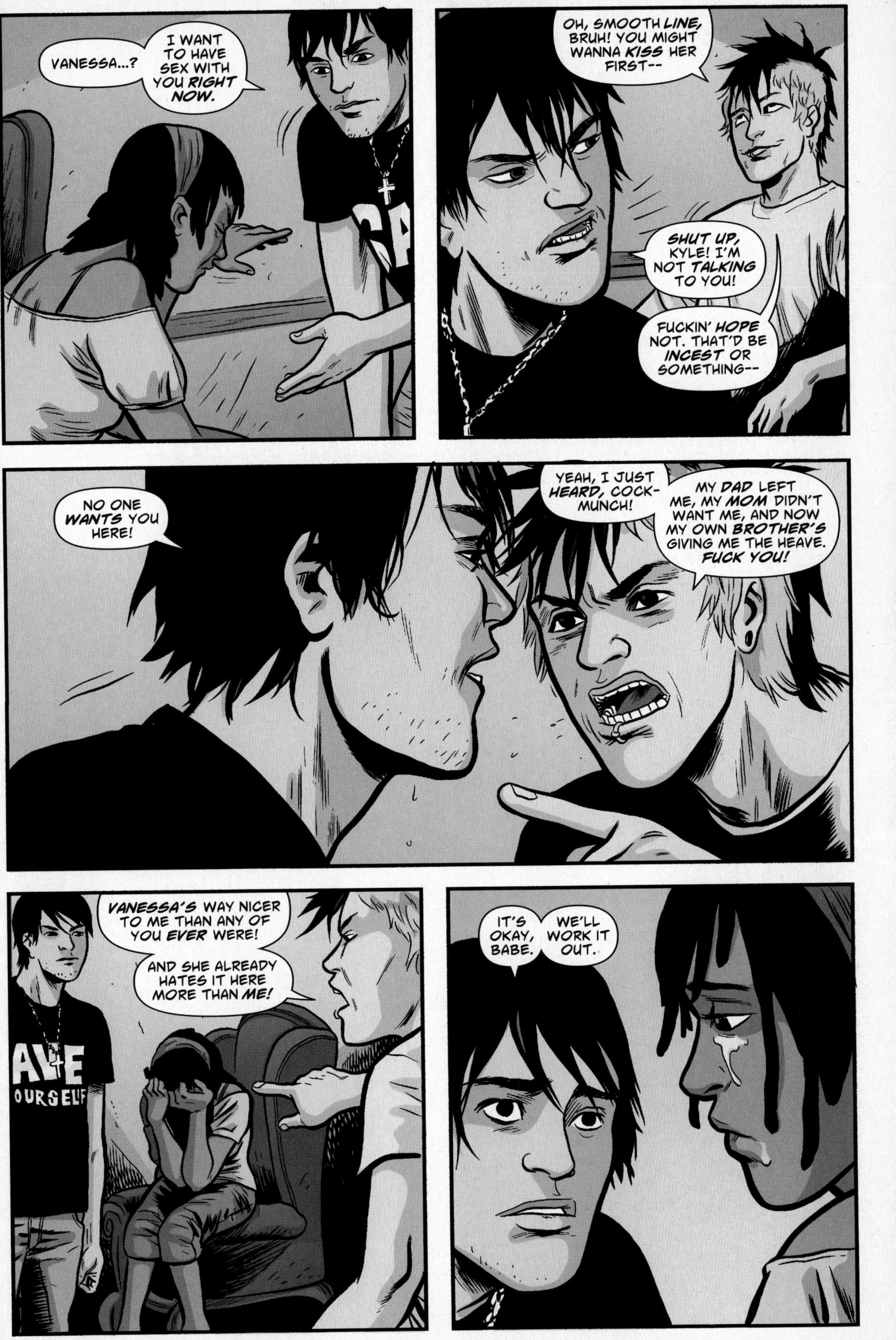
VANESSA...?
I WANT TO HAVE SEX WITH YOU RIGHT NOW.
OH, SMOOTH LINE, BRUH! YOU MIGHT WANNA KISS HER FIRST--
SHUT UP, KYLE! I'M NOT TALKING TO YOU!
FUCKIN' HOPE NOT. THAT'D BE INCEST OR SOMETHING--
NO ONE WANTS YOU HERE!
YEAH, I JUST HEARD, COCK-MUNCH!
MY DAD LEFT ME, MY MOM DIDN'T WANT ME, AND NOW MY OWN BROTHER'S GIVING ME THE HEAVE. FUCK YOU!
VANESSA'S WAY NICER TO ME THAN ANY OF YOU EVER WERE!
AND SHE ALREADY HATES IT HERE MORE THAN ME!
AVE OURSELF
IT'S OKAY, BABE.
WE'LL WORK IT OUT.

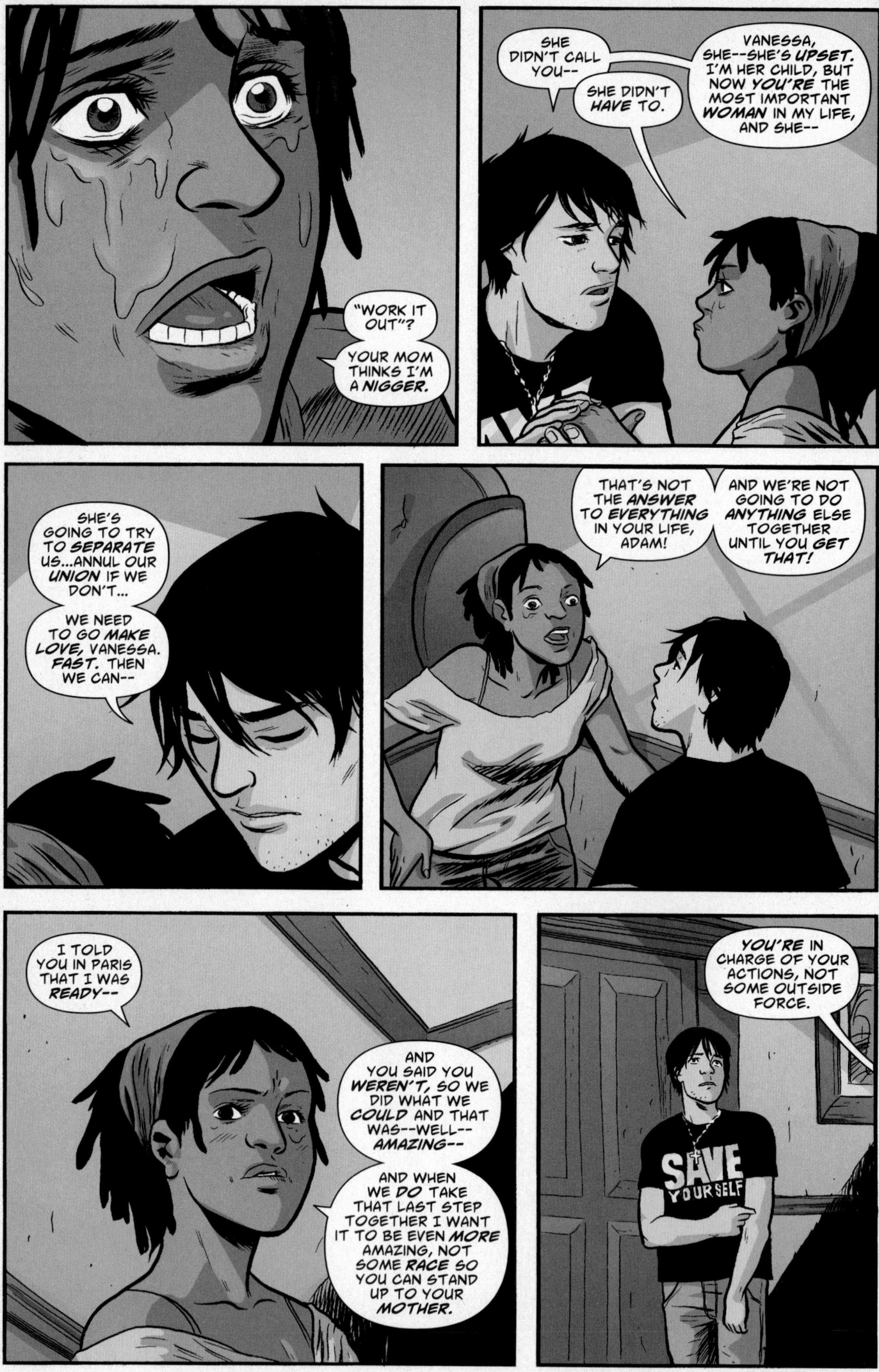
"WORK IT OUT"?
YOUR MOM THINKS I'M A NIGGER.
SHE DIDN'T CALL YOU--
SHE DIDN'T HAVE TO.
VANESSA, SHE--SHE'S UPSET. I'M HER CHILD, BUT NOW YOU'RE THE MOST IMPORTANT WOMAN IN MY LIFE, AND SHE--
SHE'S GOING TO TRY TO SEPARATE US...ANNUL OUR UNION IF WE DON'T...
WE NEED TO GO MAKE LOVE, VANESSA. FAST. THEN WE CAN--
THAT'S NOT THE ANSWER TO EVERYTHING IN YOUR LIFE, ADAM!
AND WE'RE NOT GOING TO DO ANYTHING ELSE TOGETHER UNTIL YOU GET THAT!
I TOLD YOU IN PARIS THAT I WAS READY--
AND YOU SAID YOU WEREN'T, SO WE DID WHAT WE COULD AND THAT WAS--WELL--AMAZING--
AND WHEN WE DO TAKE THAT LAST STEP TOGETHER I WANT IT TO BE EVEN MORE AMAZING, NOT SOME RACE SO YOU CAN STAND UP TO YOUR MOTHER.
YOU'RE IN CHARGE OF YOUR ACTIONS, NOT SOME OUTSIDE FORCE.
SAVE YOURSELF

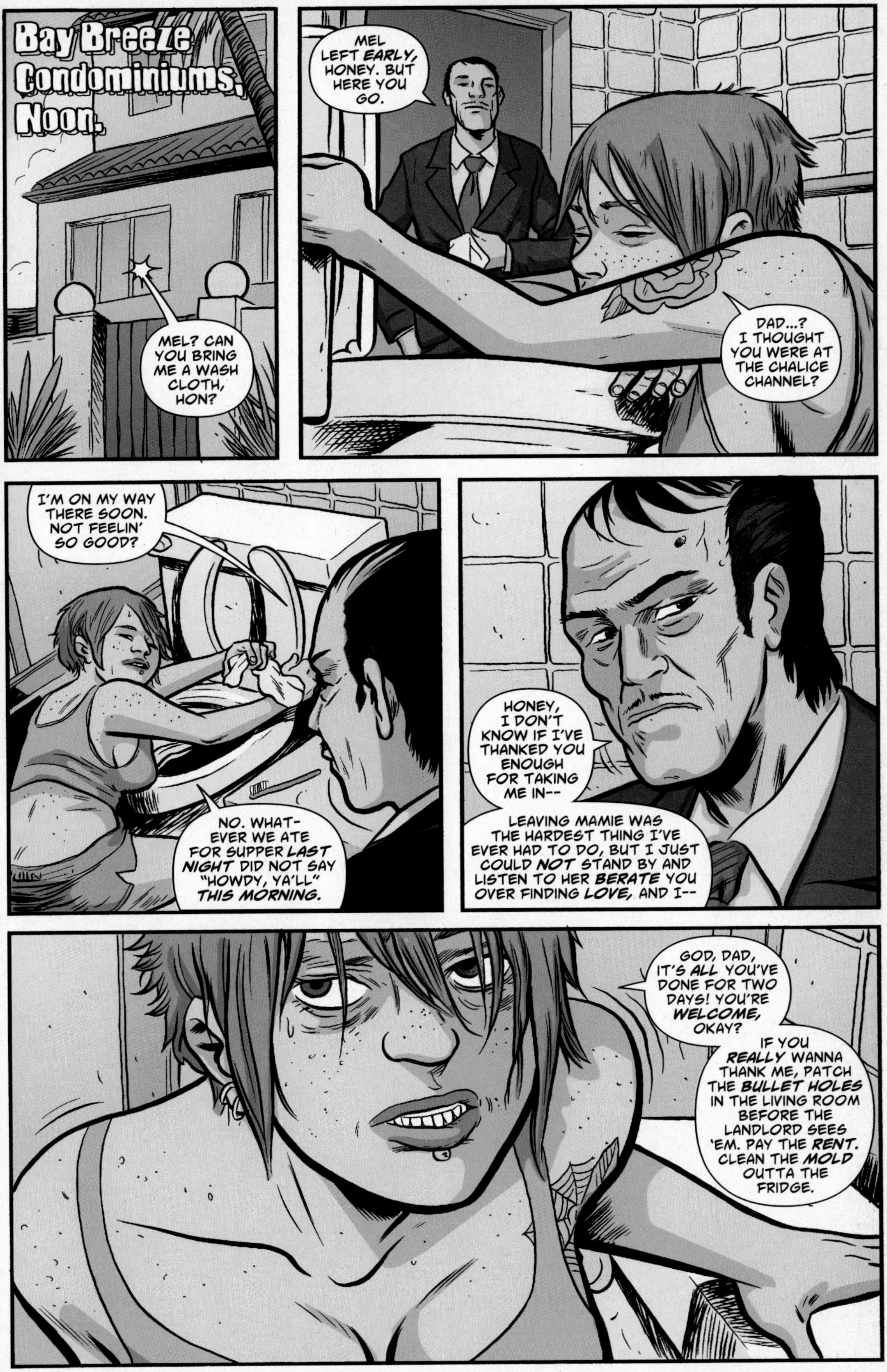
Bay Breeze Condominiums, Noon.
MEL? CAN YOU BRING ME A WASH CLOTH, HON?
MEL LEFT EARLY, HONEY. BUT HERE YOU GO.
DAD...? I THOUGHT YOU WERE AT THE CHALICE CHANNEL?
I'M ON MY WAY THERE SOON. NOT FEELIN' SO GOOD?
NO. WHATEVER WE ATE FOR SUPPER LAST NIGHT DID NOT SAY "HOWDY, YA'LL" THIS MORNING.
HONEY, I DON'T KNOW IF I'VE THANKED YOU ENOUGH FOR TAKING ME IN--
LEAVING MAMIE WAS THE HARDEST THING I'VE EVER HAD TO DO, BUT I JUST COULD NOT STAND BY AND LISTEN TO HER BERATE YOU OVER FINDING LOVE, AND I--
GOD, DAD, IT'S ALL YOU'VE DONE FOR TWO DAYS! YOU'RE WELCOME, OKAY?
IF YOU REALLY WANNA THANK ME, PATCH THE BULLET HOLES IN THE LIVING ROOM BEFORE THE LANDLORD SEES 'EM. PAY THE RENT. CLEAN THE MOLD OUTTA THE FRIDGE.

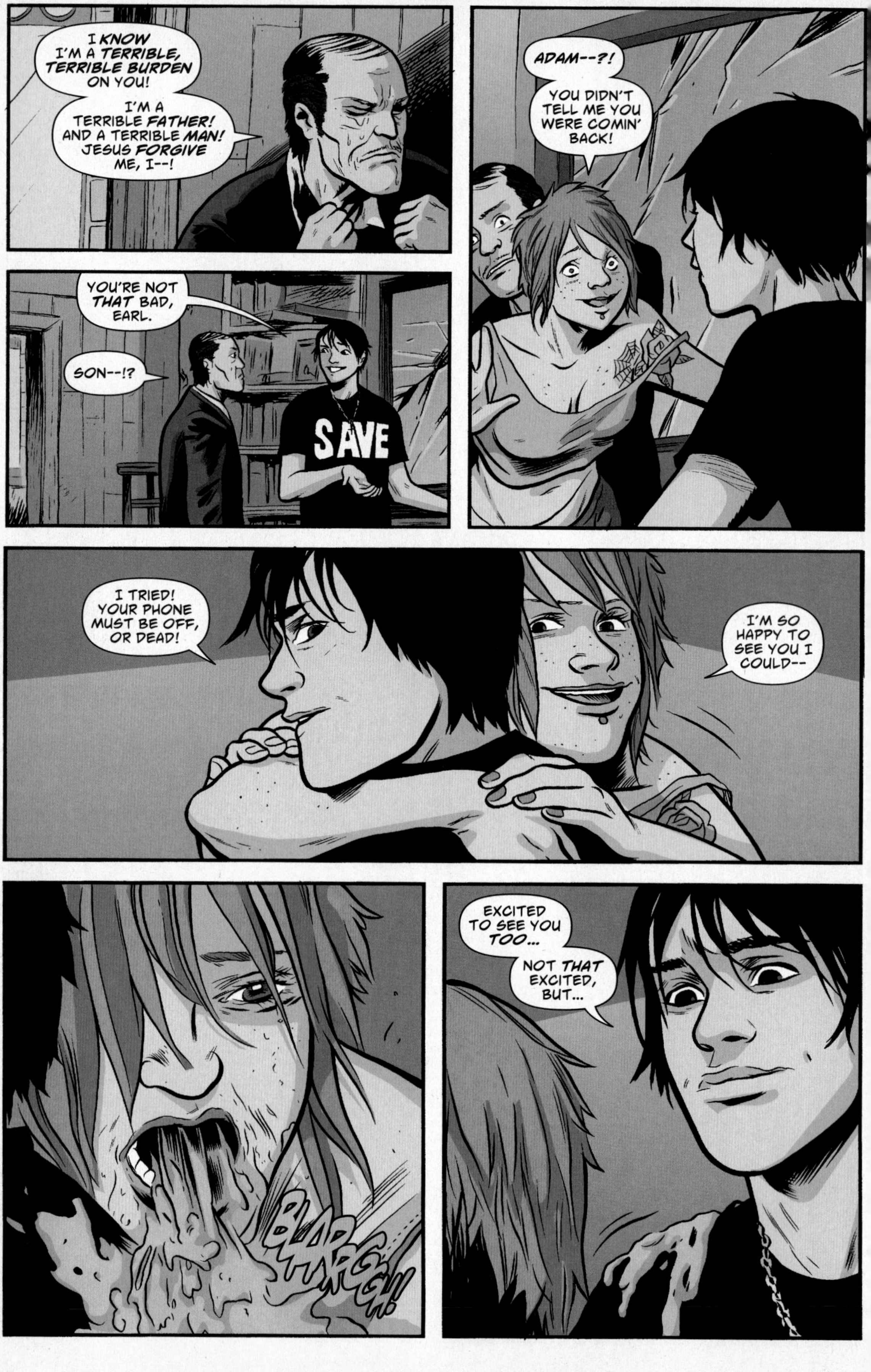
I KNOW I'M A TERRIBLE, TERRIBLE BURDEN ON YOU!
I'M A TERRIBLE FATHER! AND A TERRIBLE MAN! JESUS FORGIVE ME, I--!
ADAM--?!
YOU DIDN'T TELL ME YOU WERE COMIN' BACK!
YOU'RE NOT THAT BAD, EARL.
SON--!?
SAVE
I TRIED! YOUR PHONE MUST BE OFF, OR DEAD!
I'M SO HAPPY TO SEE YOU I COULD--
BLARGGH!
EXCITED TO SEE YOU TOO...
NOT THAT EXCITED, BUT...

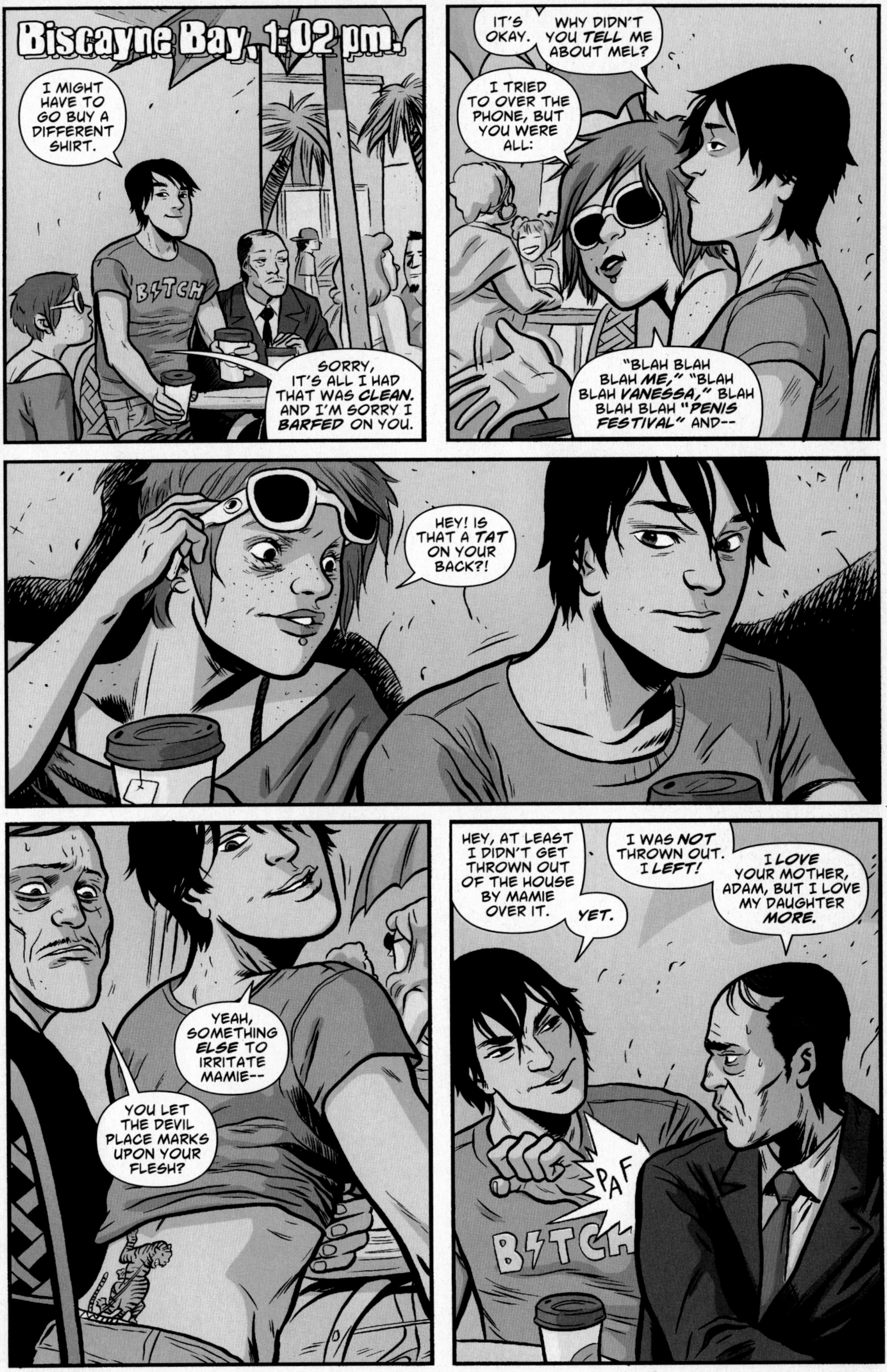
Biscayne Bay, 1:02 pm.
I MIGHT HAVE TO GO BUY A DIFFERENT SHIRT.
SORRY, IT'S ALL I HAD THAT WAS CLEAN. AND I'M SORRY I BARFED ON YOU.
IT'S OKAY.
WHY DIDN'T YOU TELL ME ABOUT MEL?
I TRIED TO OVER THE PHONE, BUT YOU WERE ALL:
"BLAH BLAH BLAH ME," "BLAH BLAH VANESSA," BLAH BLAH BLAH "PENIS FESTIVAL" AND--
HEY! IS THAT A TAT ON YOUR BACK?!
YEAH, SOMETHING ELSE TO IRRITATE MAMIE--
YOU LET THE DEVIL PLACE MARKS UPON YOUR FLESH?
HEY, AT LEAST I DIDN'T GET THROWN OUT OF THE HOUSE BY MAMIE OVER IT.
YET.
I WAS NOT THROWN OUT. I LEFT!
I LOVE YOUR MOTHER, ADAM, BUT I LOVE MY DAUGHTER MORE.
B/TCH
PAF

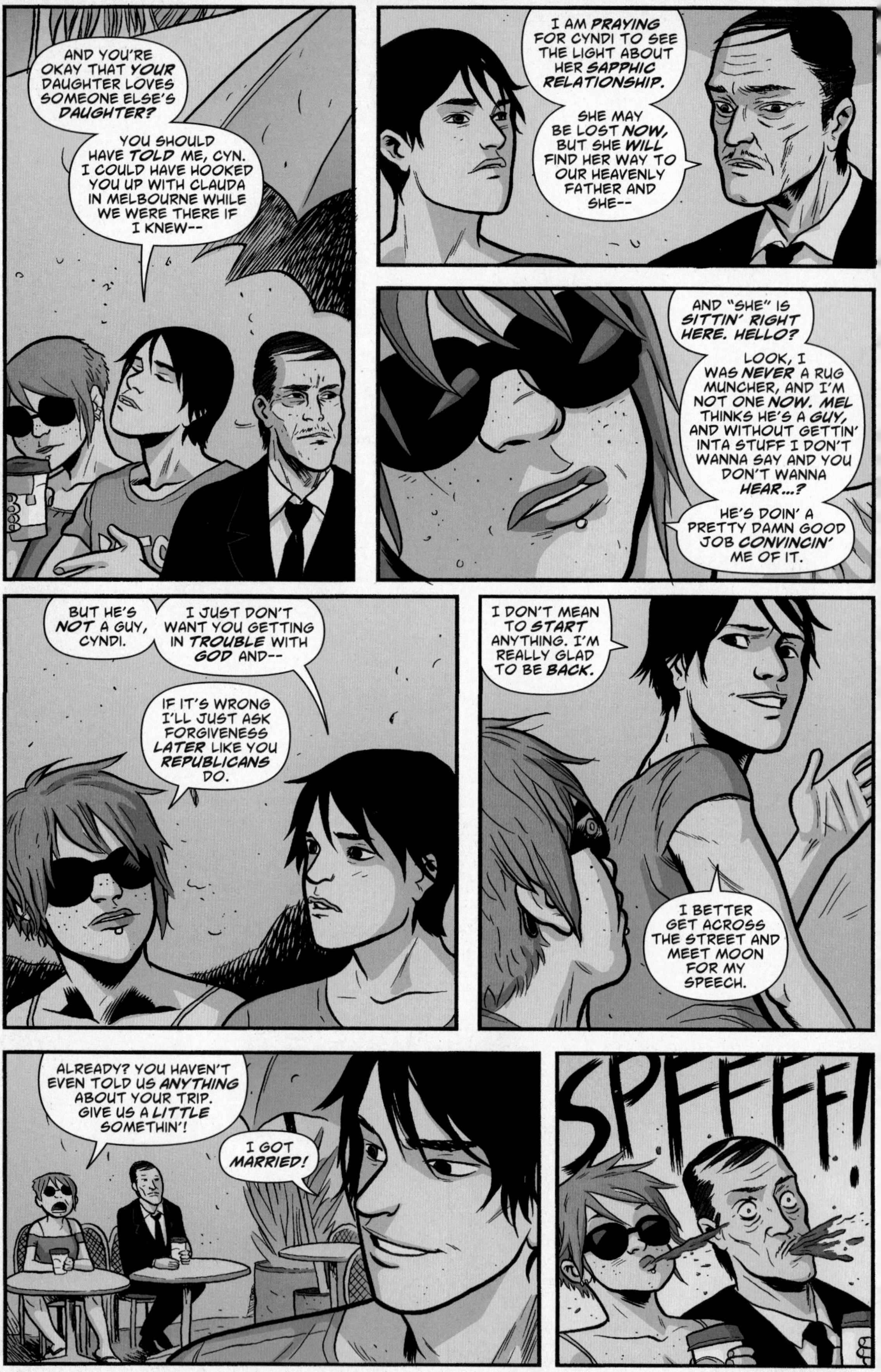
AND YOU'RE OKAY THAT YOUR DAUGHTER LOVES SOMEONE ELSE'S DAUGHTER?
YOU SHOULD HAVE TOLD ME, CYN. I COULD HAVE HOOKED YOU UP WITH CLAUDA IN MELBOURNE WHILE WE WERE THERE IF I KNEW--
I AM PRAYING FOR CYNDI TO SEE THE LIGHT ABOUT HER SAPPHIC RELATIONSHIP.
SHE MAY BE LOST NOW, BUT SHE WILL FIND HER WAY TO OUR HEAVENLY FATHER AND SHE--
AND "SHE" IS SITTIN' RIGHT HERE. HELLO?
LOOK, I WAS NEVER A RUG MUNCHER, AND I'M NOT ONE NOW. MEL THINKS HE'S A GUY, AND WITHOUT GETTIN' INTA STUFF I DON'T WANNA SAY AND YOU DON'T WANNA HEAR...?
HE'S DOIN' A PRETTY DAMN GOOD JOB CONVINCIN' ME OF IT.
BUT HE'S NOT A GUY, CYNDI.
I JUST DON'T WANT YOU GETTING IN TROUBLE WITH GOD AND--
IF IT'S WRONG I'LL JUST ASK FORGIVENESS LATER LIKE YOU REPUBLICANS DO.
I DON'T MEAN TO START ANYTHING. I'M REALLY GLAD TO BE BACK.
I BETTER GET ACROSS THE STREET AND MEET MOON FOR MY SPEECH.
ALREADY? YOU HAVEN'T EVEN TOLD US ANYTHING ABOUT YOUR TRIP. GIVE US A LITTLE SOMETHIN'!
I GOT MARRIED!
SPFFFF!

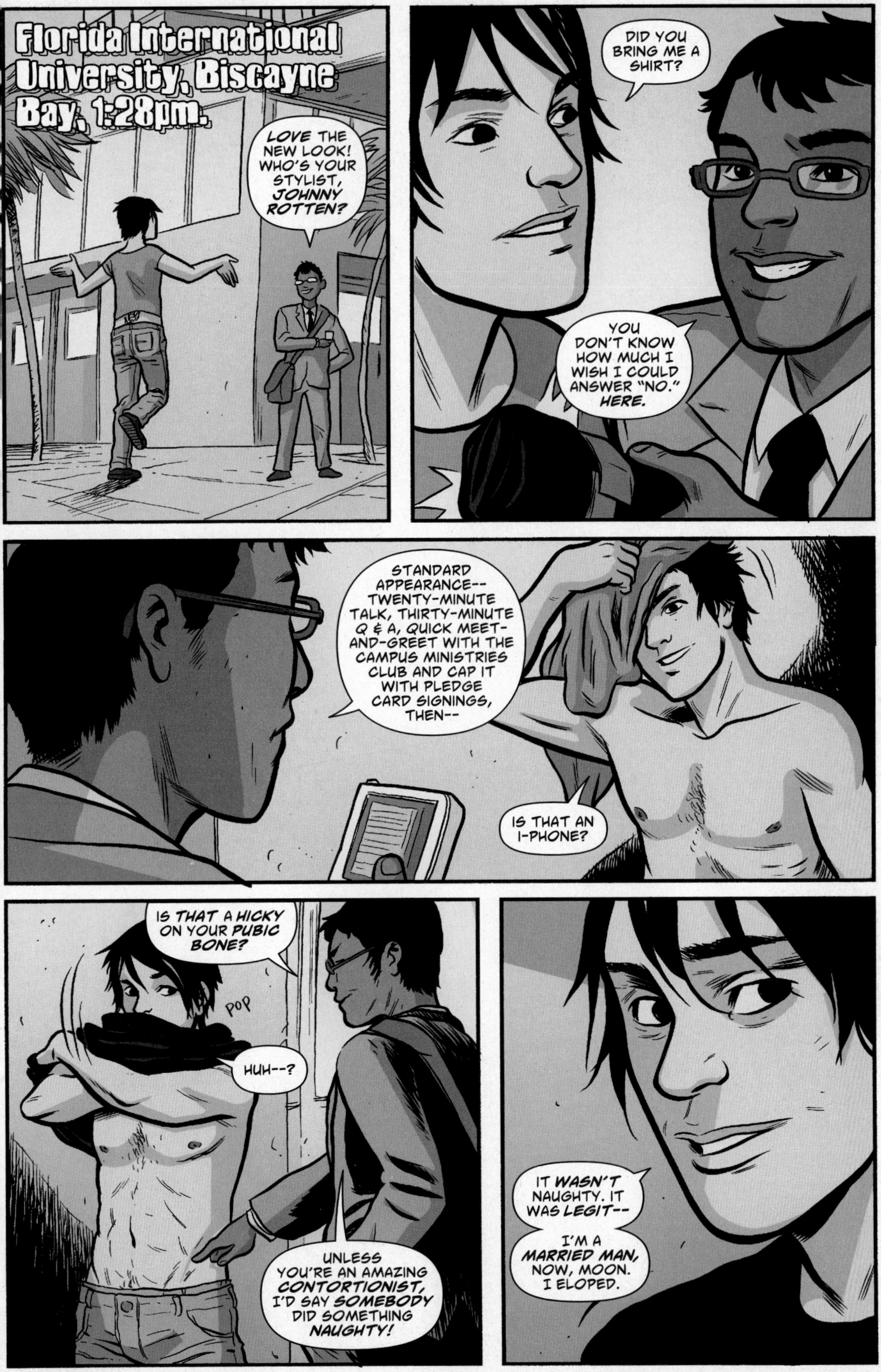
Florida International University, Biscayne Bay, 1:28pm.
LOVE THE NEW LOOK! WHO'S YOUR STYLIST, JOHNNY ROTTEN?
DID YOU BRING ME A SHIRT?
YOU DON'T KNOW HOW MUCH I WISH I COULD ANSWER "NO." HERE.
STANDARD APPEARANCE-- TWENTY-MINUTE TALK, THIRTY-MINUTE Q & A, QUICK MEET-AND-GREET WITH THE CAMPUS MINISTRIES CLUB AND CAP IT WITH PLEDGE CARD SIGNINGS, THEN--
IS THAT AN I-PHONE?
IS THAT A HICKY ON YOUR PUBIC BONE?
POP
HUH--?
UNLESS YOU'RE AN AMAZING CONTORTIONIST, I'D SAY SOMEBODY DID SOMETHING NAUGHTY!
IT WASN'T NAUGHTY. IT WAS LEGIT--
I'M A MARRIED MAN, NOW, MOON. I ELOPED.

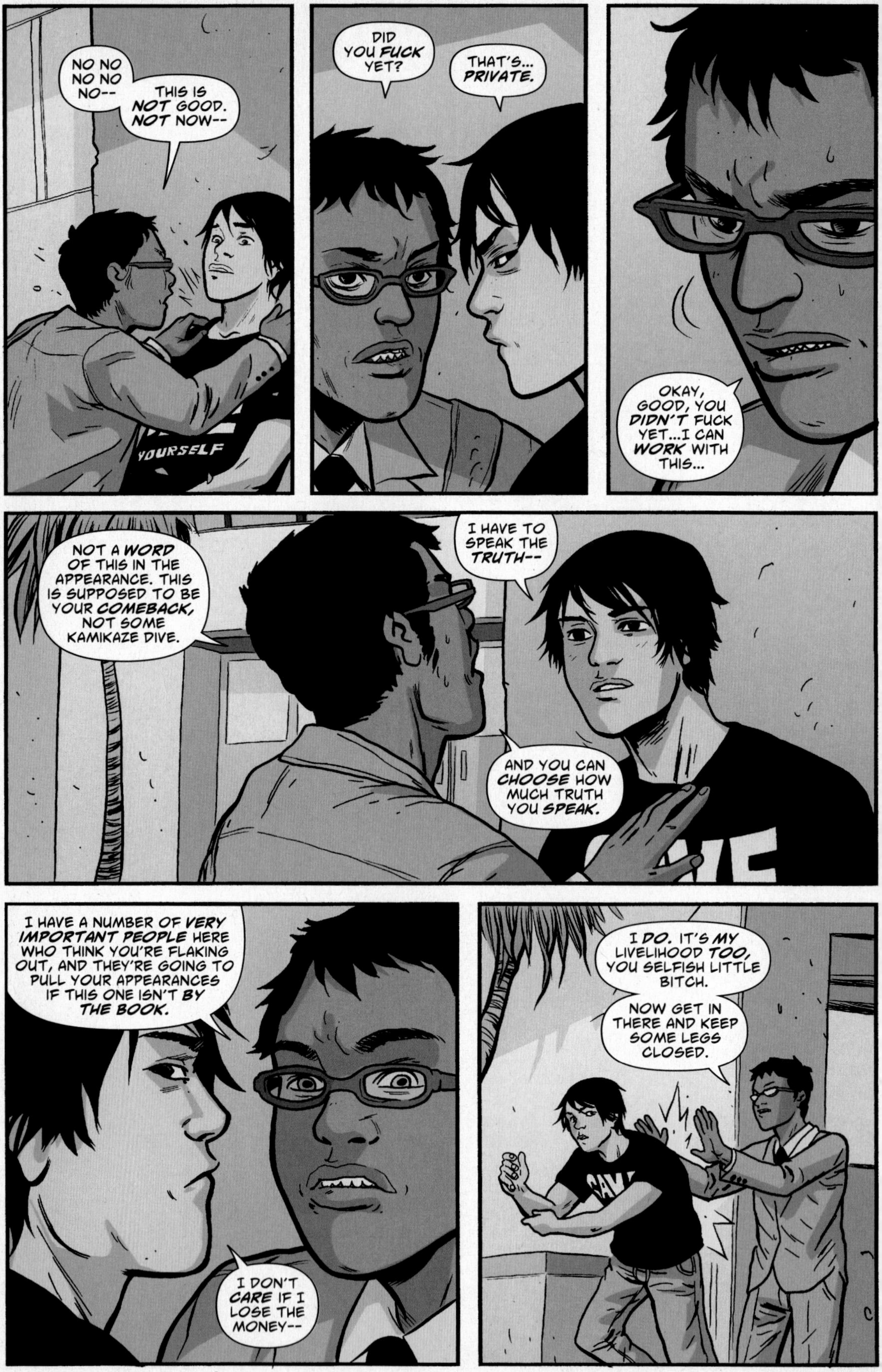
NO NO NO NO NO--
THIS IS NOT GOOD. NOT NOW--
YOURSELF
DID YOU FUCK YET?
THAT'S... PRIVATE.
OKAY, GOOD, YOU DIDN'T FUCK YET...I CAN WORK WITH THIS...
NOT A WORD OF THIS IN THE APPEARANCE. THIS IS SUPPOSED TO BE YOUR COMEBACK, NOT SOME KAMIKAZE DIVE.
I HAVE TO SPEAK THE TRUTH--
AND YOU CAN CHOOSE HOW MUCH TRUTH YOU SPEAK.
I HAVE A NUMBER OF VERY IMPORTANT PEOPLE HERE WHO THINK YOU'RE FLAKING OUT, AND THEY'RE GOING TO PULL YOUR APPEARANCES IF THIS ONE ISN'T BY THE BOOK.
I DON'T CARE IF I LOSE THE MONEY--
I DO. IT'S MY LIVELIHOOD TOO, YOU SELFISH LITTLE BITCH.
NOW GET IN THERE AND KEEP SOME LEGS CLOSED.

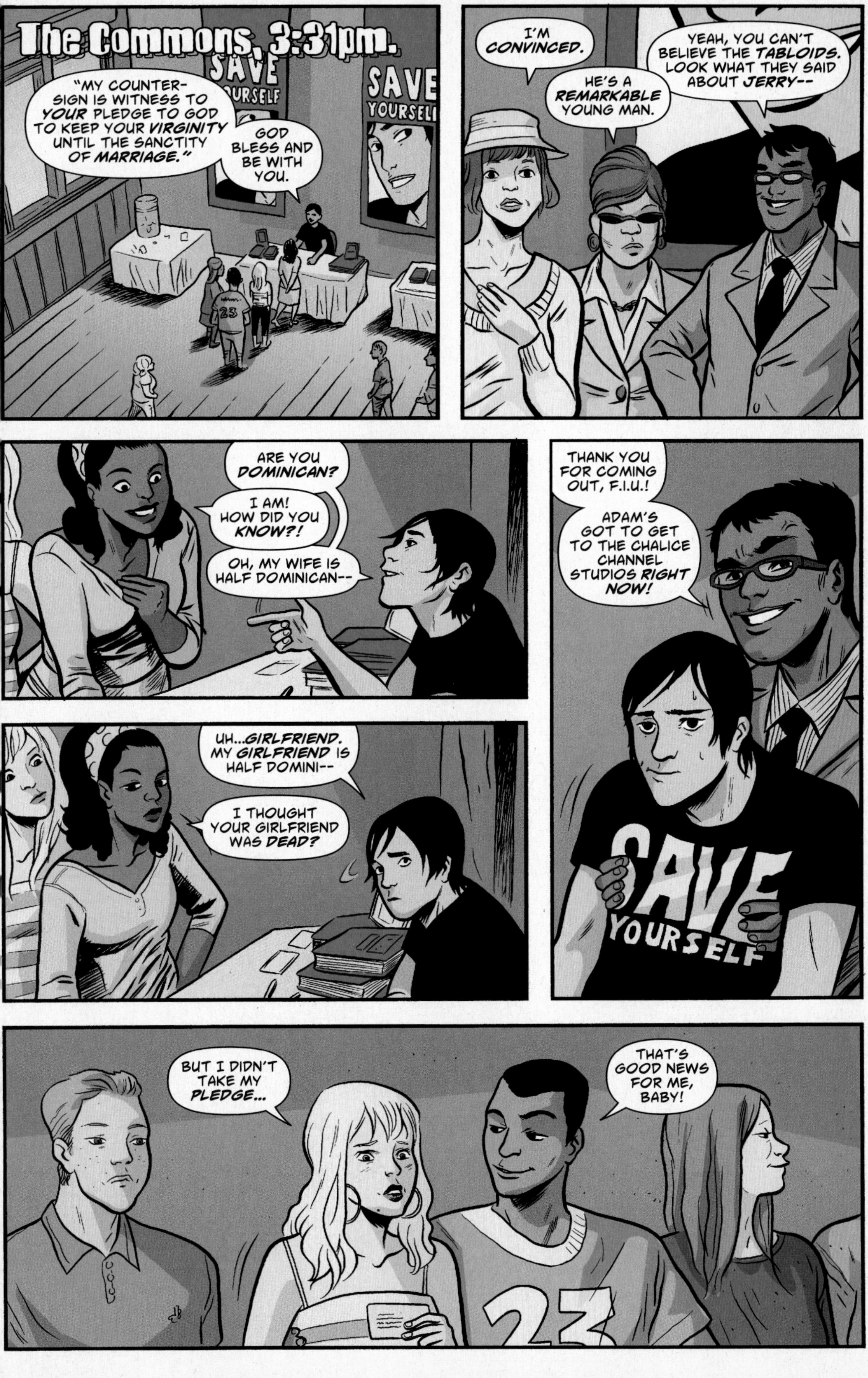
The Commons, 3:31pm.
SAVE YOURSELF
SAVE YOURSELF
"MY COUNTER-SIGN IS WITNESS TO YOUR PLEDGE TO GOD TO KEEP YOUR VIRGINITY UNTIL THE SANCTITY OF MARRIAGE."
GOD BLESS AND BE WITH YOU.
I'M CONVINCED.
HE'S A REMARKABLE YOUNG MAN.
YEAH, YOU CAN'T BELIEVE THE TABLOIDS. LOOK WHAT THEY SAID ABOUT JERRY--
ARE YOU DOMINICAN?
I AM! HOW DID YOU KNOW?!
OH, MY WIFE IS HALF DOMINICAN--
UH...GIRLFRIEND. MY GIRLFRIEND IS HALF DOMINI--
I THOUGHT YOUR GIRLFRIEND WAS DEAD?
THANK YOU FOR COMING OUT, F.I.U.!
ADAM'S GOT TO GET TO THE CHALICE CHANNEL STUDIOS RIGHT NOW!
SAVE YOURSELF
BUT I DIDN'T TAKE MY PLEDGE...
THAT'S GOOD NEWS FOR ME, BABY!

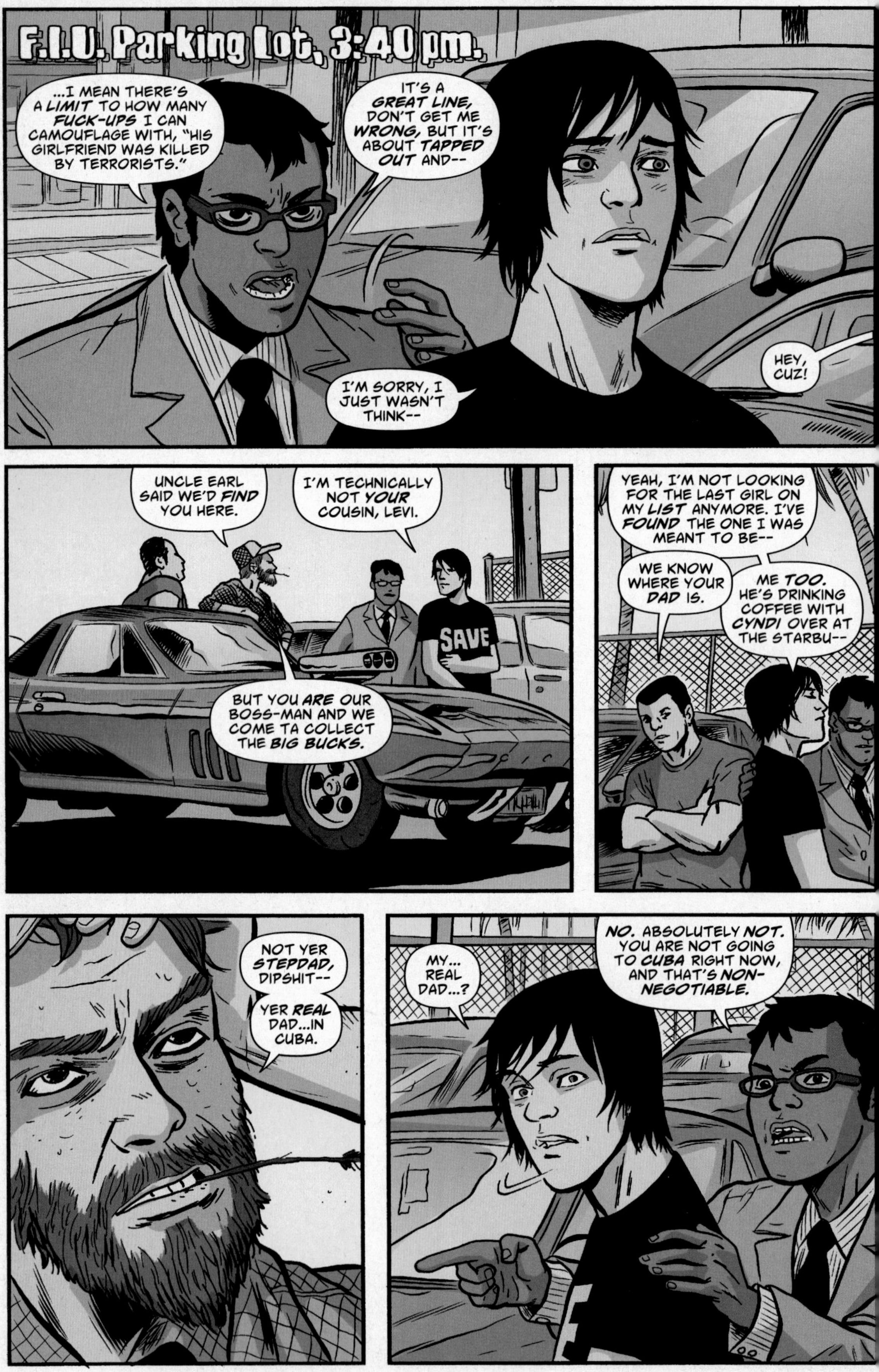
F.I.U. Parking Lot, 3:40 pm.
...I MEAN THERE'S A LIMIT TO HOW MANY FUCK-UPS I CAN CAMOUFLAGE WITH, "HIS GIRLFRIEND WAS KILLED BY TERRORISTS."
IT'S A GREAT LINE, DON'T GET ME WRONG, BUT IT'S ABOUT TAPPED OUT AND--
I'M SORRY, I JUST WASN'T THINK--
HEY, CUZ!
UNCLE EARL SAID WE'D FIND YOU HERE.
I'M TECHNICALLY NOT YOUR COUSIN, LEVI.
BUT YOU ARE OUR BOSS-MAN AND WE COME TA COLLECT THE BIG BUCKS.
SAVE
YEAH, I'M NOT LOOKING FOR THE LAST GIRL ON MY LIST ANYMORE. I'VE FOUND THE ONE I WAS MEANT TO BE--
WE KNOW WHERE YOUR DAD IS.
ME TOO. HE'S DRINKING COFFEE WITH CYNDI OVER AT THE STARBU--
NOT YER STEPDAD, DIPSHIT--
YER REAL DAD...IN CUBA.
MY... REAL DAD...?
NO. ABSOLUTELY NOT. YOU ARE NOT GOING TO CUBA RIGHT NOW, AND THAT'S NON-NEGOTIABLE.

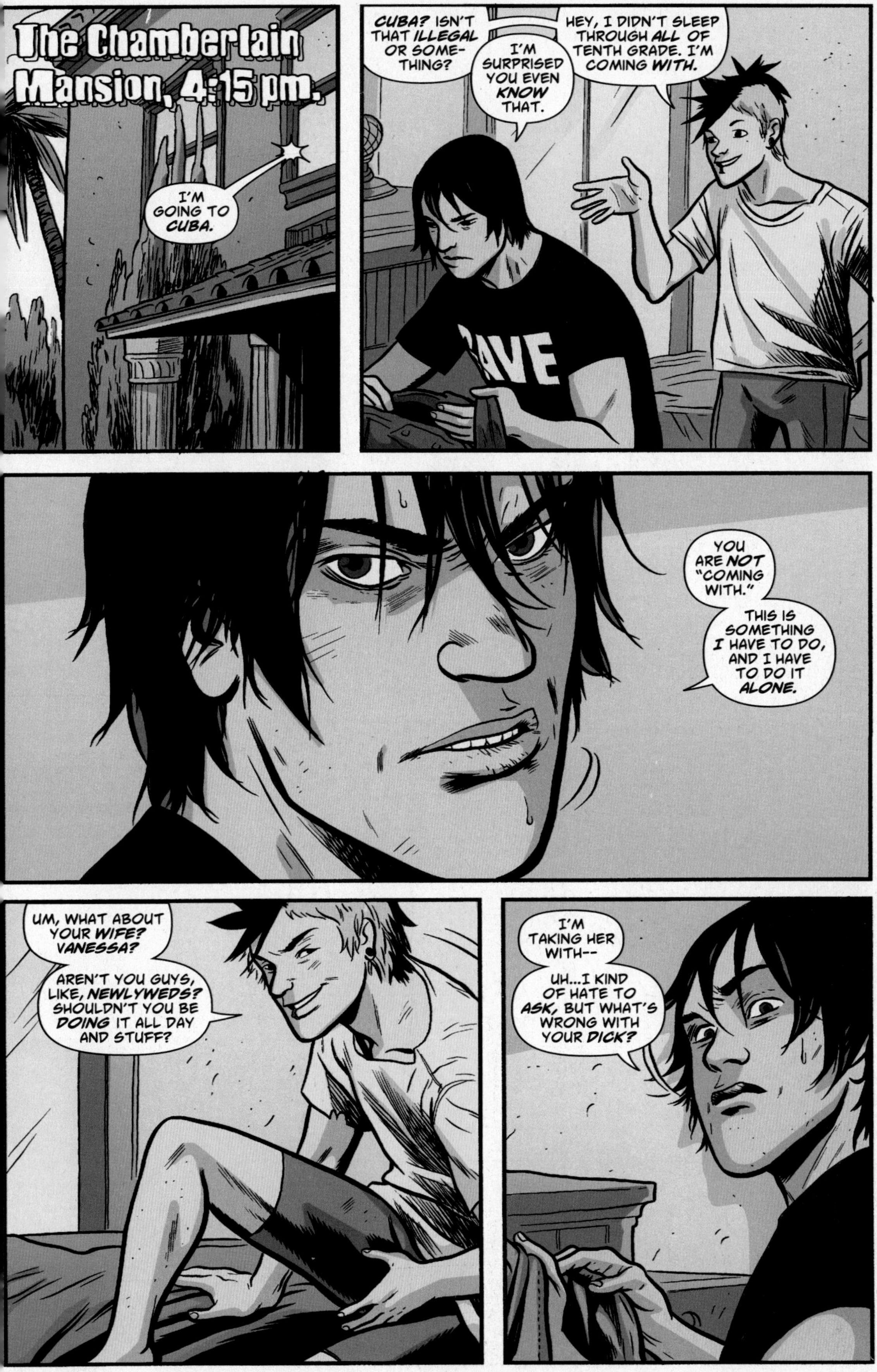
The Chamberlain Mansion, 4:15 pm.
I'M GOING TO CUBA.
CUBA? ISN'T THAT ILLEGAL OR SOME-THING?
I'M SURPRISED YOU EVEN KNOW THAT.
HEY, I DIDN'T SLEEP THROUGH ALL OF TENTH GRADE. I'M COMING WITH.
YOU ARE NOT "COMING WITH."
THIS IS SOMETHING I HAVE TO DO, AND I HAVE TO DO IT ALONE.
UM, WHAT ABOUT YOUR WIFE? VANESSA?
AREN'T YOU GUYS, LIKE, NEWLYWEDS? SHOULDN'T YOU BE DOING IT ALL DAY AND STUFF?
I'M TAKING HER WITH--
UH...I KIND OF HATE TO ASK, BUT WHAT'S WRONG WITH YOUR DICK?

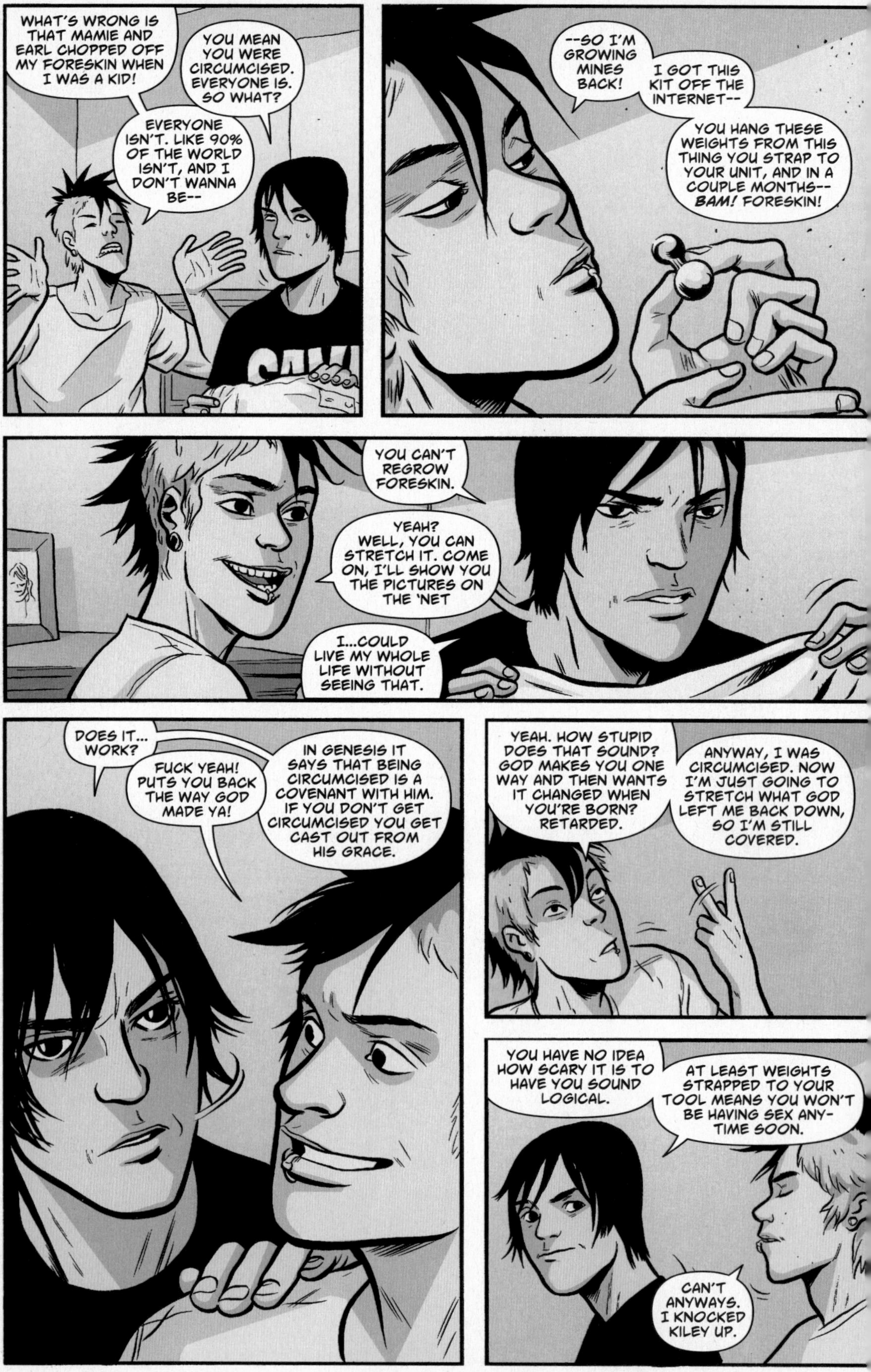
WHAT'S WRONG IS THAT MAMIE AND EARL CHOPPED OFF MY FORESKIN WHEN I WAS A KID!
YOU MEAN YOU WERE CIRCUMCISED. EVERYONE IS. SO WHAT?
EVERYONE ISN'T. LIKE 90% OF THE WORLD ISN'T, AND I DON'T WANNA BE--
--SO I'M GROWING MINES BACK!
I GOT THIS KIT OFF THE INTERNET--
YOU HANG THESE WEIGHTS FROM THIS THING YOU STRAP TO YOUR UNIT, AND IN A COUPLE MONTHS-- BAM! FORESKIN!
YOU CAN'T REGROW FORESKIN.
YEAH? WELL, YOU CAN STRETCH IT. COME ON, I'LL SHOW YOU THE PICTURES ON THE 'NET
I...COULD LIVE MY WHOLE LIFE WITHOUT SEEING THAT.
DOES IT... WORK?
FUCK YEAH! PUTS YOU BACK THE WAY GOD MADE YA!
IN GENESIS IT SAYS THAT BEING CIRCUMCISED IS A COVENANT WITH HIM. IF YOU DON'T GET CIRCUMCISED YOU GET CAST OUT FROM HIS GRACE.
YEAH. HOW STUPID DOES THAT SOUND? GOD MAKES YOU ONE WAY AND THEN WANTS IT CHANGED WHEN YOU'RE BORN? RETARDED.
ANYWAY, I WAS CIRCUMCISED. NOW I'M JUST GOING TO STRETCH WHAT GOD LEFT ME BACK DOWN, SO I'M STILL COVERED.
YOU HAVE NO IDEA HOW SCARY IT IS TO HAVE YOU SOUND LOGICAL.
AT LEAST WEIGHTS STRAPPED TO YOUR TOOL MEANS YOU WON'T BE HAVING SEX ANY-TIME SOON.
CAN'T ANYWAYS. I KNOCKED KILEY UP.

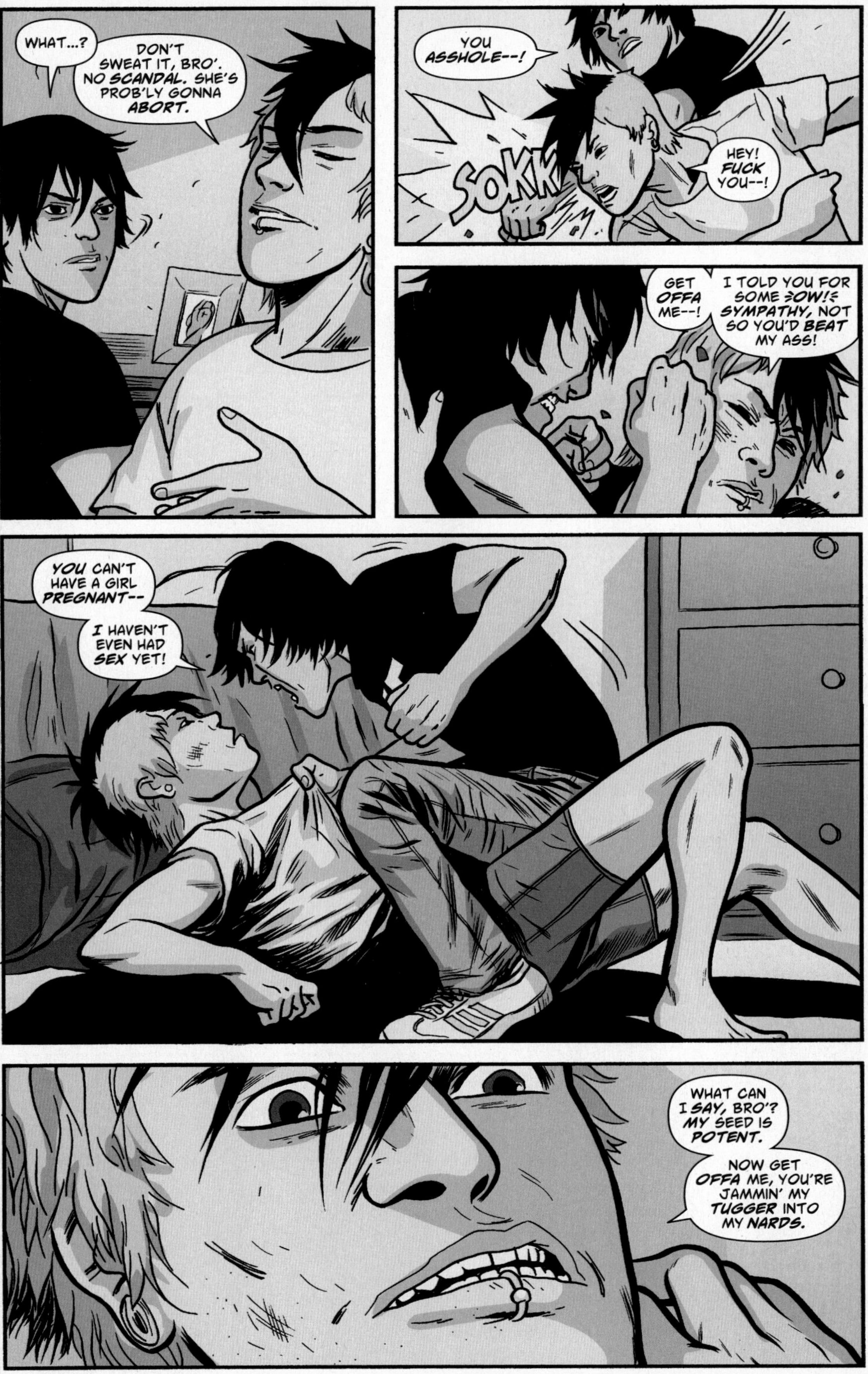
WHAT...?
DON'T SWEAT IT, BRO'. NO SCANDAL. SHE'S PROB'LY GONNA ABORT.
YOU ASSHOLE--!
SOKK
HEY! FUCK YOU--!
GET OFFA ME--!
I TOLD YOU FOR SOME ƧOW!Ƨ SYMPATHY, NOT SO YOU'D BEAT MY ASS!
YOU CAN'T HAVE A GIRL PREGNANT--
I HAVEN'T EVEN HAD SEX YET!
WHAT CAN I SAY, BRO'? MY SEED IS POTENT.
NOW GET OFFA ME, YOU'RE JAMMIN' MY TUGGER INTO MY NARDS.

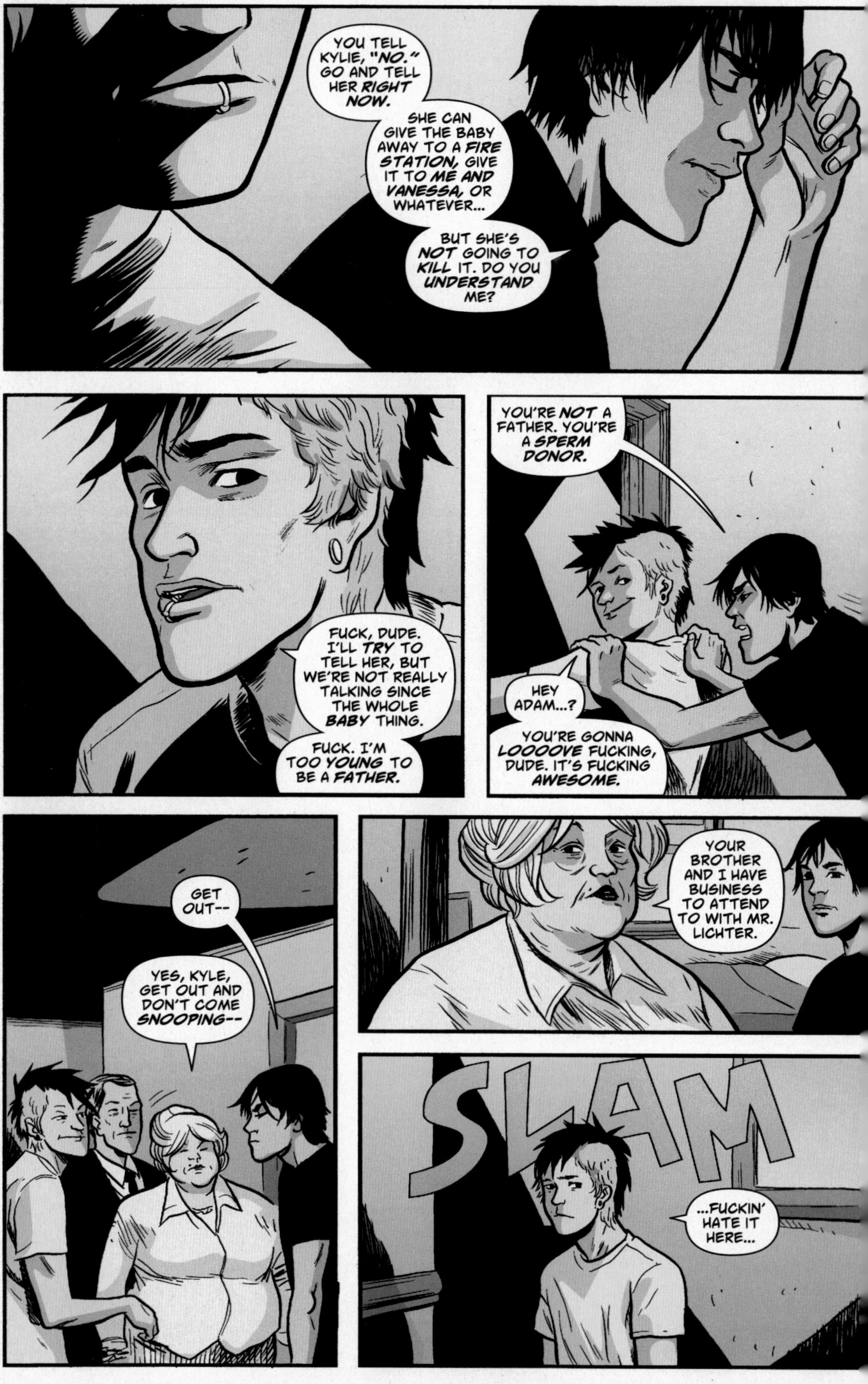
YOU TELL KYLIE, "NO." GO AND TELL HER RIGHT NOW.
SHE CAN GIVE THE BABY AWAY TO A FIRE STATION, GIVE IT TO ME AND VANESSA, OR WHATEVER...
BUT SHE'S NOT GOING TO KILL IT. DO YOU UNDERSTAND ME?
FUCK, DUDE. I'LL TRY TO TELL HER, BUT WE'RE NOT REALLY TALKING SINCE THE WHOLE BABY THING.
FUCK. I'M TOO YOUNG TO BE A FATHER.
YOU'RE NOT A FATHER. YOU'RE A SPERM DONOR.
HEY ADAM...?
YOU'RE GONNA LOOOOVE FUCKING, DUDE. IT'S FUCKING AWESOME.
GET OUT--
YES, KYLE, GET OUT AND DON'T COME SNOOPING--
YOUR BROTHER AND I HAVE BUSINESS TO ATTEND TO WITH MR. LICHTER.
SLAM
...FUCKIN' HATE IT HERE...

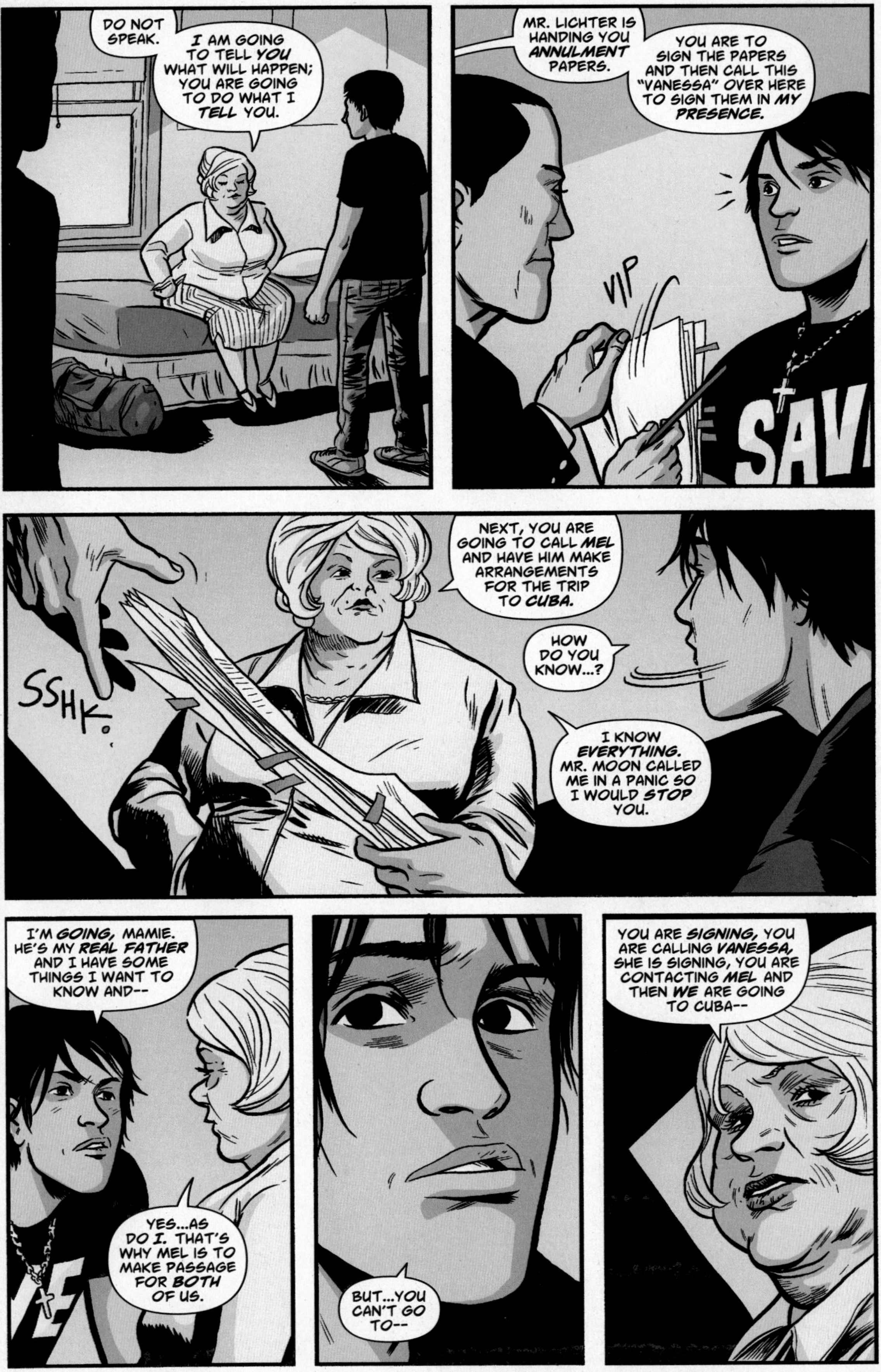
DO NOT SPEAK.
I AM GOING TO TELL YOU WHAT WILL HAPPEN; YOU ARE GOING TO DO WHAT I TELL YOU.
MR. LICHTER IS HANDING YOU ANNULMENT PAPERS.
YOU ARE TO SIGN THE PAPERS AND THEN CALL THIS "VANESSA" OVER HERE TO SIGN THEM IN MY PRESENCE.
VIP
NEXT, YOU ARE GOING TO CALL MEL AND HAVE HIM MAKE ARRANGEMENTS FOR THE TRIP TO CUBA.
SSHK.
HOW DO YOU KNOW...?
I KNOW EVERYTHING. MR. MOON CALLED ME IN A PANIC SO I WOULD STOP YOU.
I'M GOING, MAMIE. HE'S MY REAL FATHER AND I HAVE SOME THINGS I WANT TO KNOW AND--
YES...AS DO I. THAT'S WHY MEL IS TO MAKE PASSAGE FOR BOTH OF US.
BUT...YOU CAN'T GO TO--
YOU ARE SIGNING, YOU ARE CALLING VANESSA, SHE IS SIGNING, YOU ARE CONTACTING MEL AND THEN WE ARE GOING TO CUBA--

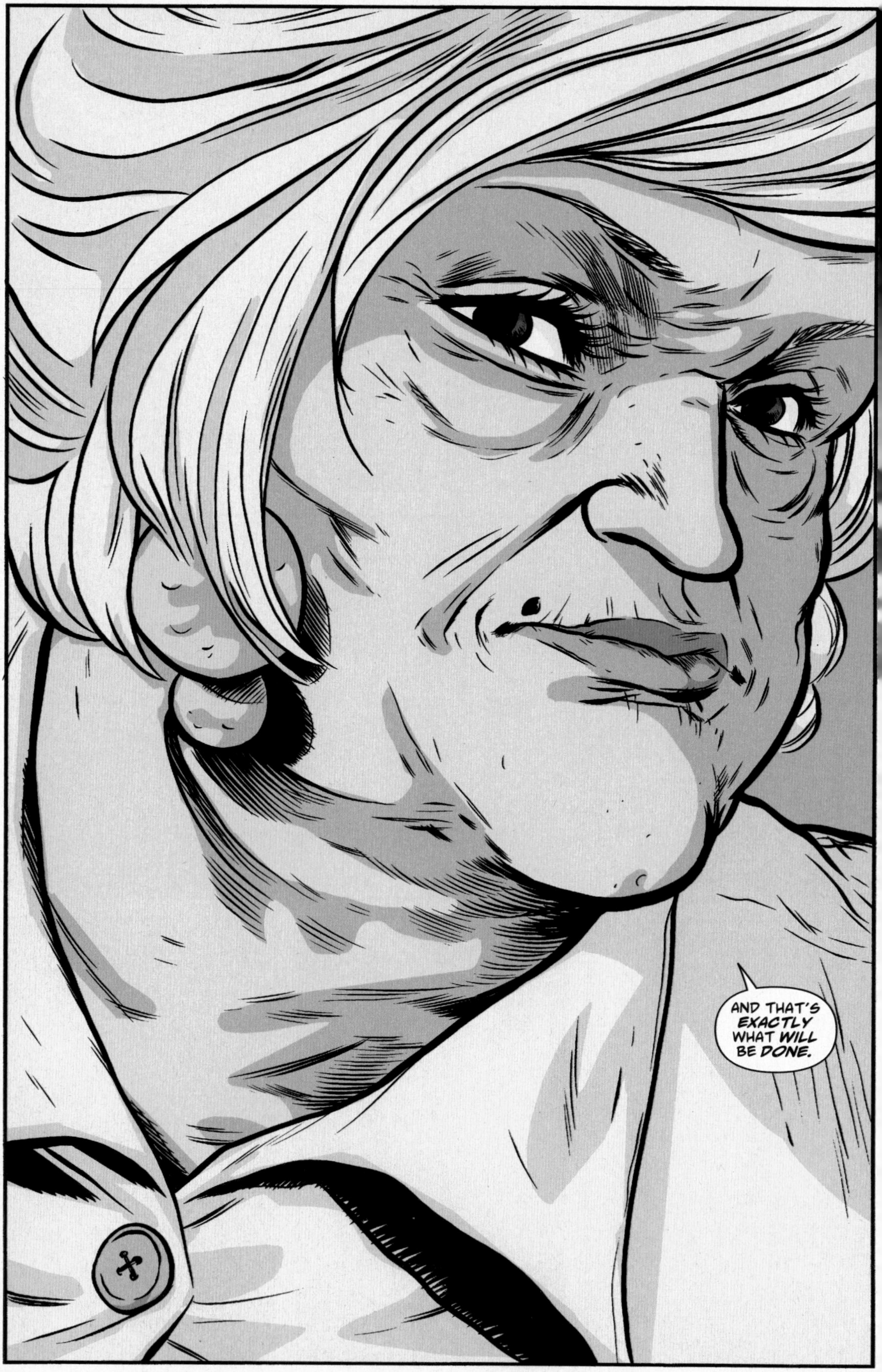
AND THAT'S EXACTLY WHAT WILL BE DONE.

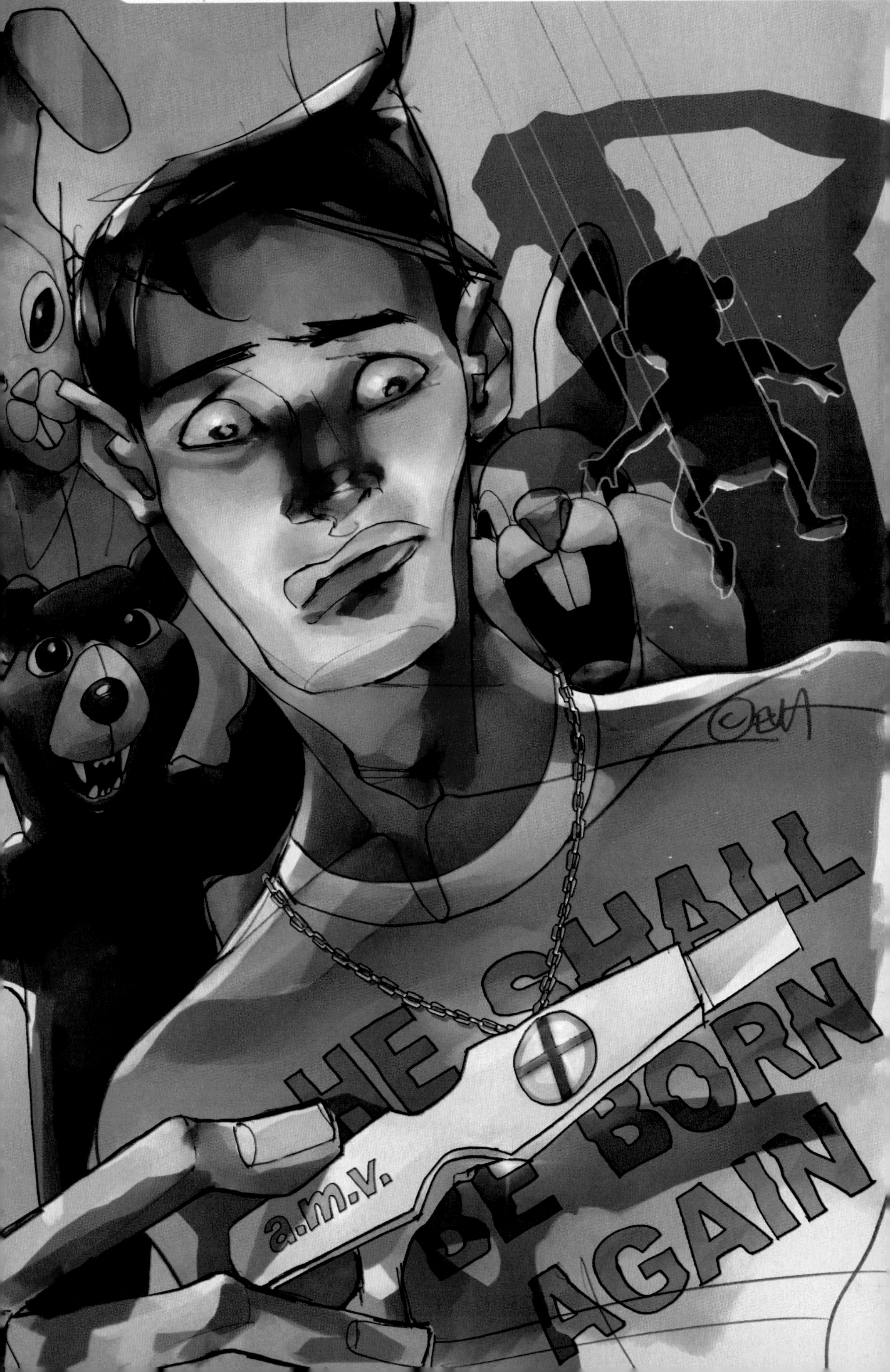
HE SHALL BE BORN AGAIN
a.m.v.

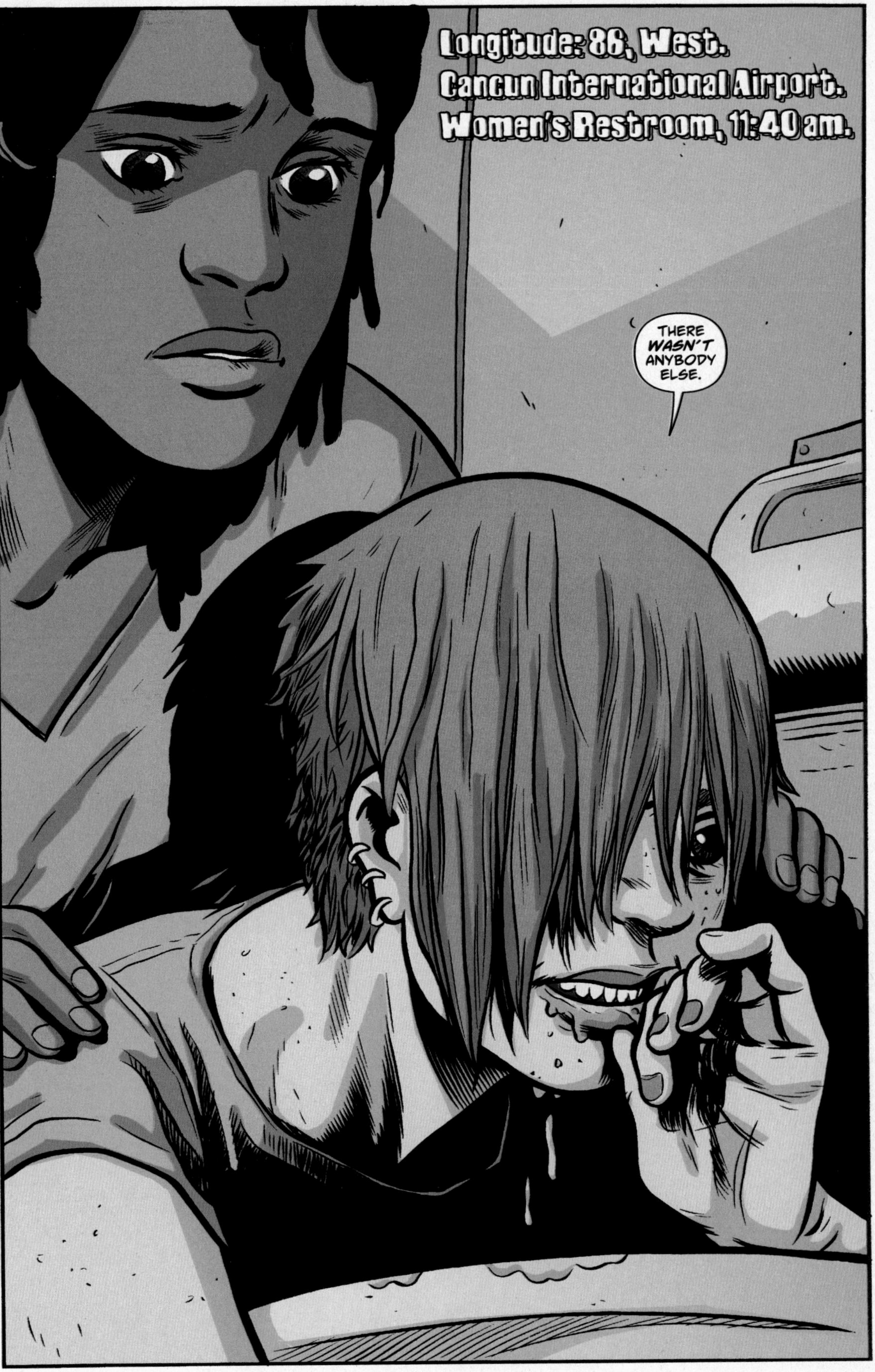
Longitude: 86, West.
Cancun International Airport.
Women's Restroom, 11:40 am.
THERE WASN'T ANYBODY ELSE.

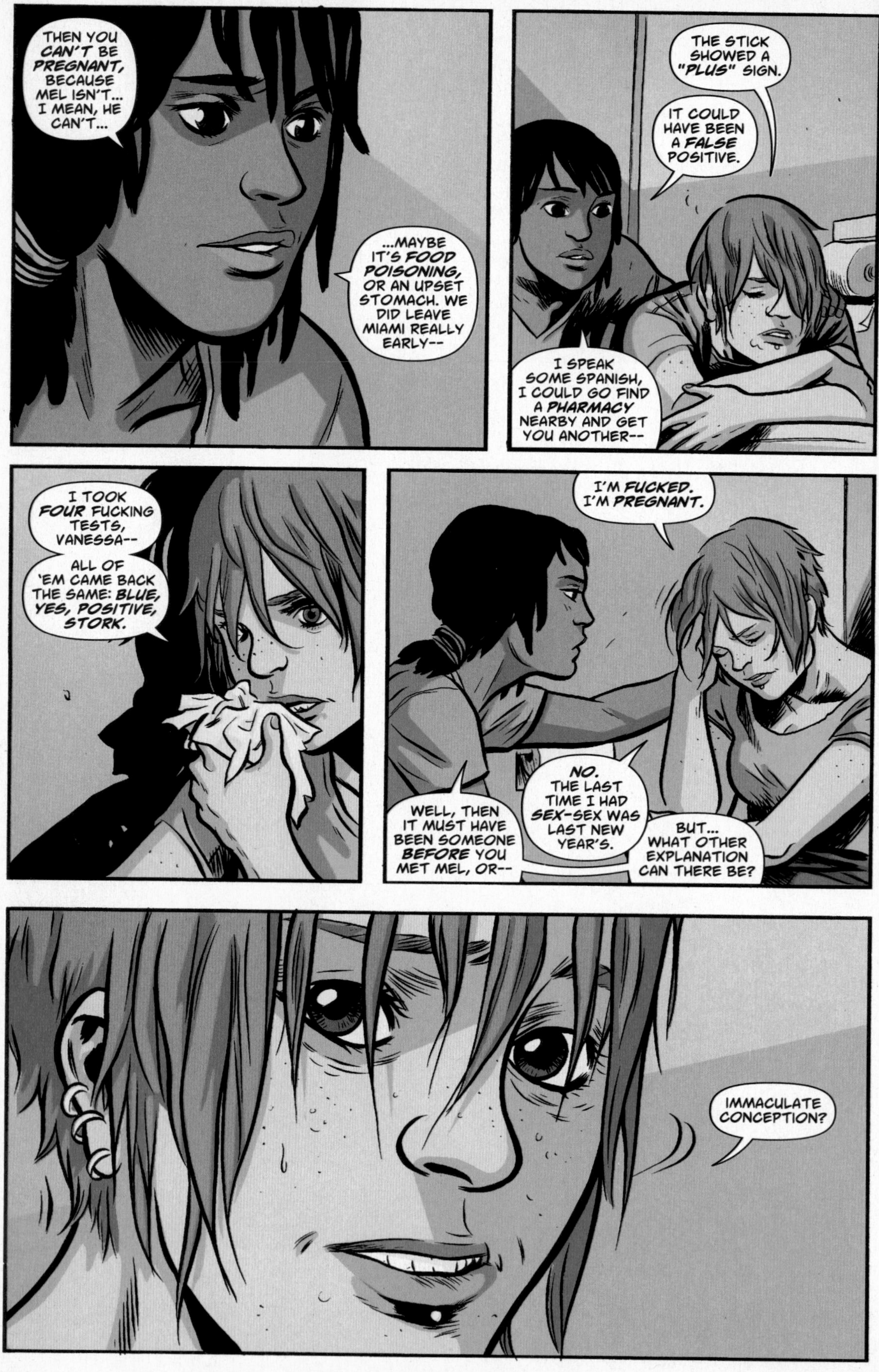
THEN YOU CAN'T BE PREGNANT, BECAUSE MEL ISN'T... I MEAN, HE CAN'T...
...MAYBE IT'S FOOD POISONING, OR AN UPSET STOMACH. WE DID LEAVE MIAMI REALLY EARLY--
THE STICK SHOWED A "PLUS" SIGN.
IT COULD HAVE BEEN A FALSE POSITIVE.
I SPEAK SOME SPANISH, I COULD GO FIND A PHARMACY NEARBY AND GET YOU ANOTHER--
I TOOK FOUR FUCKING TESTS, VANESSA--
ALL OF 'EM CAME BACK THE SAME: BLUE, YES, POSITIVE, STORK.
I'M FUCKED. I'M PREGNANT.
WELL, THEN IT MUST HAVE BEEN SOMEONE BEFORE YOU MET MEL, OR--
NO. THE LAST TIME I HAD SEX-SEX WAS LAST NEW YEAR'S.
BUT... WHAT OTHER EXPLANATION CAN THERE BE?
IMMACULATE CONCEPTION?

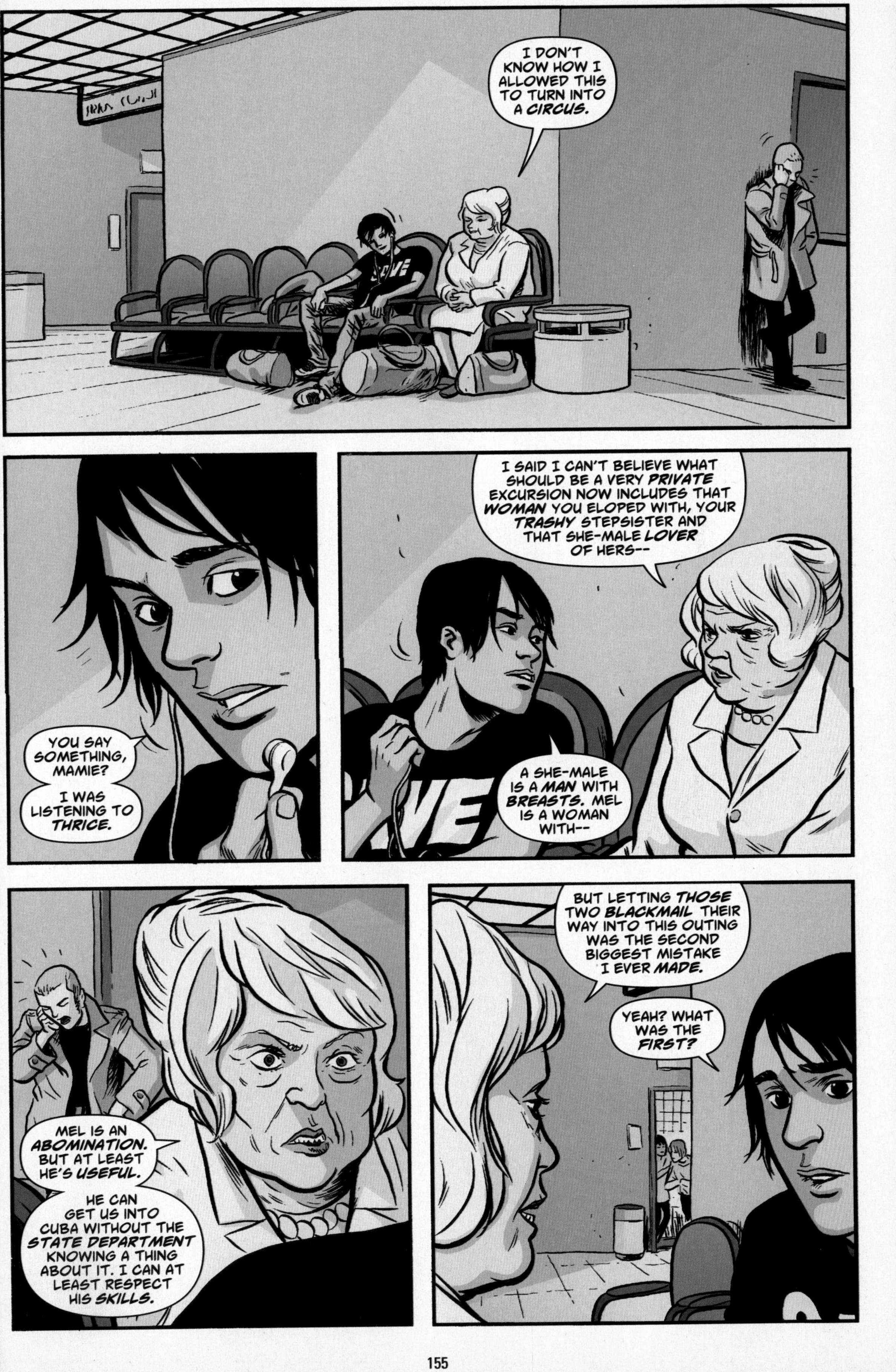
I DON'T KNOW HOW I ALLOWED THIS TO TURN INTO A CIRCUS.
YOU SAY SOMETHING, MAMIE?
I WAS LISTENING TO THRICE.
I SAID I CAN'T BELIEVE WHAT SHOULD BE A VERY PRIVATE EXCURSION NOW INCLUDES THAT WOMAN YOU ELOPED WITH, YOUR TRASHY STEPSISTER AND THAT SHE-MALE LOVER OF HERS--
A SHE-MALE IS A MAN WITH BREASTS. MEL IS A WOMAN WITH--
MEL IS AN ABOMINATION. BUT AT LEAST HE'S USEFUL.
HE CAN GET US INTO CUBA WITHOUT THE STATE DEPARTMENT KNOWING A THING ABOUT IT. I CAN AT LEAST RESPECT HIS SKILLS.
BUT LETTING THOSE TWO BLACKMAIL THEIR WAY INTO THIS OUTING WAS THE SECOND BIGGEST MISTAKE I EVER MADE.
YEAH? WHAT WAS THE FIRST?

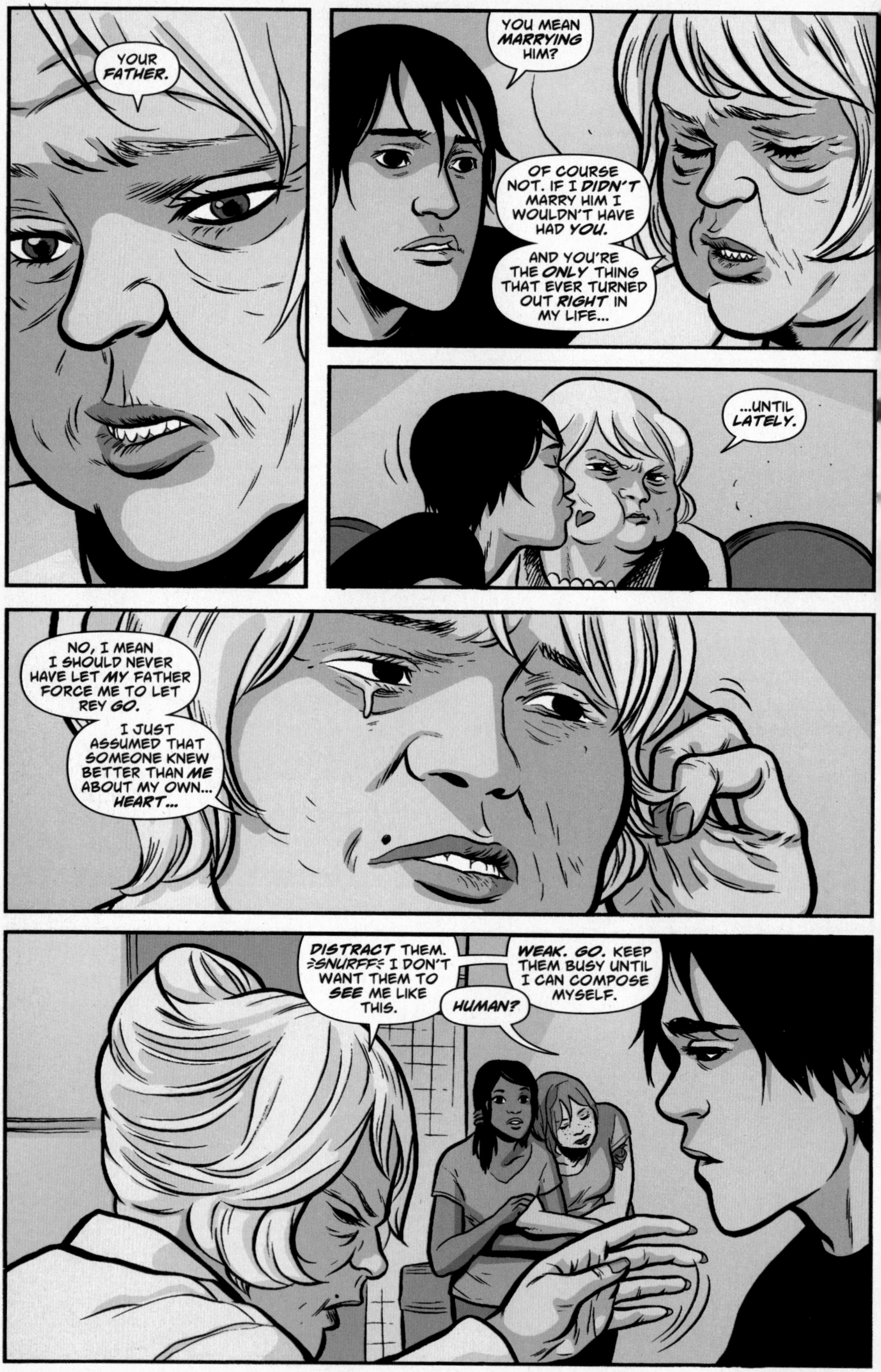

YOUR FATHER.
YOU MEAN MARRYING HIM?
OF COURSE NOT. IF I DIDN'T MARRY HIM I WOULDN'T HAVE HAD YOU.
AND YOU'RE THE ONLY THING THAT EVER TURNED OUT RIGHT IN MY LIFE...
...UNTIL LATELY.
NO, I MEAN I SHOULD NEVER HAVE LET MY FATHER FORCE ME TO LET REY GO.
I JUST ASSUMED THAT SOMEONE KNEW BETTER THAN ME ABOUT MY OWN... HEART...
DISTRACT THEM. SNURFF I DON'T WANT THEM TO SEE ME LIKE THIS.
HUMAN?
WEAK. GO. KEEP THEM BUSY UNTIL I CAN COMPOSE MYSELF.

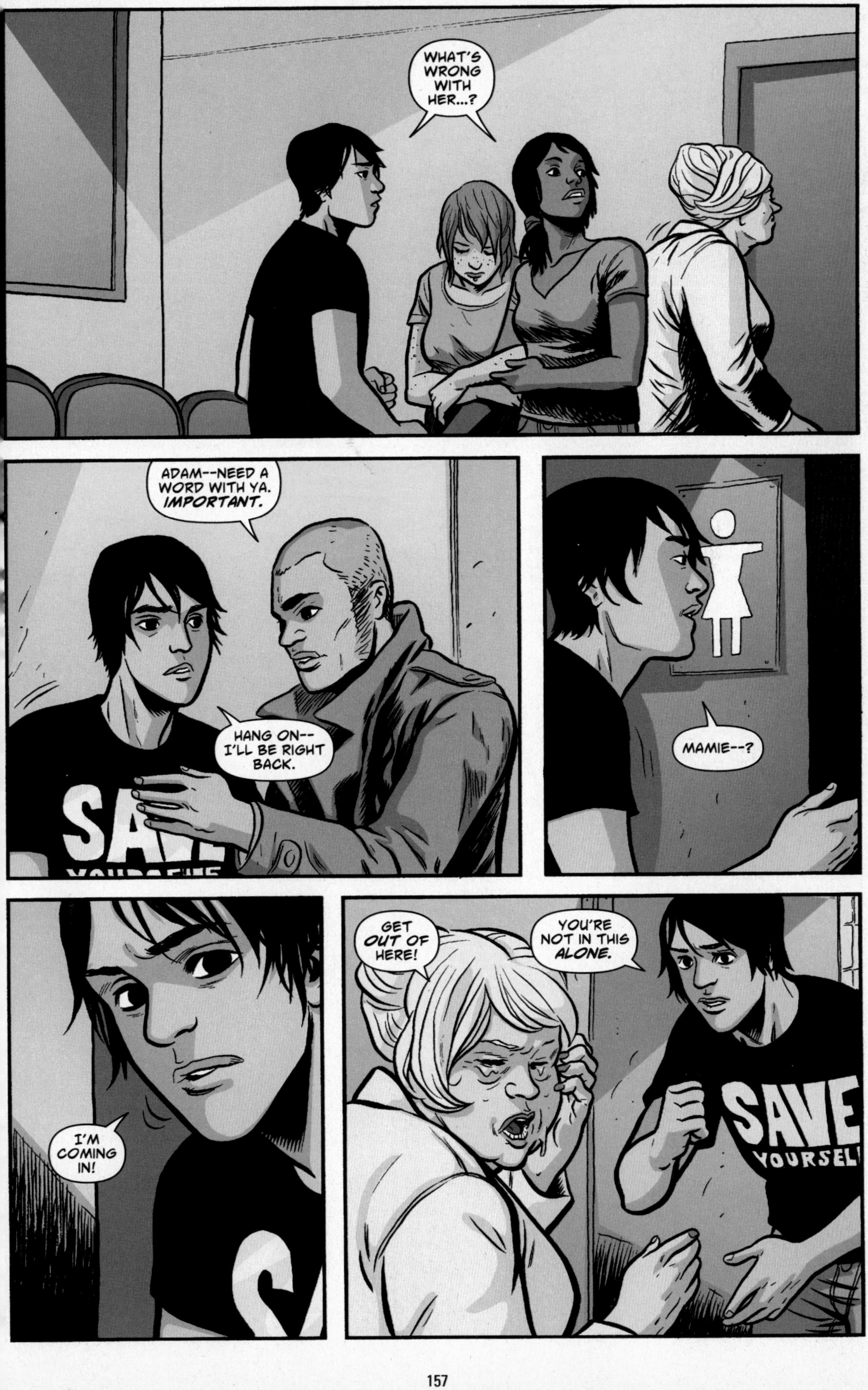
WHAT'S WRONG WITH HER...?
ADAM--NEED A WORD WITH YA. IMPORTANT.
HANG ON-- I'LL BE RIGHT BACK.
SAVE
MAMIE--?
I'M COMING IN!
GET OUT OF HERE!
YOU'RE NOT IN THIS ALONE.
SAVE
YOURSEL

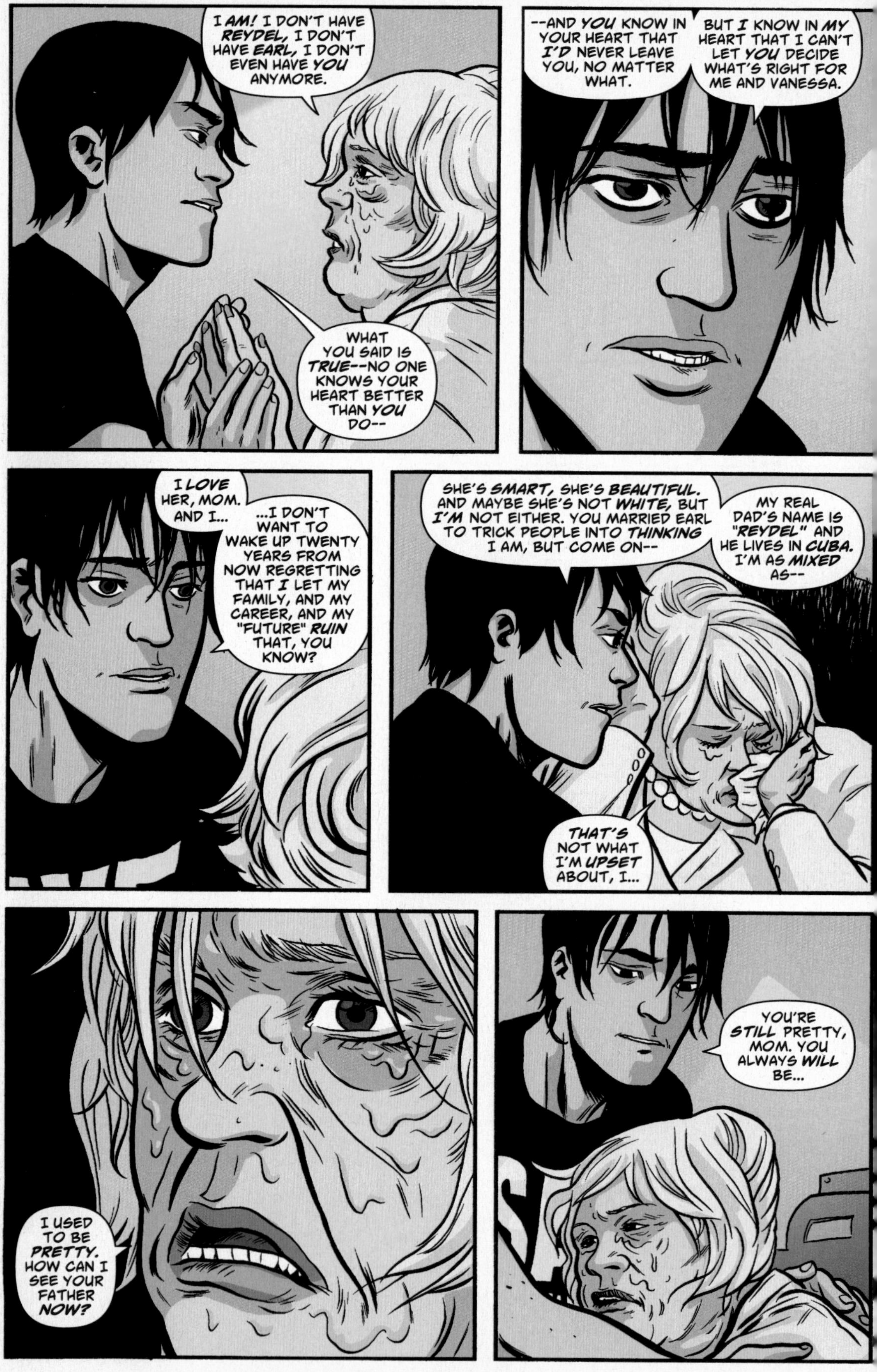
I AM! I DON'T HAVE REYDEL, I DON'T HAVE EARL, I DON'T EVEN HAVE YOU ANYMORE.
WHAT YOU SAID IS TRUE--NO ONE KNOWS YOUR HEART BETTER THAN YOU DO--
--AND YOU KNOW IN YOUR HEART THAT I'D NEVER LEAVE YOU, NO MATTER WHAT.
BUT I KNOW IN MY HEART THAT I CAN'T LET YOU DECIDE WHAT'S RIGHT FOR ME AND VANESSA.
I LOVE HER, MOM. AND I...
...I DON'T WANT TO WAKE UP TWENTY YEARS FROM NOW REGRETTING THAT I LET MY FAMILY, AND MY CAREER, AND MY "FUTURE" RUIN THAT, YOU KNOW?
SHE'S SMART, SHE'S BEAUTIFUL. AND MAYBE SHE'S NOT WHITE, BUT I'M NOT EITHER. YOU MARRIED EARL TO TRICK PEOPLE INTO THINKING I AM, BUT COME ON--
MY REAL DAD'S NAME IS "REYDEL" AND HE LIVES IN CUBA. I'M AS MIXED AS--
THAT'S NOT WHAT I'M UPSET ABOUT, I...
I USED TO BE PRETTY. HOW CAN I SEE YOUR FATHER NOW?
YOU'RE STILL PRETTY, MOM. YOU ALWAYS WILL BE...

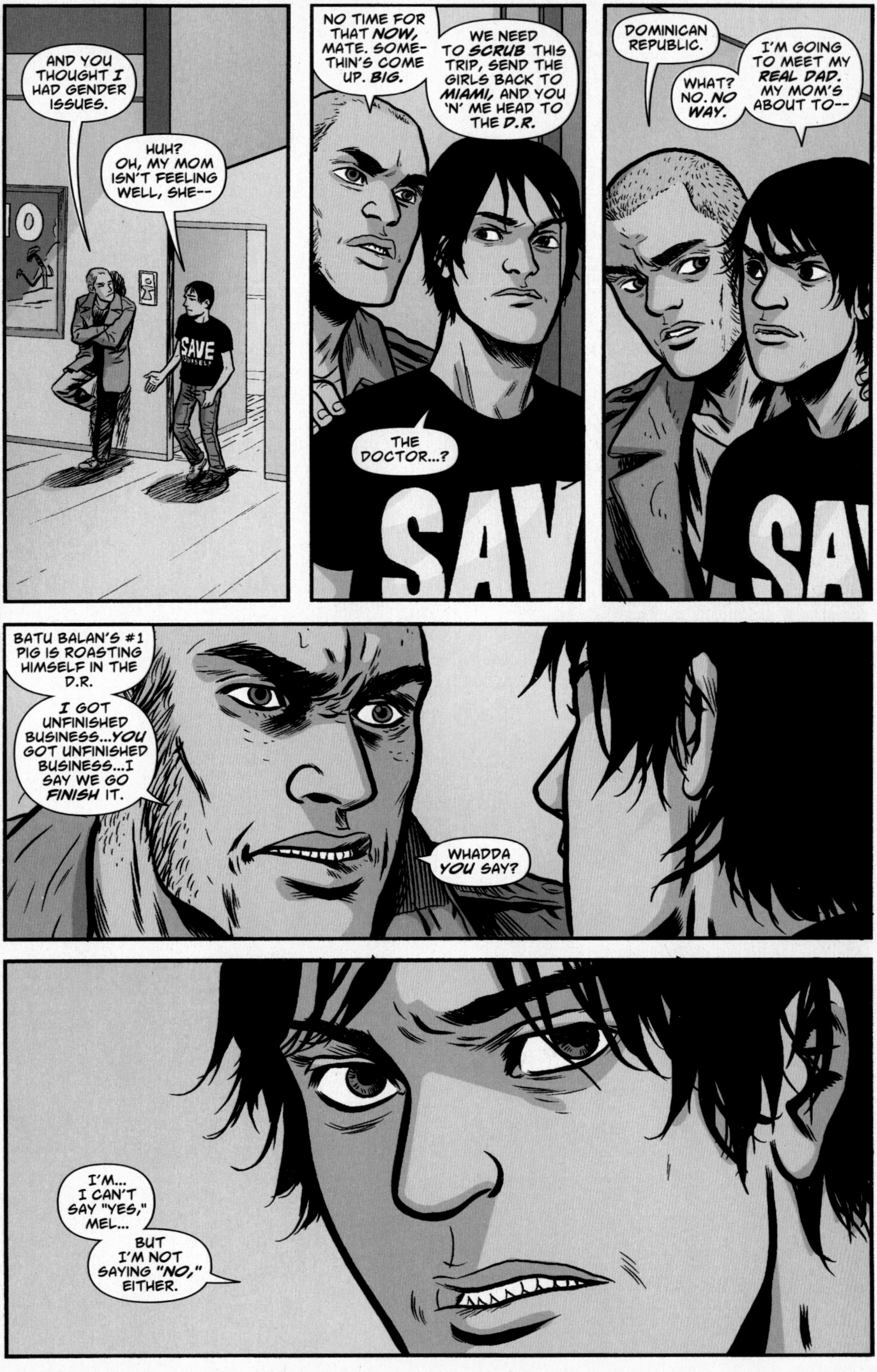
AND YOU THOUGHT *I* HAD GENDER ISSUES.
HUH? OH, MY MOM ISN'T FEELING WELL, SHE--
SAVE YOURSELF
NO TIME FOR THAT *NOW,* MATE. SOME-THIN'S COME UP. *BIG.*
WE NEED TO *SCRUB* THIS TRIP, SEND THE GIRLS BACK TO *MIAMI,* AND YOU 'N' ME HEAD TO THE *D.R.*
THE DOCTOR...?
DOMINICAN REPUBLIC.
WHAT? NO. *NO WAY.*
I'M GOING TO MEET MY *REAL DAD.* MY MOM'S ABOUT TO--
BATU BALAN'S #1 PIG IS ROASTING HIMSELF IN THE D.R.
I GOT UNFINISHED BUSINESS...*YOU* GOT UNFINISHED BUSINESS...I SAY WE GO *FINISH* IT.
WHADDA *YOU* SAY?
I'M... I CAN'T SAY "YES," MEL...
BUT I'M NOT SAYING *"NO,"* EITHER.

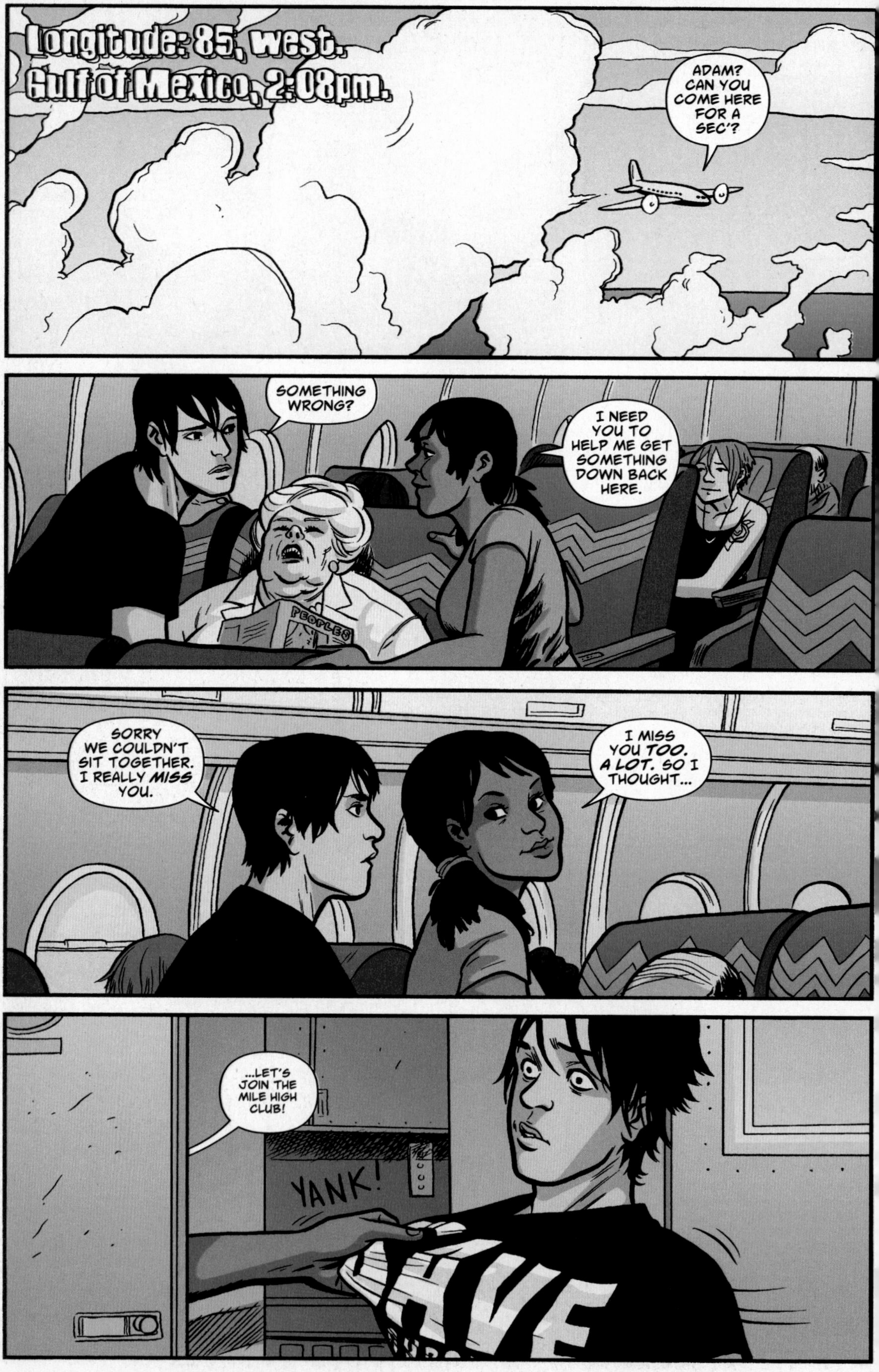
Longitude: 85, west.
Gulf of Mexico, 2:08pm.
ADAM? CAN YOU COME HERE FOR A SEC'?
SOMETHING WRONG?
I NEED YOU TO HELP ME GET SOMETHING DOWN BACK HERE.
PEOPLE
SORRY WE COULDN'T SIT TOGETHER. I REALLY MISS YOU.
I MISS YOU TOO. A LOT. SO I THOUGHT...
...LET'S JOIN THE MILE HIGH CLUB!
YANK!

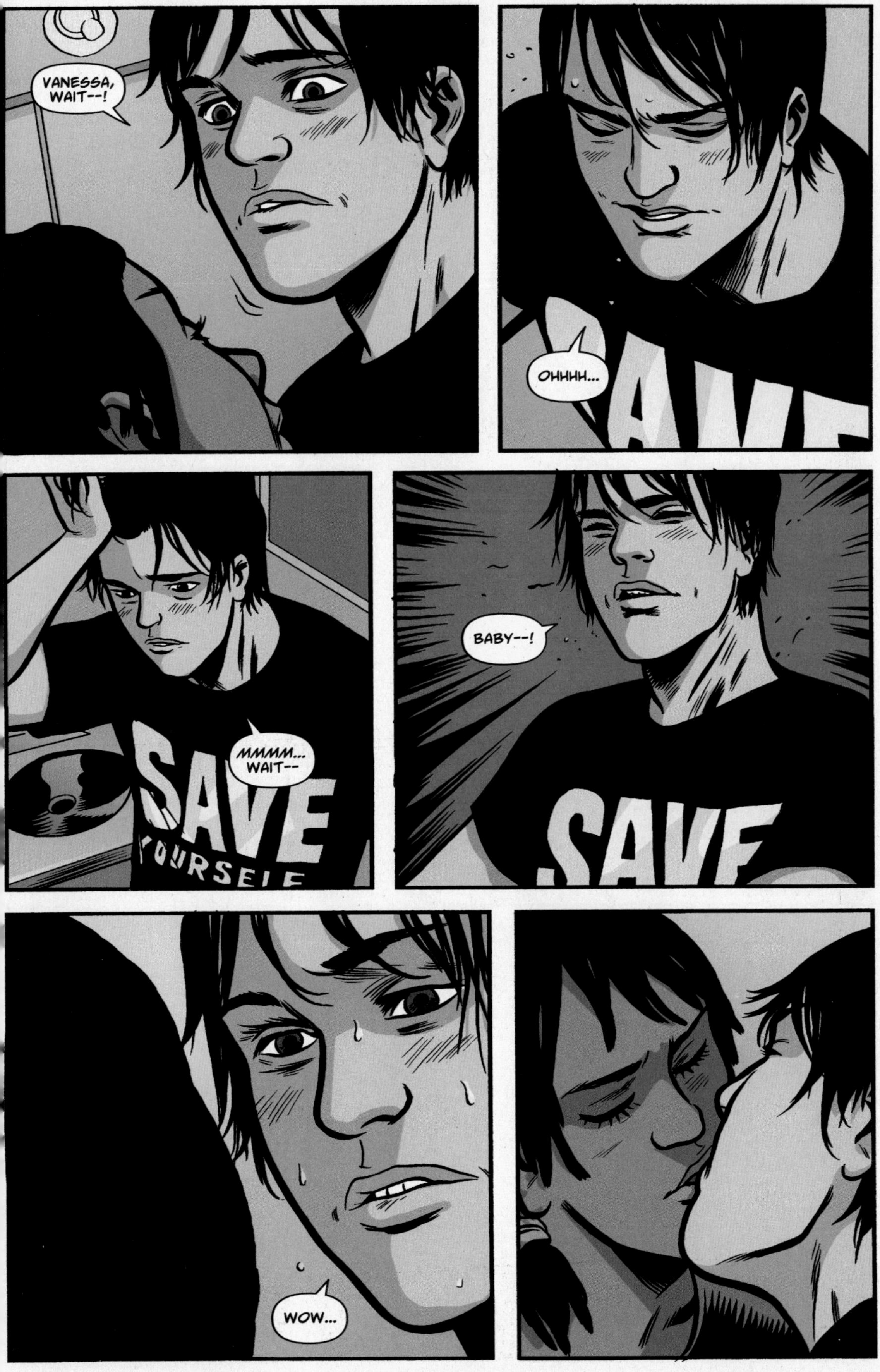

VANESSA, WAIT--!
OHHHH...
SAVE
MMMM... WAIT--
SAVE
YOURSELF
BABY--!
SAVE
WOW...

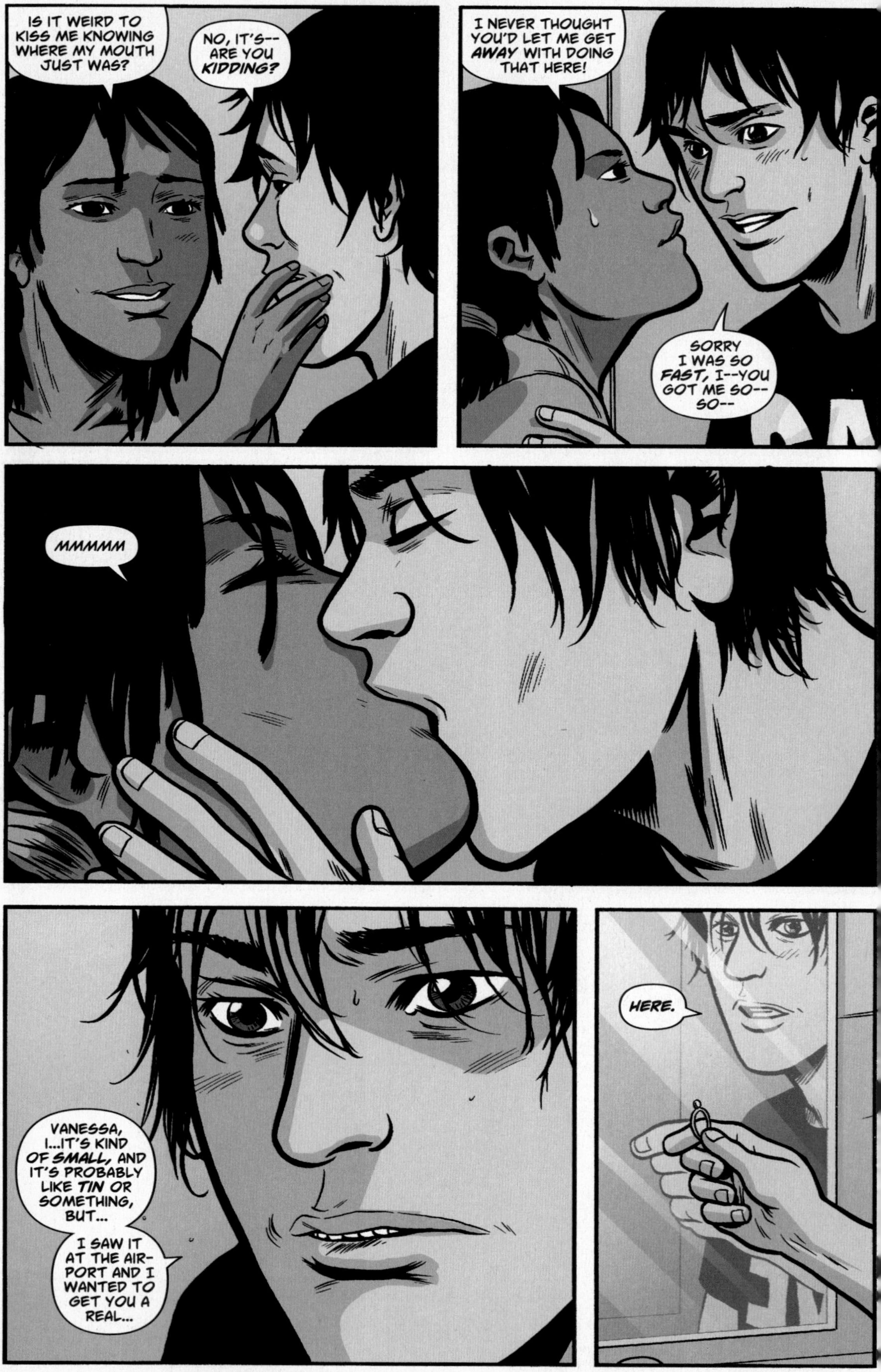
IS IT WEIRD TO KISS ME KNOWING WHERE MY MOUTH JUST WAS?
NO, IT'S-- ARE YOU *KIDDING?*
I NEVER THOUGHT YOU'D LET ME GET *AWAY* WITH DOING THAT HERE!
SORRY I WAS SO *FAST,* I--YOU GOT ME SO-- SO--
MMMMM
VANESSA, I...IT'S KIND OF *SMALL,* AND IT'S PROBABLY LIKE *TIN* OR SOMETHING, BUT...
I SAW IT AT THE AIR-PORT AND I WANTED TO GET YOU A REAL...
HERE.

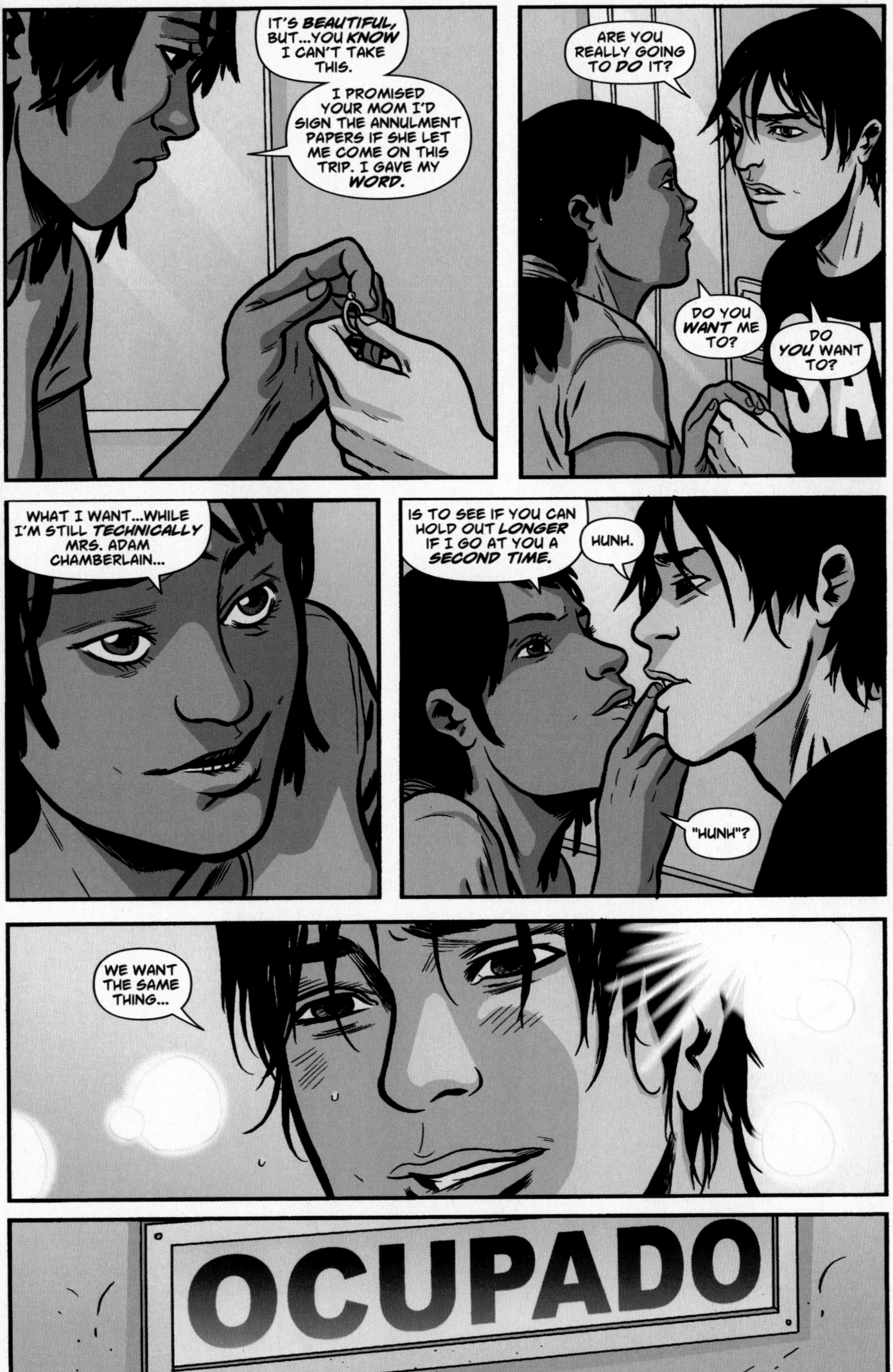

IT'S BEAUTIFUL, BUT...YOU KNOW I CAN'T TAKE THIS.
I PROMISED YOUR MOM I'D SIGN THE ANNULMENT PAPERS IF SHE LET ME COME ON THIS TRIP. I GAVE MY WORD.
ARE YOU REALLY GOING TO DO IT?
DO YOU WANT ME TO?
DO YOU WANT TO?
WHAT I WANT...WHILE I'M STILL TECHNICALLY MRS. ADAM CHAMBERLAIN...
IS TO SEE IF YOU CAN HOLD OUT LONGER IF I GO AT YOU A SECOND TIME.
HUNH.
"HUNH"?
WE WANT THE SAME THING...
OCUPADO

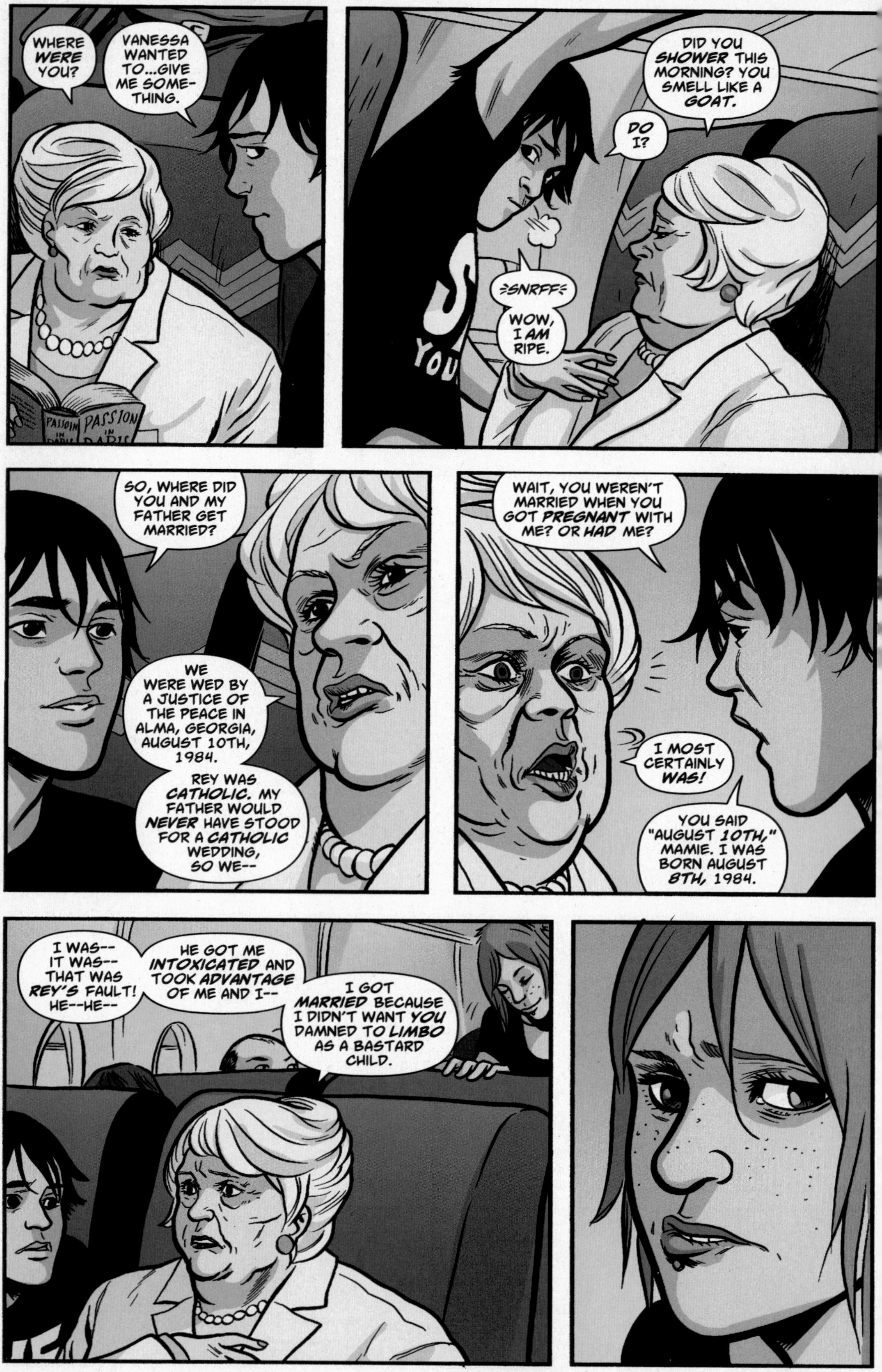
WHERE WERE YOU?
VANESSA WANTED TO...GIVE ME SOME-THING.
PASSION IN PARIS
DID YOU SHOWER THIS MORNING? YOU SMELL LIKE A GOAT.
DO I?
SNRFF
WOW, I AM RIPE.
SO, WHERE DID YOU AND MY FATHER GET MARRIED?
WE WERE WED BY A JUSTICE OF THE PEACE IN ALMA, GEORGIA, AUGUST 10TH, 1984.
REY WAS CATHOLIC. MY FATHER WOULD NEVER HAVE STOOD FOR A CATHOLIC WEDDING, SO WE--
WAIT, YOU WEREN'T MARRIED WHEN YOU GOT PREGNANT WITH ME? OR HAD ME?
I MOST CERTAINLY WAS!
YOU SAID "AUGUST 10TH," MAMIE. I WAS BORN AUGUST 8TH, 1984.
I WAS-- IT WAS-- THAT WAS REY'S FAULT! HE--HE--
HE GOT ME INTOXICATED AND TOOK ADVANTAGE OF ME AND I--
I GOT MARRIED BECAUSE I DIDN'T WANT YOU DAMNED TO LIMBO AS A BASTARD CHILD.

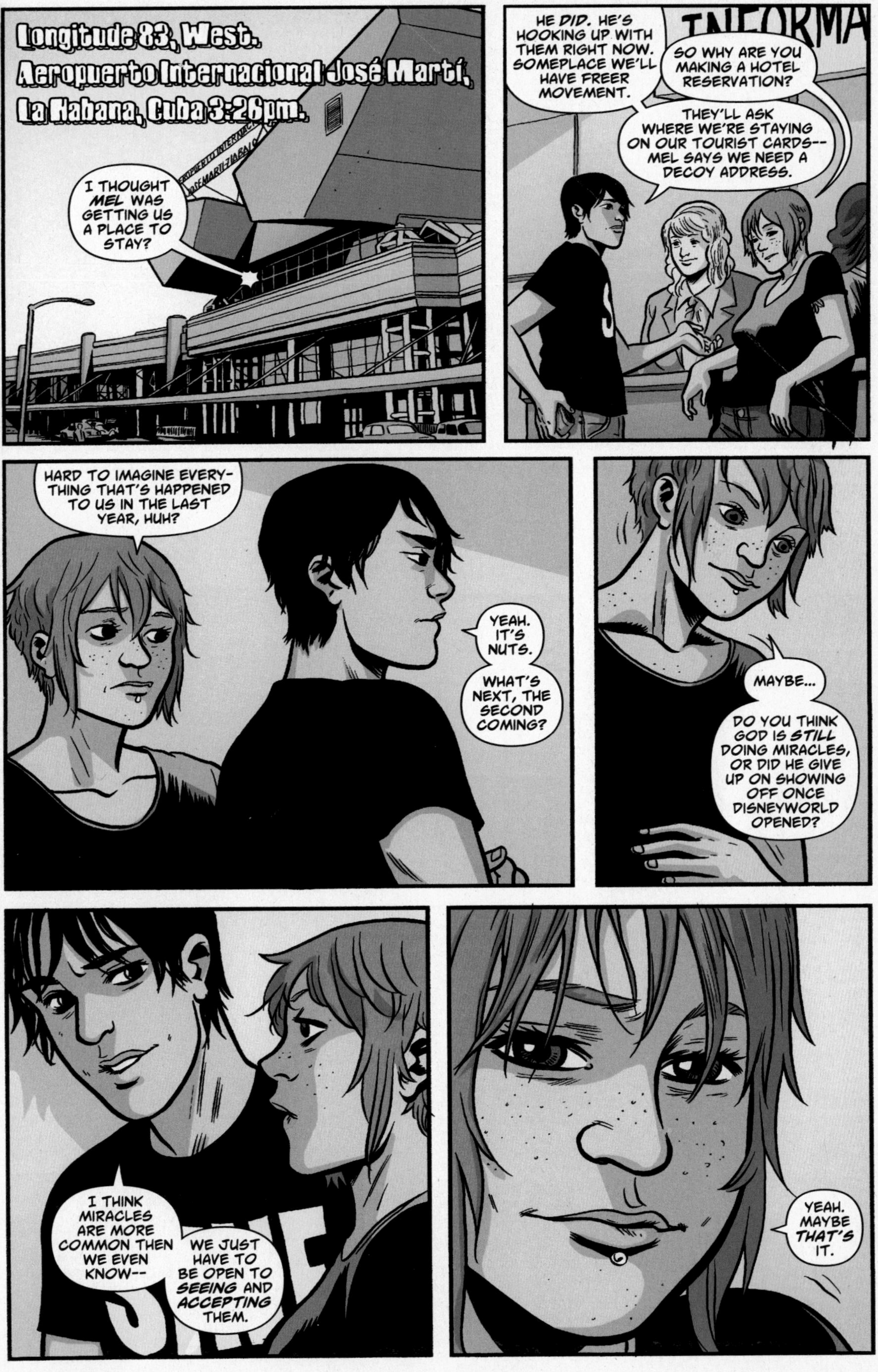
Longitude 83, West.
Aeropuerto Internacional José Martí,
La Habana, Cuba 3:26pm.
AEROPUERTO INTERNACIONAL JOSE MARTI-HABANA
I THOUGHT MEL WAS GETTING US A PLACE TO STAY?
INFORMA
HE DID. HE'S HOOKING UP WITH THEM RIGHT NOW. SOMEPLACE WE'LL HAVE FREER MOVEMENT.
SO WHY ARE YOU MAKING A HOTEL RESERVATION?
THEY'LL ASK WHERE WE'RE STAYING ON OUR TOURIST CARDS-- MEL SAYS WE NEED A DECOY ADDRESS.
HARD TO IMAGINE EVERYTHING THAT'S HAPPENED TO US IN THE LAST YEAR, HUH?
YEAH. IT'S NUTS.
WHAT'S NEXT, THE SECOND COMING?
MAYBE...
DO YOU THINK GOD IS STILL DOING MIRACLES, OR DID HE GIVE UP ON SHOWING OFF ONCE DISNEYWORLD OPENED?
I THINK MIRACLES ARE MORE COMMON THEN WE EVEN KNOW--
WE JUST HAVE TO BE OPEN TO SEEING AND ACCEPTING THEM.
YEAH. MAYBE THAT'S IT.

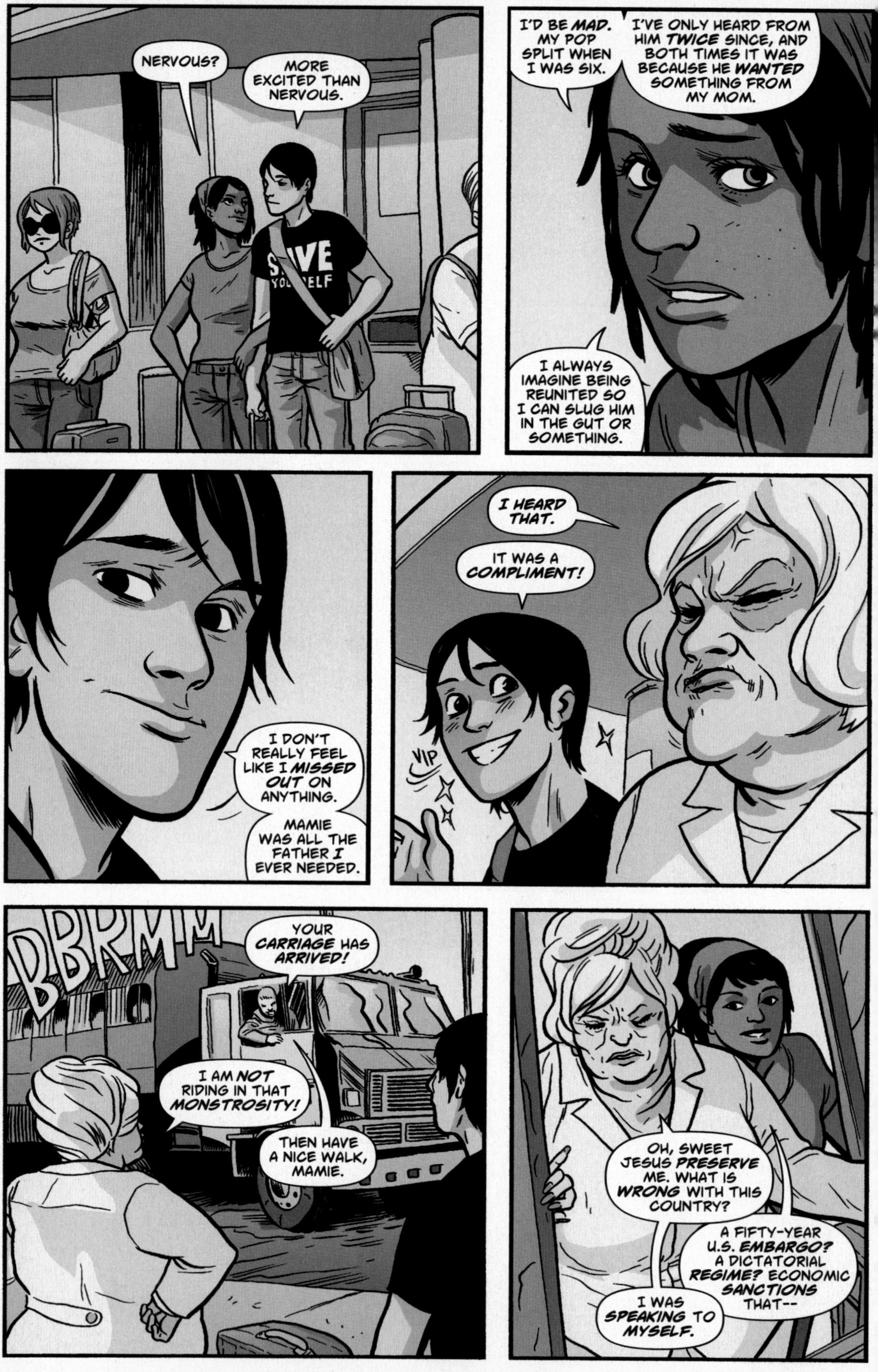
NERVOUS?
MORE EXCITED THAN NERVOUS.
SAVE YOURSELF
I'D BE MAD. MY POP SPLIT WHEN I WAS SIX.
I'VE ONLY HEARD FROM HIM TWICE SINCE, AND BOTH TIMES IT WAS BECAUSE HE WANTED SOMETHING FROM MY MOM.
I ALWAYS IMAGINE BEING REUNITED SO I CAN SLUG HIM IN THE GUT OR SOMETHING.
I DON'T REALLY FEEL LIKE I MISSED OUT ON ANYTHING.
MAMIE WAS ALL THE FATHER I EVER NEEDED.
I HEARD THAT.
IT WAS A COMPLIMENT!
VIP
BBRMM
YOUR CARRIAGE HAS ARRIVED!
I AM NOT RIDING IN THAT MONSTROSITY!
THEN HAVE A NICE WALK, MAMIE.
OH, SWEET JESUS PRESERVE ME. WHAT IS WRONG WITH THIS COUNTRY?
A FIFTY-YEAR U.S. EMBARGO? A DICTATORIAL REGIME? ECONOMIC SANCTIONS THAT--
I WAS SPEAKING TO MYSELF.

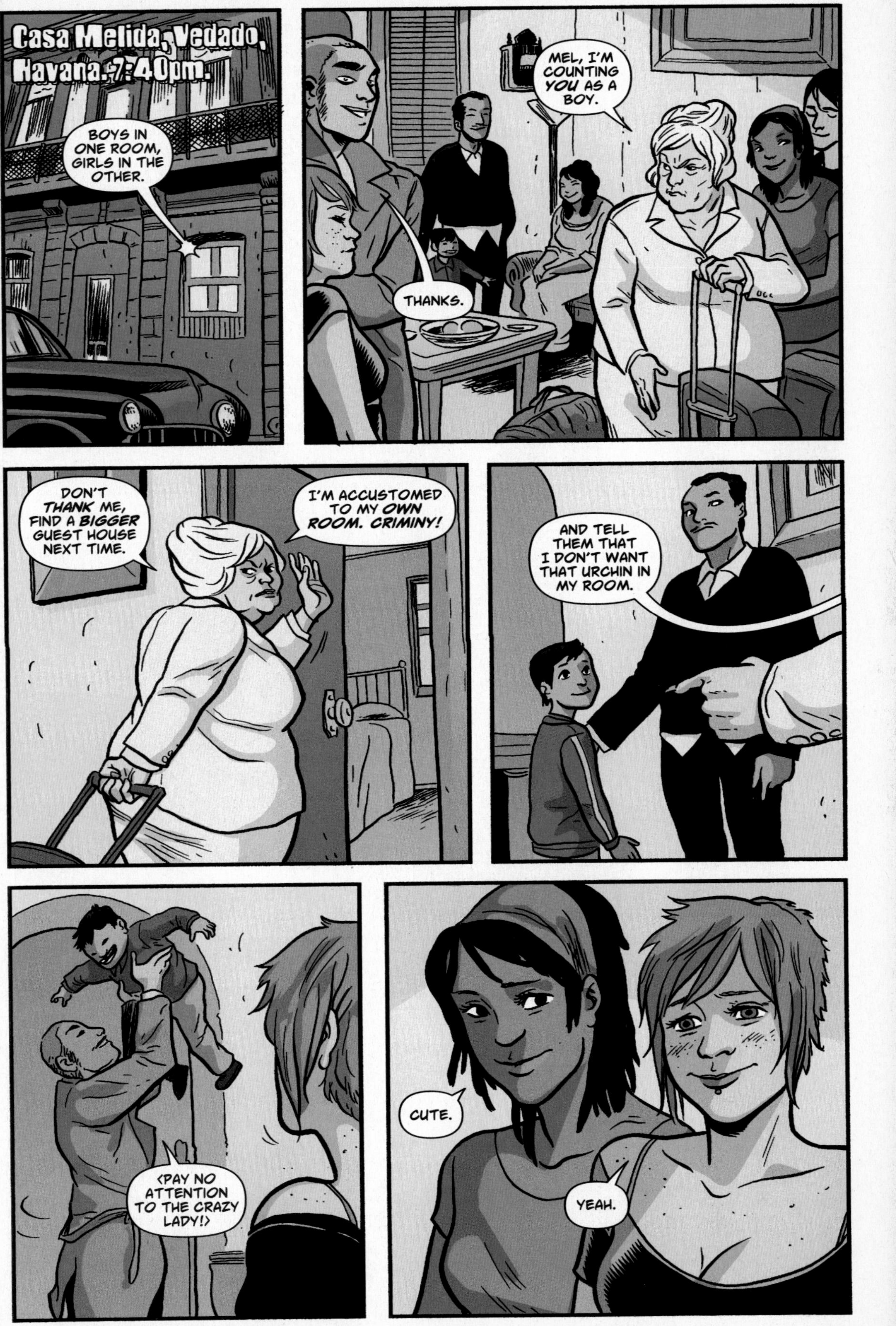
Casa Melida, Vedado, Havana. 7:40pm.
BOYS IN ONE ROOM, GIRLS IN THE OTHER.
MEL, I'M COUNTING YOU AS A BOY.
THANKS.
DON'T THANK ME, FIND A BIGGER GUEST HOUSE NEXT TIME.
I'M ACCUSTOMED TO MY OWN ROOM. CRIMINY!
AND TELL THEM THAT I DON'T WANT THAT URCHIN IN MY ROOM.
<PAY NO ATTENTION TO THE CRAZY LADY!>
CUTE.
YEAH.

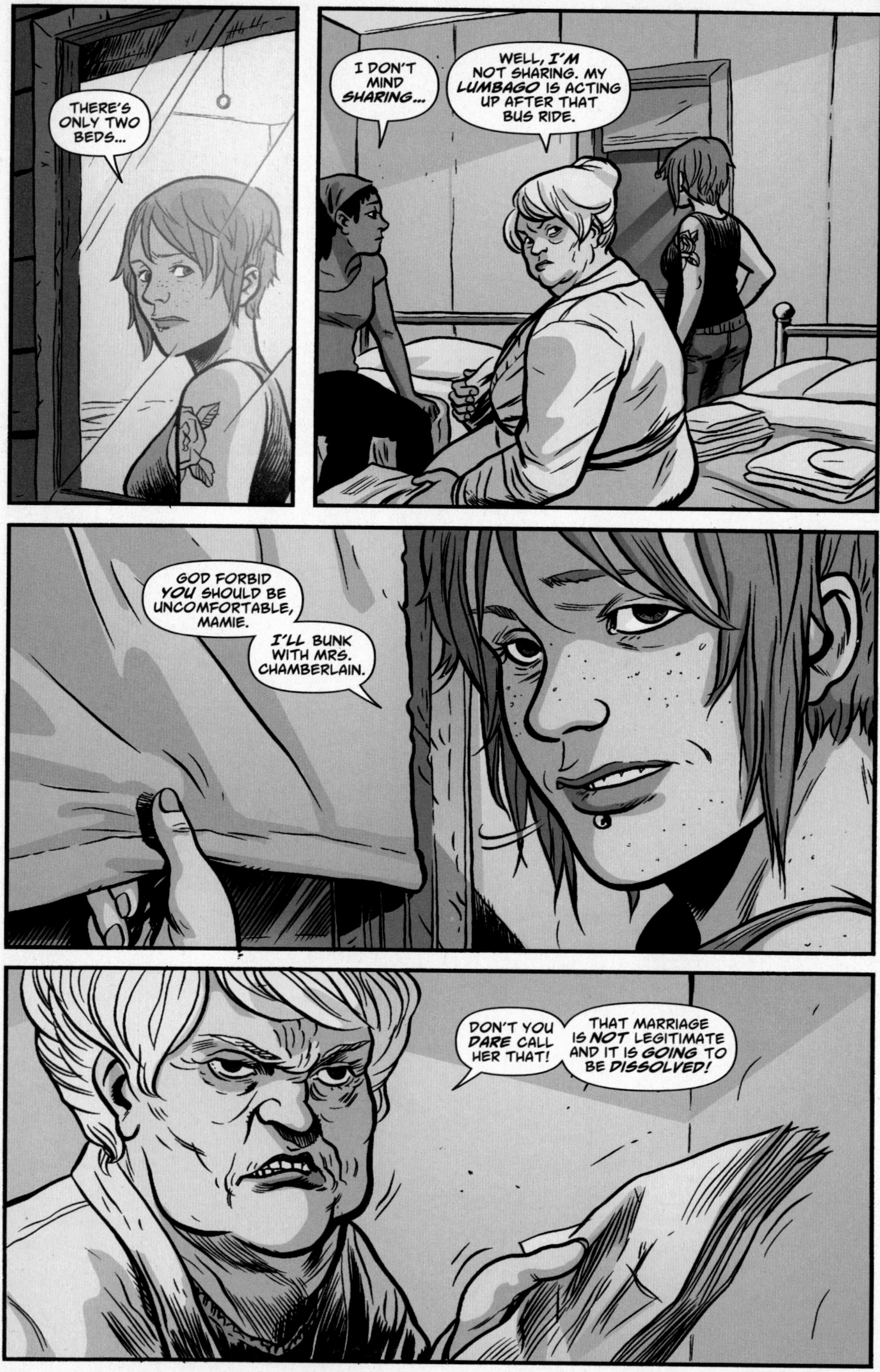
THERE'S ONLY TWO BEDS...
I DON'T MIND SHARING...
WELL, I'M NOT SHARING. MY LUMBAGO IS ACTING UP AFTER THAT BUS RIDE.
GOD FORBID YOU SHOULD BE UNCOMFORTABLE, MAMIE.
I'LL BUNK WITH MRS. CHAMBERLAIN.
DON'T YOU DARE CALL HER THAT!
THAT MARRIAGE IS NOT LEGITIMATE AND IT IS GOING TO BE DISSOLVED!

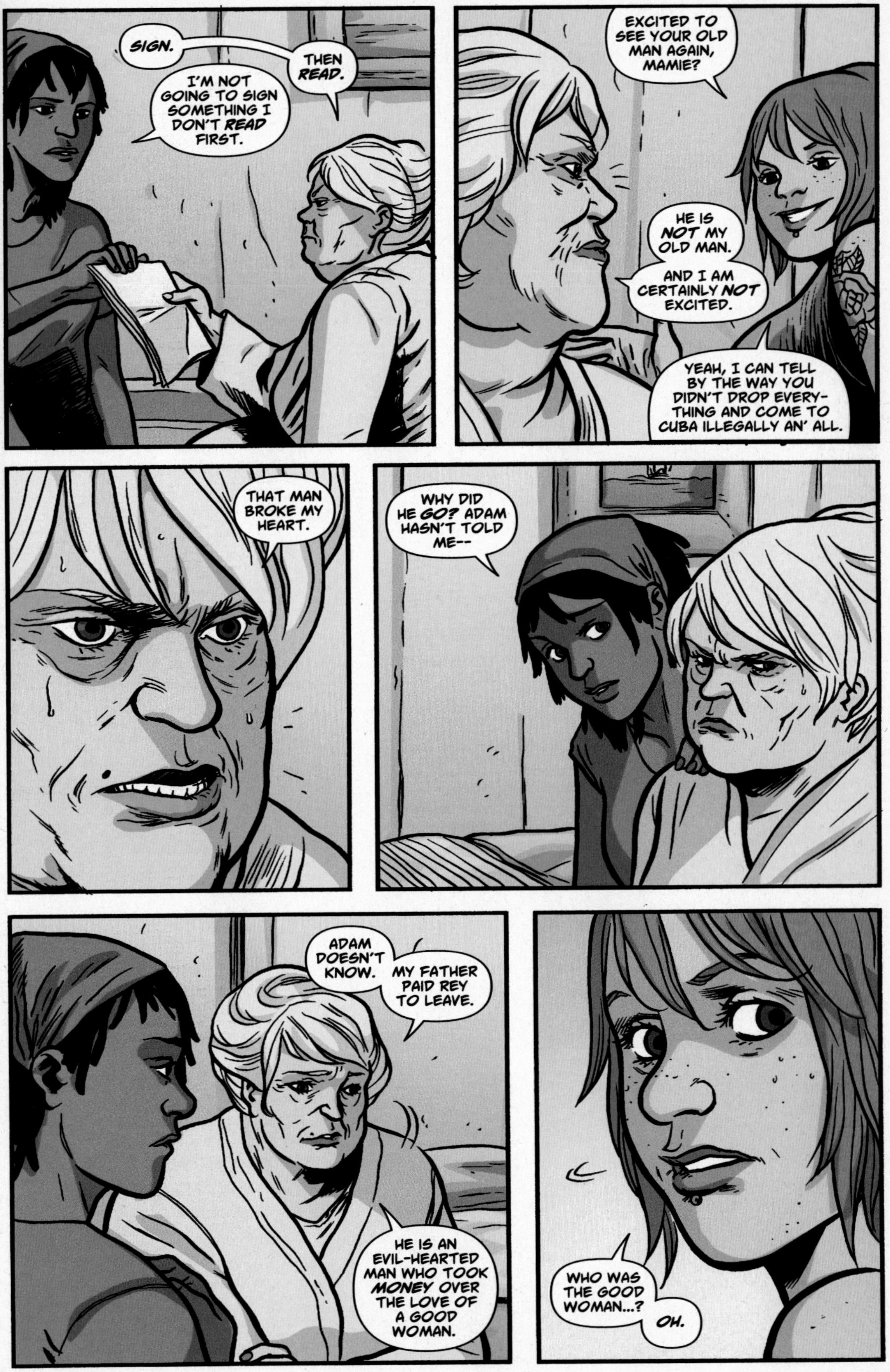
SIGN.
I'M NOT GOING TO SIGN SOMETHING I DON'T READ FIRST.
THEN READ.
EXCITED TO SEE YOUR OLD MAN AGAIN, MAMIE?
HE IS NOT MY OLD MAN.
AND I AM CERTAINLY NOT EXCITED.
YEAH, I CAN TELL BY THE WAY YOU DIDN'T DROP EVERY-THING AND COME TO CUBA ILLEGALLY AN' ALL.
THAT MAN BROKE MY HEART.
WHY DID HE GO? ADAM HASN'T TOLD ME--
ADAM DOESN'T KNOW.
MY FATHER PAID REY TO LEAVE.
HE IS AN EVIL-HEARTED MAN WHO TOOK MONEY OVER THE LOVE OF A GOOD WOMAN.
WHO WAS THE GOOD WOMAN...?
OH.

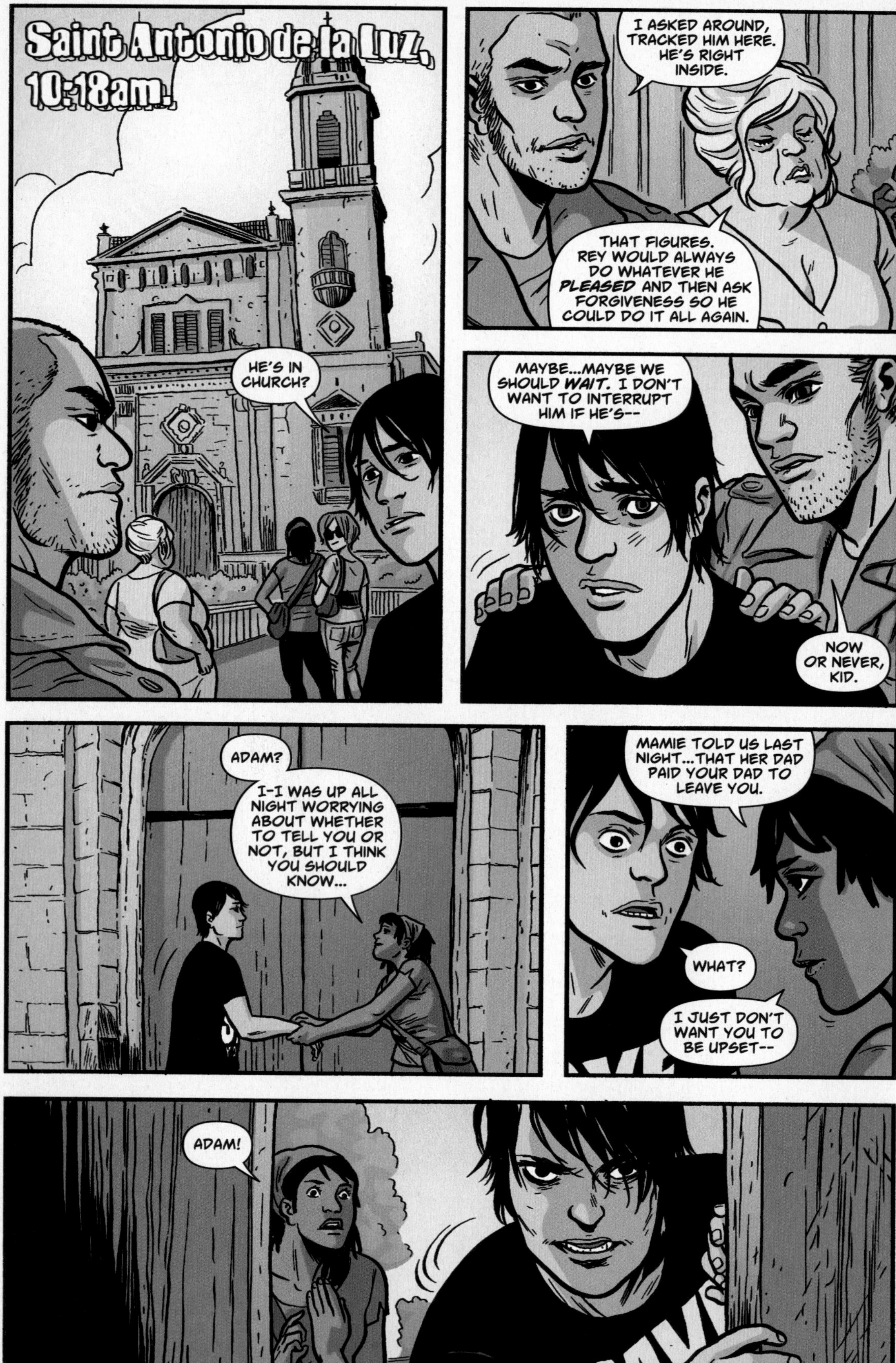
Saint Antonio de la Luz, 10:18am.
HE'S IN CHURCH?
I ASKED AROUND, TRACKED HIM HERE. HE'S RIGHT INSIDE.
THAT FIGURES. REY WOULD ALWAYS DO WHATEVER HE PLEASED AND THEN ASK FORGIVENESS SO HE COULD DO IT ALL AGAIN.
MAYBE...MAYBE WE SHOULD WAIT. I DON'T WANT TO INTERRUPT HIM IF HE'S--
NOW OR NEVER, KID.
ADAM?
I-I WAS UP ALL NIGHT WORRYING ABOUT WHETHER TO TELL YOU OR NOT, BUT I THINK YOU SHOULD KNOW...
MAMIE TOLD US LAST NIGHT...THAT HER DAD PAID YOUR DAD TO LEAVE YOU.
WHAT?
I JUST DON'T WANT YOU TO BE UPSET--
ADAM!

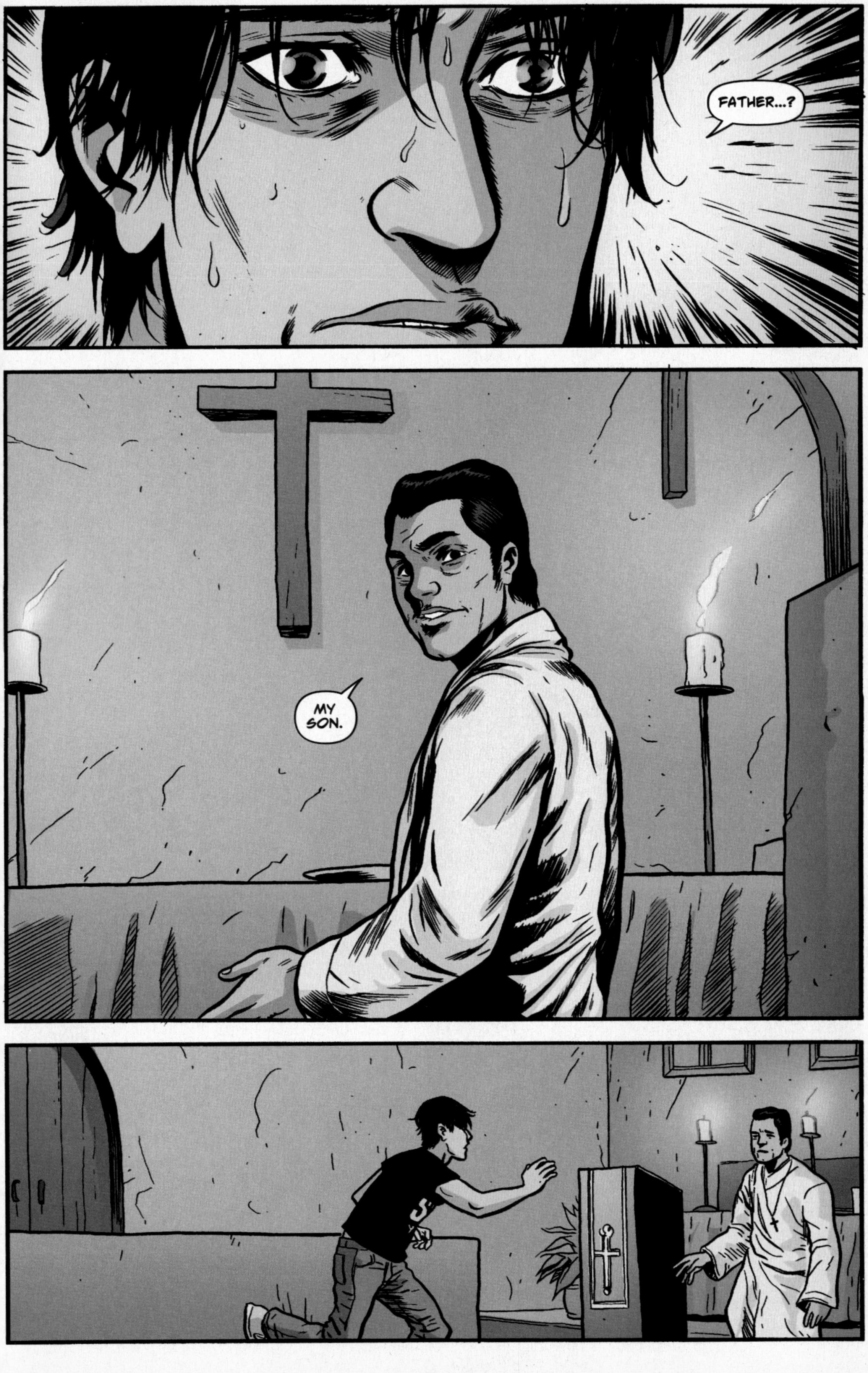
FATHER...?
MY SON.

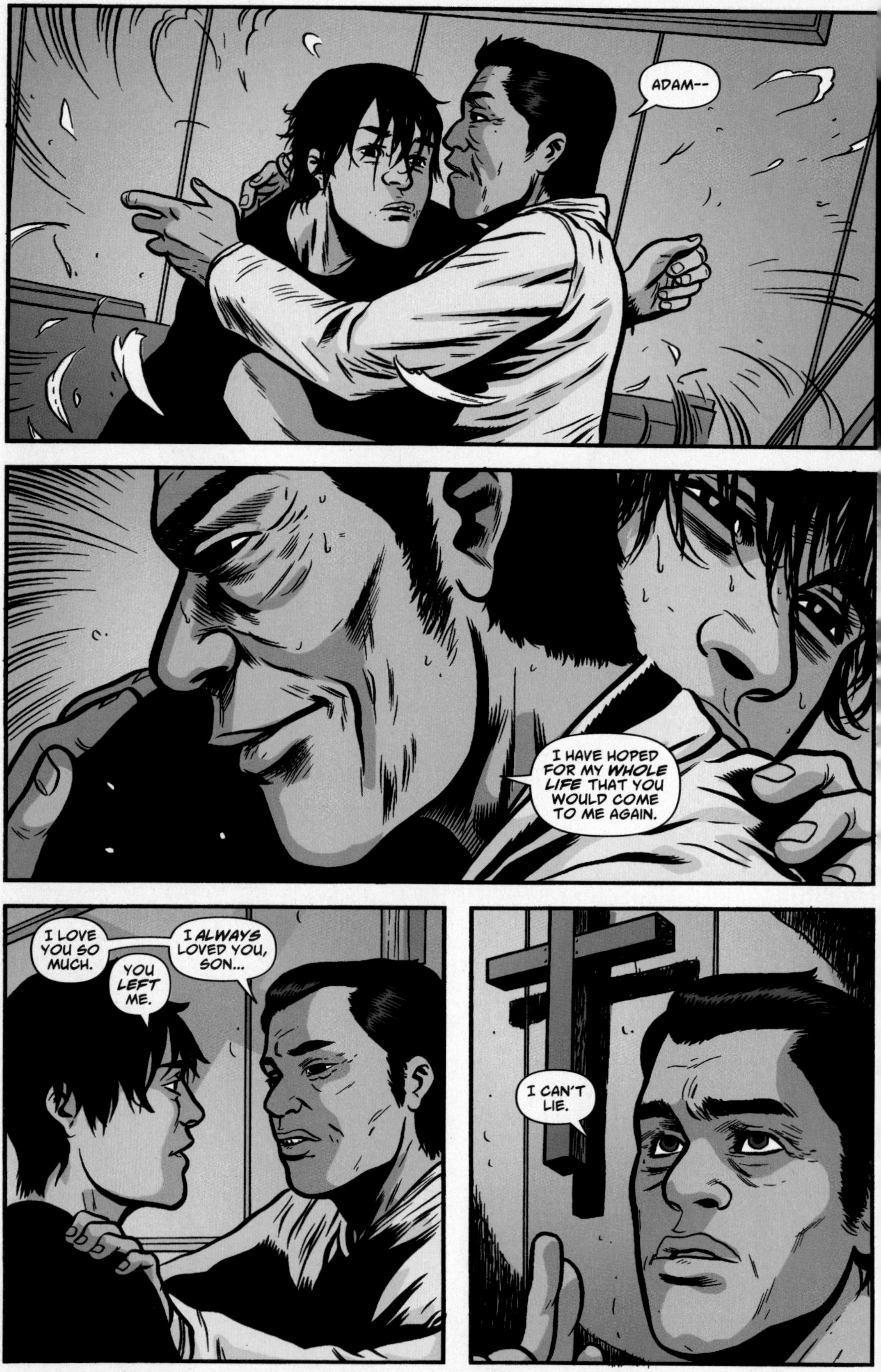
ADAM--
I HAVE HOPED FOR MY WHOLE LIFE THAT YOU WOULD COME TO ME AGAIN.
I LOVE YOU SO MUCH.
I ALWAYS LOVED YOU, SON...
YOU LEFT ME.
I CAN'T LIE.

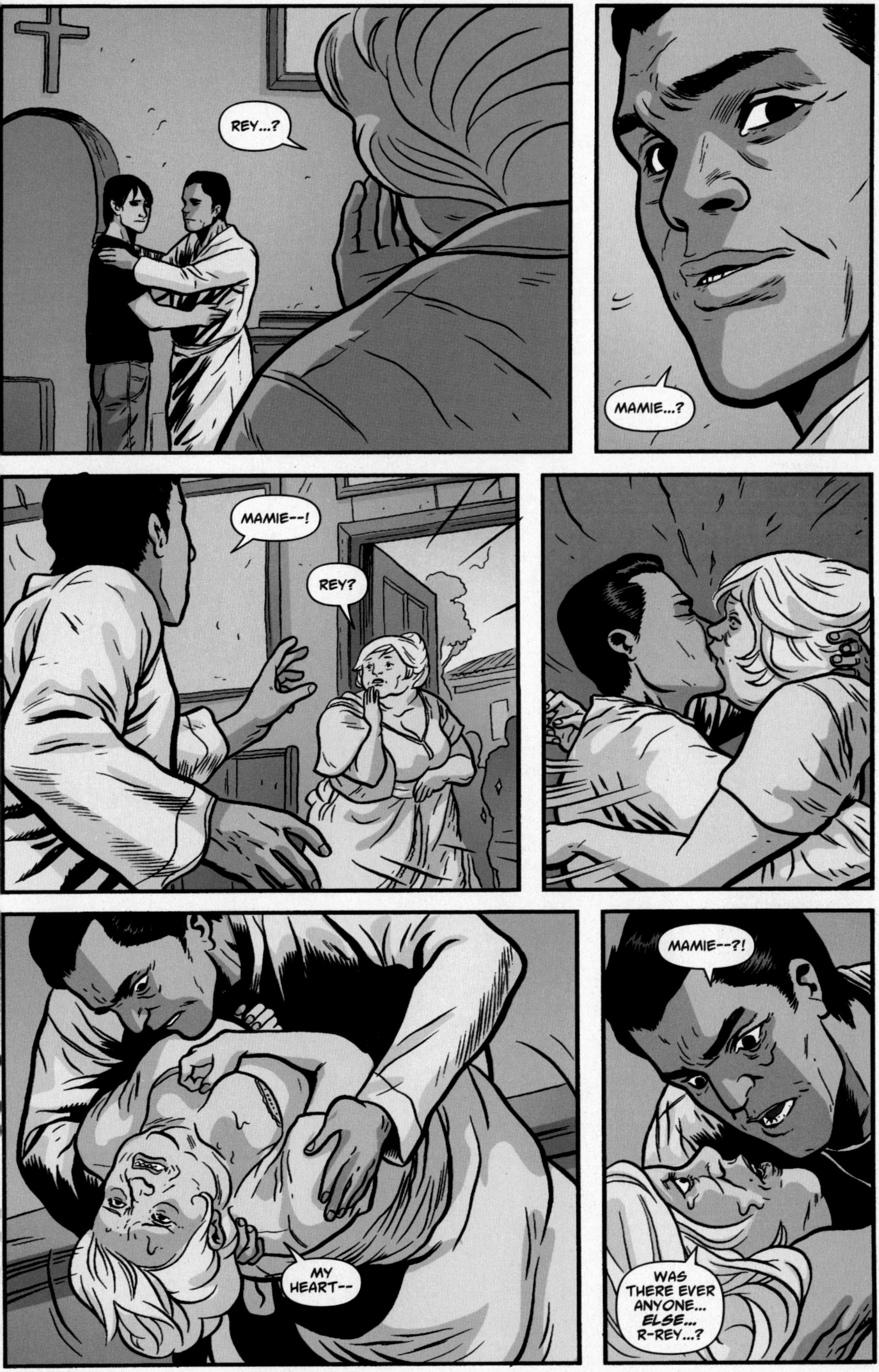
REY...?
MAMIE...?
MAMIE--!
REY?
MAMIE--?!
MY HEART--
WAS THERE EVER ANYONE... ELSE... R-REY...?

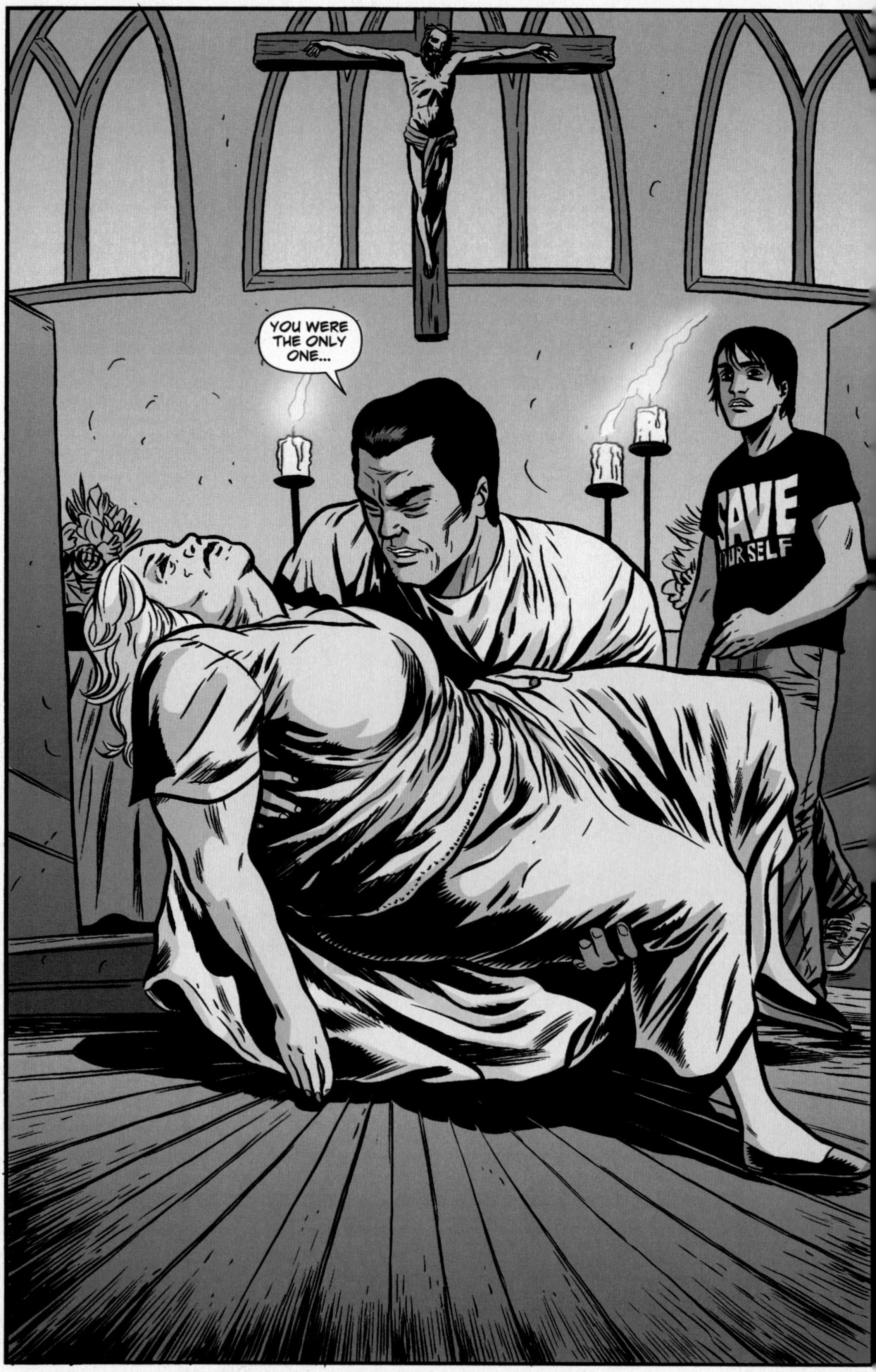
YOU WERE THE ONLY ONE...
SAVE
YOURSELF

CHAPTER THREE

Chapter pencils by Becky Cloonan and Ryan Kelly   Chapter inks by Jim Rugg

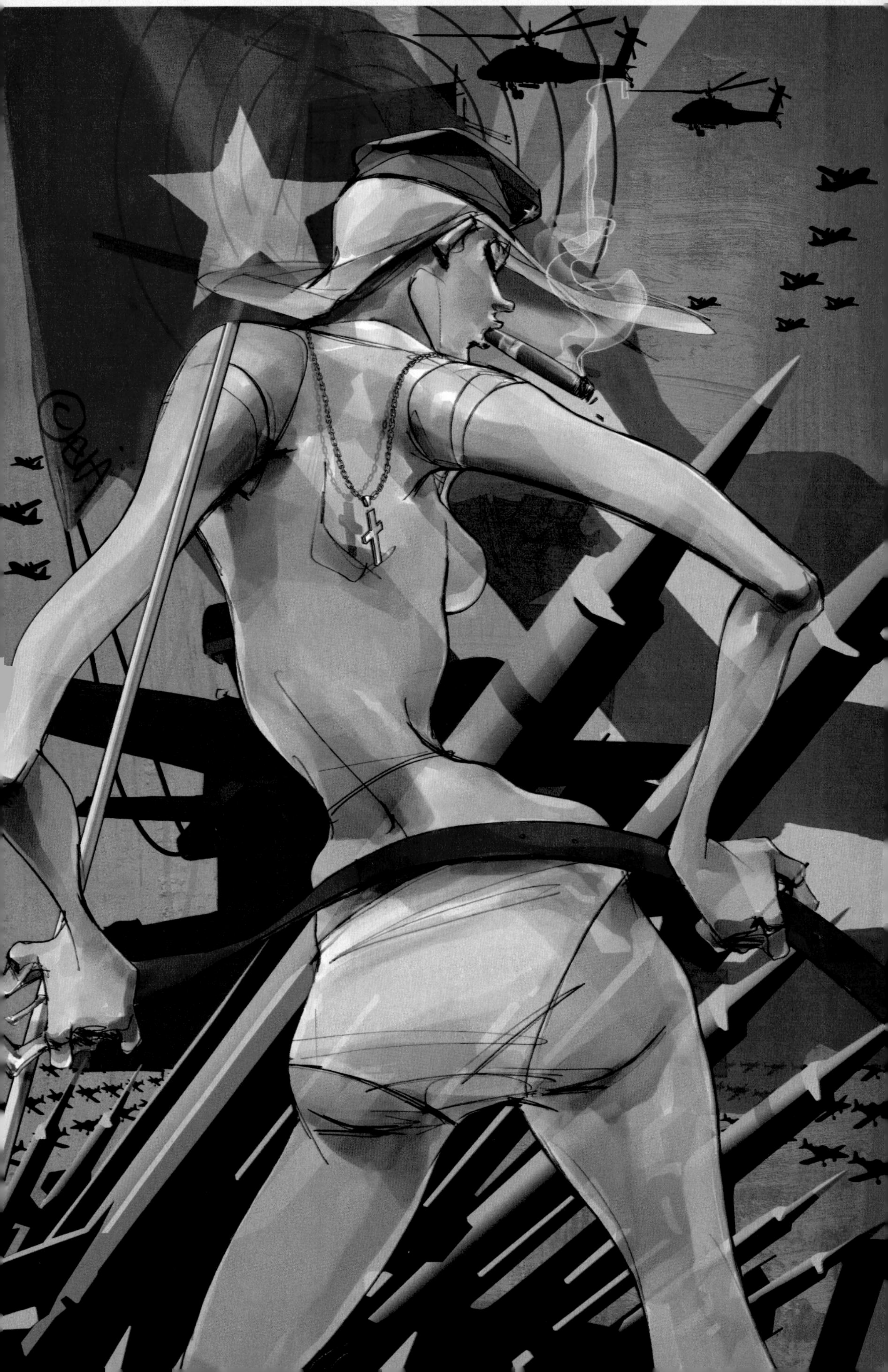

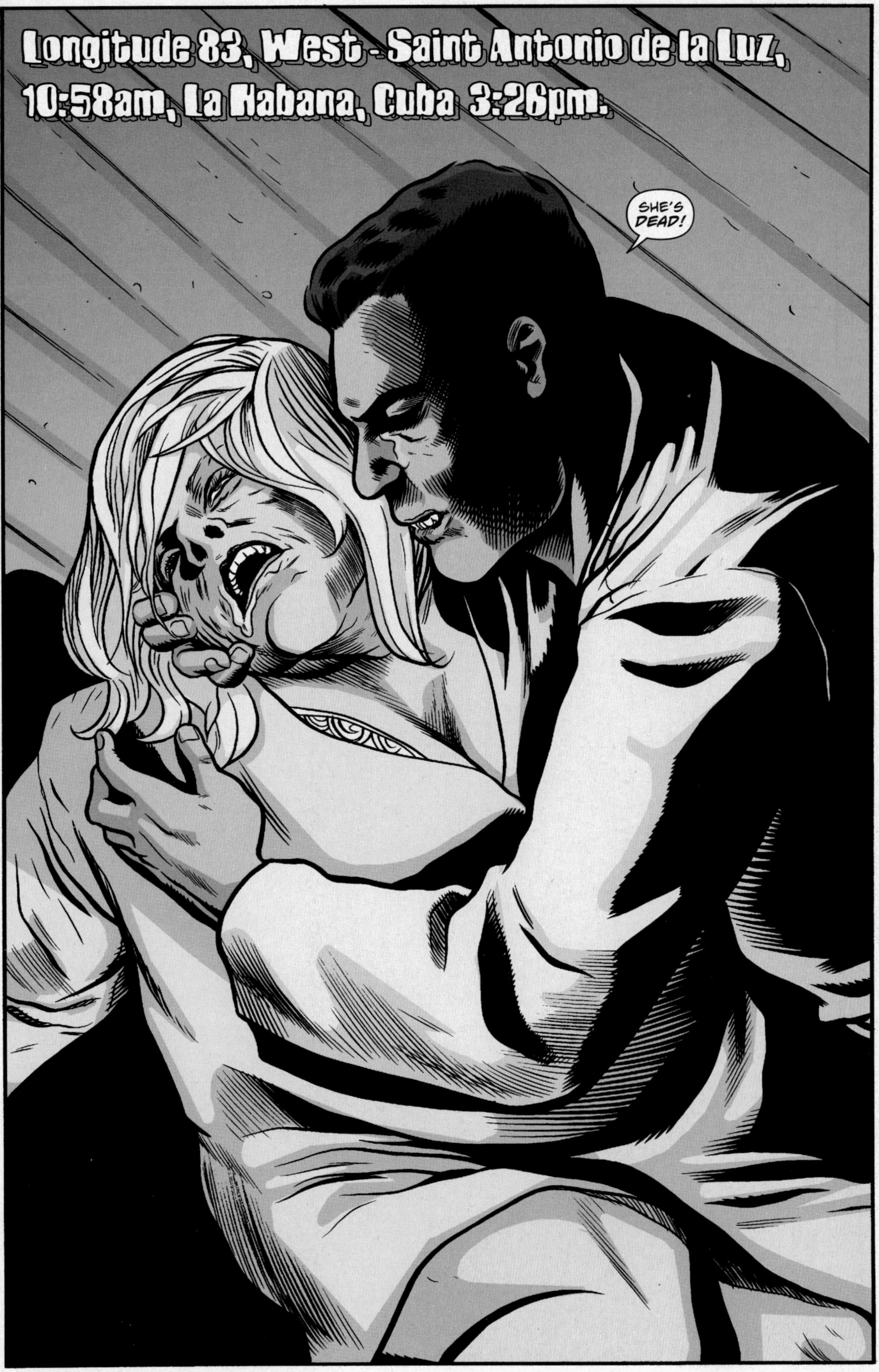
Longitude 83, West - Saint Antonio de la Luz,
10:58am, La Habana, Cuba 3:26pm.
SHE'S DEAD!

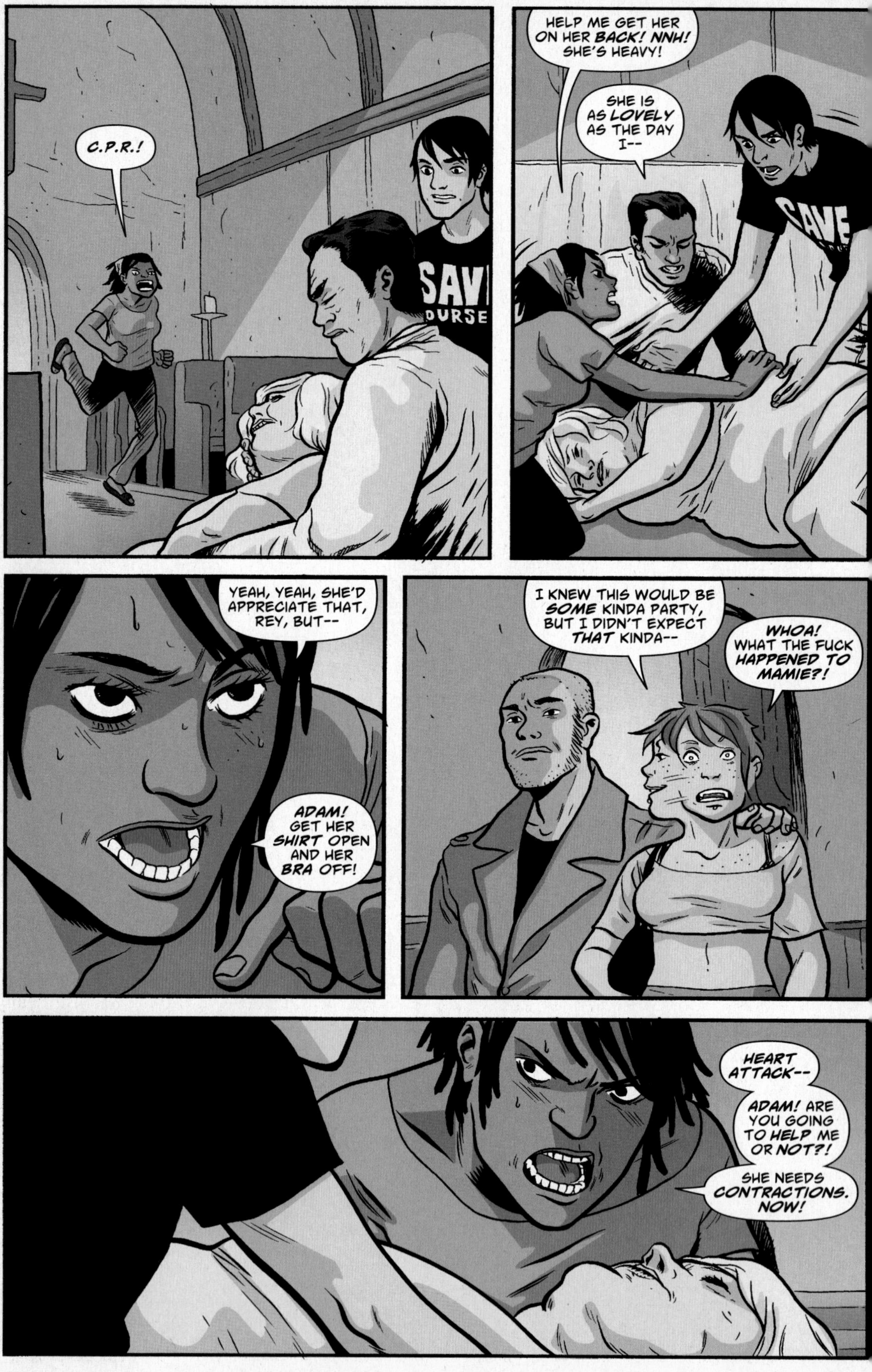
C.P.R.!
SAVE YOURSE
HELP ME GET HER ON HER BACK! NNH! SHE'S HEAVY!
SHE IS AS LOVELY AS THE DAY I--
SAVE
YEAH, YEAH, SHE'D APPRECIATE THAT, REY, BUT--
ADAM! GET HER SHIRT OPEN AND HER BRA OFF!
I KNEW THIS WOULD BE SOME KINDA PARTY, BUT I DIDN'T EXPECT THAT KINDA--
WHOA! WHAT THE FUCK HAPPENED TO MAMIE?!
HEART ATTACK--
ADAM! ARE YOU GOING TO HELP ME OR NOT?!
SHE NEEDS CONTRACTIONS. NOW!

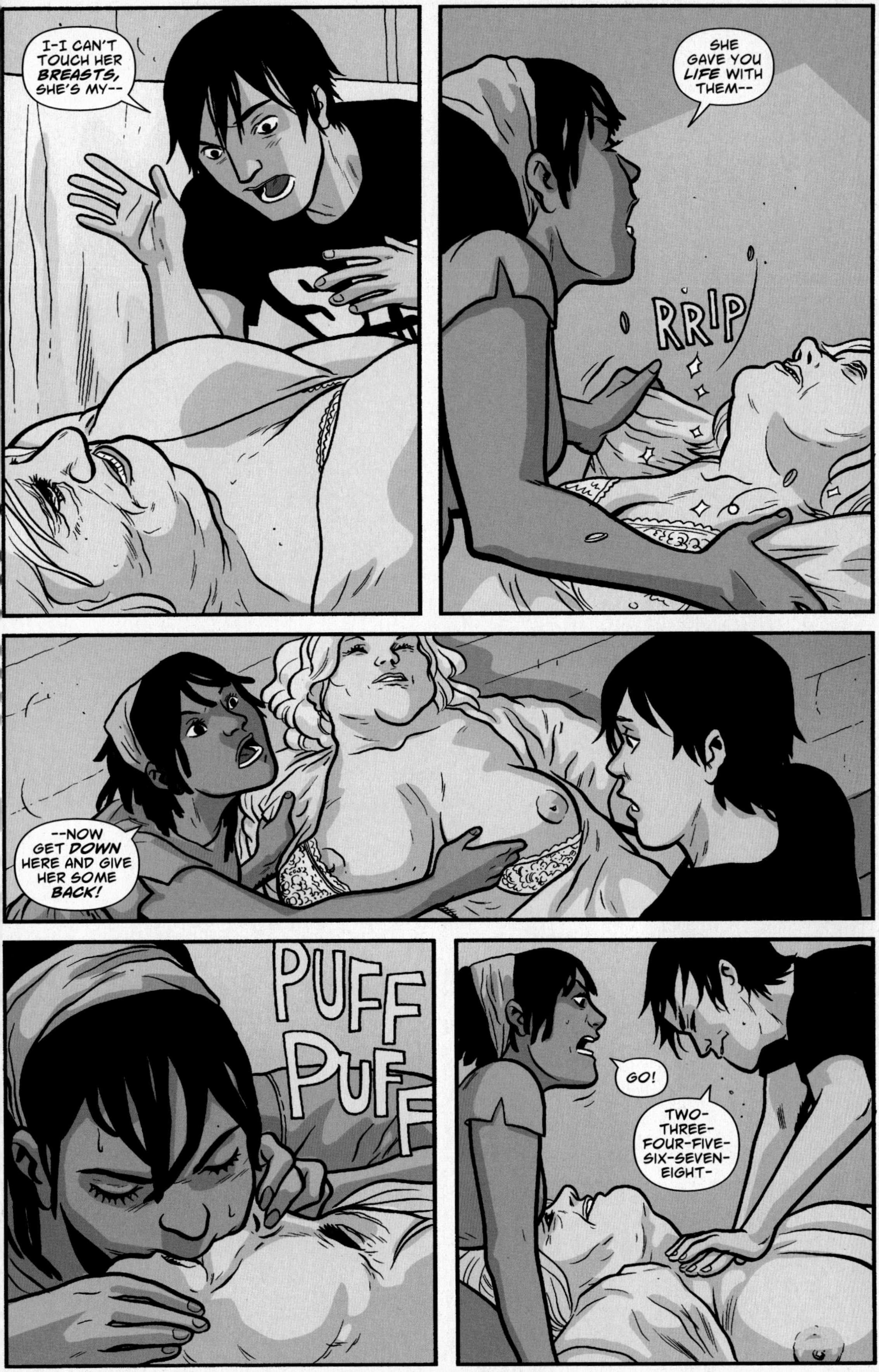
I-I CAN'T TOUCH HER BREASTS, SHE'S MY--
SHE GAVE YOU LIFE WITH THEM--
RRIP
--NOW GET DOWN HERE AND GIVE HER SOME BACK!
PUFF
PUFF
GO!
TWO-THREE-FOUR-FIVE-SIX-SEVEN-EIGHT-

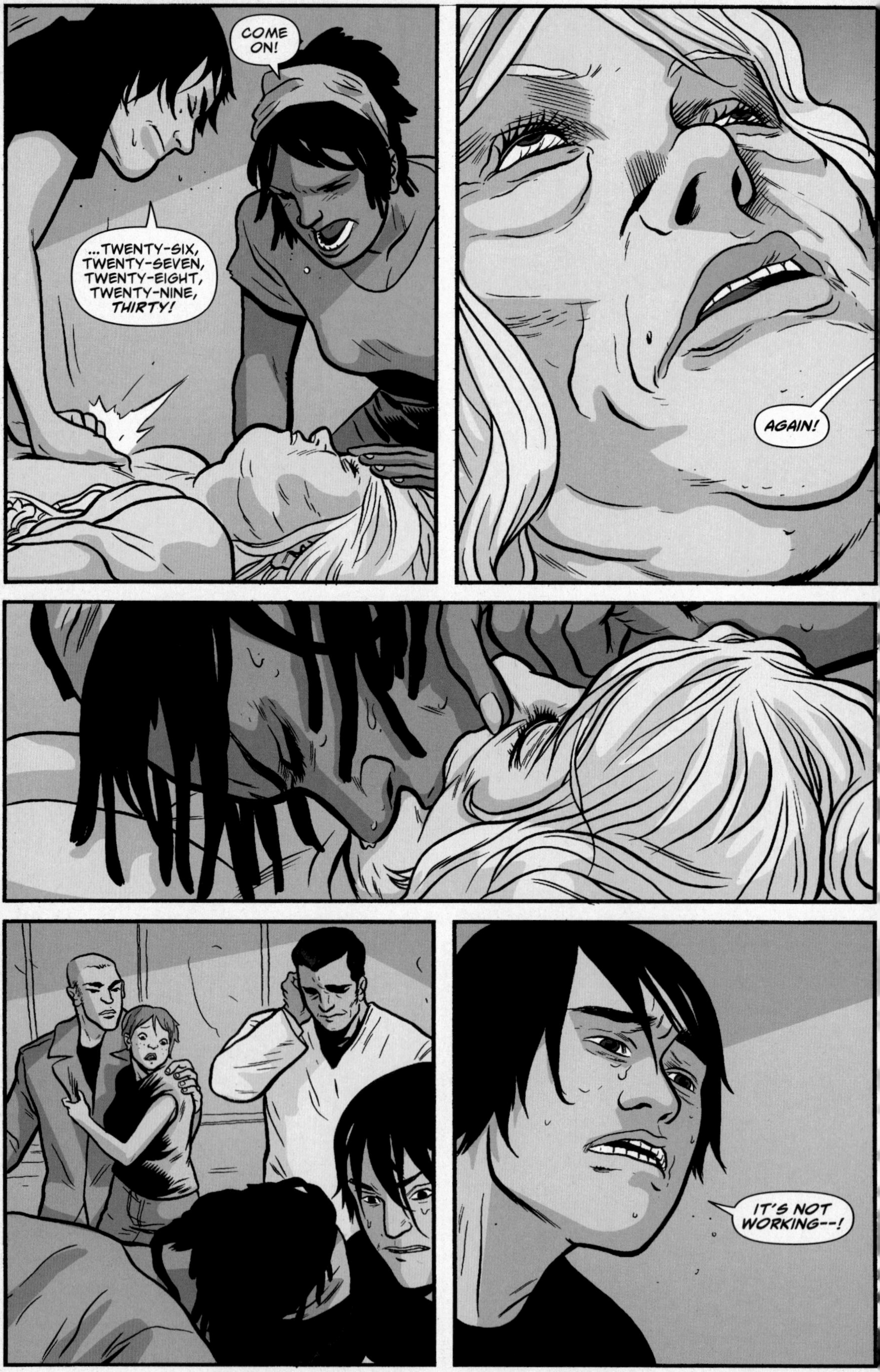
COME ON!
...TWENTY-SIX, TWENTY-SEVEN, TWENTY-EIGHT, TWENTY-NINE, THIRTY!
AGAIN!
IT'S NOT WORKING--!

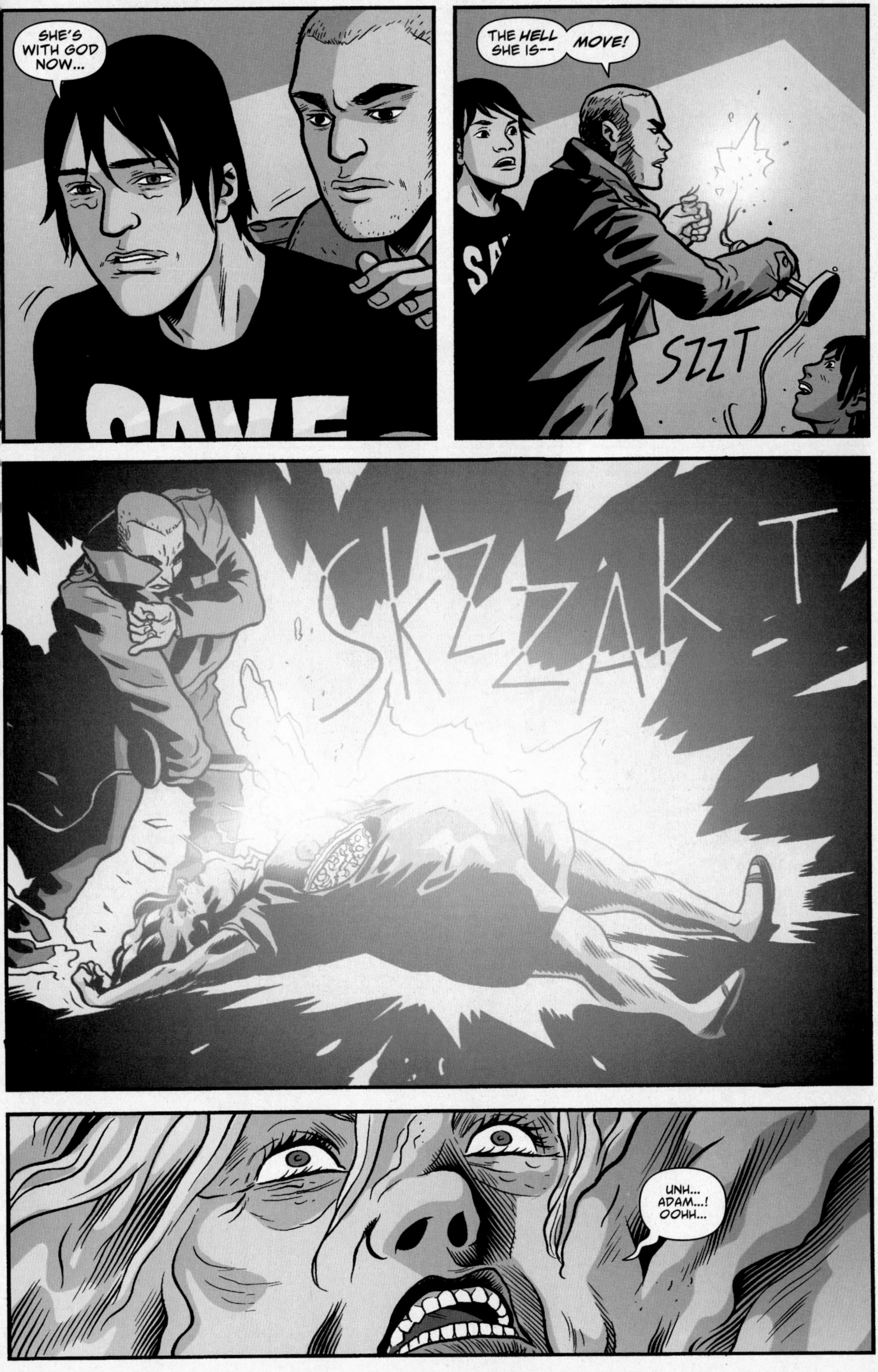
SHE'S WITH GOD NOW...
THE HELL SHE IS--
MOVE!
SZZT
SKZZAKT
UNH... ADAM...! OOHH...

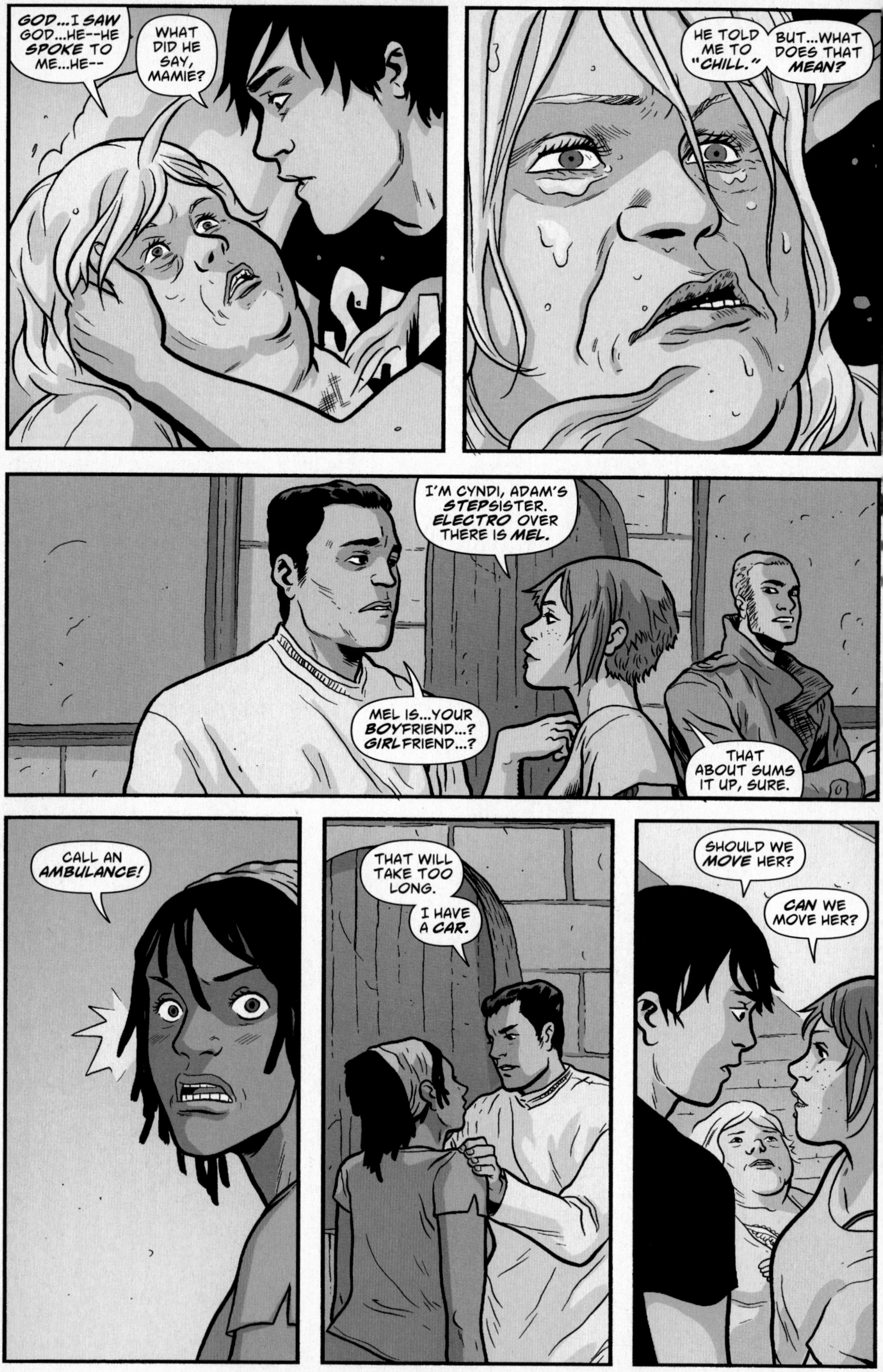
GOD...I SAW GOD...HE--HE SPOKE TO ME...HE--
WHAT DID HE SAY, MAMIE?
HE TOLD ME TO "CHILL."
BUT...WHAT DOES THAT MEAN?
I'M CYNDI, ADAM'S STEPSISTER. ELECTRO OVER THERE IS MEL.
MEL IS...YOUR BOYFRIEND...? GIRLFRIEND...?
THAT ABOUT SUMS IT UP, SURE.
CALL AN AMBULANCE!
THAT WILL TAKE TOO LONG.
I HAVE A CAR.
SHOULD WE MOVE HER?
CAN WE MOVE HER?

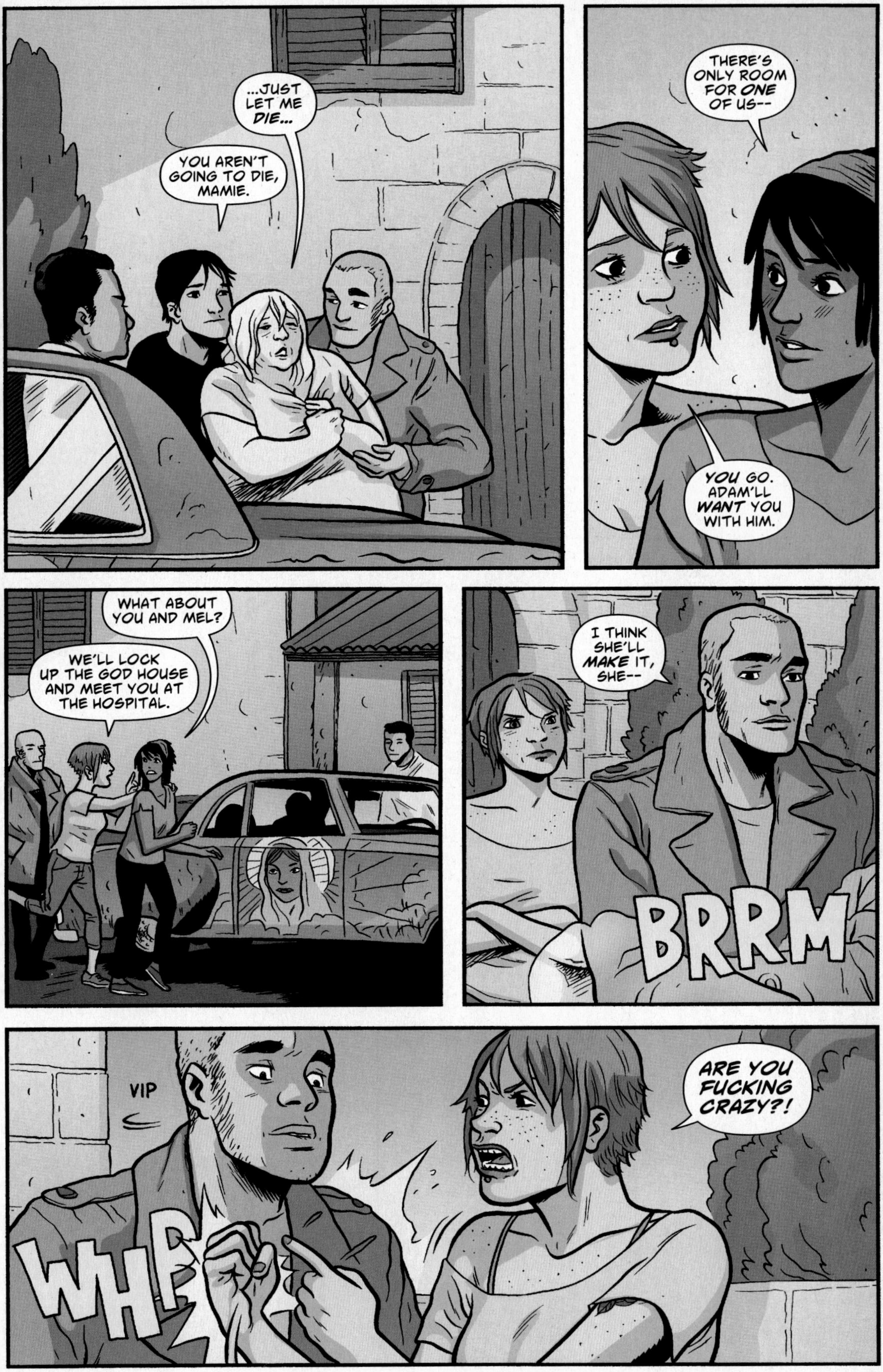
...JUST LET ME DIE...
YOU AREN'T GOING TO DIE, MAMIE.
THERE'S ONLY ROOM FOR ONE OF US--
YOU GO. ADAM'LL WANT YOU WITH HIM.
WHAT ABOUT YOU AND MEL?
WE'LL LOCK UP THE GOD HOUSE AND MEET YOU AT THE HOSPITAL.
I THINK SHE'LL MAKE IT, SHE--
BRRM
VIP
WHP
ARE YOU FUCKING CRAZY?!

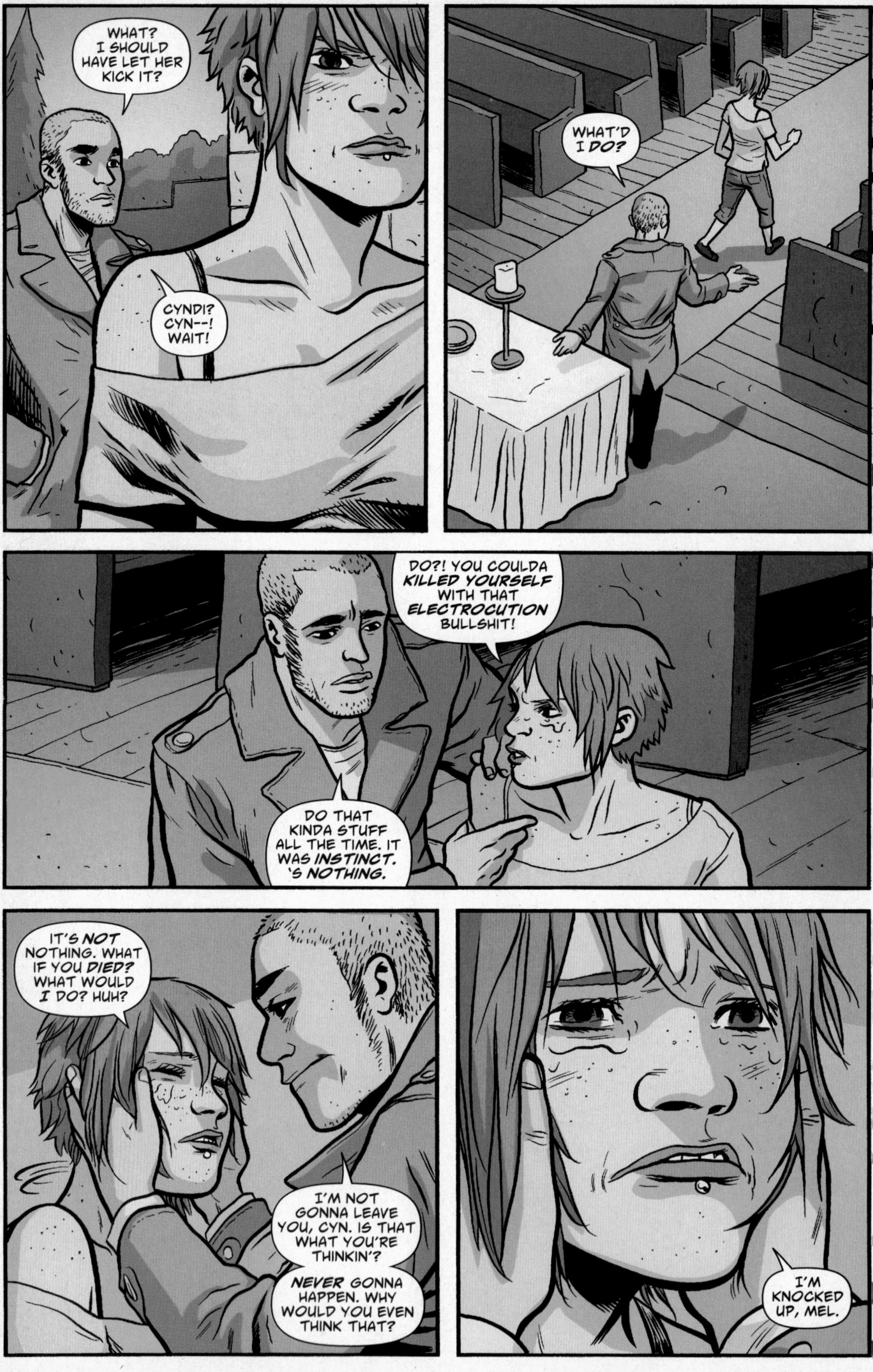
WHAT? I SHOULD HAVE LET HER KICK IT?
CYNDI? CYN--! WAIT!
WHAT'D I DO?
DO?! YOU COULDA KILLED YOURSELF WITH THAT ELECTROCUTION BULLSHIT!
DO THAT KINDA STUFF ALL THE TIME. IT WAS INSTINCT. 'S NOTHING.
IT'S NOT NOTHING. WHAT IF YOU DIED? WHAT WOULD I DO? HUH?
I'M NOT GONNA LEAVE YOU, CYN. IS THAT WHAT YOU'RE THINKIN'?
NEVER GONNA HAPPEN. WHY WOULD YOU EVEN THINK THAT?
I'M KNOCKED UP, MEL.

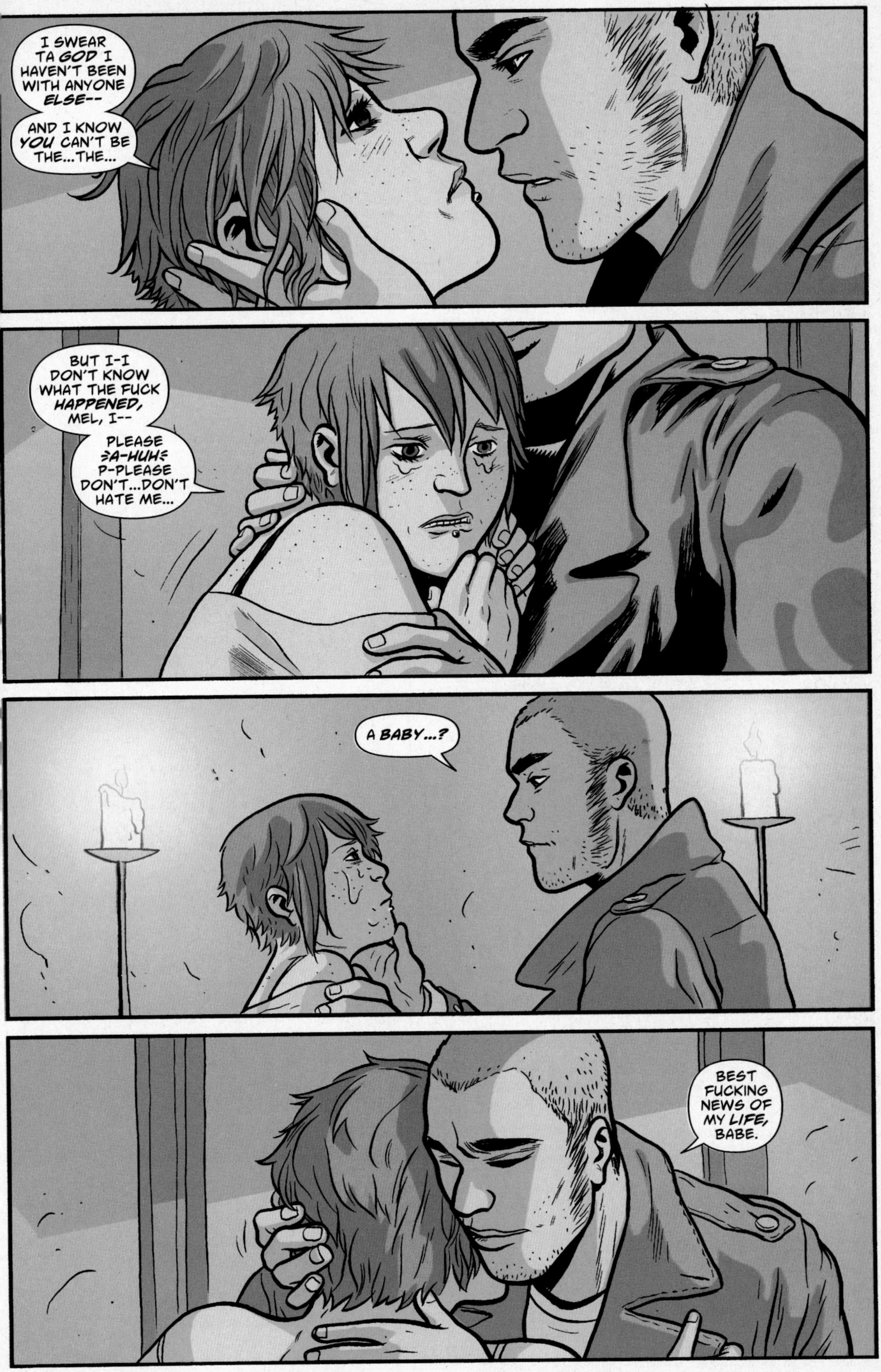
I SWEAR TA GOD I HAVEN'T BEEN WITH ANYONE ELSE--
AND I KNOW YOU CAN'T BE THE...THE...
BUT I-I DON'T KNOW WHAT THE FUCK HAPPENED, MEL, I--
PLEASE ≈A-HUH≈ P-PLEASE DON'T...DON'T HATE ME...
A BABY...?
BEST FUCKING NEWS OF MY LIFE, BABE.

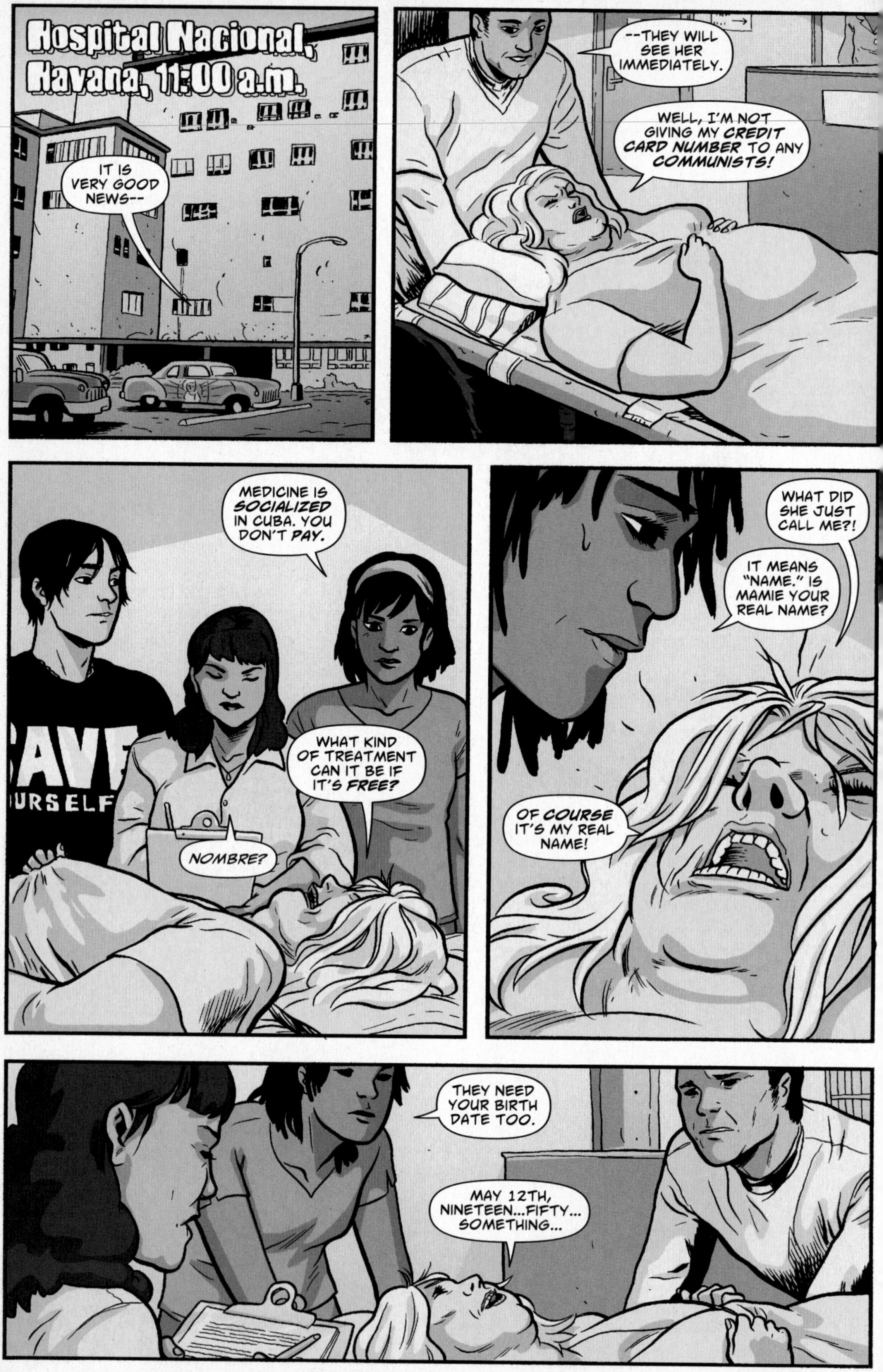
Hospital Nacional, Havana, 11:00 a.m.
IT IS VERY GOOD NEWS--
--THEY WILL SEE HER IMMEDIATELY.
WELL, I'M NOT GIVING MY CREDIT CARD NUMBER TO ANY COMMUNISTS!
MEDICINE IS SOCIALIZED IN CUBA. YOU DON'T PAY.
WHAT KIND OF TREATMENT CAN IT BE IF IT'S FREE?
NOMBRE?
WHAT DID SHE JUST CALL ME?!
IT MEANS "NAME." IS MAMIE YOUR REAL NAME?
OF COURSE IT'S MY REAL NAME!
THEY NEED YOUR BIRTH DATE TOO.
MAY 12TH, NINETEEN...FIFTY... SOMETHING...

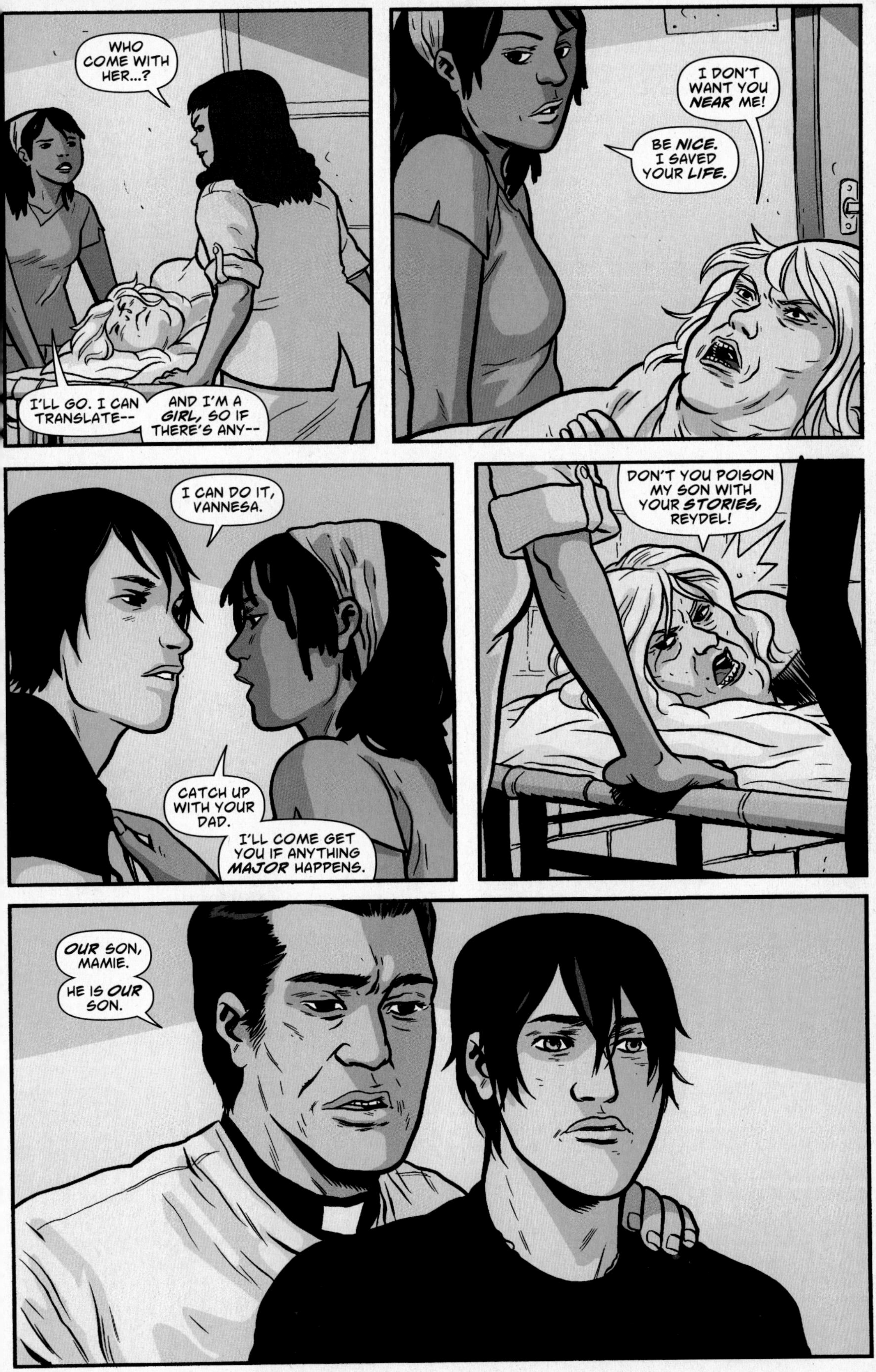
WHO COME WITH HER...?
I'LL GO. I CAN TRANSLATE--
AND I'M A GIRL, SO IF THERE'S ANY--
I DON'T WANT YOU NEAR ME!
BE NICE. I SAVED YOUR LIFE.
I CAN DO IT, VANNESA.
CATCH UP WITH YOUR DAD.
I'LL COME GET YOU IF ANYTHING MAJOR HAPPENS.
DON'T YOU POISON MY SON WITH YOUR STORIES, REYDEL!
OUR SON, MAMIE.
HE IS OUR SON.

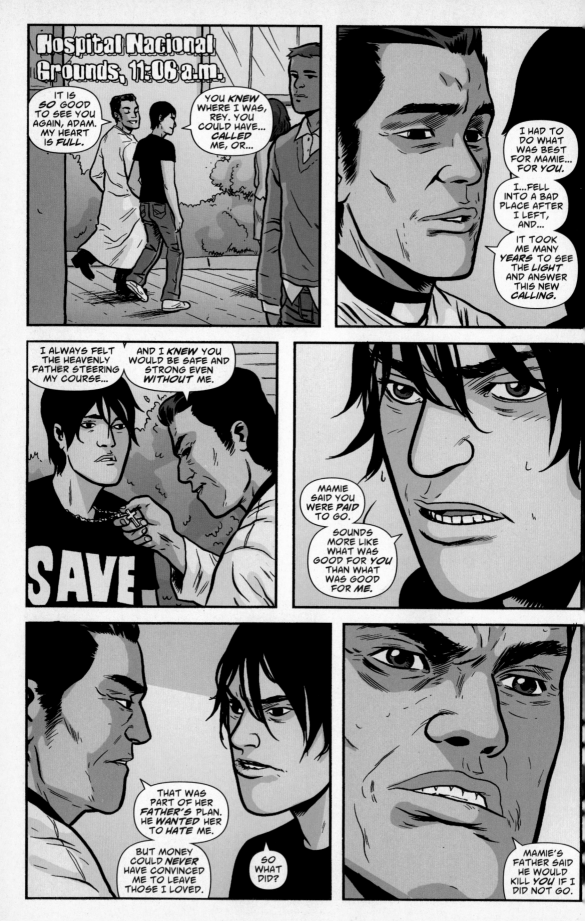

Hospital Nacional Grounds, 11:06 a.m.

IT IS SO GOOD TO SEE YOU AGAIN, ADAM. MY HEART IS *FULL*.

YOU *KNEW* WHERE I WAS, REY. YOU COULD HAVE... *CALLED* ME, OR...

I HAD TO DO WHAT WAS BEST FOR MAMIE... FOR *YOU*.

I...FELL INTO A BAD PLACE AFTER I LEFT, AND...

IT TOOK ME MANY *YEARS* TO SEE THE *LIGHT* AND ANSWER THIS NEW *CALLING*.

I ALWAYS FELT THE HEAVENLY FATHER STEERING MY COURSE...

AND I *KNEW* YOU WOULD BE SAFE AND STRONG EVEN *WITHOUT* ME.

SAVE.

MAMIE SAID YOU WERE *PAID* TO GO.

SOUNDS MORE LIKE WHAT WAS GOOD FOR *YOU* THAN WHAT WAS GOOD FOR *ME*.

THAT WAS PART OF HER *FATHER'S* PLAN. HE *WANTED* HER TO HATE ME.

BUT MONEY COULD *NEVER* HAVE CONVINCED ME TO LEAVE THOSE I LOVED.

SO WHAT DID?

MAMIE'S *FATHER* SAID HE WOULD KILL *YOU* IF I DID NOT GO.

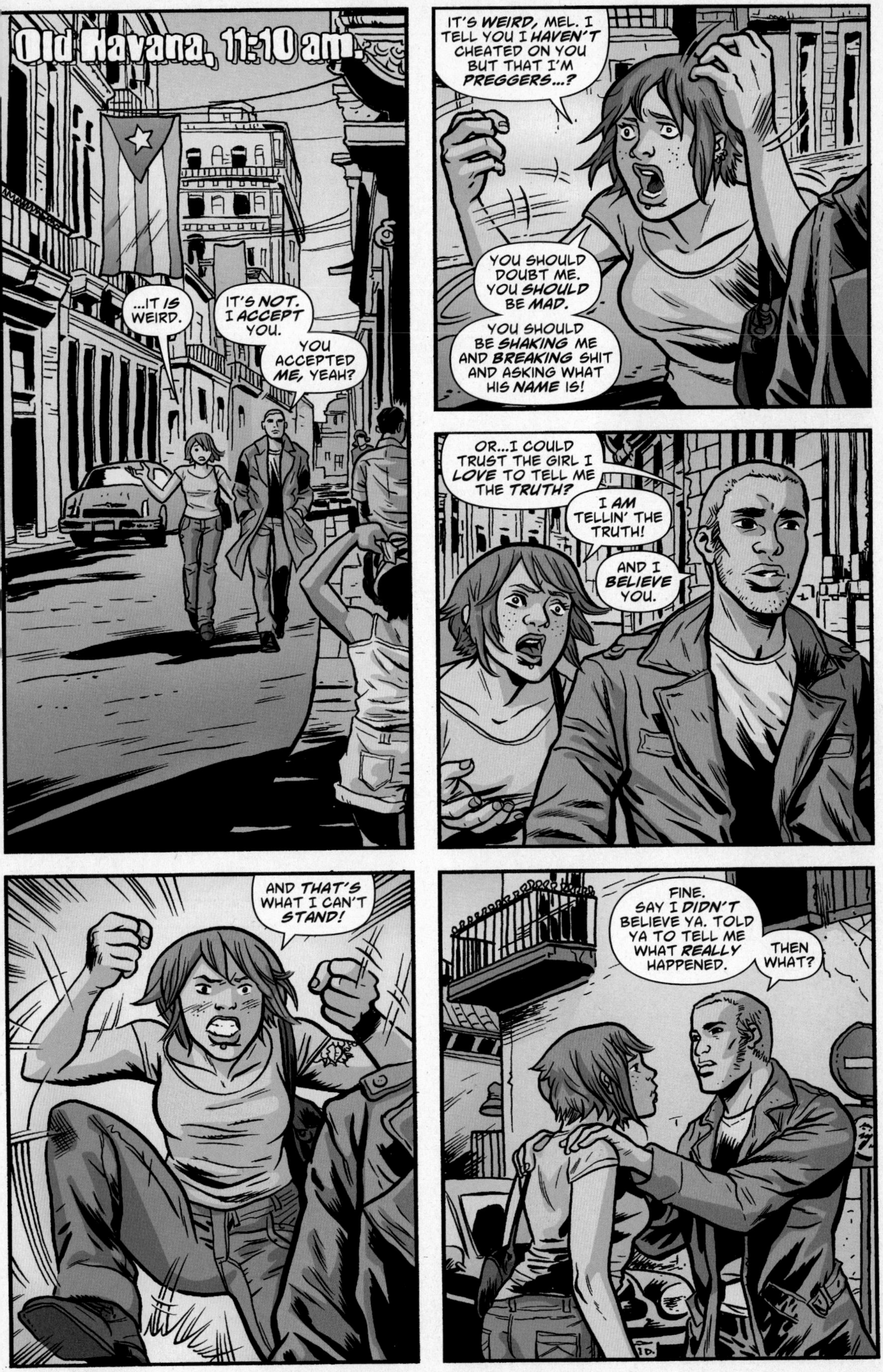
Old Havana, 11:10 am.
...IT IS WEIRD.
IT'S NOT. I ACCEPT YOU.
YOU ACCEPTED ME, YEAH?
IT'S WEIRD, MEL. I TELL YOU I HAVEN'T CHEATED ON YOU BUT THAT I'M PREGGERS...?
YOU SHOULD DOUBT ME. YOU SHOULD BE MAD.
YOU SHOULD BE SHAKING ME AND BREAKING SHIT AND ASKING WHAT HIS NAME IS!
OR...I COULD TRUST THE GIRL I LOVE TO TELL ME THE TRUTH?
I AM TELLIN' THE TRUTH!
AND I BELIEVE YOU.
AND THAT'S WHAT I CAN'T STAND!
FINE. SAY I DIDN'T BELIEVE YA. TOLD YA TO TELL ME WHAT REALLY HAPPENED.
THEN WHAT?

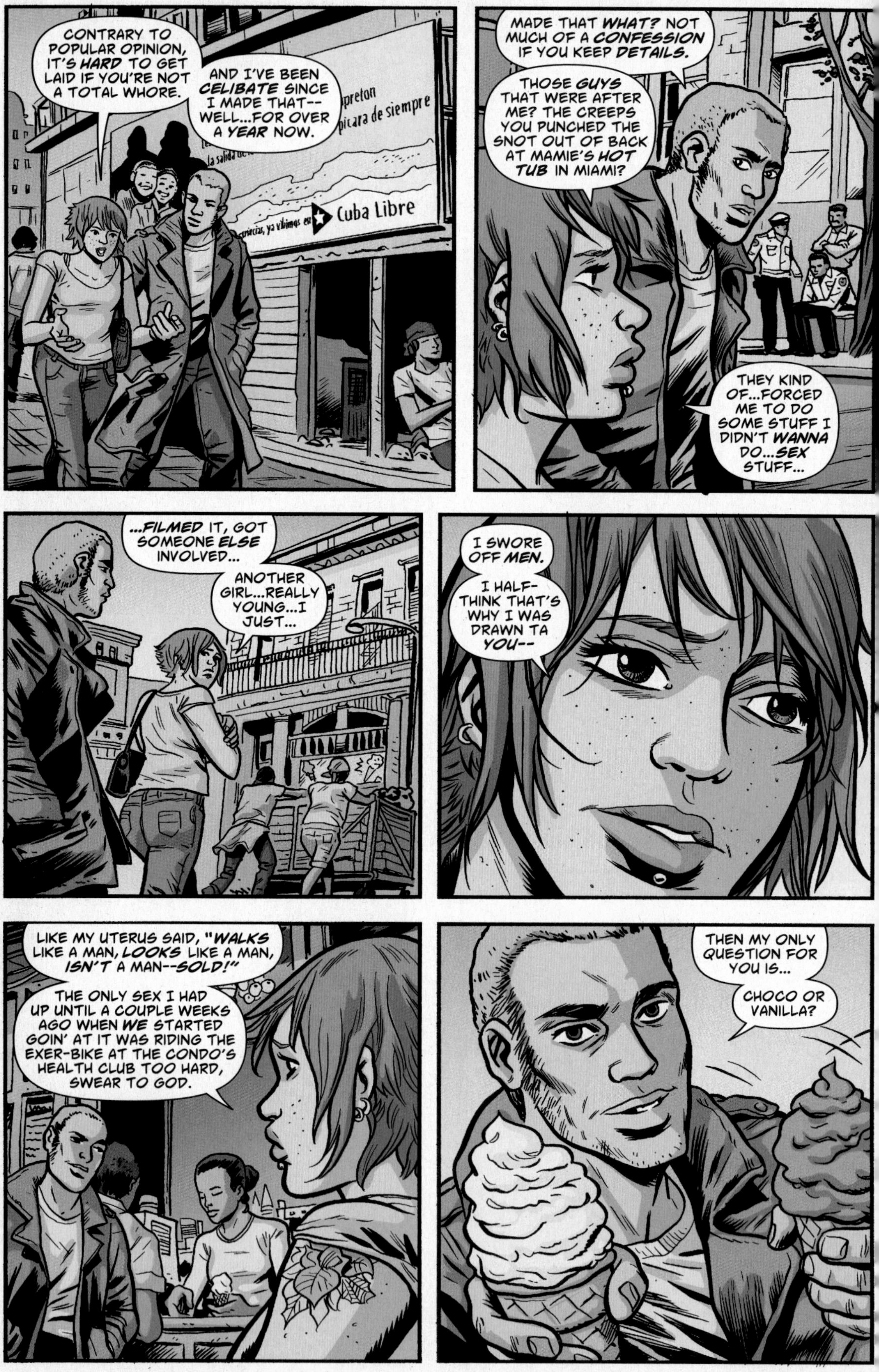

CONTRARY TO POPULAR OPINION, IT'S HARD TO GET LAID IF YOU'RE NOT A TOTAL WHORE.
AND I'VE BEEN CELIBATE SINCE I MADE THAT-- WELL...FOR OVER A YEAR NOW.
picara de siempre
Cuba Libre
MADE THAT WHAT? NOT MUCH OF A CONFESSION IF YOU KEEP DETAILS.
THOSE GUYS THAT WERE AFTER ME? THE CREEPS YOU PUNCHED THE SNOT OUT OF BACK AT MAMIE'S HOT TUB IN MIAMI?
THEY KIND OF...FORCED ME TO DO SOME STUFF I DIDN'T WANNA DO...SEX STUFF...
...FILMED IT, GOT SOMEONE ELSE INVOLVED...
ANOTHER GIRL...REALLY YOUNG...I JUST...
I SWORE OFF MEN.
I HALF-THINK THAT'S WHY I WAS DRAWN TA YOU--
LIKE MY UTERUS SAID, "WALKS LIKE A MAN, LOOKS LIKE A MAN, ISN'T A MAN--SOLD!"
THE ONLY SEX I HAD UP UNTIL A COUPLE WEEKS AGO WHEN WE STARTED GOIN' AT IT WAS RIDING THE EXER-BIKE AT THE CONDO'S HEALTH CLUB TOO HARD, SWEAR TO GOD.
THEN MY ONLY QUESTION FOR YOU IS...
CHOCO OR VANILLA?

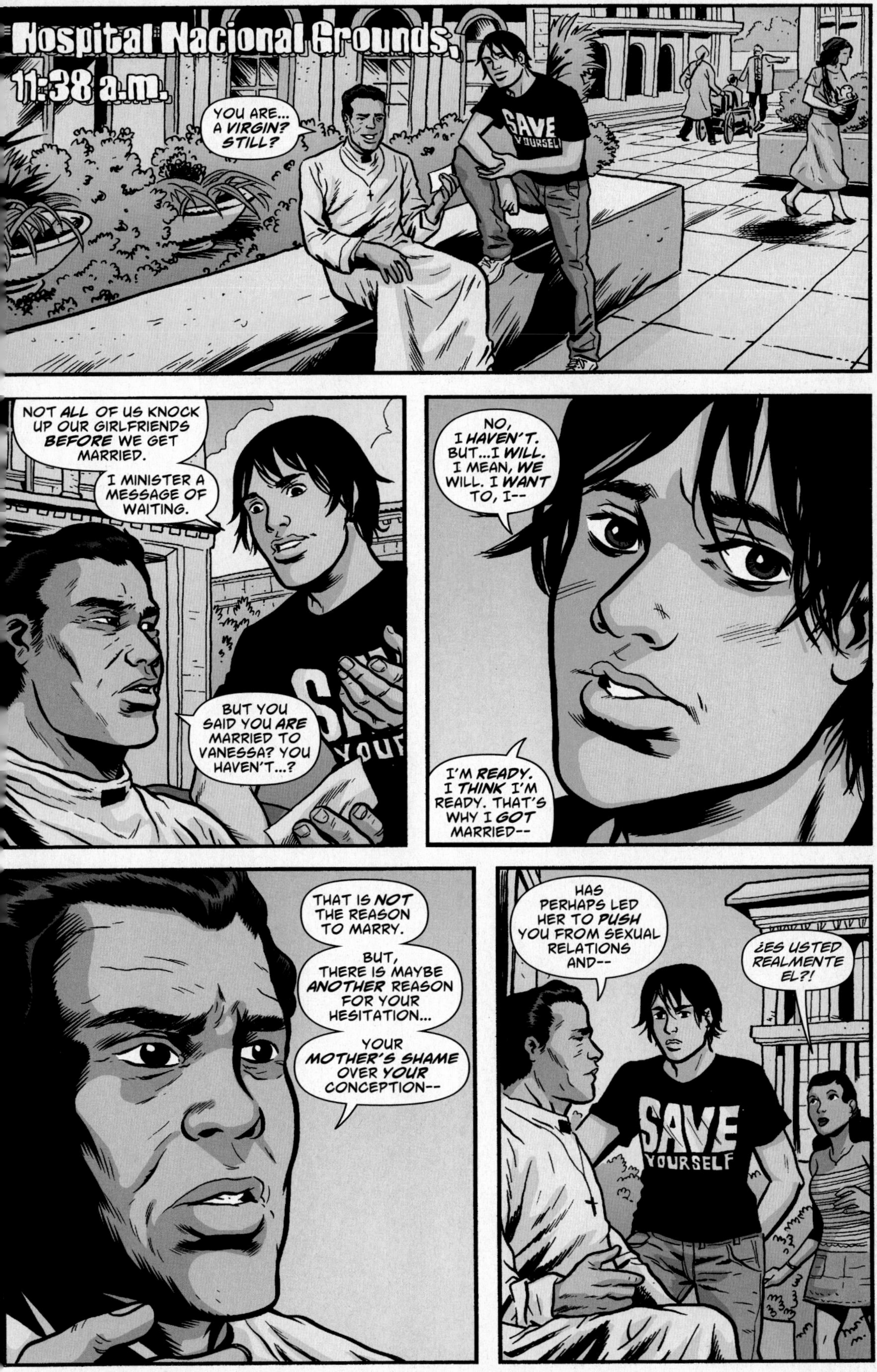
Hospital Nacional Grounds, 11:38 a.m.
YOU ARE... A VIRGIN? STILL?
SAVE YOURSELF
NOT ALL OF US KNOCK UP OUR GIRLFRIENDS BEFORE WE GET MARRIED.
I MINISTER A MESSAGE OF WAITING.
BUT YOU SAID YOU ARE MARRIED TO VANESSA? YOU HAVEN'T...?
NO, I HAVEN'T. BUT...I WILL. I MEAN, WE WILL. I WANT TO, I--
I'M READY. I THINK I'M READY. THAT'S WHY I GOT MARRIED--
THAT IS NOT THE REASON TO MARRY.
BUT, THERE IS MAYBE ANOTHER REASON FOR YOUR HESITATION...
YOUR MOTHER'S SHAME OVER YOUR CONCEPTION--
HAS PERHAPS LED HER TO PUSH YOU FROM SEXUAL RELATIONS AND--
¿ES USTED REALMENTE EL?!
SAVE YOURSELF

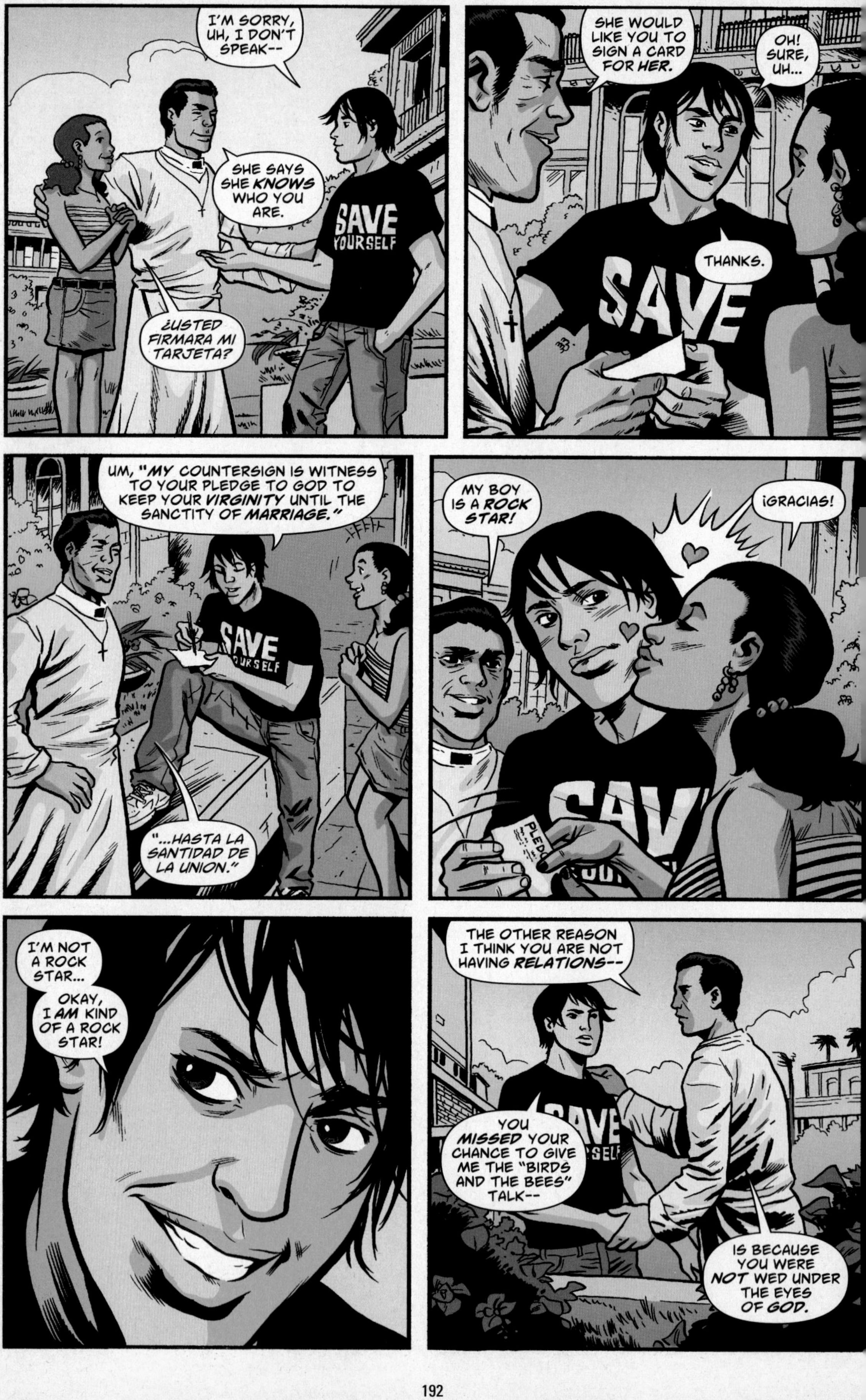
I'M SORRY, UH, I DON'T SPEAK--
SHE SAYS SHE KNOWS WHO YOU ARE.
SAVE YOURSELF
¿USTED FIRMARA MI TARJETA?
SHE WOULD LIKE YOU TO SIGN A CARD FOR HER.
OH! SURE, UH...
THANKS.
SAVE
UM, "MY COUNTERSIGN IS WITNESS TO YOUR PLEDGE TO GOD TO KEEP YOUR VIRGINITY UNTIL THE SANCTITY OF MARRIAGE."
"...HASTA LA SANTIDAD DE LA UNION."
MY BOY IS A ROCK STAR!
¡GRACIAS!
I'M NOT A ROCK STAR...
OKAY, I AM KIND OF A ROCK STAR!
THE OTHER REASON I THINK YOU ARE NOT HAVING RELATIONS--
YOU MISSED YOUR CHANCE TO GIVE ME THE "BIRDS AND THE BEES" TALK--
IS BECAUSE YOU WERE NOT WED UNDER THE EYES OF GOD.

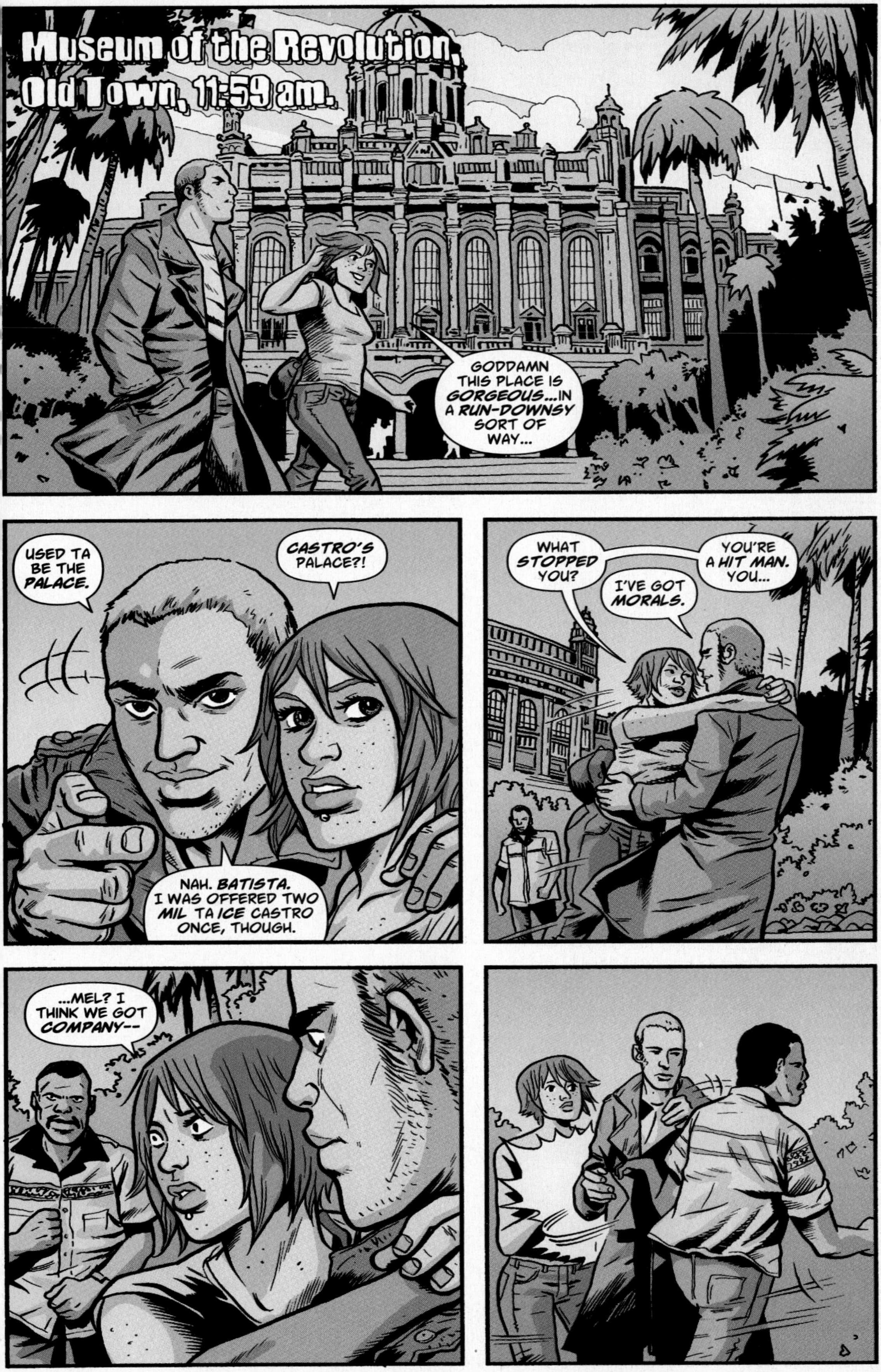
Museum of the Revolution, Old Town, 11:59 am.
GODDAMN THIS PLACE IS GORGEOUS...IN A RUN-DOWNSY SORT OF WAY...
USED TA BE THE PALACE.
CASTRO'S PALACE?!
NAH. BATISTA. I WAS OFFERED TWO MIL TA ICE CASTRO ONCE, THOUGH.
WHAT STOPPED YOU?
YOU'RE A HIT MAN. YOU...
I'VE GOT MORALS.
...MEL? I THINK WE GOT COMPANY--

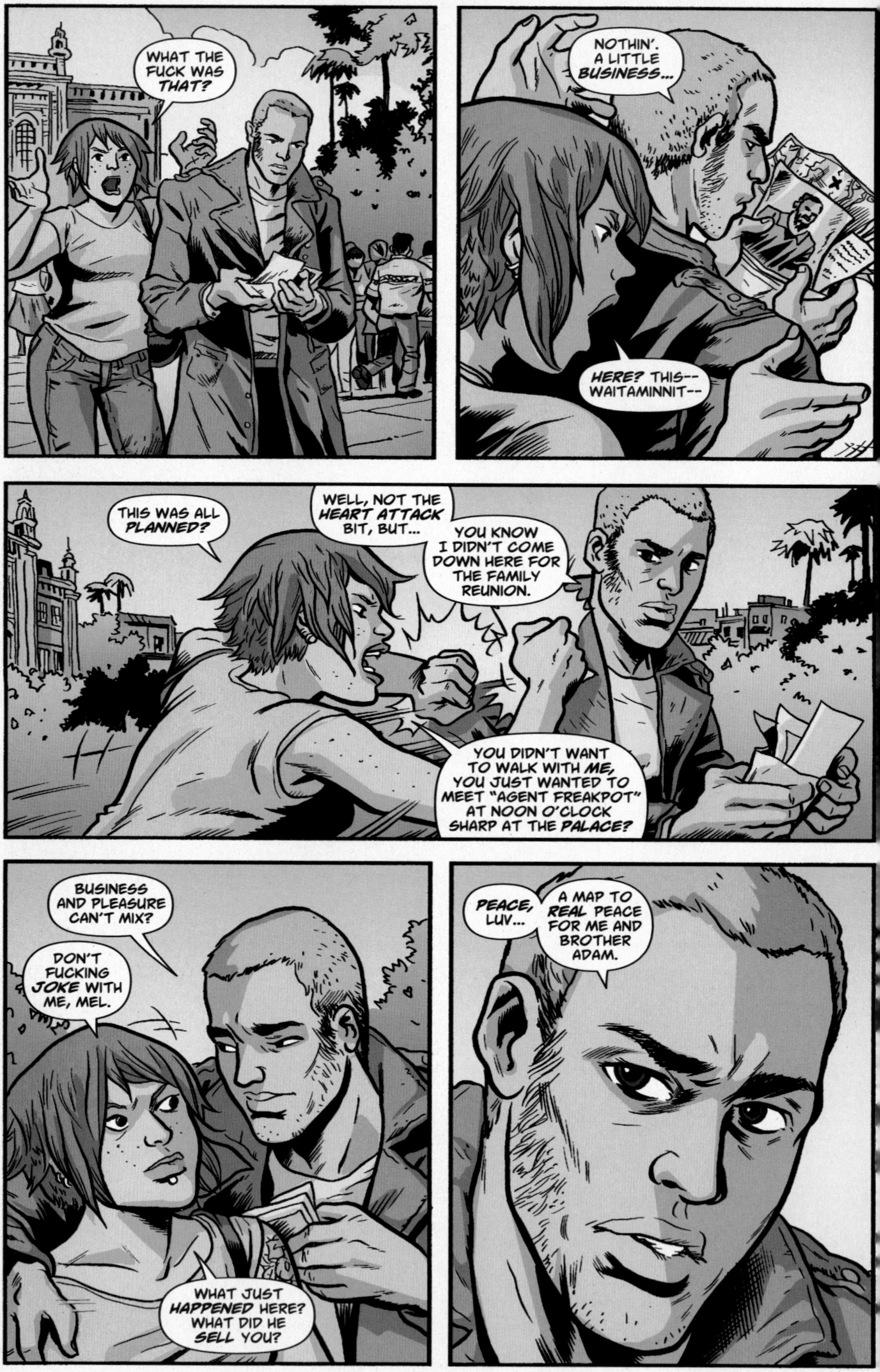
WHAT THE FUCK WAS THAT?
NOTHIN'. A LITTLE BUSINESS...
HERE? THIS-- WAITAMINNIT--
THIS WAS ALL PLANNED?
WELL, NOT THE HEART ATTACK BIT, BUT...
YOU KNOW I DIDN'T COME DOWN HERE FOR THE FAMILY REUNION.
YOU DIDN'T WANT TO WALK WITH ME, YOU JUST WANTED TO MEET "AGENT FREAKPOT" AT NOON O'CLOCK SHARP AT THE PALACE?
BUSINESS AND PLEASURE CAN'T MIX?
DON'T FUCKING JOKE WITH ME, MEL.
WHAT JUST HAPPENED HERE? WHAT DID HE SELL YOU?
PEACE, LUV...
A MAP TO REAL PEACE FOR ME AND BROTHER ADAM.

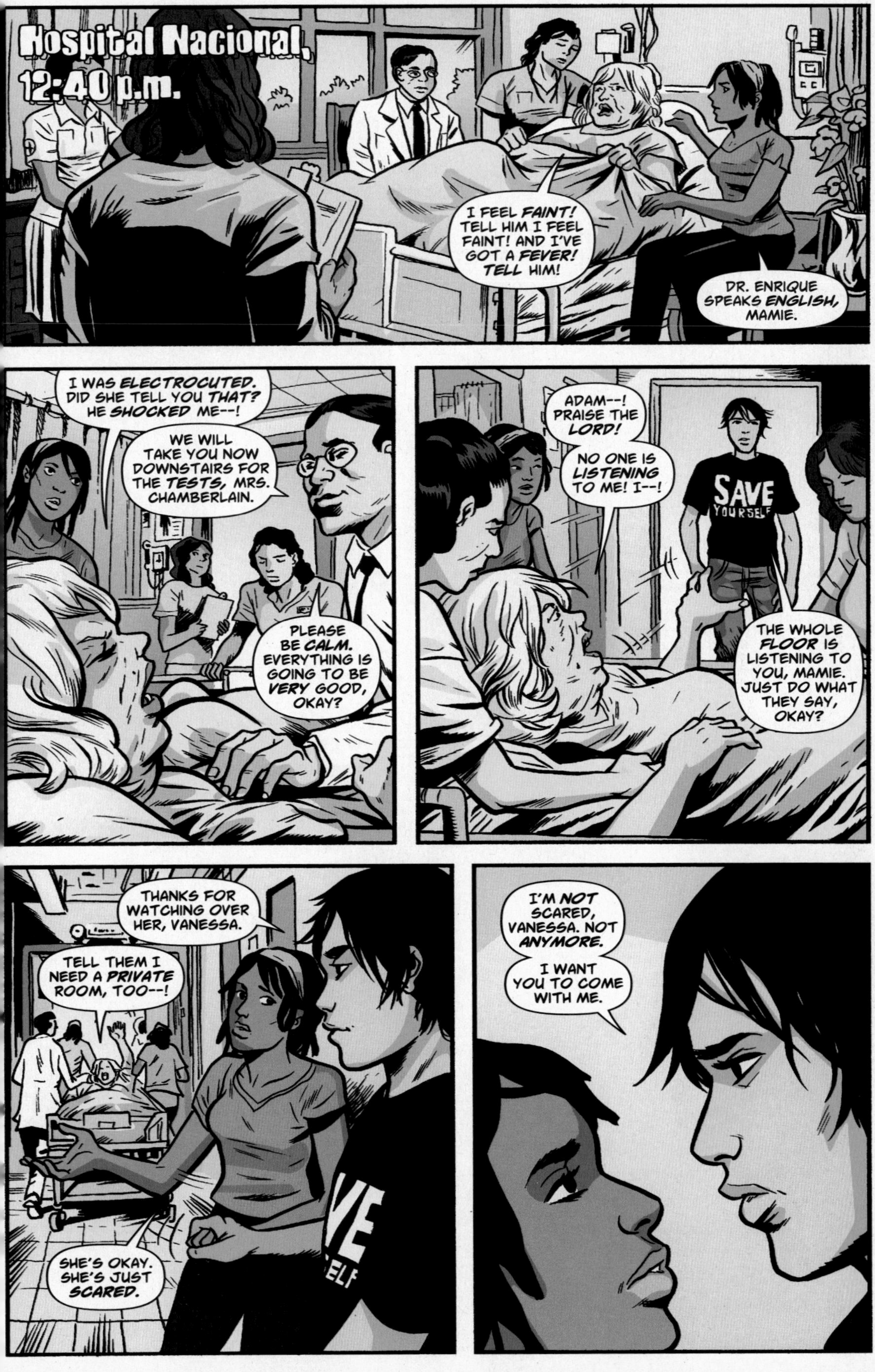
Hospital Nacional, 12:40 p.m.
I FEEL FAINT! TELL HIM I FEEL FAINT! AND I'VE GOT A FEVER! TELL HIM!
DR. ENRIQUE SPEAKS ENGLISH, MAMIE.
I WAS ELECTROCUTED. DID SHE TELL YOU THAT? HE SHOCKED ME--!
WE WILL TAKE YOU NOW DOWNSTAIRS FOR THE TESTS, MRS. CHAMBERLAIN.
PLEASE BE CALM. EVERYTHING IS GOING TO BE VERY GOOD, OKAY?
ADAM--! PRAISE THE LORD!
NO ONE IS LISTENING TO ME! I--!
SAVE YOURSELF
THE WHOLE FLOOR IS LISTENING TO YOU, MAMIE. JUST DO WHAT THEY SAY, OKAY?
THANKS FOR WATCHING OVER HER, VANESSA.
TELL THEM I NEED A PRIVATE ROOM, TOO--!
SHE'S OKAY. SHE'S JUST SCARED.
I'M NOT SCARED, VANESSA. NOT ANYMORE.
I WANT YOU TO COME WITH ME.

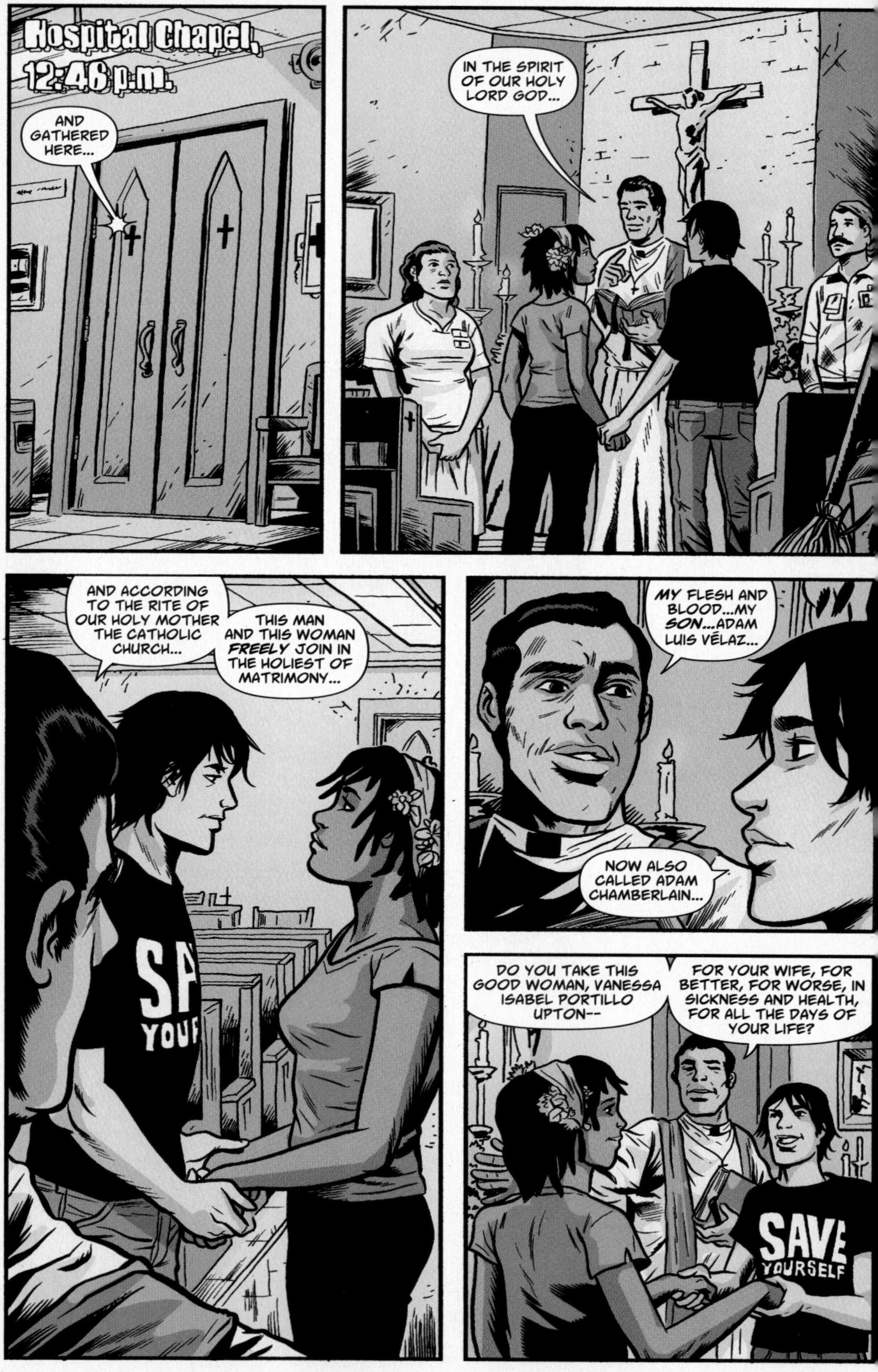
Hospital Chapel, 12:46 p.m.
AND GATHERED HERE...
IN THE SPIRIT OF OUR HOLY LORD GOD...
AND ACCORDING TO THE RITE OF OUR HOLY MOTHER THE CATHOLIC CHURCH...
THIS MAN AND THIS WOMAN FREELY JOIN IN THE HOLIEST OF MATRIMONY...
MY FLESH AND BLOOD...MY SON...ADAM LUIS VÉLAZ...
NOW ALSO CALLED ADAM CHAMBERLAIN...
DO YOU TAKE THIS GOOD WOMAN, VANESSA ISABEL PORTILLO UPTON--
FOR YOUR WIFE, FOR BETTER, FOR WORSE, IN SICKNESS AND HEALTH, FOR ALL THE DAYS OF YOUR LIFE?
SAVE YOURSELF

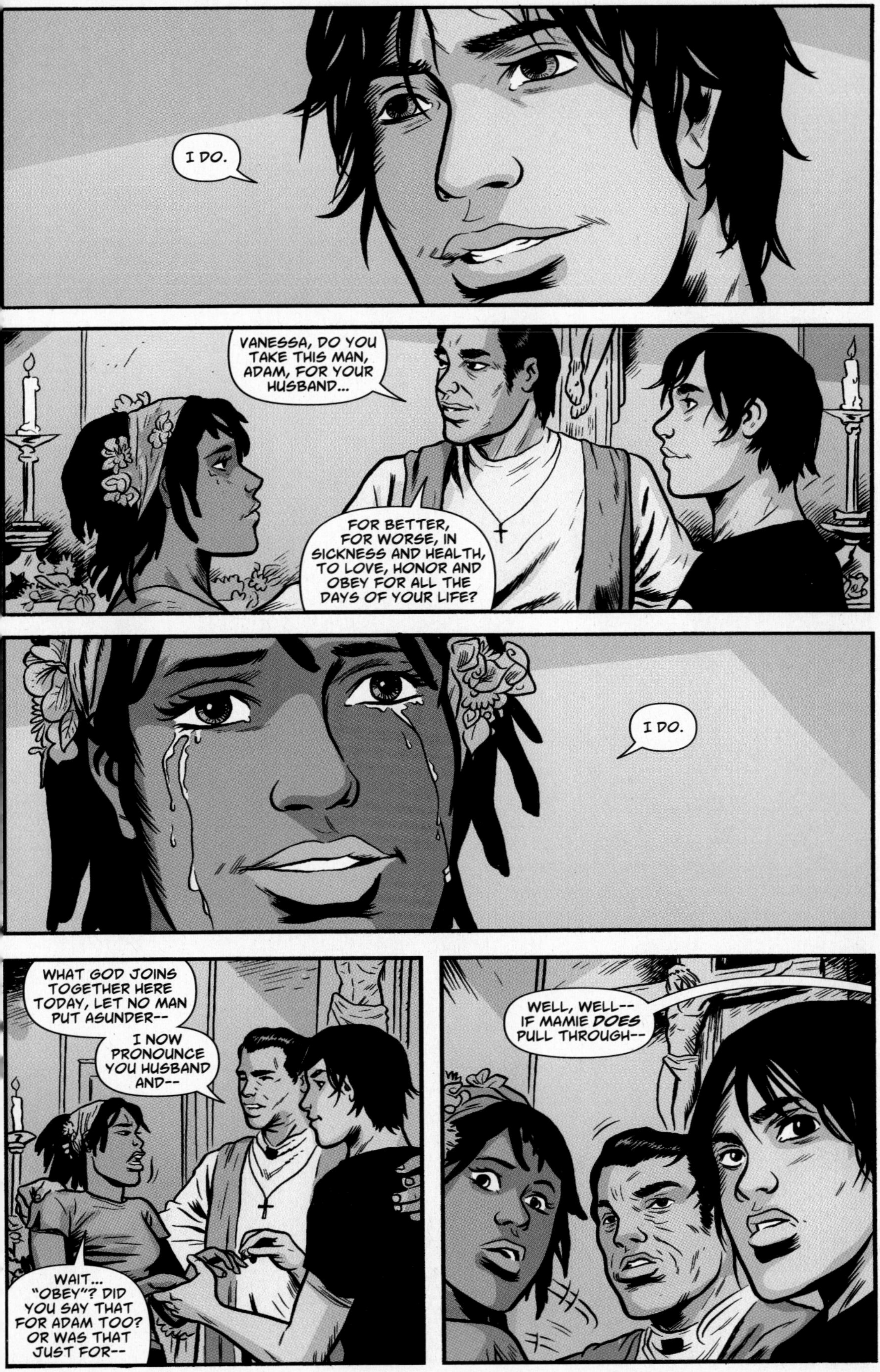
I DO.
VANESSA, DO YOU TAKE THIS MAN, ADAM, FOR YOUR HUSBAND...
FOR BETTER, FOR WORSE, IN SICKNESS AND HEALTH, TO LOVE, HONOR AND OBEY FOR ALL THE DAYS OF YOUR LIFE?
I DO.
WHAT GOD JOINS TOGETHER HERE TODAY, LET NO MAN PUT ASUNDER--
I NOW PRONOUNCE YOU HUSBAND AND--
WAIT... "OBEY"? DID YOU SAY THAT FOR ADAM TOO? OR WAS THAT JUST FOR--
WELL, WELL-- IF MAMIE DOES PULL THROUGH--

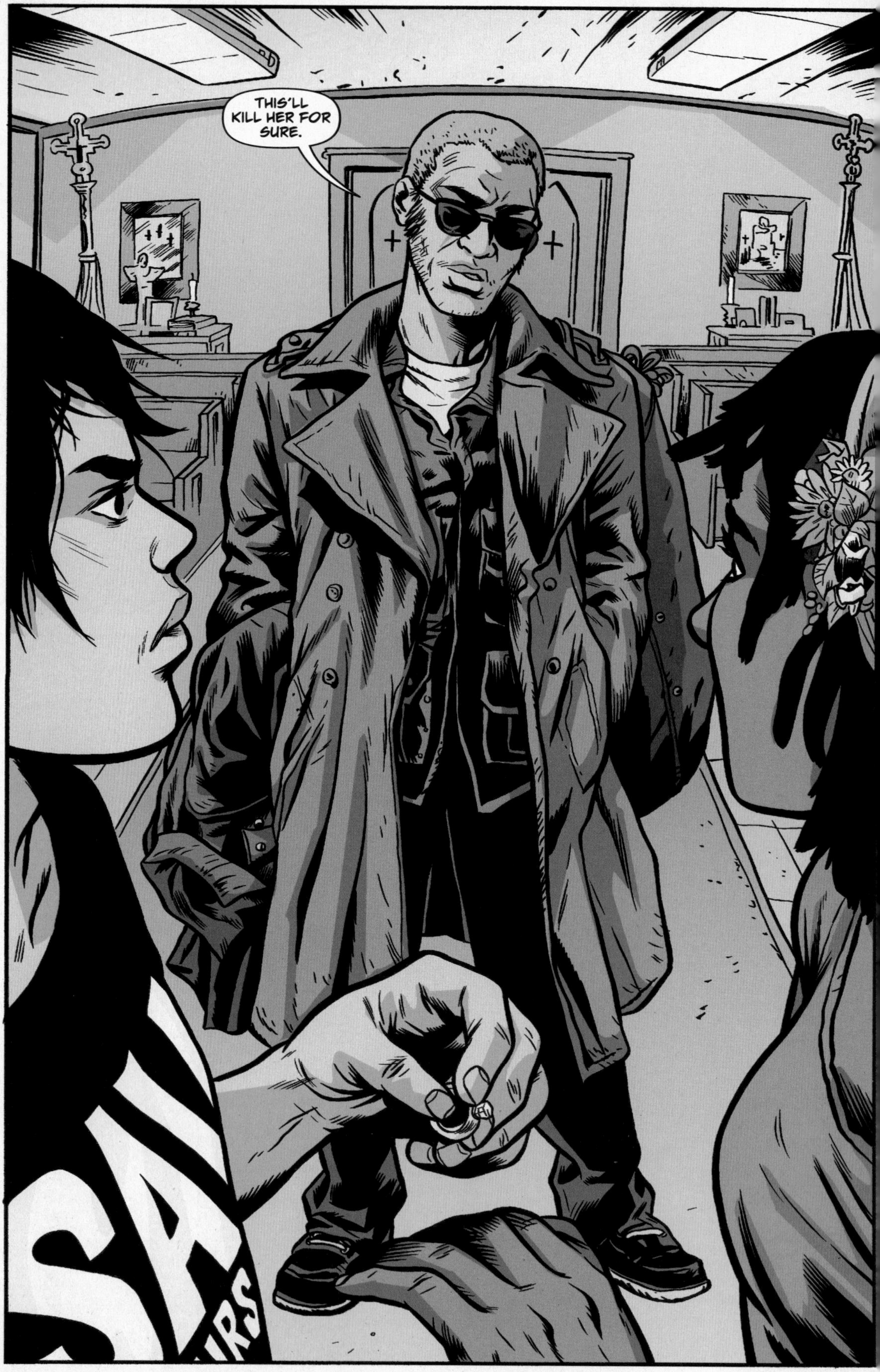
THIS'LL KILL HER FOR SURE.

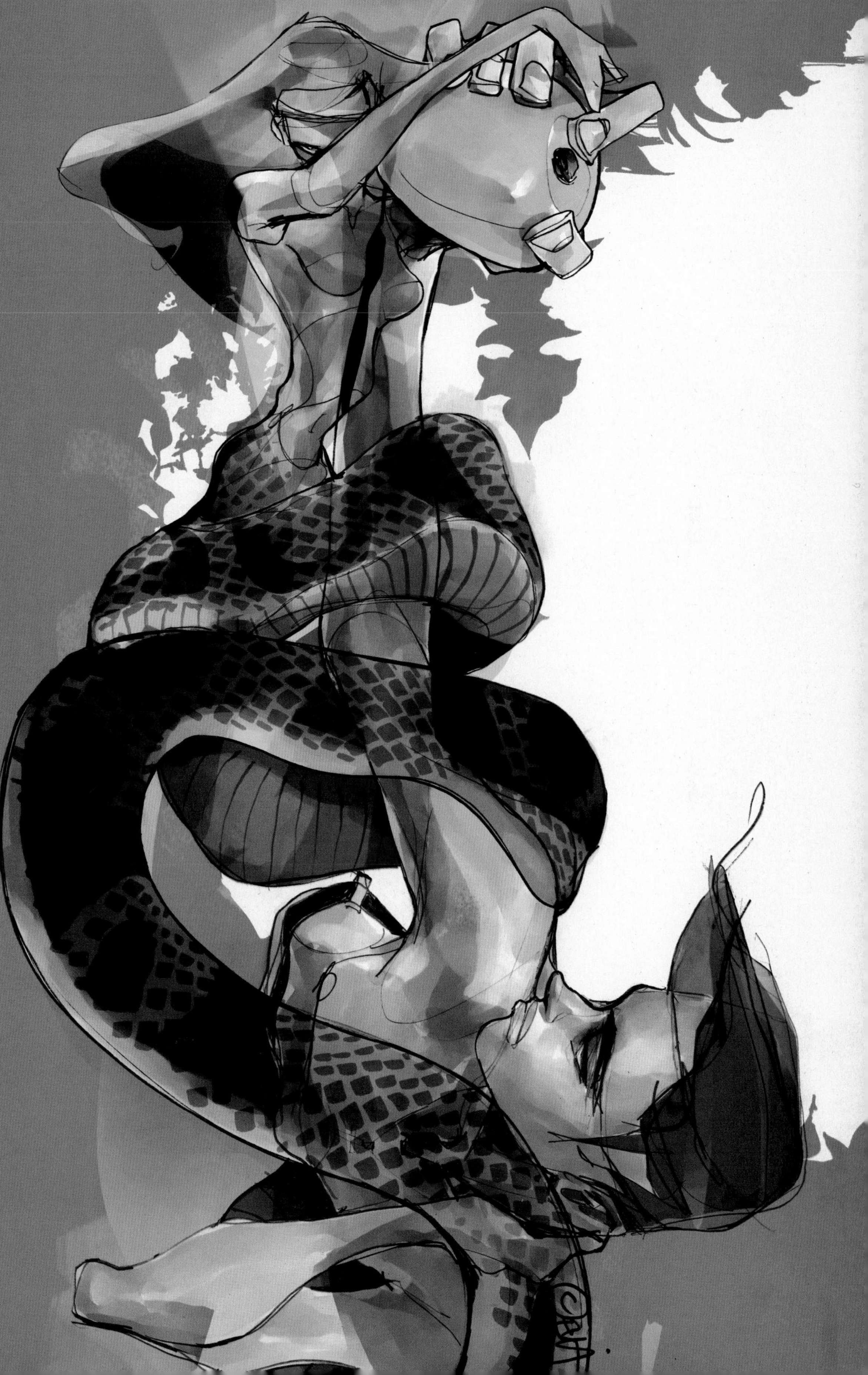

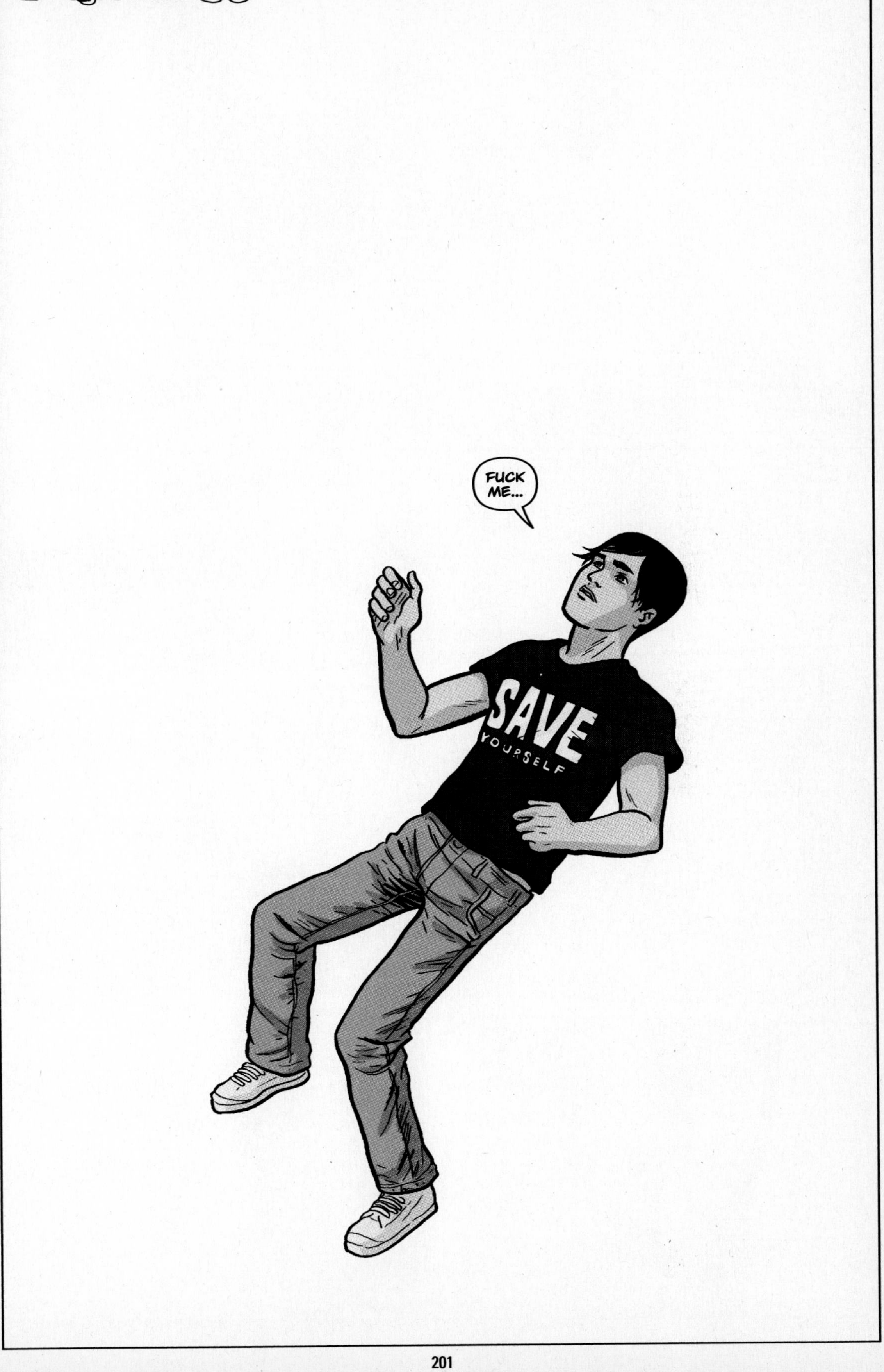
FUCK ME...
SAVE YOURSELF

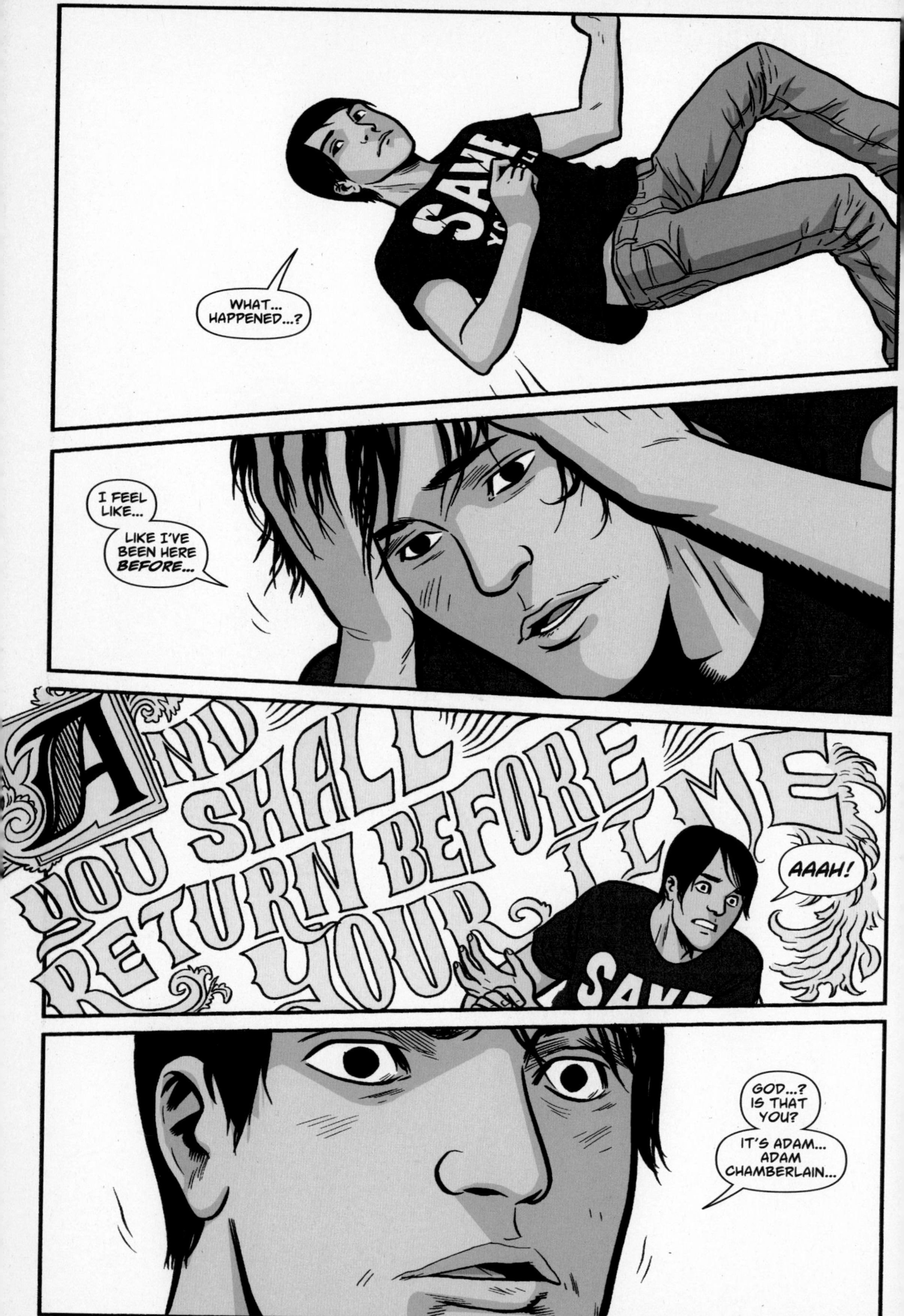
WHAT... HAPPENED...?
I FEEL LIKE...
LIKE I'VE BEEN HERE *BEFORE...*
AND YOU SHALL RETURN BEFORE YOUR TIME
AAAH!
GOD...? IS THAT YOU?
IT'S ADAM... ADAM CHAMBERLAIN...

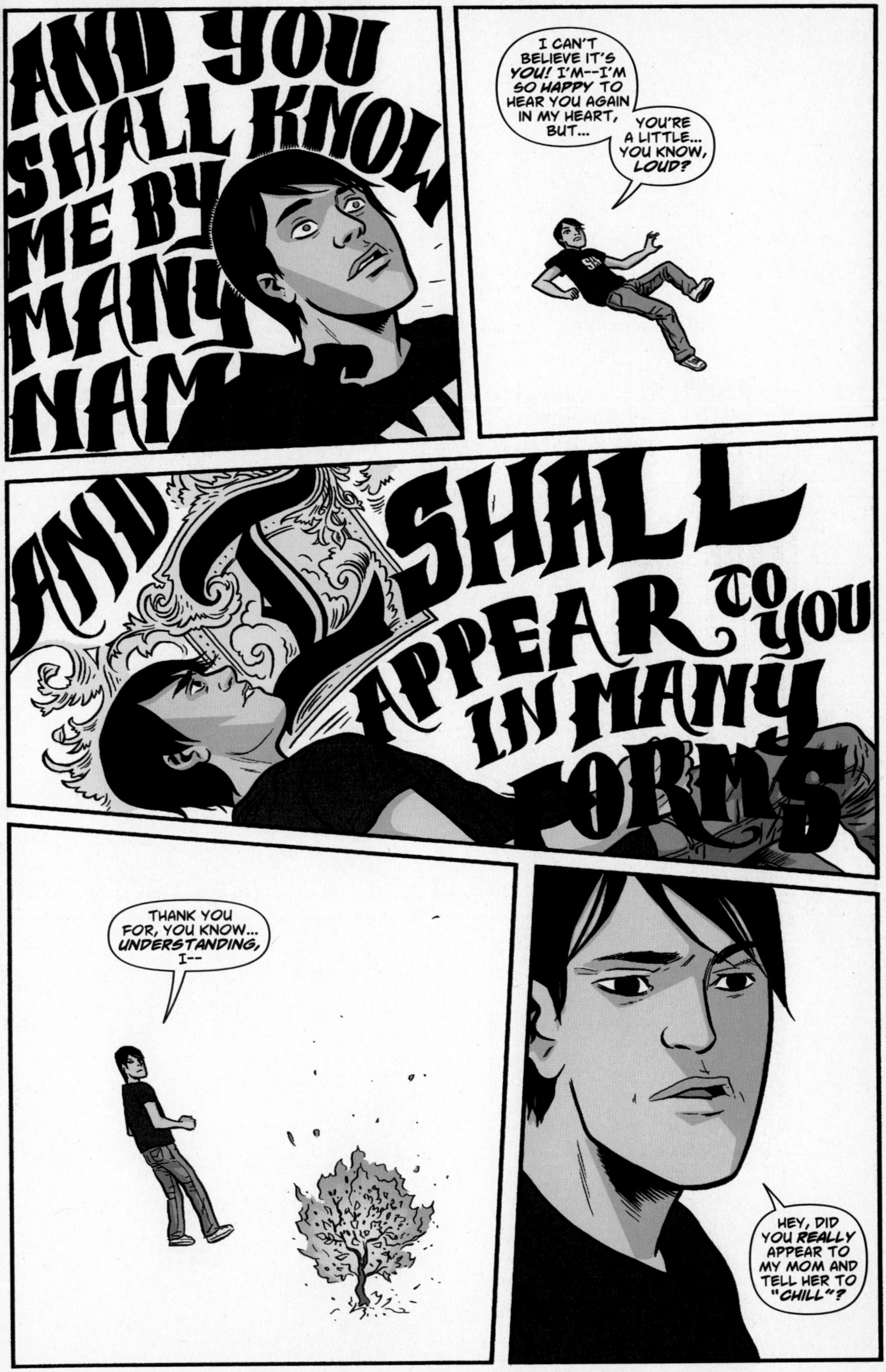
AND YOU SHALL KNOW ME BY MANY NAM
I CAN'T BELIEVE IT'S YOU! I'M--I'M SO HAPPY TO HEAR YOU AGAIN IN MY HEART, BUT...
YOU'RE A LITTLE... YOU KNOW, LOUD?
AND SHALL APPEAR TO YOU IN MANY FORMS
THANK YOU FOR, YOU KNOW... UNDERSTANDING, I--
HEY, DID YOU REALLY APPEAR TO MY MOM AND TELL HER TO "CHILL"?

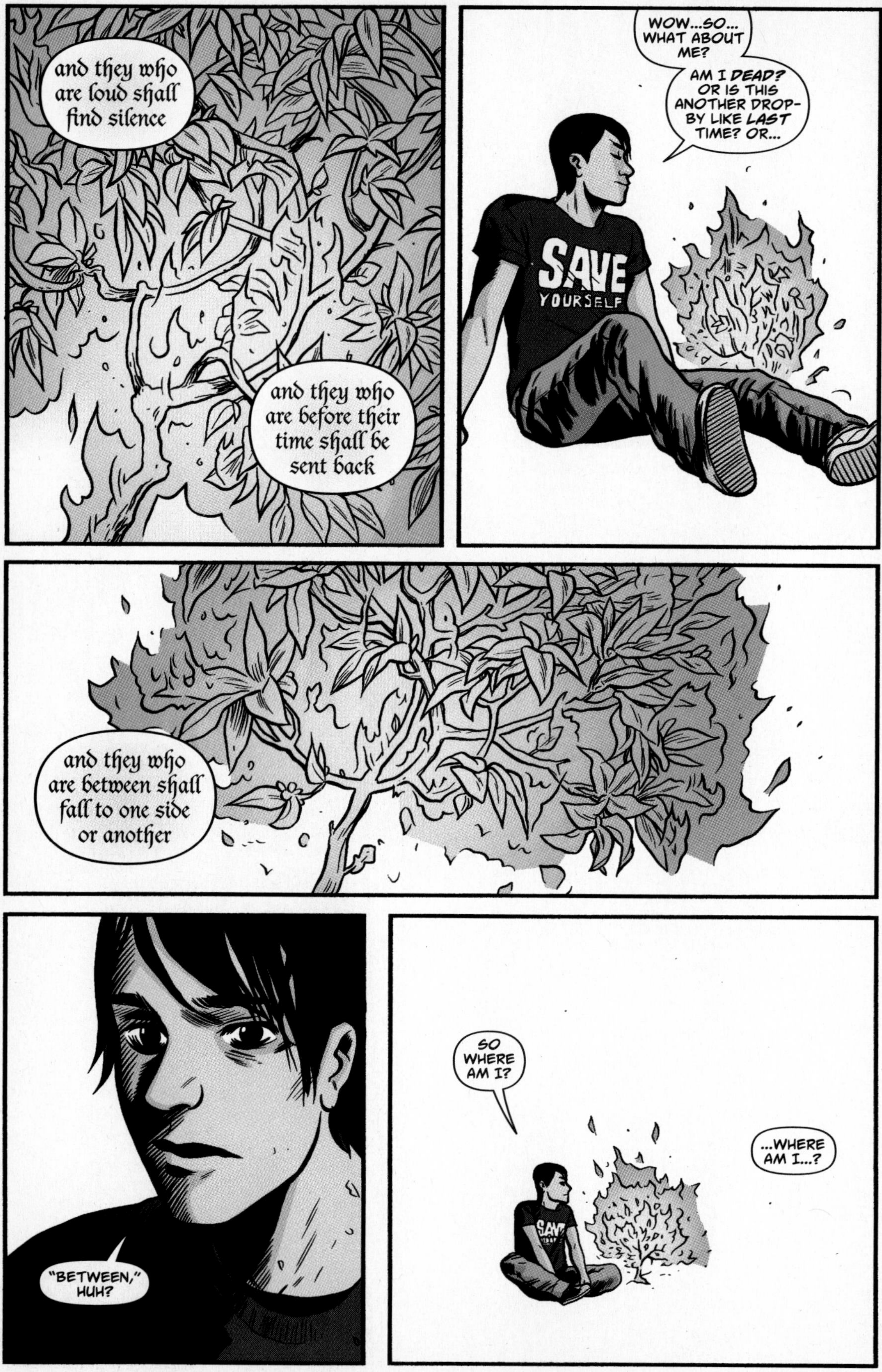
and they who are loud shall find silence
and they who are before their time shall be sent back
WOW...SO... WHAT ABOUT ME?
AM I DEAD? OR IS THIS ANOTHER DROP-BY LIKE LAST TIME? OR...
SAVE YOURSELF
and they who are between shall fall to one side or another
"BETWEEN," HUH?
SO WHERE AM I?
...WHERE AM I...?

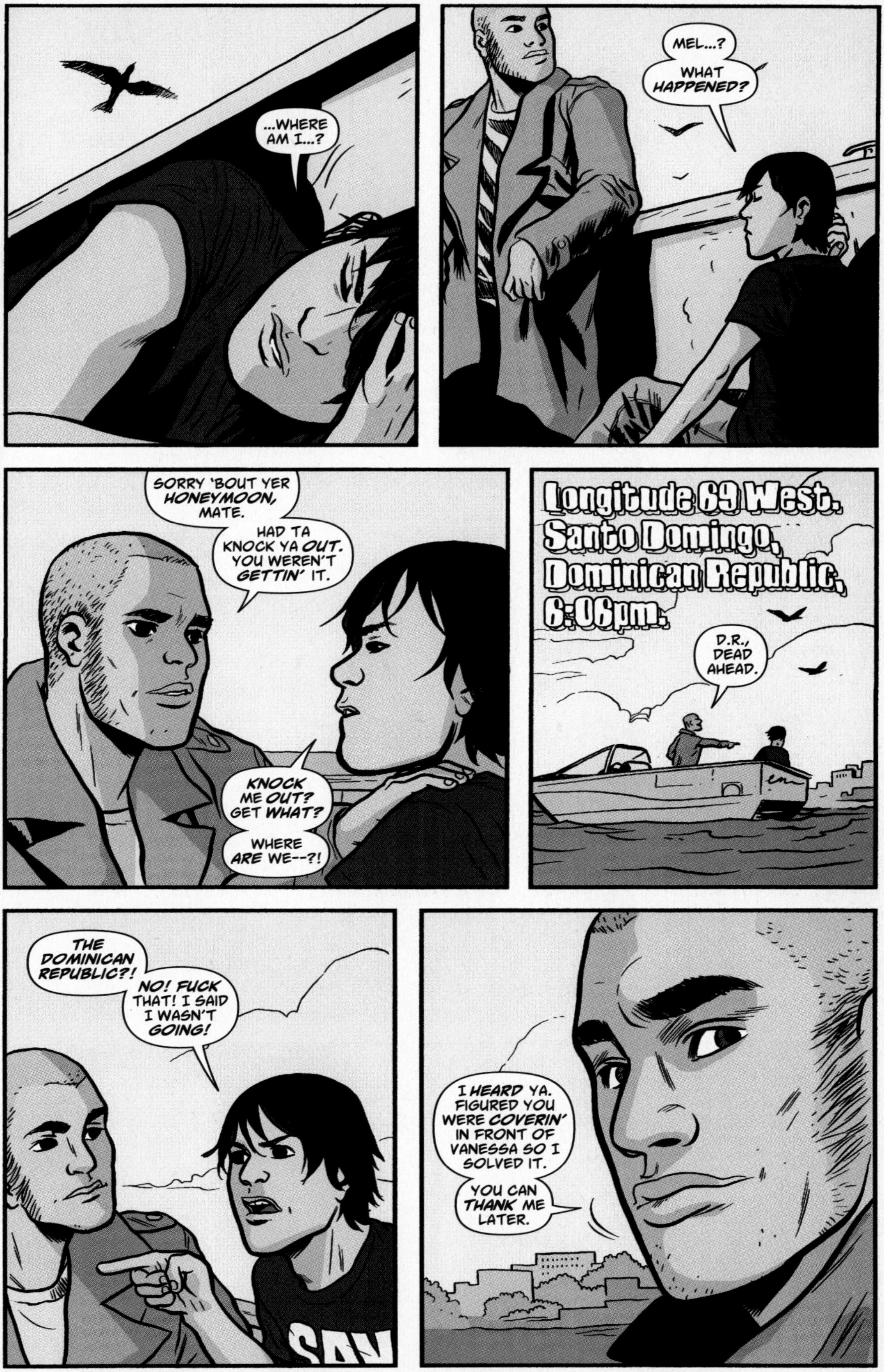

...WHERE AM I...?
MEL...? WHAT HAPPENED?
SORRY 'BOUT YER HONEYMOON, MATE.
HAD TA KNOCK YA OUT. YOU WEREN'T GETTIN' IT.
KNOCK ME OUT? GET WHAT?
WHERE ARE WE--?!
Longitude 69 West. Santo Domingo, Dominican Republic, 6:06pm.
D.R., DEAD AHEAD.
THE DOMINICAN REPUBLIC?!
NO! FUCK THAT! I SAID I WASN'T GOING!
I HEARD YA. FIGURED YOU WERE COVERIN' IN FRONT OF VANESSA SO I SOLVED IT.
YOU CAN THANK ME LATER.

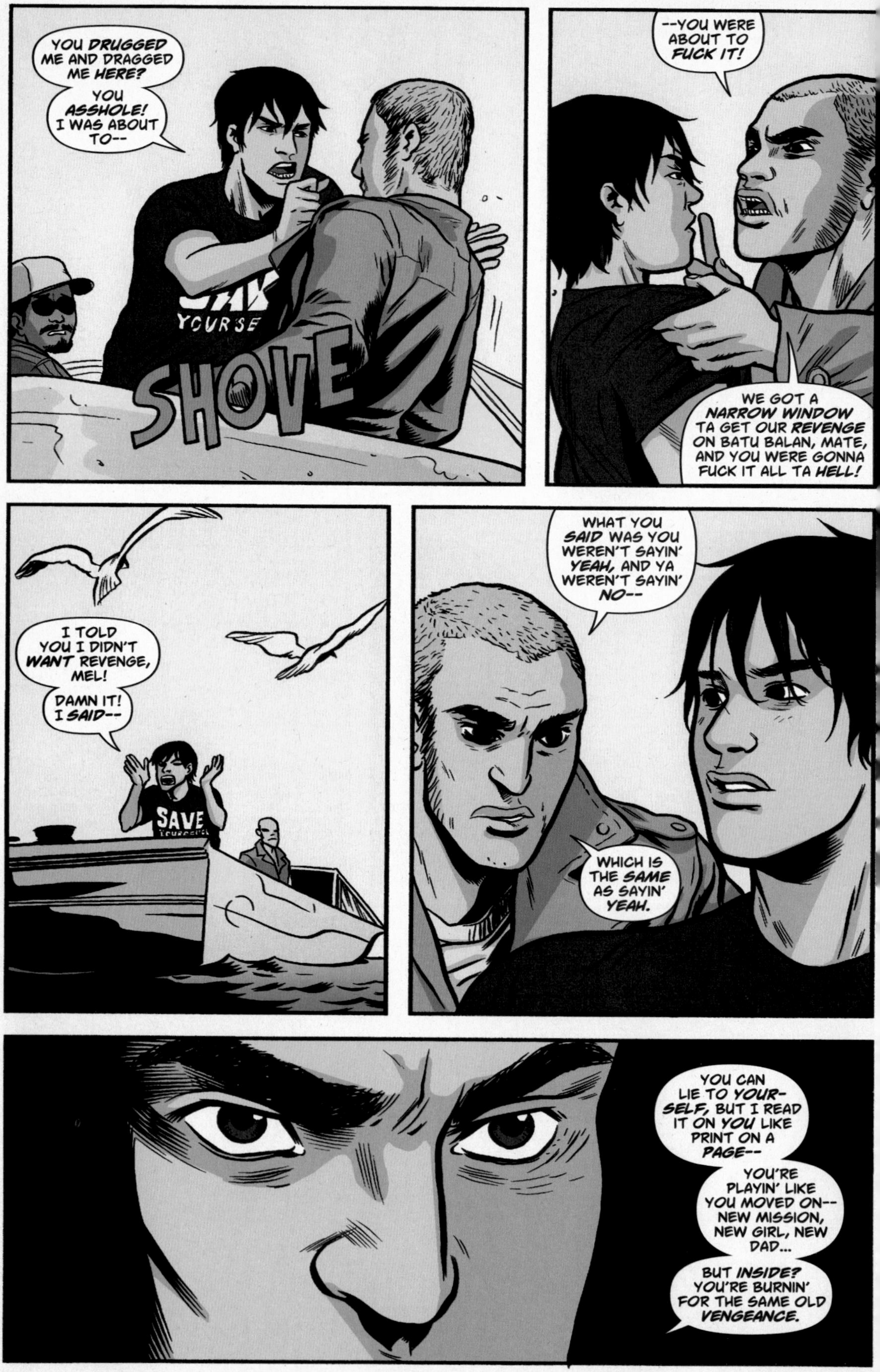
YOU DRUGGED ME AND DRAGGED ME HERE?
YOU ASSHOLE! I WAS ABOUT TO--
SHOVE
--YOU WERE ABOUT TO FUCK IT!
WE GOT A NARROW WINDOW TA GET OUR REVENGE ON BATU BALAN, MATE, AND YOU WERE GONNA FUCK IT ALL TA HELL!
I TOLD YOU I DIDN'T WANT REVENGE, MEL!
DAMN IT! I SAID--
SAVE
WHAT YOU SAID WAS YOU WEREN'T SAYIN' YEAH, AND YA WEREN'T SAYIN' NO--
WHICH IS THE SAME AS SAYIN' YEAH.
YOU CAN LIE TO YOURSELF, BUT I READ IT ON YOU LIKE PRINT ON A PAGE--
YOU'RE PLAYIN' LIKE YOU MOVED ON-- NEW MISSION, NEW GIRL, NEW DAD...
BUT INSIDE? YOU'RE BURNIN' FOR THE SAME OLD VENGEANCE.

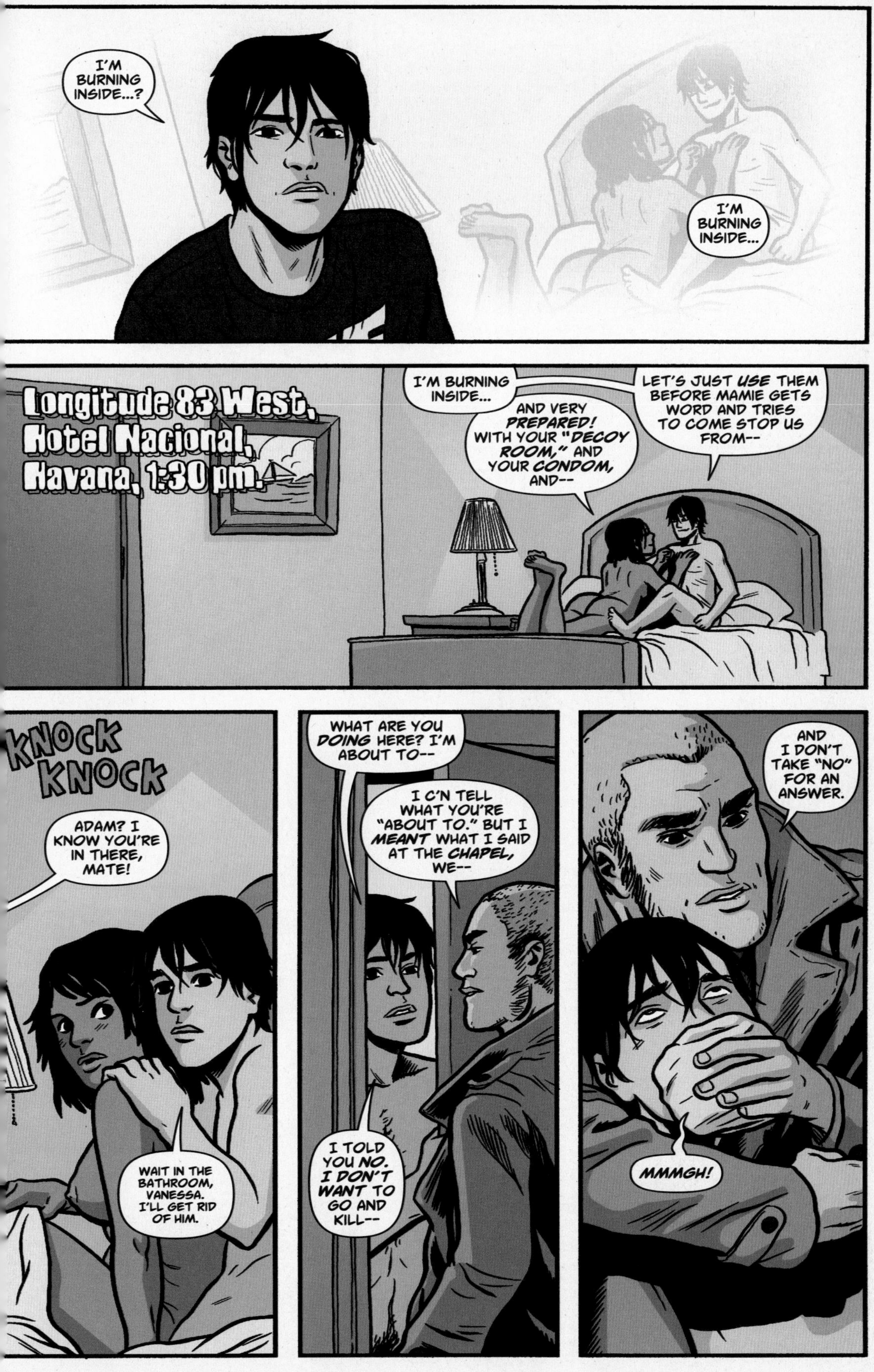
I'M BURNING INSIDE...?
I'M BURNING INSIDE...
Longitude 83 West, Hotel Nacional, Havana, 1:30 pm.
I'M BURNING INSIDE...
AND VERY PREPARED! WITH YOUR "DECOY ROOM," AND YOUR CONDOM, AND--
LET'S JUST USE THEM BEFORE MAMIE GETS WORD AND TRIES TO COME STOP US FROM--
KNOCK KNOCK
ADAM? I KNOW YOU'RE IN THERE, MATE!
WAIT IN THE BATHROOM, VANESSA. I'LL GET RID OF HIM.
WHAT ARE YOU DOING HERE? I'M ABOUT TO--
I C'N TELL WHAT YOU'RE "ABOUT TO." BUT I MEANT WHAT I SAID AT THE CHAPEL, WE--
I TOLD YOU NO. I DON'T WANT TO GO AND KILL--
AND I DON'T TAKE "NO" FOR AN ANSWER.
MMMGH!

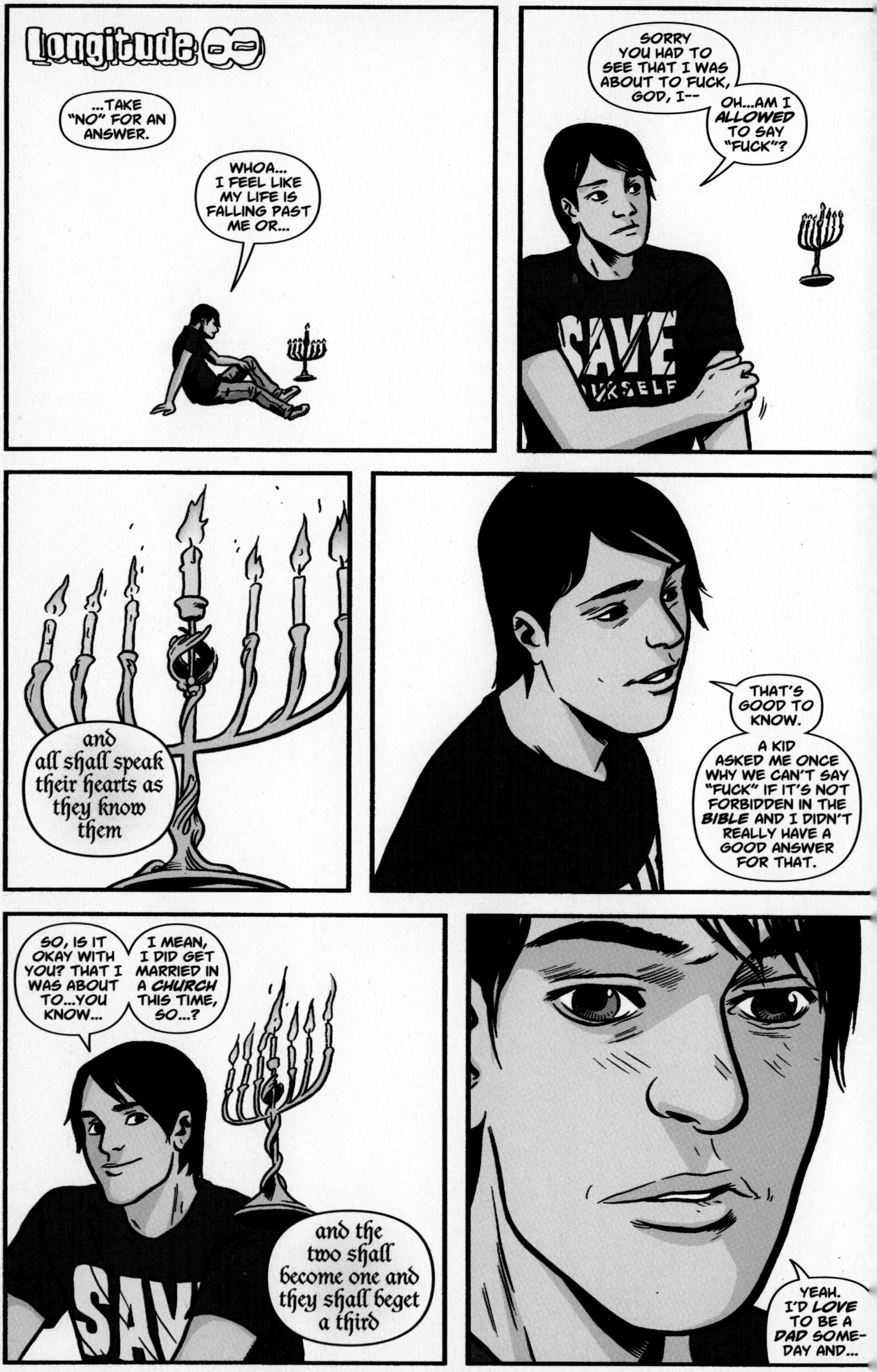
Longitude -∞
...TAKE "NO" FOR AN ANSWER.
WHOA... I FEEL LIKE MY LIFE IS FALLING PAST ME OR...
SORRY YOU HAD TO SEE THAT I WAS ABOUT TO FUCK, GOD, I--
OH...AM I ALLOWED TO SAY "FUCK"?
SAVE YOURSELF
and all shall speak their hearts as they know them
THAT'S GOOD TO KNOW.
A KID ASKED ME ONCE WHY WE CAN'T SAY "FUCK" IF IT'S NOT FORBIDDEN IN THE BIBLE AND I DIDN'T REALLY HAVE A GOOD ANSWER FOR THAT.
SO, IS IT OKAY WITH YOU? THAT I WAS ABOUT TO...YOU KNOW...
I MEAN, I DID GET MARRIED IN A CHURCH THIS TIME, SO...?
and the two shall become one and they shall beget a third
YEAH. I'D LOVE TO BE A DAD SOME-DAY AND...

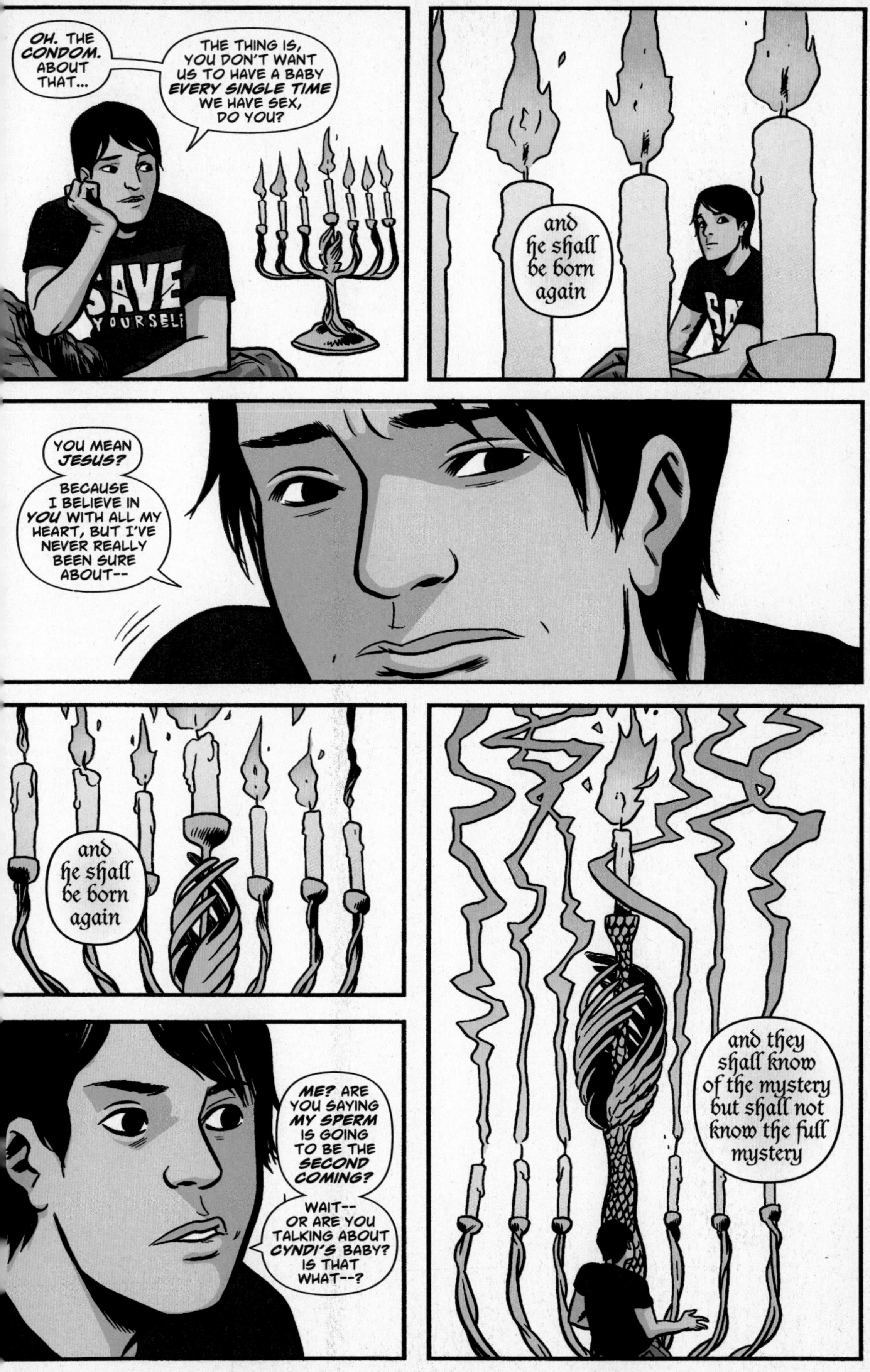

OH. THE CONDOM. ABOUT THAT...
THE THING IS, YOU DON'T WANT US TO HAVE A BABY EVERY SINGLE TIME WE HAVE SEX, DO YOU?
SAVE YOURSELF
and he shall be born again
YOU MEAN JESUS?
BECAUSE I BELIEVE IN YOU WITH ALL MY HEART, BUT I'VE NEVER REALLY BEEN SURE ABOUT--
and he shall be born again
and they shall know of the mystery but shall not know the full mystery
ME? ARE YOU SAYING MY SPERM IS GOING TO BE THE SECOND COMING?
WAIT-- OR ARE YOU TALKING ABOUT CYNDI'S BABY? IS THAT WHAT--?

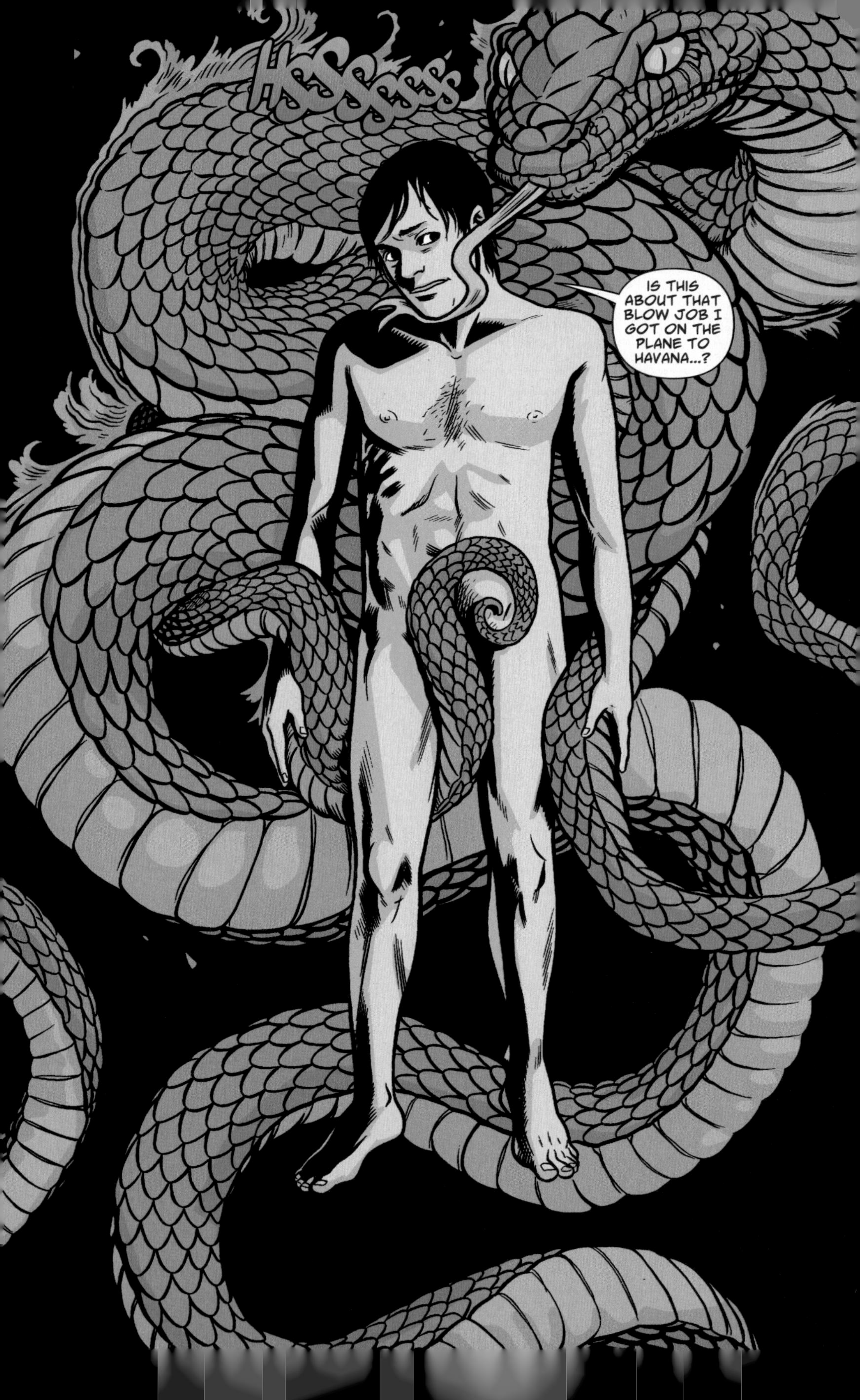
HSSSSSS
IS THIS ABOUT THAT BLOW JOB I GOT ON THE PLANE TO HAVANA...?

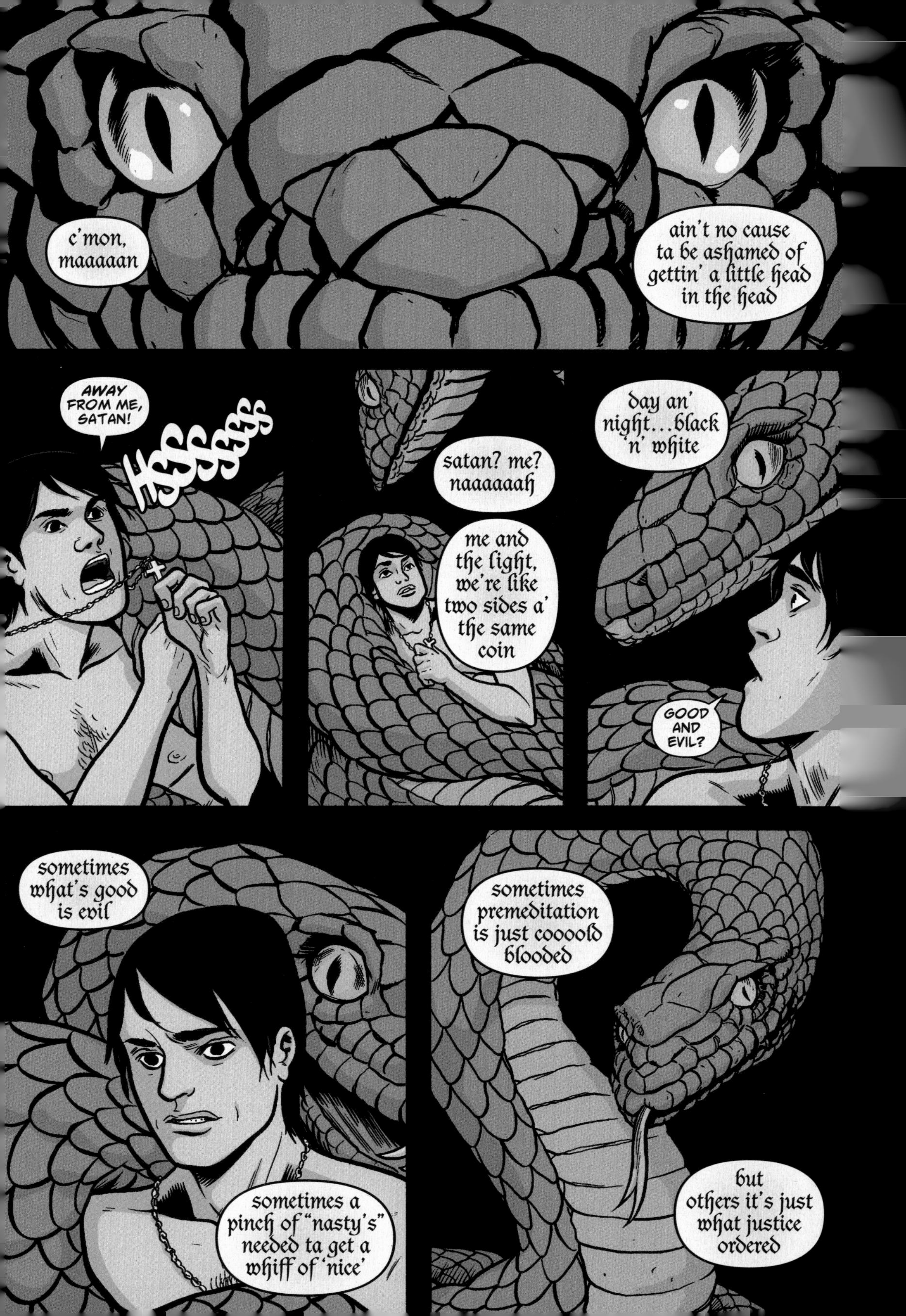
c'mon, maaaaan
ain't no cause ta be ashamed of gettin' a little head in the head
AWAY FROM ME, SATAN!
HSSSSSS
satan? me? naaaaaah
me and the light, we're like two sides a' the same coin
day an' night...black 'n' white
GOOD AND EVIL?
sometimes what's good is evil
sometimes a pinch of "nasty's" needed ta get a whiff of 'nice'
sometimes premeditation is just coooold blooded
but others it's just what justice ordered

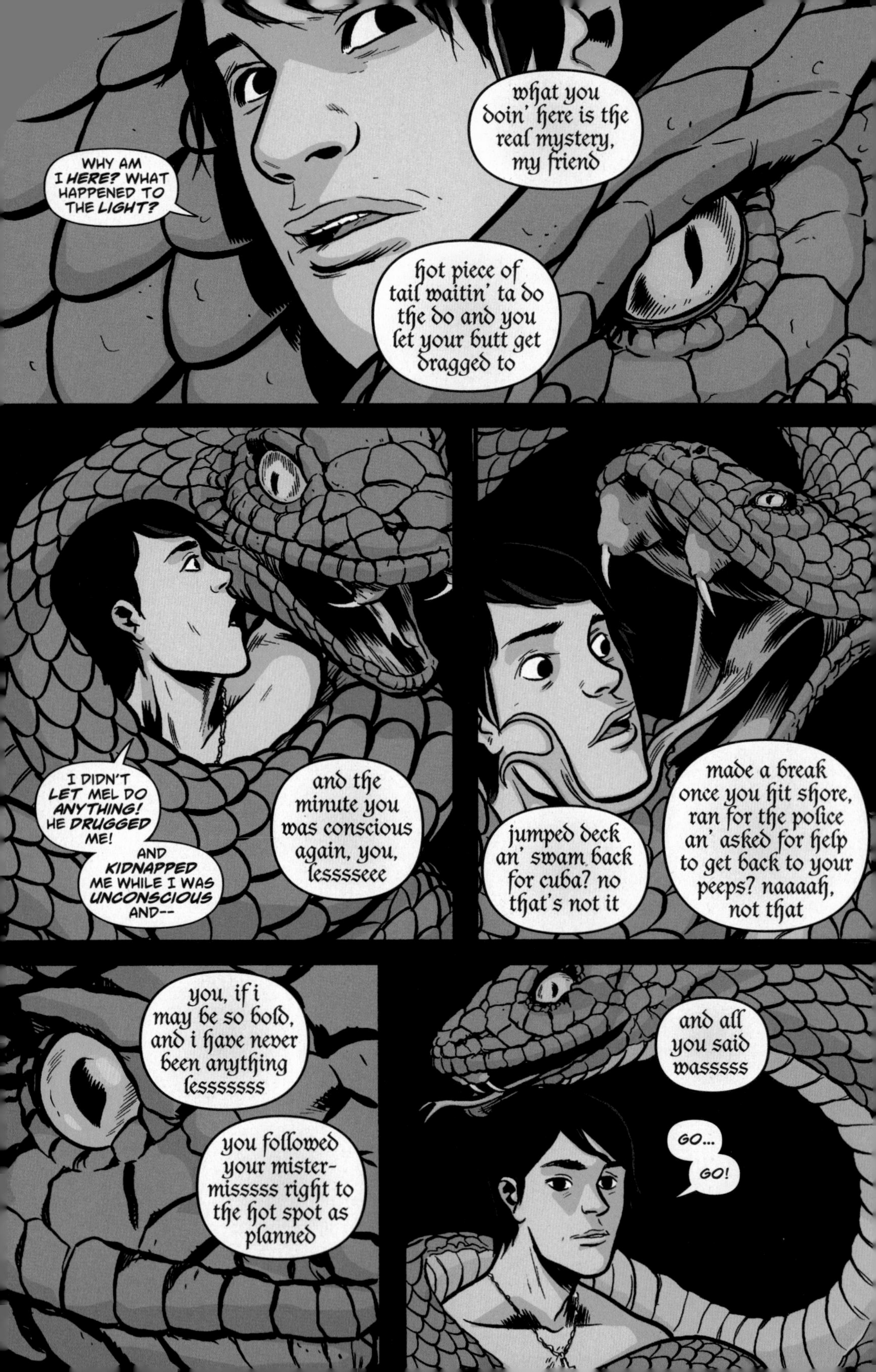
WHY AM I HERE? WHAT HAPPENED TO THE LIGHT?
what you doin' here is the real mystery, my friend
hot piece of tail waitin' ta do the do and you let your butt get dragged to
I DIDN'T LET MEL DO ANYTHING! HE DRUGGED ME!
AND KIDNAPPED ME WHILE I WAS UNCONSCIOUS AND--
and the minute you was conscious again, you, lessssеее
jumped deck an' swam back for cuba? no that's not it
made a break once you hit shore, ran for the police an' asked for help to get back to your peeps? naaaah, not that
you, if i may be so bold, and i have never been anything lesssssss
you followed your mister-misssss right to the hot spot as planned
and all you said wasssss
GO...
GO!

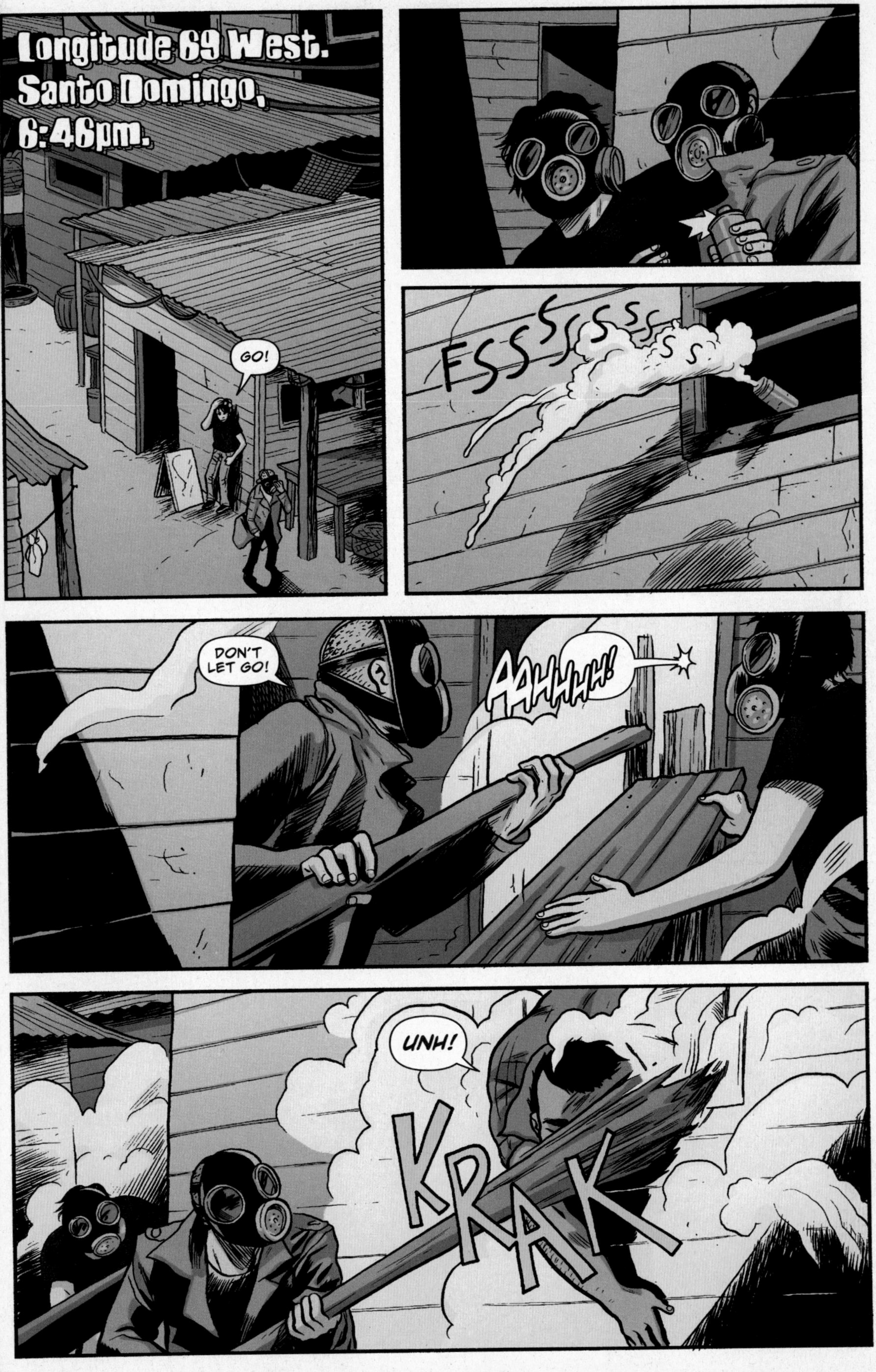
Longitude 69 West. Santo Domingo, 6:46pm.
GO!
FSSSSSSSSS
DON'T LET GO!
AAHHHH!
UNH!
KRAK

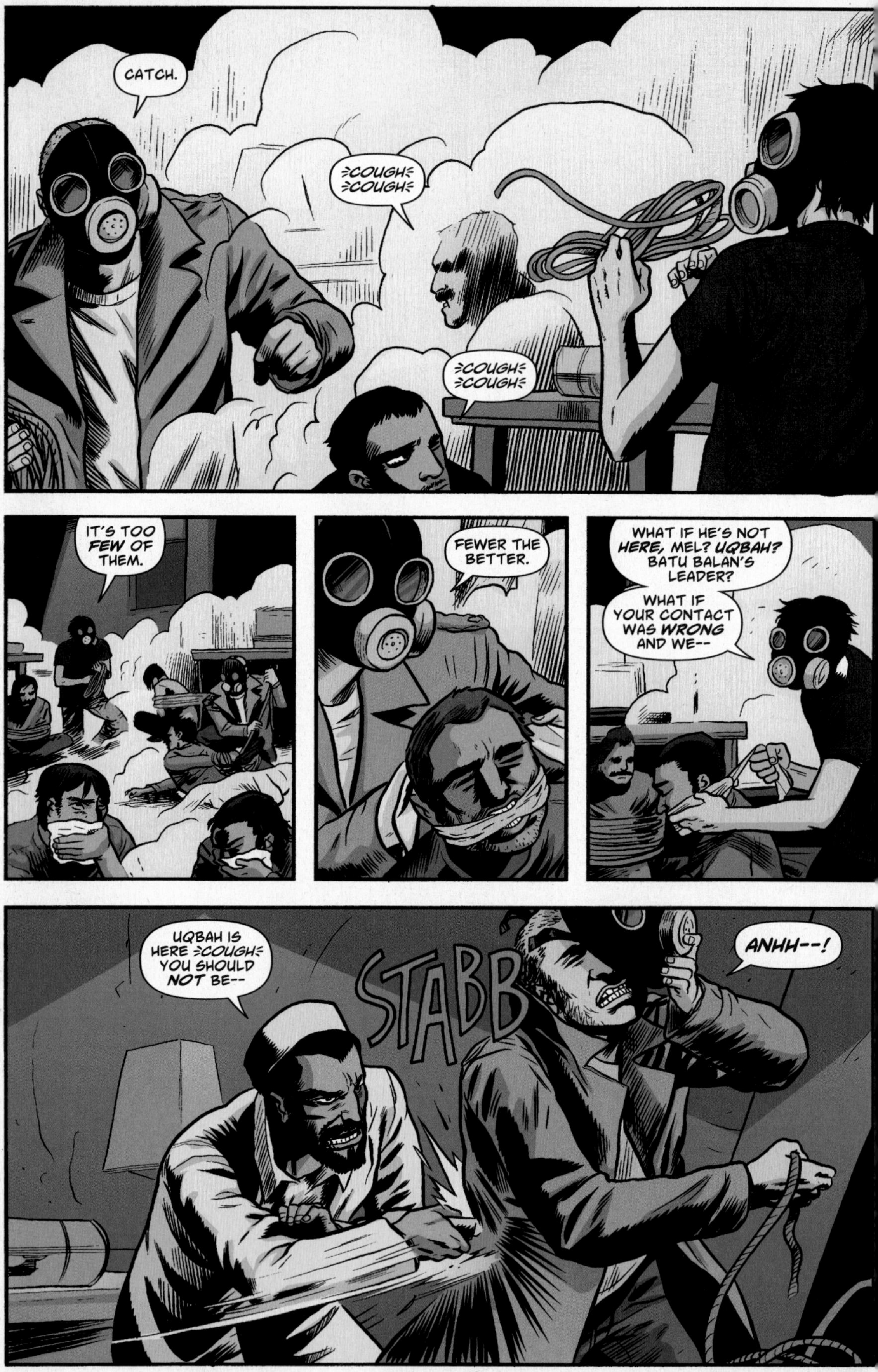
CATCH.
COUGH COUGH
COUGH COUGH
IT'S TOO FEW OF THEM.
FEWER THE BETTER.
WHAT IF HE'S NOT HERE, MEL? UQBAH? BATU BALAN'S LEADER?
WHAT IF YOUR CONTACT WAS WRONG AND WE--
UQBAH IS HERE COUGH YOU SHOULD NOT BE--
STABB
ANHH--!

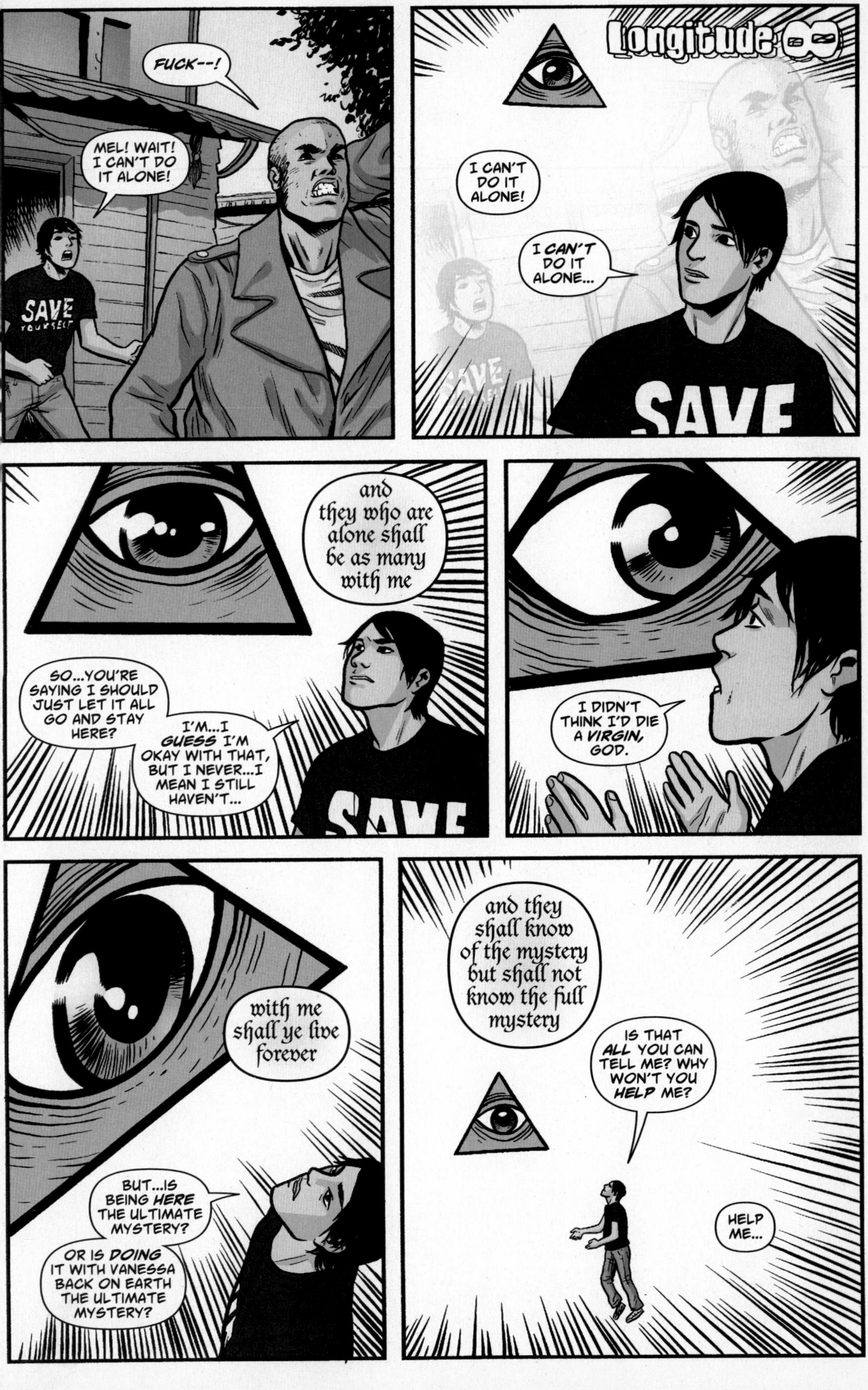
FUCK--!
MEL! WAIT! I CAN'T DO IT ALONE!
SAVE YOURSELF
Longitude ∞
I CAN'T DO IT ALONE!
I CAN'T DO IT ALONE...
SAVE
and they who are alone shall be as many with me
SO...YOU'RE SAYING I SHOULD JUST LET IT ALL GO AND STAY HERE?
I'M...I GUESS I'M OKAY WITH THAT, BUT I NEVER...I MEAN I STILL HAVEN'T...
I DIDN'T THINK I'D DIE A VIRGIN, GOD.
with me shall ye live forever
BUT...IS BEING HERE THE ULTIMATE MYSTERY?
OR IS DOING IT WITH VANESSA BACK ON EARTH THE ULTIMATE MYSTERY?
and they shall know of the mystery but shall not know the full mystery
IS THAT ALL YOU CAN TELL ME? WHY WON'T YOU HELP ME?
HELP ME...

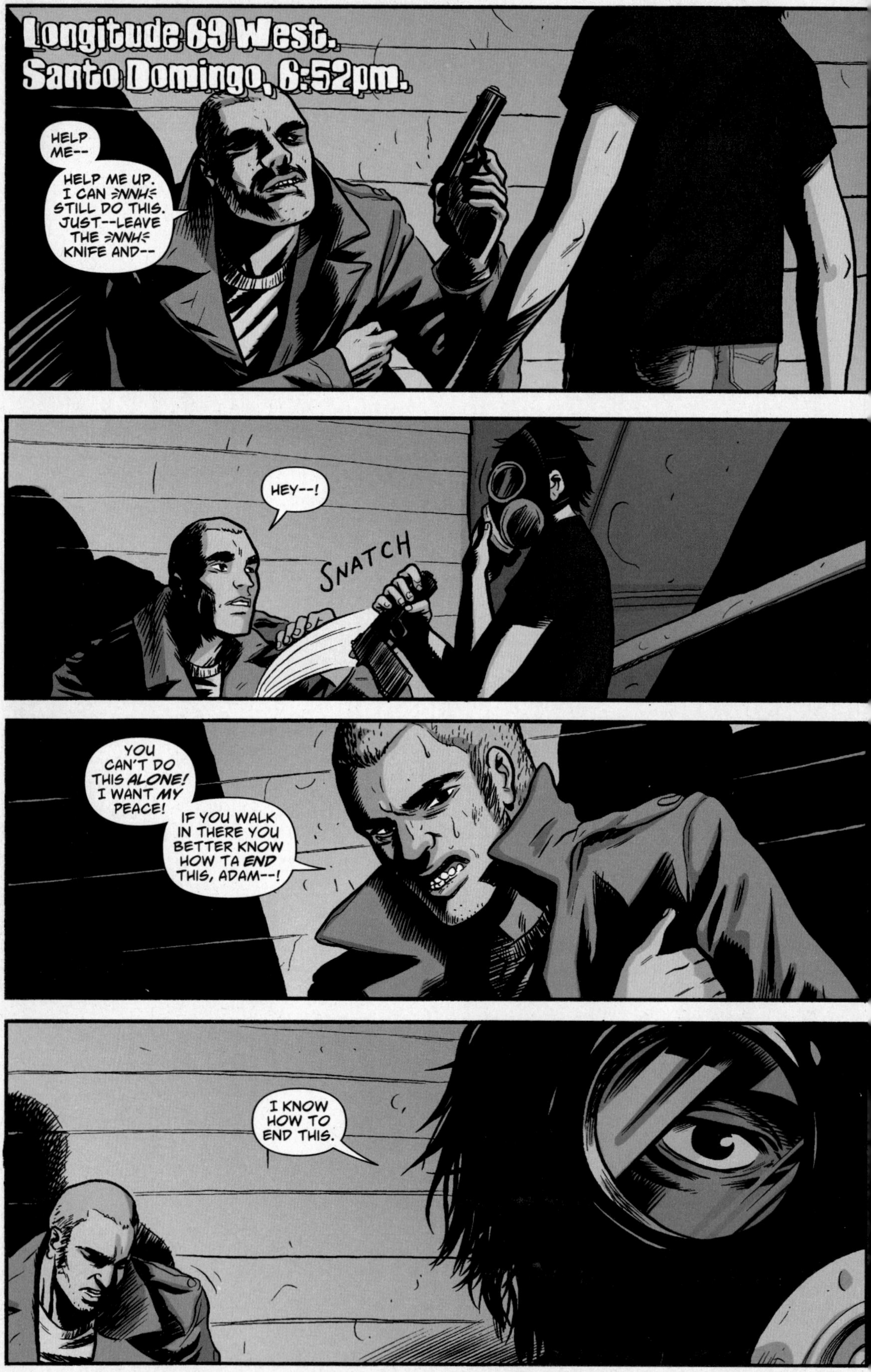
Longitude 69 West.
Santo Domingo, 6:52pm.
HELP ME--
HELP ME UP. I CAN ≋NNH≋ STILL DO THIS. JUST--LEAVE THE ≋NNH≋ KNIFE AND--
HEY--!
SNATCH
YOU CAN'T DO THIS ALONE! I WANT MY PEACE!
IF YOU WALK IN THERE YOU BETTER KNOW HOW TA END THIS, ADAM--!
I KNOW HOW TO END THIS.

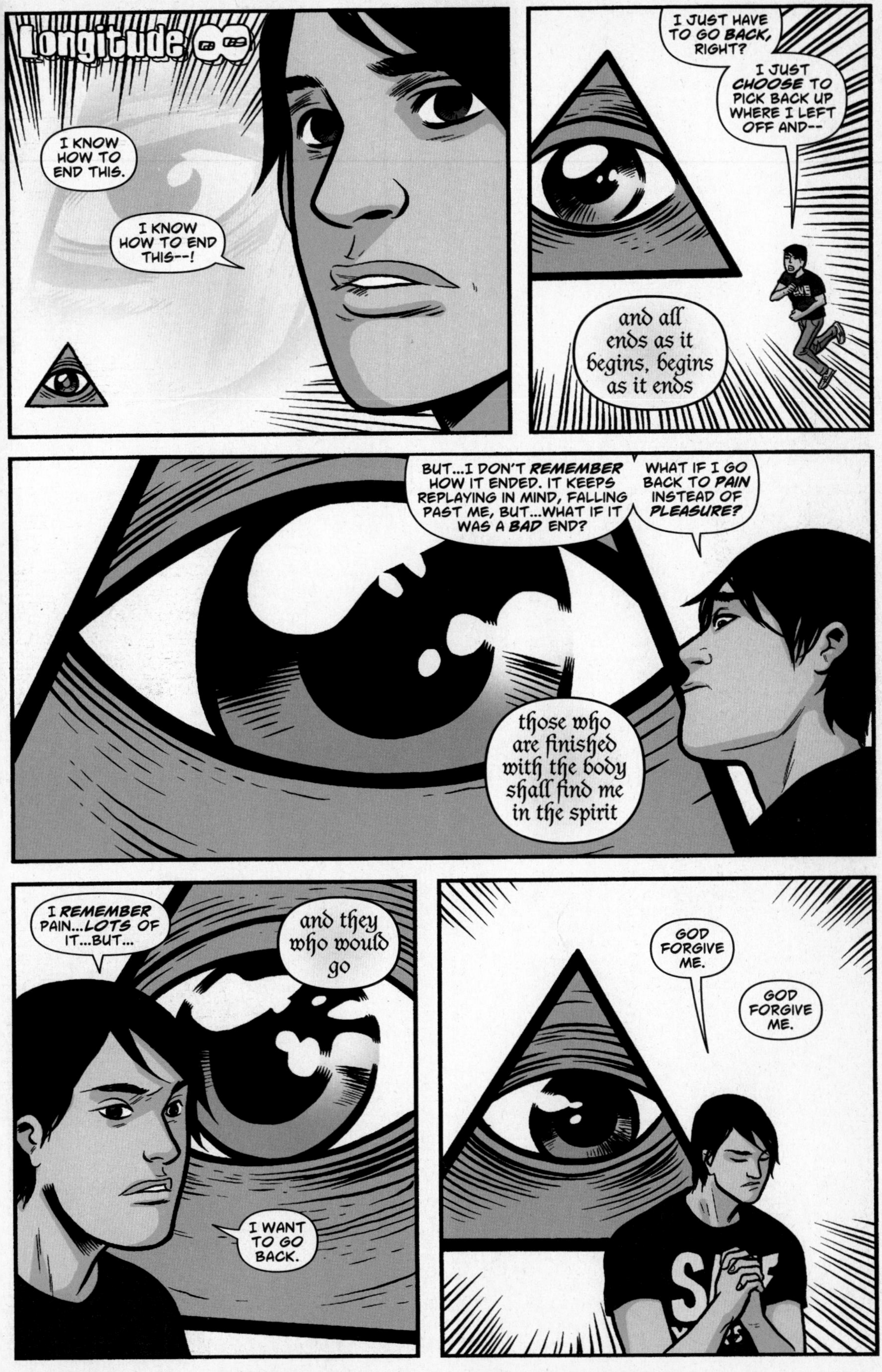
Longitude ∞
I KNOW HOW TO END THIS.
I KNOW HOW TO END THIS--!
I JUST HAVE TO GO BACK, RIGHT?
I JUST CHOOSE TO PICK BACK UP WHERE I LEFT OFF AND--
and all ends as it begins, begins as it ends
BUT...I DON'T REMEMBER HOW IT ENDED. IT KEEPS REPLAYING IN MIND, FALLING PAST ME, BUT...WHAT IF IT WAS A BAD END?
WHAT IF I GO BACK TO PAIN INSTEAD OF PLEASURE?
those who are finished with the body shall find me in the spirit
I REMEMBER PAIN...LOTS OF IT...BUT...
and they who would go
I WANT TO GO BACK.
GOD FORGIVE ME.
GOD FORGIVE ME.

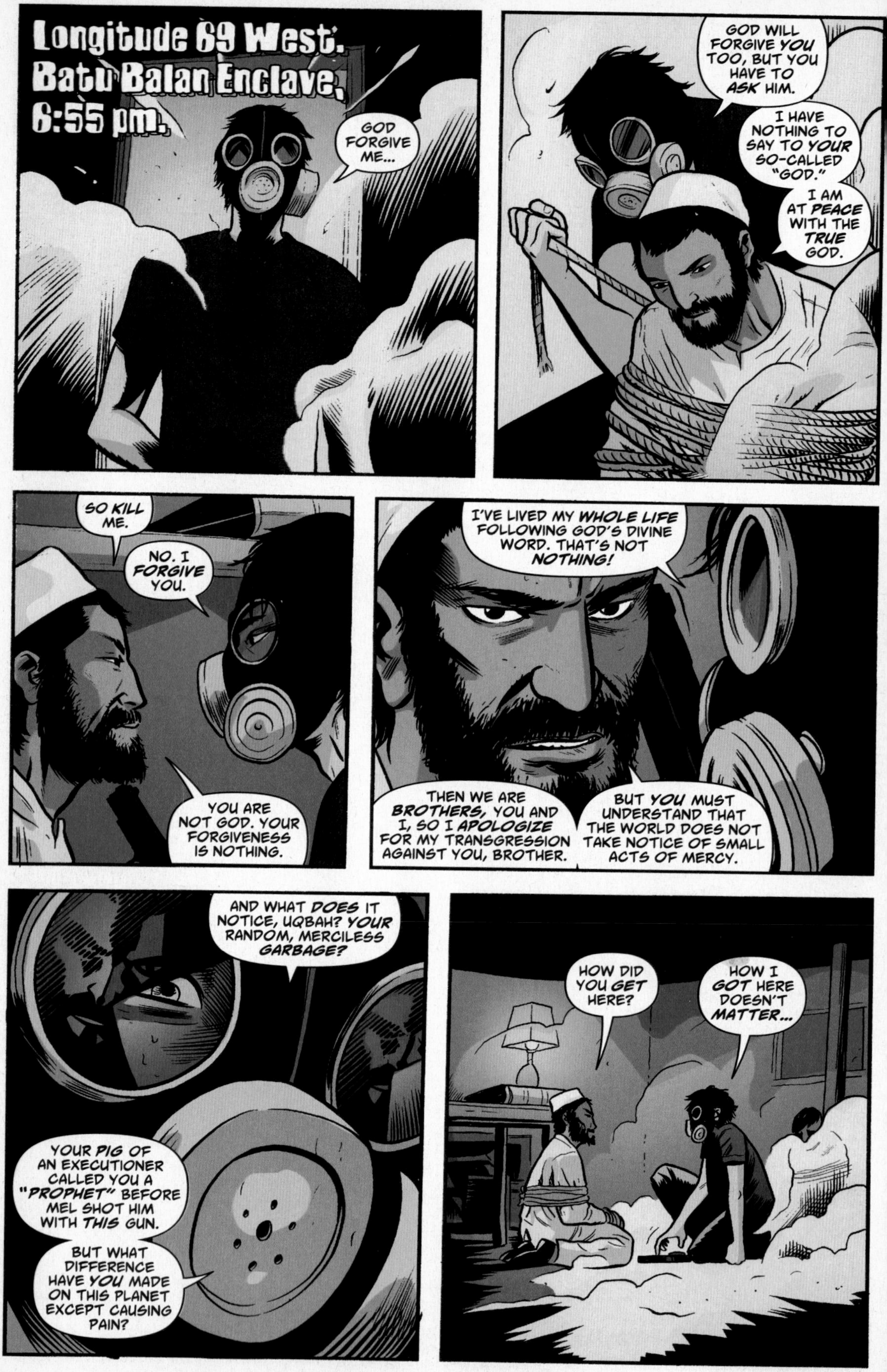

Longitude 69 West. Batu Balan Enclave, 6:55 pm.
GOD FORGIVE ME...
GOD WILL FORGIVE YOU TOO, BUT YOU HAVE TO ASK HIM.
I HAVE NOTHING TO SAY TO YOUR SO-CALLED "GOD."
I AM AT PEACE WITH THE TRUE GOD.
SO KILL ME.
NO. I FORGIVE YOU.
YOU ARE NOT GOD. YOUR FORGIVENESS IS NOTHING.
I'VE LIVED MY WHOLE LIFE FOLLOWING GOD'S DIVINE WORD. THAT'S NOT NOTHING!
THEN WE ARE BROTHERS, YOU AND I, SO I APOLOGIZE FOR MY TRANSGRESSION AGAINST YOU, BROTHER.
BUT YOU MUST UNDERSTAND THAT THE WORLD DOES NOT TAKE NOTICE OF SMALL ACTS OF MERCY.
AND WHAT DOES IT NOTICE, UQBAH? YOUR RANDOM, MERCILESS GARBAGE?
YOUR PIG OF AN EXECUTIONER CALLED YOU A "PROPHET" BEFORE MEL SHOT HIM WITH THIS GUN.
BUT WHAT DIFFERENCE HAVE YOU MADE ON THIS PLANET EXCEPT CAUSING PAIN?
HOW DID YOU GET HERE?
HOW I GOT HERE DOESN'T MATTER...

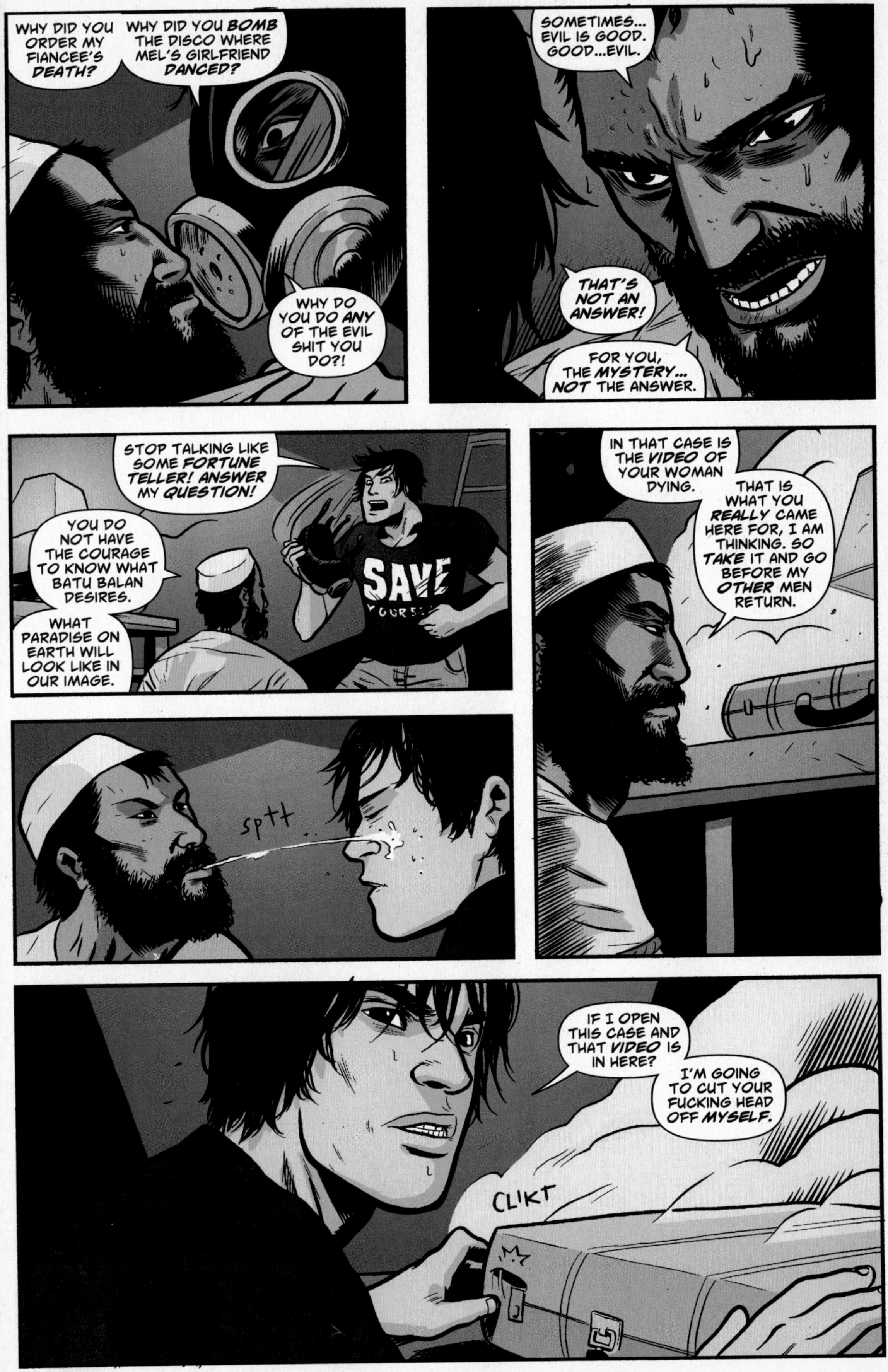
WHY DID YOU ORDER MY FIANCEE'S DEATH?
WHY DID YOU BOMB THE DISCO WHERE MEL'S GIRLFRIEND DANCED?
WHY DO YOU DO ANY OF THE EVIL SHIT YOU DO?!
SOMETIMES... EVIL IS GOOD. GOOD...EVIL.
THAT'S NOT AN ANSWER!
FOR YOU, THE MYSTERY... NOT THE ANSWER.
STOP TALKING LIKE SOME FORTUNE TELLER! ANSWER MY QUESTION!
YOU DO NOT HAVE THE COURAGE TO KNOW WHAT BATU BALAN DESIRES.
WHAT PARADISE ON EARTH WILL LOOK LIKE IN OUR IMAGE.
SAVE
IN THAT CASE IS THE VIDEO OF YOUR WOMAN DYING.
THAT IS WHAT YOU REALLY CAME HERE FOR, I AM THINKING. SO TAKE IT AND GO BEFORE MY OTHER MEN RETURN.
sptt
IF I OPEN THIS CASE AND THAT VIDEO IS IN HERE?
I'M GOING TO CUT YOUR FUCKING HEAD OFF MYSELF.
CLIKT

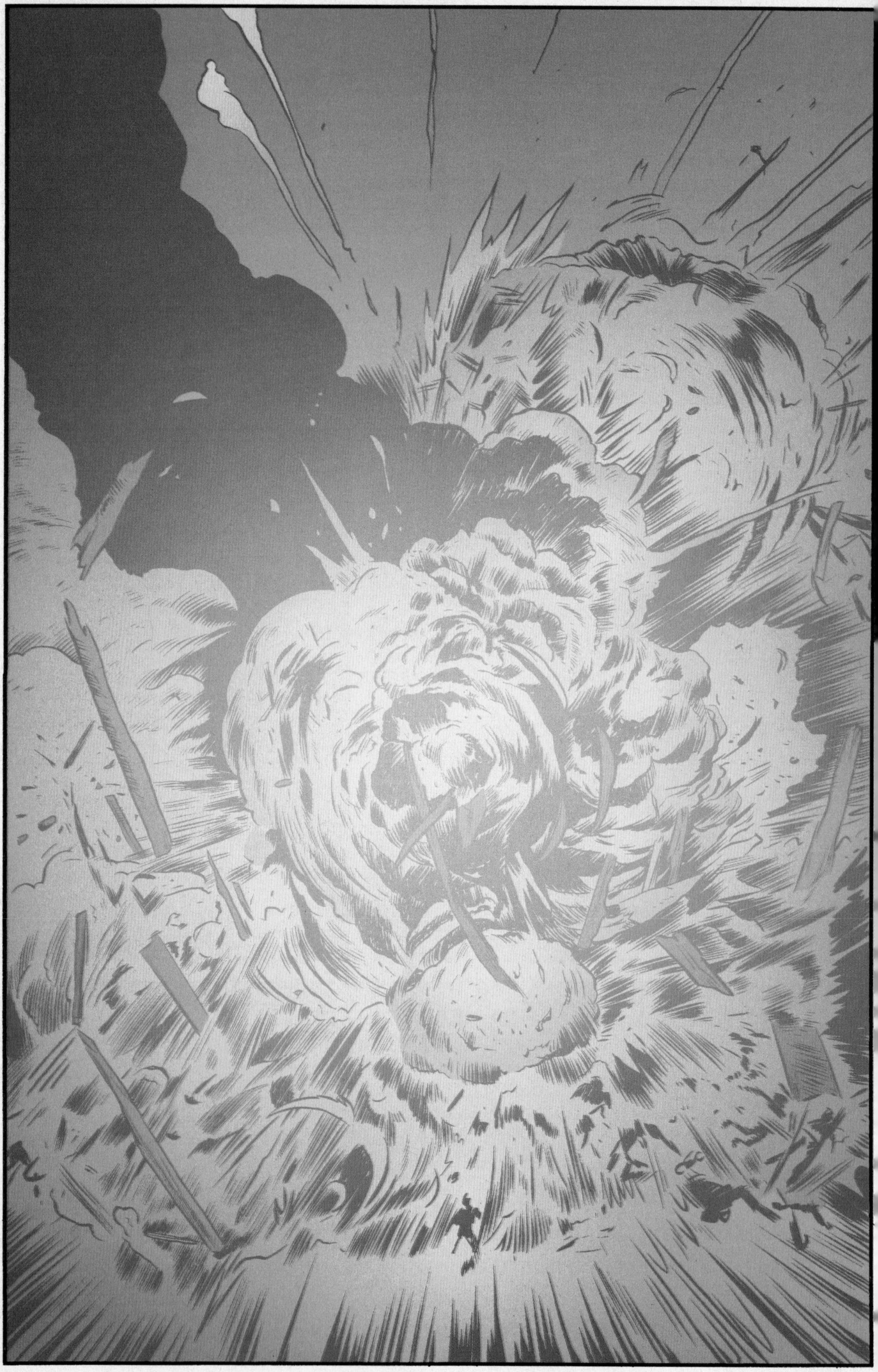

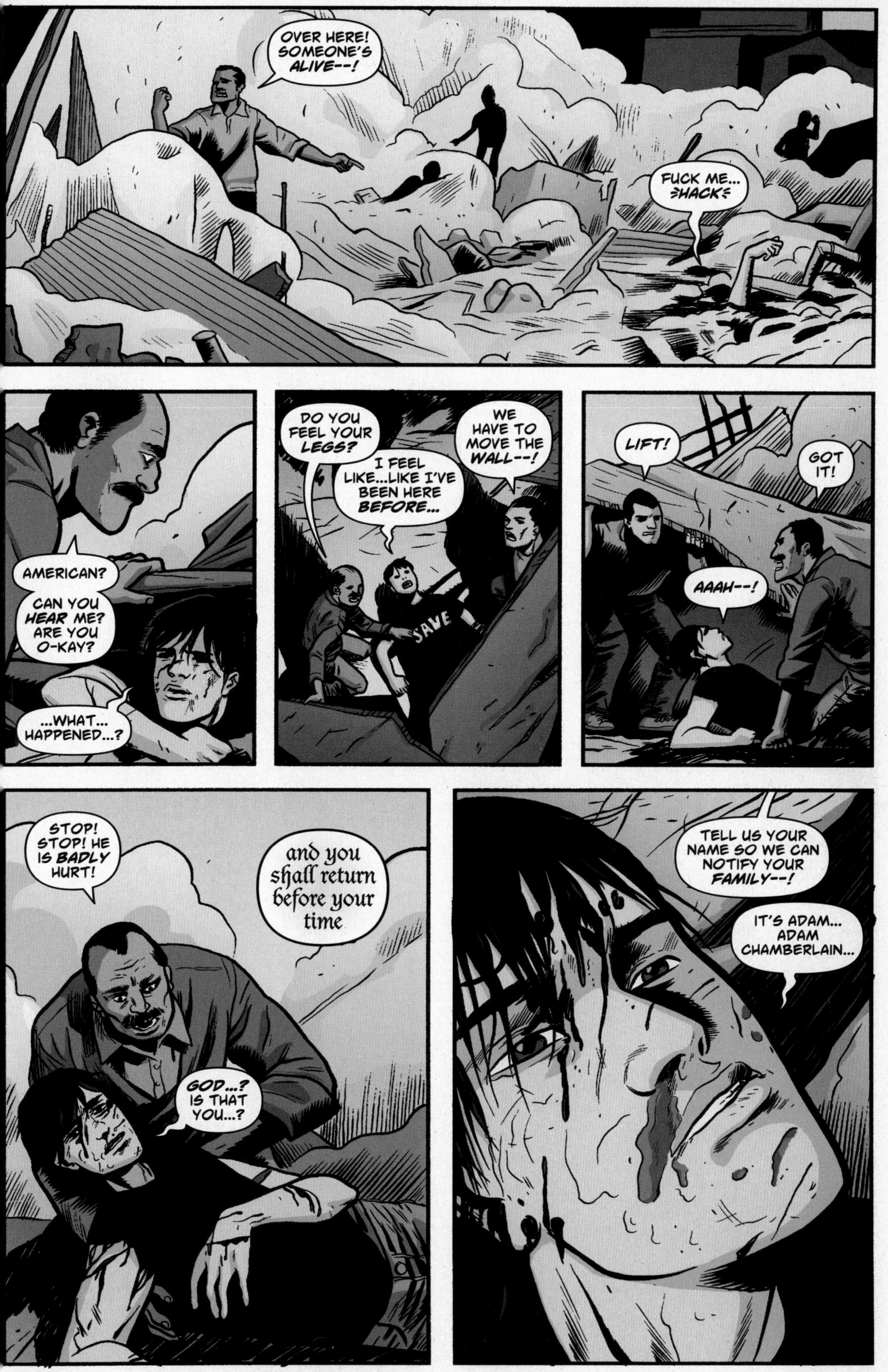
OVER HERE! SOMEONE'S ALIVE--!
FUCK ME... ≈HACK≈
AMERICAN?
CAN YOU HEAR ME? ARE YOU O-KAY?
...WHAT... HAPPENED...?
DO YOU FEEL YOUR LEGS?
I FEEL LIKE...LIKE I'VE BEEN HERE BEFORE...
WE HAVE TO MOVE THE WALL--!
SAVE
LIFT!
GOT IT!
AAAH--!
STOP! STOP! HE IS BADLY HURT!
and you shall return before your time
GOD...? IS THAT YOU...?
TELL US YOUR NAME SO WE CAN NOTIFY YOUR FAMILY--!
IT'S ADAM... ADAM CHAMBERLAIN...

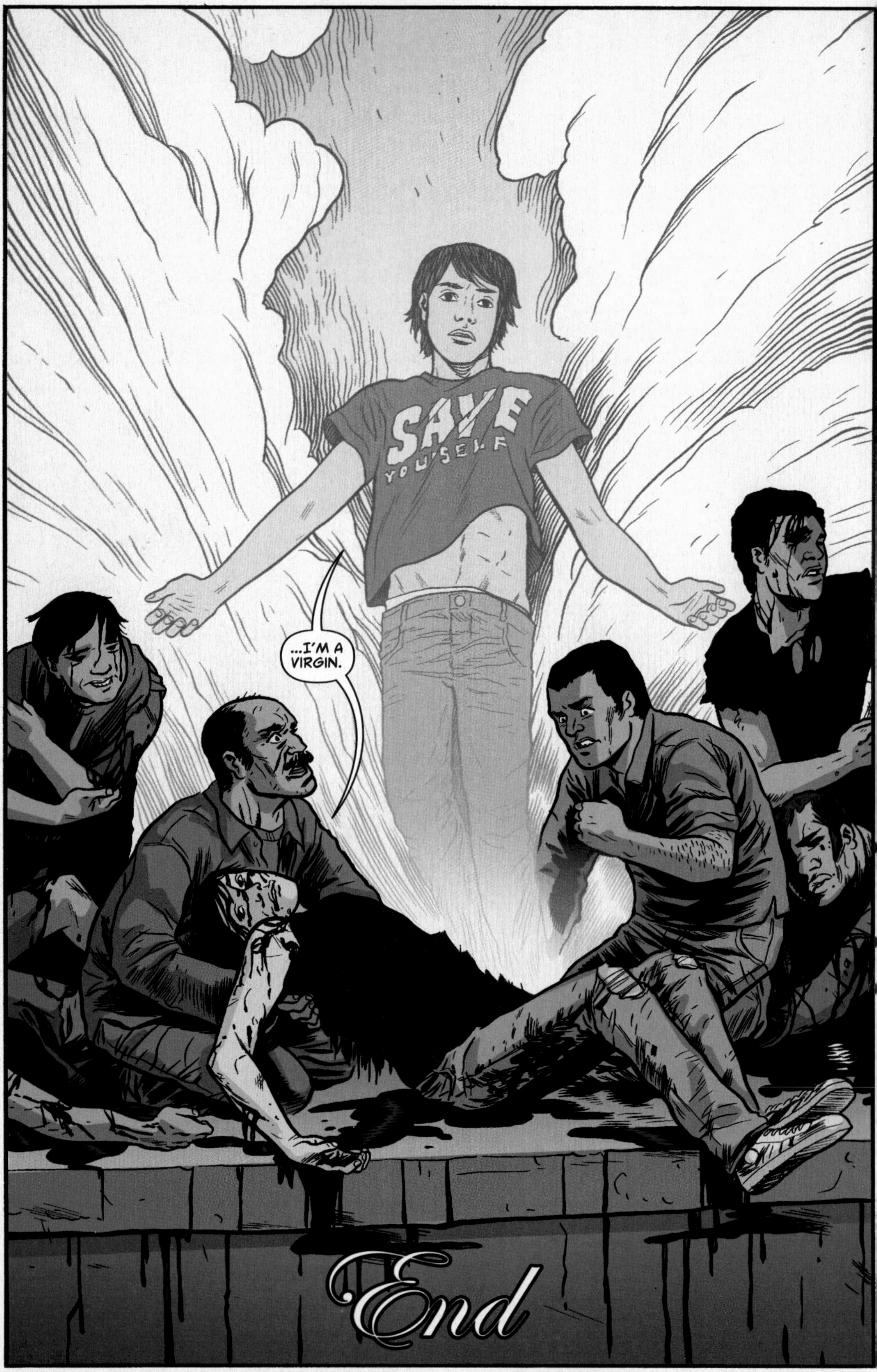
SAVE YOURSELF
...I'M A VIRGIN.
End